A Spiritual Treasury for the Children of God

A MEDITATION FOR EACH DAY OF THE YEAR

WILLIAM MASON

BAKER BOOK HOUSE
Grand Rapids, Michigan

Reprinted 1977 by
Baker Book House

ISBN: 0-8010-6040-0

PHOTOLITHOPRINTED BY CUSHING - MALLOY, INC.
ANN ARBOR, MICHIGAN, UNITED STATES OF AMERICA
1977

These devout meditations were written, towards the close of the last century, with "the chief aim to exalt the Lord Jesus, the perfection of his atonement and righteousness, and the glory of his salvation." An eminent divine of that age, acknowledging the benefits he had derived from them to his own soul, adds, "They will be profitable to thee, Reader, if thou art hungering and thirsting after righteousness—if, being taught by the Holy Ghost that Jesus is the Lord, thou art desiring to grow in the knowledge of his adorable person, and in the love of the Father through him. May the Lord the Spirit witness to thy heart of Jesus whilst thou art reading them, and render them the means of glorifying Him in thy life and conversation, that thou mayest learn from every page to trust him more, to hope more in him, and to love Him more who is thy ALL; and if thou livest upon him *in all*, he will be thy heaven upon earth, and thy heaven of heavens in eternal glory."

AN INDEX

OF THE

TEXTS OF SCRIPTURE TREATED OF

SPIRITUAL TREASURY

January.

Jan. 1.—*We see Jesus.* Heb. 2 : 9

Fine sights of human pomp and worldly grandeur captivate and ravish worldly minds. It is common to hear persons say, O, I could sit all night to see a fine play! But one sight of the matchless charms and dazzling glories of our Saviour makes all other things appear mean and contemptible. We turn our eyes from them and say, " I put away these childish things ; I have a heavenly object, infinitely superior to such low and perishing vanities."

I know one, who having heard that faithful minister of Christ, Mr. Whitefield, when he first preached in the fields, upwards of thirty years ago, on being asked which he liked best, to hear him preach, or see Vauxhall? profanely replied, " Whitefield only preaches of heaven, but Vauxhall is heaven itself." Poor soul! he was then blind to his want of Christ, and to his glory and excellency. But, to the glory of his rich grace, that poor sinner is out of hell, and can now happily join the faithful in saying, WE SEE JESUS. So then, the once profane sinner is changed into the " enthusiast." Enthusiasm to see Jesus !

> "Enthusiastic this ?
> " Then all are blind but rank enthusiasts."

The essence of the Gospel, the joy of sinners, and the glory of faith consist in this sight. What is life itself without it ? Alas, we have lost all righteousness, holiness, and happiness, in ourselves; but we see all these, with heaven and glory, restored to us in Christ. O blessed day! happy hour! joyful moment! when the sight of our inestimably precious Saviour first saluted the eyes of our mind and became the object of our faith! It was the beginning of days; yea, our birth-day to eternal blessedness.

This sight is a feast to our souls all the year. We delight to begin the year with seeing Jesus. We salute one another with, "I wish you a happy new year." What mean we, but I wish you to see Jesus? What can make the year happy without this? This creates heaven in the soul. Then it is a happy year indeed. But without this precious view of faith we can get no ease from the burden of sin, and our souls must be miserable. This world can afford us no real happiness. The thoughts of death will torment us; and the view of judgment fill us with dread and terror. But, O happy sinners, who can bless God with Simeon, and say, "Mine eyes have seen thy salvation!" Luke 2 : 30. I see Christ: he is all *my* salvation and all *my* desire. Ye heaven-born, highly-favored souls, well may ye say, "Time, hasten on; years, roll round; moments, fly swiftly; and bring me to the full enjoyment of my beloved Saviour in his kingdom of glory."

We see Jesus, who saw us, loved us, pitied and saved us when dead in our sins, cursed by the law, and polluted in our blood. We look back and see him an outcast babe, a despised MAN, crucified as a vile malefactor, bearing our sins on the cross, made a sacrifice for our souls, and redeeming us to GOD by his blood. We glory in him as the only atonement for our sins and our one righteousness to justify our souls; for he is *the Lord our righteousness*. Jer. 23 : 6. We look up and see Jesus crowned with glory and honor, pleading our cause and interceding for our persons at the right hand of God, and ever living to save us to the uttermost. We look forward to judgment; awful day! we see

> "A trembling world, and a devouring God."

But, O how bright the prospect! we see Jesus coming with power and great glory to receive us to his kingdom, that where he is there we may be also.

Do we thus see Jesus by faith as revealed in the word of truth? Then we are new creatures in him. We are called, with Moses, "to endure as seeing Him who is invisible." Heb. 11 : 27. We are exhorted to "lay aside every weight, and the sin which doth so easily beset us, and run with patience the race set before us, *looking unto Jesus*, the author and finisher of our faith." Heb. 12 : 1, 2. Thus we obey the will of God our Father, who commands us, "Behold mine elect, in whom my soul delighteth," Isa. 42 : 1, "my beloved Son, in whom I am well pleased." Matt. 3 : 17.

JAN. 2.—*I will go in the strength of the Lord God : I will make mention of thy righteousness, even of thine only.* Psalm 71 : 16

Wise travellers provide things needful for their journey, and guard against such as lie in wait, by the way, to rob them. Our gracious God calls not his dear children to forsake their native country, to travel to the heavenly city, without furnishing them with a rich supply of all things necessary for their comfort, and also strength to protect them from the power of every enemy. No soldier of his goeth a warfare at his own charge. Christ being both their righteousness and strength, they can want nothing : neither riches nor power. Hence they go on from day to day, glorying in him as their richest treasure, and trusting in him as their almighty strength; and this is their constant song in the house of their pilgrimage, and all their journey through :

"Surely, in the Lord have I righteousness and strength."
Isa. 45 : 24. Jesus' righteousness inspires the soul with
boldness before God. Jesus' strength obtains victory
over every enemy. This is the triumph of faith. So believers walk safely and comfortably. Children of grace
are not called to be idle speculatists in doctrines; but
to a life of activity, to holy walking with Jesus, constant
hearing of his love, cheerful obedience to his will, diligent search of the Scriptures, steadfast resistance of Satan, striving daily against sin, and praying always with
all prayer and supplication.

But well may one ask, "Who is sufficient for these
things?" As to natural power and inherent strength, we
must all sit down in despair. But faith leads from self
to Jesus. I can do all things through Christ strengthening me; so will I go on against my enemies; thus I shall
be enabled to walk in the paths of every duty. Yet after
I have done all, my Saviour bids me confess the truth,
that I am an unprofitable servant.

But is not this discouraging to the soul? No; for it
works not to obtain *righteousness*. It is already clothed
with that, and, in the view of faith, rejoices in it; ab-
jures all other, and will make mention of Jesus' righteousness, and his only, for acceptance with God, perfect justification before him, from every condemnation
of the law and accusation of Satan. True, doubts and
fears may arise, distressing thoughts deject; but happily
are we conducted, joyful shall be our experience, while
the righteousness of Christ is held by faith, as our only
hope, our only joy, our only crown of rejoicing. For we
are made the righteousness of God in Christ. 2 Cor. 5 : 21.

JAN. 3.—*Because thy loving-kindness is better than life, my
lips shall praise thee.* Psalm 63 : 3

Forsake all, and possess all; give up all, and enjoy

all—This is the doctrine of Jesus, and the experience of faith. So we overcome the world, by preferring the love of Christ to every thing beside. Most blessed enthusiasm! really tasting that the Lord is gracious, truly feeling the comforts of his love, actually partaking of fellowship with Jesus, communion of the Holy Spirit, freely conversing with the Father of all consolations— O how transporting to the spirit; how ravishing to the soul! With what holy indifference does the enraptured heart look down upon the objects of sense! The gilded toys of time, that so attract the view; the glittering vanities of life, that so enslave earthly minds; the empty shadows of sense, that so bewitch the heart; yea, life itself, with all its comforts, what are all, compared to one moment's enjoyment of the loving-kindness of the Lord? In competition, as shadow to substance; in worth, as the dust of the earth to the gold of Ophir. Sense is but short-lived fancy. Faith is reality and substance. For it brings love, the kindness of love, yea, the God of loving-kindness himself into the sinner's heart. This changes a fallen son of Adam into a glorious saint in Christ: a miserable sinner into a comfortable, holy, humble praiser of our covenant Lord.

Thus it is when the soul has found God in Christ, who is its life, its glory, its treasure, its heaven, its all. But this knowledge consists, not merely in ecstasy of soul and rapturous sensations: faith is an habitual principle, love is an active grace, hope has a purifying efficacy. Not only are the lips opened in praise, the tongue loosed to speak of the glory of Jesus; but the life, the practice, the conversation will also be savored with the grace of truth, as an evidence that we know his love, and have been with Jesus. Thus we prove that he has taught us wisdom, not to prefer heaven to earth in word only, but in conduct. Having received all from him freely, in love and by grace, we desire to do what he

has commanded, to avoid what he has forbidden. The
fruits of righteousness are by him, to the glory of God
the Father; therefore we pray to be filled with them.
The works of the flesh, the works of darkness, we desire
to mortify, to have no fellowship with them; because
contrary to love, and the enjoyment of it. "We have
known and believed the love that God hath to us. God
is love; and he that dwelleth in love dwelleth in God,
and God in him." 1 John 4 : 16.

> "Of all the joys we mortals know,
> " Jesus, thy love exceeds the rest;
> "Love, the best blessing here below,
> " The highest rapture of the blest."

JAN. 4.—*Jesus said, Ye know not what ye ask.* Mark 10:38

Strange! what, James and John, two disciples of a
despised and rejected Master who had not where to lay
his head, petitioning for nothing less than the right hand
of pre-eminence, and the left hand of power! What are
the best of men when left to their own spirits? Truly,
we know not what to pray for as we ought. Jesus, Master, instruct us. Teach us what to pray for. Let thy
word, "My kingdom is not of this world," be ever uppermost in our minds!

Poor Baruch could not be honored of God, and commissioned to read the roll to the princes of Judah, but
he thinks, Now I am somebody; I have got in the way
to earthly honor and preferment. But his brother, Jeremiah, is sent to him with this question and reproof,
"Seekest thou great things for thyself? seek them not."
Jer. 45 : 5. How many distresses were brought upon
the children of Israel by the mixed multitude that went
with them! So the swarms of earthly affections and carnal desires which are found with us, are ever opposing
the glory of Jesus, and exciting us to seek that happi-

ness, in nature and sense, which can only be found in the spiritual reign of Jesus in the heart.

But so kind and gracious is our dear Saviour, that he crosses our will and denies our request, when contrary to our spiritual interest. Thus in love he answers our prayers: he withholds what we ask; he gives what he knows is best for us. If disciples ask what it is unfit for them to receive, or unlawful to beg, shall we complain of God's love, if he denies? Granting is not always the effect of love. If so, Paul had been less loved than Satan. Satan asked but once concerning Job, and his request was granted. Paul besought the Lord thrice that the messenger of Satan might depart, yet was denied in that. Yea, the blessed Jesus thrice prayed his Father that the cup might pass from him, but that could not be. The Lord delights in the prosperity of his people; therefore withholds no good thing from them. Not our judgment, but his wisdom must determine this. We pray to be in the height of comfort, and on the pinnacle of joy. But love answers by keeping us in the safe vale of humility and self-abasement. Lord, what proud aspiring creatures are we! enable us to obey thee: "Humble yourselves under the mighty hand of God." 1 Pet. 5 : 6.

JAN. 5.—*I will bear the indignation of the Lord, because I have sinned against him, until he plead my cause and execute judgment for me: he will bring me forth to the light, and I shall behold his righteousness.* MICAH 7 : 9

Though sin be atoned for by the blood of Jesus, and the soul be made holy and happy by believing this, yet, alas! sin dwelleth in us. Hence all our griefs, our sufferings, our wretchedness. God's judgments are sometimes secret, always just, ever in love to his own. Misery would never afflict us if sin did not infect us. God disciplines by afflictions, for our profit and his glory.

The faith, patience, and valor of God's soldiers are best known in times of exercise; then how animating to view the love and trust to the faithfulness of a covenant God! To see a Father's love to the soul, in the rod of his displeasure against sin, how supporting! I will bear the chastisements of my Father, my sins deserve them; yea, wrath and hell are my desert. My mouth is stopped; I have nothing to plead; guilt silences me.

But see, hear, and rejoice, O soul. The church beholds a Blessed Person. Who is it that she thinks upon and mentions? "Until He plead my cause." It is the dear Advocate Jesus, the ever-precious pleader for poor sinners. How reviving are the sacred pages! they ever testify of his blessed name and soul-comforting work. He never intermits his plea for the life of the soul. He prevails over all the desert of sin, by his atonement and intercession. Shortly he will speak destruction to all sin by the word of his power.

In the meantime he sends his Spirit, the Comforter, the third person in the glorious Trinity. "He will bring me forth to the light." Here see Old Testament faith in New Testament love. It is the Spirit's office to bring souls out of the dark dungeon of nature's sorrows, to see Jesus the Light of life. "I shall behold his righteousness." Then it is a day of comfort after a night of distress. Is the righteousness of Jesus mine? am I righteous by that in the sight of God? Then, truly, it is in righteousness God dealeth with me, and will save me. This faith humbles the soul to the dust, strips it of proud murmurings and self-righteous pleas, and inspires it with boldness at a throne of grace. This is the confident plea of faith: "For thy righteousness' sake bring my soul out of trouble. Destroy all them that afflict my soul: for I am thy servant." Psalm 143 : 11, 12

JAN. 6.—*Love as brethren.* 1 Peter 3 : 8

Love without reason is a mad passion. Profession

without love is but "a sounding brass or a tinkling cymbal;" unmeaning noise to others; unprofitable to him that makes it. Love is of God. It is that precious ointment which is poured forth from the Father of love upon the head of our spiritual Aaron, and runs down to the skirts of his garment, even upon all his brethren, the children of love. Love descends from God, through Jesus, to us, spreads itself among the brethren, and ascends in grateful odors to the God of love.

The prophet asks, "Have we not all one Father?" Mal. 2 : 10. Yes, saith Christ. "I ascend unto my Father, and your Father." John 20 : 17. Hence the Holy Spirit draws the image of Jesus, "the first-born of many brethren," upon each of their souls, and possesses them with the faith of Jesus ; and "whosoever believeth that Jesus is the Christ is born of God; and every one that loveth him that begat, loveth him also that is begotten of him." 1 John 5 : 1. Faith in Jesus is the band or cement of brotherly love. Are we the brethren of Jesus, beloved and chosen by one Father, born again of the same Spirit, partakers of the same grace, heirs of the same promises, travellers to the same kingdom, and shall we not love each other? Alas! alas! we mourn for the loss of health or of property, but how much greater cause is there to lament the loss of love amongst God's dear children and Christ's beloved brethren!

But we are all, like Simeon and Levi, brethren in iniquity ; and as with them, so anger and self-will are found with us. Gen. 49 : 5, 6. Both are the effect of pride, and are contrary to faith and love. The question is not, Are we perfectly freed from every passion and temper contrary to love? This we are not to expect in our brethren. God loves us, not as sinless, but as he views us in Christ. Do we really love the children of God as such, love the members of Jesus purely for his sake? Instead of indulging, do we curb and resist, watch

and pray against our tempers which are contrary to
love? This is a blessed evidence that the root of love
is in us. Let us be importunate with Christ, that the
fruits may abound more and more to the glory of God,
"whom we love, because he first loved us." Love
creates happiness, yea, heaven in the heart; it restores
paradise to the soul; for "he who dwelleth in love,
dwelleth in God and God in him." 1 John, 4 : 16. "Covet earnestly the best gifts, and yet I show unto you a
more excellent way:" "Walk in love, as Christ also
hath loved us." Ephesians 5 : 2. Love as brethren.

> "Love is the grace that keeps her power
> "In all the realms above:
> "There faith and hope are known no more,
> "But saints for ever love."

Jan. 7.—*Mine iniquities are gone over mine head: as an heavy
burden they are too heavy for me.* Psalm 38 : 4

They who think lightly of sin, and account iniquity
a trifling thing, evidently show that the God of this
world hath blinded their eyes to the infinite atonement
of Jesus, and hardened their hearts through the deceitfulness of sin; therefore they are insensible of grief, and
have no godly sorrow for sin. But when Jesus is known in
the heart, sin is truly abhorred, forsaken, and overcome.

It is most distressing to the regenerate soul, when
the load of guilt and the burden of sin are suffered to
lie, day after day, upon the conscience. The insupportable agony of such a state none know but those who
have experienced it. One may ask, is not this contra-
dictory to that comforting assertion, "There is now no
condemnation to them that are in Christ Jesus?" Rom.
8 : 1; inconsistent with that triumphant challenge,
"Who shall lay any thing to the charge of God's elect?"
Rom. 8 : 33. We answer, No, for though charge and
condemnation for sin may be brought by Satan, the ac-

cuser of the brethren ; the law may condemn, and our own spirits must confess we are sinners; yet our covenant God hath no condemnation against us. He hath laid all our iniquities upon Jesus ; and this is the full and free charter of his covenant concerning all his children, "Their sins and their iniquities I will remember no more." Jer. 31 : 34. O, say some, this will take away all fear of sinning, and all dread of guilt! Most impious charge against the God of grace and love! But who say this? They who reject God's truth, and believe not his everlasting love ; but judge from their own corrupt principles. But regenerate souls groan under the burden of sin; and because love prevails, sin is hated and self abhorred.

Jesus is the only balm of Gilead, the only Physician for sin-distressed, sore-burdened, heavy-ladened souls. We may seek rest from other objects, but all in vain. Nothing can quiet and relieve the distressed soul but this one truth : Jesus hath actually borne, fully suffered, perfectly atoned for all the sins of his people. So that the Lord has discharged all their sins, and will remember not one sin against them. O, when one beholds this general release! every debt cancelled by Jesus' blood, and God acquitting from every accusation of law and conscience, then our souls return to their rest. This is the faith of God's elect. And while kept simple, loving, faithful to him, we live by his grace, feast on his love, and holy longings inspire our hearts to enjoy him in glory.   O then

" Sin (my worst enemy before)
" Shall vex my eyes and ears no more :
" My inward foes shall all be slain,
" Nor Satan break my peace again.

" Then shall I see, and hear, and know
" All I desired and wished below ;
" And every power find sweet employ
" In that eternal world of joy."

Jan. 8.—*Search me, O God, and know my heart: try me, and know my thoughts: and see if there be any wicked way in me, and lead me in the way everlasting.* Psalm 139: 23, 24.

"He that doeth truth cometh to the light, that his deeds may be made manifest that they are wrought in God:" this is an infallible touchstone of true conversion, given by the Oracle of truth. "He that trusteth to his own heart is a fool." Prov. 28 : 26. Sincere, upright souls know they have to do with a heart-searching God: to him they appeal, and desire to be tried and searched by him. What avails it to the soul, to obtain a favorable opinion from our vain fellow-mortals, if we are conscious that all is not right within? What peace, what comfort, what joy, though men approve, and the soul itself be ever so confident, while conscience testifies, My ways do not please the Lord, my walk is contrary to his will? True love to Jesus will ever excite godly jealousy in the heart.

While in the flesh we are ever exposed to deceits from a subtle foe, a deceitful heart, and an insnaring world; yea, and from false teachers also. Our paths may be intricate, darkness may overtake, and Satan may thrust sore at the soul, that it may fall, or be driven into by-ways of error and wickedness. Here is the wisdom and patience of saints: when they cannot see their way, to cry to their Guide. Jesus is the way, the only way, the way everlasting in which the saints in all ages have walked to glory. Faith in Jesus is inconsistent with every wicked way, though in our present state there is no entire freedom from sin, which dwelleth in us; consequently no perfection in righteousness performed by us. Yet, the more we abide in Jesus, the closer we cleave to him, the more steadfastly we behold him; so much the more, through the grace of his Holy Spirit, we shall be dead to sin, and alive to holiness. We shall experience the ways of wisdom to be ways of pleasantness, and all her paths to be paths of peace. Prov. 3 : 17. This is the end of simple-hearted, sincere souls, in their appeals at a throne of grace, that, " with open face, beholding as in a glass the glory of the Lord," they may be " changed into the same image from glory to glory, even as by the Spirit of the Lord." 2 Cor. 3 : 18. Thus the new creature appeals to the God of all grace to be searched, tried, and led. Thus our new state and new life in Christ are manifested : "we walk not after the flesh, but after the Spirit." Rom. 8 : 1.

JAN. 9.—*Let us go forth unto Him without the camp, bearing his reproach.* Heb. 13 : 13

The profession of the Gospel of Christ is easy to nature. There is nothing irksome to the flesh in being called a christian. But to know Jesus in heart, to confess him with the tongue, and to follow him in our life, will ever expose us to reproach and contempt. Yet if, with Philip, we have really found HIM of whom Moses and the prophets wrote, we must, we shall speak of him to others. We shall esteem Jesus as our beloved, and choose him as our richest treasure. Our hearts and affections will be going out after him. Moses' choice will be ours : we shall esteem " the reproach of Christ greater riches than the treasures of Egypt."

But fleshly wisdom is contrary to all this. That ever prompts : " Save thyself ; take care of thy good name ; fear lest that be cast out as evil ; beware of thy character ; go not too far, thou wilt sustain damage. In the camp of this world, riches, pleasures, and honors are enjoyed. Study the happy mean. Thou mayest hold with the world, and yet not quit Jesus." Nay, but thou canst not love and serve two such contrary masters : thou wilt soon grow tired of the one or the other. The inward glory and peace of Jesus will not, cannot be enjoyed but while the heart and affections are placed on him. The faith of Jesus is contrary to the world, it cannot be reconciled to its vain customs and sinful maxims. Nay, faith is the victory that overcometh the world. The world is an enemy's camp. A despised Nazarene is the christian's glory. To bear his reproach is our highest honor.

The heaven-born soul, though like a captive imprisoned in flesh, yet hath free access to Jesus by faith. So it endures present reproaches, seeing Him who is invisible. And do we hope for the future sight and eternal fruition of Him who endured the cross and despised the shame for us? Let us take and bear his cross: despised disciples let us be. Look down on the world with contempt. Look up to Christ with joy. Go forth to meet him in love. Ever remember, Jesus went forth cheerfully to meet all his conflicts and agonies for us. It is but a little while ere we shall go forth from the body "to meet the Lord in the air: and so shall we be ever with the Lord." 1 Thess. 4 : 17. Is this really our faith? Is this truly our hope? O let us more than ever dwell on it! For it will not only make reproach for Christ easy, but excite longings to be with him : " The Lord Jesus Christ be with our spirits." 2 Tim. 4 : 22.

JAN. 10.—*For his anger endureth but a moment; in his favor is life: weeping may endure for a night, but joy cometh in the morning.* Psalm 30 : 5

Verily, here is a glorious assemblage of comforting truths, like a reviving cordial of rich compounds, to enliven drooping spirits. Too often do God's children judge of their Father's love from corrupt ideas. Through the carnality of their natures, the depravity of their judgment, the weakness of their faith, the uncertainty of their frames and feelings, and the artful insinuations of Satan, their loving Father is considered as an implacable Being, full of wrath and anger against them. But this is contrary to God's revelation of himself in Christ, as a God of love. So also is it injurious and hurtful to the souls of his children. For it damps their love, distresses their spirits, deadens the exercise of their graces, and hinders their increase in holiness, the essence of which is founded in the love of God. Therefore, such views come not from God. But hereby Satan gains an advantage, and triumphs over poor souls with " There, there, so would I have it."

What can the trembling sinner do ? whither can he fly ? what course can he take ? All legal efforts are vain ; from self and nature no hope can spring. What can he think ? Truly, stand amazed that he is out of hell. He cannot sink lower in his views of himself than are his just deserts; yet he can never be in his own sight so miserable but that the grace of God in Christ is all-sufficient to afford hope and help. In nature's despair grace triumphs. A sense of momentary anger heightens returning favor. The joy of the morning is improved by a past night of sorrow. God ever rests unchangeable in his love to his people. This is the essence of Gospel grace and truth. That we vary and fluctuate in our apprehension of his love is natural to our very existence. "But we have a more sure word of prophecy, whereunto ye do well that ye take heed, as unto a light that shineth in a dark place, until the day dawn, and the day-star arise in your hearts." 2 Peter 1 : 19. " The testimony of Jesus is the spirit of prophecy." Rev. 19 : 10. The favor of God to sinners is in Christ, that is their life ; the life and spring of all their graces and comforts. God in Christ is the christian's highest glory and greatest triumph. For his love is unchangeably the same to Christ, and to all who are united to him by the Holy Spirit, and one with him by precious faith. "Rejoice in the Lord alway : and again I say, rejoice." Philippians. 4 : 4.

JAN. 11.—*O my God, my soul is cast down within me : therefore will I remember thee from the land of Jordan, and of the Hermonites, from the hill Mizar.* Psalm 42 : 6

In times of dejection and distress, the thought of a dear friend, who has comforted us in times past, tends to alleviate the mind. If we are assured of his love to us, we question not his readiness to assist us. So, under the affecting loss of a dear brother, Martha addresses the Saviour, "Lord, if thou hadst been here, my brother had not died." John 11 : 21.

Inexpressible blessedness to live in a holy familiarity with the God of love ! How simple are David's words ! how freely doth he pour out his complaints, and tell God of his sorrows ! though his soul was bowed down within him, heaviness of mind beset him, the sweet sunshine of joy was overcast by the dark cloud of sorrow, yet faith's piercing eye looks through all. Regardless of his own frames and feelings, he has direct recourse to God.

O *my* God ! how sweet, how animating are appropriating views of thee to the soul ! Though cast down, though dejected in self, and all within heightens the gloom, yet all above is hopeful and encouraging. Though no confidence about us, yet Jesus is before the throne for us. "I will not, I cannot, I dare not forget this. Rejoice not over me, O mine enemy ; I will still remember my God ; my thoughts shall be yet towards him ; my hope is in him ; my expectations from him. Though it is now dark, I will remember past times of light and love. Though now bowed down, yet my God has been the lifter-up of my head. The light of his reconciled face, in Jesus, hath shined upon me. Clouds may intercept my joyful views of this, but not prevent his sight of me, nor turn away his love from me. My case is before him. My soul lies open to his view. The times of refreshing shall come from his presence. He rests in his love." Such are the reasonings of faith. The experience of departed saints should encourage the confidence of living saints. Down-cast, mourning souls, when they enjoy not God's comforts, should meditate on his loving purposes, rich promises, and free grace in Christ; holding fast the word of his truth. Of what singular and blessed use is the memory to retain divine truths, and bring back a fresh and lively sense of God's past dealings with us! "Remember this, and show yourselves men." "God is faithful, by whom ye were called unto the fellowship of his Son Jesus Christ our Lord." 1 Cor. 1 : 9.

"Amidst temptations sharp and long,
  "My soul to this dear Refuge flies:
"Hope is my anchor, firm and strong,
  "While tempests blow and billows rise.

"The Gospel bears my spirit up:
  "A faithful and unchanging God
"Lays the foundation for my hope,
  "In oaths, and promises, and blood."

Jan. 12.—*Sanctify them through thy truth.* John 17 : 17

Thus prayed our great High Priest on earth. What he asked in his humiliation, is founded upon the word and will of his Father, and he hath power to effect it in his exaltation. Hence we have the fullest assurance of the final perfect sanctification of all his members. Hence the desires and breathings of souls after holiness are encouraged, and our prayers gather the strongest confidence of success.

While our Beloved expresses his affectionate concern for his people's salvation, we see his equal regard for the honor and glory of his Father's word. Love for holiness and love of the truth are inseparable. As the Gospel prevails in the heart, holiness is increased. It is first life, then liveliness in the soul. It is the ministration of the Spirit in the sanctification of the Spirit. Whatever workings of the Spirit we find in the heart, all are by the word of truth. The life of believers is from Christ, who is *the Truth;* therefore increasing light, refreshing comforts, stronger affections shall abound, and all by that same law of grace and truth whereby the soul was at first converted to the faith of Jesus. " The law of the Lord is perfect, converting the soul, making wise the simple, rejoicing the heart, enlightening the eyes." Psalm 19 : 7, 8.

There is a peculiar glory in the order of salvation. " God hath from the beginning chosen us to salvation." But how is this made manifest? Only " through sanctification of the Spirit and belief of the truth." 2 Thess. 2 : 13. Thus faith and holiness flow from electing love. So every word of God's truth is prized, and the fulfilment of every promise is expected. We love the truth of the word, because it discovers God's love to us in Christ : it reveals Christ's righteousness to us for our justification ; revives our hearts with the knowledge of pardon by his blood, and the certainty of full sanctification, and perfect glory, through his intercession. So Jesus prayed, so we believe, so we poor sinners are saved. Saved, unspeakable mercy! from the power of sin and the prevalence of pride. Happy the heart where the love of holiness prevails agreeably to the word of truth. Glory to the Father for his everlasting love ; to Jesus, for his justifying righteousness and atoning blood ; and to the Spirit, for his sanctifying influences This will ever be ascribed, by truly sanctified hearts. "What God hath joined together, let not man put asunder." Matt. 19 : 6.

JAN. 13.—*Whosoever he be of you that forsaketh not all that he hath, he cannot be my disciple.* Luke, 14 : 33

There must be the heart of a disciple, before there can be the conduct of a disciple. Hence, says Christ, "Marvel not that I said unto thee, Ye must be born again." John 3 : 7. The blessed effects of this spiritual birth will be evident in choosing Christ as our Lord, and becoming his disciples. Earthly objects will be forsaken; heavenly ones prized. Jesus being esteemed our treasure and our hope, our hearts will be with him, our affections set on him ; and it will be our chief delight to hear his voice and follow him.

Coming to Christ, is turning our backs upon the "lust of the flesh, the lust of the eye, and the pride of life." By the faith of Jesus we renounce and forsake all these things as our curse and shame. The clearer views we have of Christ's glory, and the stronger our faith is in him, so much the more we become dead to all things beside him. Thus it is manifest who are the disciples of Jesus. Their Master so teacheth them. We have need to pray daily, Sun of righteousness, shine brighter on our minds! Lord, increase our faith! For the flesh, with its affections and lusts, still abides with us ; and as the life of Jesus increases, through faith in the heart, so shall we, more and more, groan under whatever is contrary thereto.

The victory is obtained only through faith : in its nature very simple, but in its fruits and effects most comprehensive. For hereby we enjoy more happiness and comfort in Christ, than all this present world can give. Ye sons of earth, ye disdain us; we pity you. As ye are now, so once were we. We enjoyed your

sinful gratifications, and feasted on your vain delights
too long. We confess it, and grieve for it. Now we
have found Jesus, we have another and a better life. In
divine pleasures, spiritual joys from Christ, and sweet
communion with him, we anticipate future glory. We
enjoy a heaven of comfort in a world of sorrow. Therefore, in seeking all, we gain all. In following Jesus,
though painful and grievous to the flesh, we reap spiritual consolation and joy to our souls. Our greatest honor
upon earth is to be his disciples; our greatest glory
is to confess him; and our chief happiness is to walk
worthy of him. Experience will ever prove, that he
who walks most by faith will be most comforted. He
who lives nearest Christ in faith, will follow him closest
in love ; and, consequently, keep at the greatest distance
from the world's vain pleasures, and the carnal delights
of the flesh. "For if ye live after the flesh, ye shall
die." Rom. 8 : 13.

JAN. 14.—*He that believeth on him is not condemned.* John 3 : 18

Dost thou believe on the Son of God ? This is the
most important question in the world. Faith in Jesus is
the " one thing needful." Without this, the day of life
is a state of sin and condemnation ; the night of death
will be full of terror, and the day of judgment most
dreadful. It cannot be otherwise. For as we are all
malefactors, under the sentence of the law, the thoughts
of such an execution must be most awful and alarming.
But sin blinds men's eyes, hardens their hearts ; and
vain, self-righteous hopes deceive their souls into an insensibility to their lost and ruined state.

What a special mercy to know one's self! what distinguishing grace to know Jesus ! what peculiar favor
to know one is delivered from condemnation by him !
This is the joyful privilege of every believer. Though

he be a sinner, yet God doth not impute sin, but imputeth righteousness unto him; a righteousness which is equivalent to every demand of the law; even the perfect righteousness of the ever-blessed man and Mediator Jesus, our Surety in the flesh. Faith humbly receives this glorious righteousness. The believer is thankful to God the Son who wrought it out, to God the Father who freely bestows it, and to God the Spirit who showed him his want of it. Therefore he is not condemned.

Sin cannot condemn us: it is atoned for by the blood of Jesus. The law cannot condemn us: that is satisfied; yea more, it is magnified and made honorable by the perfect obedience of the God-man Jesus; infinitely more so than it could have been by all the obedience of a world of innocent spotless saints, or of the whole company of the heavenly host of angels and archangels. The justice of God cannot condemn us, being "accepted in the Beloved." God's faithfulness and truth cannot condemn, they are engaged for the righteous. "God is faithful and just to forgive us our sins and to cleanse from all unrighteousness."

Lo, thus is the man blessed that believeth in Jesus: he is righteous in him, through faith; yet not faith, but Jesus alone is his righteousness. He that abides in Jesus, enjoys—what? perfect freedom from the being of sin? No; but this blessedness, perfect freedom from all condemnation for sin. Being passed from death to life, he brings forth fruit to the glory of God: and has inheritance among them who are sanctified by faith which is in Jesus. Acts 26: 18.

Jan. 15.—*Who can understand his errors? cleanse thou me from secret faults. Keep back thy servant also from presumptuous sins; let them not have dominion over me.* Psa. 19: 12, 13

As faith gives a holy boldness at the throne of grace,

so the regenerate soul is open and ingenuous in confession of sin. When sin is dethroned in the heart, the most secret faults bow it in humility before the Lamb. To his precious blood the believer has recourse for cleansing; he finds daily need of it. He cannot understand all his errors. Many secret faults cleave unto him. He is sensible that even these must be washed away, lest they defile his conscience and spread a cloud over his mind. It is the peculiar wisdom of disciples not only to observe the bud, blossom, and fruit of sin; but also to consider the evil root, the polluted nature from which it springs. Here is the exercise of watchfulness. This calls for their daily prayer to be kept by the power of God.

Happy souls! who, under a sense of peace, through the blood of Jesus, are daily praying to be kept by the grace of the Spirit. Such truly know themselves, see their danger of falling, will not, dare not palliate the odious nature of sin, nor lessen its hateful deformity. They will not give a softer name to sin than it deserves, lest they depreciate the infinite value of Jesus' precious blood, which was shed to atone its guilt. Far will they be from flattering themselves into a deceitful notion that they are perfect, and have no sin in them. The Spirit of truth delivers them from such errors; he teaches them, as poor sinners, to look to the Saviour, and beseech him to keep back the head-strong passions, the unruly lusts, which dwell in their sinful natures. Alas! the most exalted saint, the most established believer, if left to himself, how soon might the blackest crimes, the most presumptuous sins, get dominion over him! David had woful experience of this for a season. He prays from a heart-felt sense of past misery and dread of future danger. And he found the blessing of that covenant promise—O believer, may it be the exercise of thy faith, daily to live upon it, daily to plead it before thy

Saviour—"Sin shall not have dominion over you; for ye are not under the law, but under grace." Rom. 6 : 14. Why shall not sin lord it over the conscience of a believer? Because the grace of Jesus reigns for him, and in him. He saith, "I will put my fear in their hearts, that they shall not depart from me." Jer. 32 : 40. O soul! ever cherish this blessed fear. "Happy is the man who feareth alway : but he who hardeneth his heart shall fall into mischief." Prov. 28 : 14.

"O who can ever find
 "The errors of his ways?
"Yet with a bold presumptuous mind
 "I would not dare transgress.

"Warn me of every sin,
 "Forgive my secret faults,
"And cleanse this guilty soul of mine,
 "Whose crimes exceed my thoughts."

JAN. 16.—*If ye love me, keep my commandments. And I will pray the Father, and he shall give you another Comforter, that he may abide with you for ever ; even the Spirit of truth.* John 14 : 15, &c.

He would be a traitor and a rebel, who should dare set up his standard, demand allegiance from the king's subjects, and require obedience to his commands, having no right to the crown. So Jesus, if he were not King of kings and Lord of lords, the living and true God ; but only a mere man, a prophet mighty in word and in deed, a very good man, who taught the best morals and set a good example, as some vainly and ignorantly pretend—verily, if this were all, we christians could see no goodness in him ; but he would be a bold usurper against the one eternal Jehovah, striving to alienate the affections of the heart and the obedience of the life from God, whom alone we are commanded to love and serve. Therefore, "If ye love me keep my commandments,'

saith Jehovah the mighty God in the wonderful man
Christ Jesus. Disciples know his voice. In love he
hath done all things for our salvation. From love he
requires all duty from us. Obedience without love is
slavery : love without obedience is dissimulation. "In
keeping his commandments there is great reward," enjoyed in present peace, expected in future hope ; both
are the fruits of free grace and unmerited love, and secured by precious promises.

While others might hear of Jesus, and talk of the
miracles he wrought in the days of his flesh ; yet those
disciples only, who were obedient to his call and followed him, saw his glory and enjoyed the comforts of his
presence. So, the closer disciples walk with Jesus in
love and obedience, the more they enjoy of the comforts
of faith. And besides the gift of faith, as an evidence,
they shall also receive the comforting witness of their
being the children of God, even from the Spirit of truth ;
another Comforter, who shall abide with them for ever,
as a seal, earnest, and pledge of their future glory. So
Jesus prays : so the Father bestows : so the Spirit applies and comforts. Glory be to the ever-blessed Three
who thus agree in one, and bear witness on earth of salvation, to the comfort and joy of poor sinners. Love
to Jesus is the spring of obedience. Keeping his commandments is the way *in* which, though not *for* which,
the Spirit assures and comforts our hearts. "What God
hath joined together, let not man put asunder." Matt.
19 : 6. "If any man have not the Spirit of Christ, he is
none of his." Rom. 8 : 9.

> "To praise the Father, and the Son,
>   " And Spirit all divine,
> " The one in three, and three in one,
> " Let saints and angels join."

JAN. 17.—*God, who commanded the light to shine out of darkness, hath shined into our hearts, to give us the knowledge of the glory of God in the face of Jesus Christ.* 2 Cor. 4 : 6

This is a glorious confession of faith, worthy to be written in letters of gold, set with the most precious jewels, and ever to be worn, as the believer's ornament and glory. For here is the rich display of sovereign grace, and the glory of almighty power, in producing light in the heart of sinners, who are by nature not only in the dark, but even darkness itself. The knowledge of Jesus is commanded by the same Omnipotent Agent who called forth light in the beginning upon this dark globe. Light gladdens the whole creation of nature : and this spiritual light causeth joy in the whole soul; for it gives the knowledge of God's glory. In what respect? that God is glorious in majesty? O this strikes us with horror. Glorious in power? That fills us with terror. Glorious in holiness? This causes black despair. So every other attribute and perfection of Jehovah must sink sinners into dread, astonishment, and death.

But here is our relief—It is the knowledge of the glory of God *in the person of the anointed Saviour.* In him, God's glorious favor, eternal love, everlasting counsel of peace, covenant of grace, promises of mercy, scheme of salvation, shine with the most resplendent lustre. Hence pardon, love, peace, joy, holiness, hope, security, heaven in possession, glory in reversion ; all, all centre in the person of Jesus. Thus we behold the glory of God : God in Christ ! This is the only comfortable knowledge, the only reviving experience of the christian heart. And here we see how inseparably connected are God's glory and his people's welfare. Each leads to the other, and both tend to lay sinners low in humility, and sink them to nothing before a sovereign.

gracious Lord. Could a dark chaos contribute any thing to the production of light? Canst thou, O worm of the earth, exert any power to cause that glorious luminary the sun to send forth its reviving beams of light? No; the first is by the command of the Sovereign Agent; the latter acts by the laws of its wise Creator. So as to spiritual light, saving knowledge, it is given to those who sought it not; it is made manifest to those who askd d not after it. What then becomes of human merits in the business of our salvation? O thou once spiritually blind and dead soul, if God hath commanded the light and knowledge of Jesus in thine heart, all boasting is excluded; all glorying in self is at an end. Surely thou wilt say, Thine is the power; to thee, to thee alone, Jehovah, be all the glory!

JAN. 18.—*Who being the brightness of his glory, and the express image of his person, and upholding all things by the word of his power, when he had by himself purged our sins, sat down on the right hand of the Majesty on high.* Hebrews 1 : 3

What St. Paul says of the resurrection of Jesus, (1 Cor. 15,) may, with equal truth, be applied to his divinity : if Jesus be not truly and essentially the self-existing God, " all preaching is vain; all faith is vain;" all the saints of God must perish in their sins. But we have not so learned Christ, if so be we have heard him, and know the truth as it is in him. His eternal power and Godhead angels adore, while devils tremble and saints rejoice. Only poor, blinded, proud sinners dare cavil against and deny it.

That Jesus is both Lord and God, lies at the foundation of our faith. That he upholds all things by the word of his power, is the joy of our hearts. That, as man, he hath purged our sins, causes all our hope and comfort.

That he is entered into heaven for us, and there pleads our cause, is the glory of our souls. For our hope entereth into that within the veil. There Jesus, our forerunner, is for us entered. On this rock Christ's church is built, and neither the powers of earth and sin, nor the gates of hell shall prevail against it. When the Spirit brings the soul up to Nebo, the mount of prospect and prophecy, it has glorious views of the inheritance, it speaks of it, and the graces of faith, hope, love, peace, and joy abound in the heart.

But, alas! all is barren as a wilderness, unfruitful as a desert, while sin, in its guilt and punishment, is not known and believed to have been purged by the blood of Jesus. This is the only remedy for sin-burdened souls, the most reviving cordial for drooping spirits. That same blood, which was all-sufficient to purge away sin in the court of heaven, is also all-sufficient to cleanse the guilt of it from the conscience. Sweet consolation for the members of Jesus! Their living Head, in human form, is at the right hand of the Majesty in glory; the blessed object to whom we are ever to look, through whom every comfort flows, and in whom is our hope in every conflict with sin and Satan. What then doth this doctrine teach us? That our hearts should ascend up to our Saviour. But how? By faith. "Christ dwells in our hearts by faith." Eph. 3 : 17. And by faith our hearts ascend to and dwell with him. And this is the reasoning of faith : "If, when we were enemies, we were reconciled to God by the death of his Son, much more, being reconciled, we shall be saved by his life." Romans 5 : 10.

Jan. 19.—*Keep yourselves in the love of God.* Jude 21

The love of God, like every other attribute and perfection of Jehovah, is everlasting and unchangeable :

even as the essence of God himself. This love is manifested to his people in Christ Jesus. He is the object
in whom they are viewed and loved by the Father. As
" Jesus is the same yesterday, to-day, and for ever ;"
so is God's love towards them. Time, with all its con-
curring circumstances, can make no alteration or change,
increase or diminution herein. But, as to the sense and
enjoyment of this love, the word of truth and experience of saints plainly testify of its ebbing and flowing,
its fervor and abatement in the soul. Hence the necessity of those tender calls, kind warnings, and loving counsels, addressed to believers in the word of truth ; because they are ever to be active, as those who are made
alive to God, and have their senses exercised to discern
between good and evil. Exhortations excite jealousy
and quicken diligence. The enjoyment of the love of
God is our heaven below ; to keep ourselves in the happy sense of it is our highest privilege, our greatest happiness. Keep ourselves in the love of God ! Yes. How ?
Use every means which love commands. Avoid all things
which love forbids. Account not this legal. Those who
do, have only the notion of love in the head, but are
strangers to the constraints of God's love in the heart.

Wouldst thou ever enjoy love, O christian ? Be much
in meditation upon it, think daily, constantly of that
unparalleled instance of it : God so loved the world as
to give his only begotten Son Jesus, to atone for sin by
his precious blood, to justify sinners by his perfect
righteousness. Dost thou know this by the Gospel ?
This is love revealed. Dost thou believe this, in thine
heart, by the Spirit ? This is love felt and enjoyed. All,
al flows from the rich, transcendently rich love of God
in Christ Jesus. O be concerned daily to keep thy soul
in and under a lively sense of this love ! and also keep
thyself, by this love, from all worldly and forbidden in-
du'gences. Thy flesh may covet them ; but by the love

of God, by his mercies in Christ Jesus, and for thy soul's sake, abstain from them. Know verily, as hurtful food will impair the health of thy body; so these things will as certainly rob thy soul of its peace, damp the warm sense of God's love, and render thee indifferent and lifeless to the enjoyment of the love of God. Thus saith the God of love, " Consider your ways." Haggai 1 : 5.

Jan. 20.—*But Jesus answered her not a word.* Matt. 15: 23.

What! not a word from the compassionate Saviour, who is touched with a feeling of our infirmities? Is he deaf to the cries and dumb to the entreaties of a distressed, sorrowful heart? No: love in the heart has always an ear open to complaints, a tongue ready to speak comfort, and a kind hand to relieve. But love afflicts, to bring his children to him, and make them call upon him: he forbears to answer, that they may be the more importunate. God's delays prove faith's vigor, make love cling closer, prayer more fervent, and patience shine brighter. By these means the graces of God's children are drawn forth into lively exercise, and are made manifest that they are wrought by God. Perseverance obtains the blessing in due time. Jesus honors and applauds the grace of his beloved members with, O man, O woman, great is thy faith!

Christ well knew what work he had wrought in this poor humble supplicant's heart, whereby she knew Jesus to be Lord and God; therefore he proved her, and tried her, that her faith might shine brighter to his glory and her soul's comfort. As she possessed the same faith, so she discovers the same resolution as Job, " Though he slay me, yet will I trust in him." Job 13 : 15. And, with Jacob, she would wrestle, and her heart determined, ' I will not let thee go except thou bless me." Genesis 32 : 26.

But the silence of Jesus was very disheartening; when he spake, it was quite discouraging. Though she worshipped him, and sighed out, "Lord, help me;" yet Jesus seems rather to repulse than comfort her. But true faith ever sinks the soul low in humility, while it clings close to the most high God. The soul owns its vileness and utter unworthiness, and fixes all its plea upon mere mercy, all its hopes upon Jesus only. Thus Christ empties whom he delights to fill. He makes us see and confess ourselves to be dogs, fit only to feed under the table; though he loves us as children, and all that he hath is ours by free gift, precious promise, and rich grace. Thou poor, fearing, doubting soul, who hast long been seeking, waiting, and praying for comfort by a word or look from Jesus, take courage. Ever trust in him who saith, "I have satiated the weary soul, and I have replenished every sorrowful soul." Jer. 31 : 25. Mark the result to this believing, importunate, waiting woman: "Be it unto thee, even as thou wilt," was the answer, replete with all comfort and joy. "The Lord is a God of judgment; blessed are all they who wait for him." Isaiah 30 : 18.

> " My spirit looks to God alone:
> " My rock and refuge is his throne:
> " In all my fears, in all my straits,
> " My soul on his salvation waits."

JAN. 21.—*Our Gospel came not to you in word only, but also in power, and in the Holy Ghost, and in much assurance.* 1 Thessalonians 1 : 5

Though sin, salvation, death, judgment, eternity, are subjects of the highest moment to us all, yet we naturally think of them with little concern, speak of them with great indifference, and treat the consideration of them as Felix did Paul, " Go thy way for this time;

when I have a convenient season I will call for thee."
Acts 24 : 25. And yet, perhaps, such have long sat under
a preached Gospel; greatly applaud the preachers, and
are ready to condemn others who do not see and admire
their excellency. But, alas! what are the most excellent words of man without the power of the Spirit?
Light as air; ineffectual, to the saving of the soul, as
sounding brass or a tinkling cymbal.

The grand question is, Have I inwardly known and
felt the power of the Gospel? It *has* an internal voice:
it speaks glad tidings, good news, of life and salvation
to the very soul: it is the word of power, to quicken
dead souls to life: it is a revelation to the heart, of pardon and peace by Jesus Christ. Thus it brings the
clearest evidence, the fullest assurance along with it,
that it is God's word of life and salvation. The Holy
Ghost bears witness to it, in power and demonstration.
Blessed souls! who are divinely assured of the truths
of Gospel grace and love by Christ; who embrace the
Gospel as their only hope, flee and cleave to Jesus as
their only refuge. But more blessed, yea, most happy
those believing souls who are upon the delectable mountains, and enjoy much assurance of their own personal
interest in Jesus, and eternal life through him; and by
the Holy Ghost are enabled to say, "I know that Jesus
loved me and died for me." O this privilege is most
highly to be prized! it deserves the most earnest pressing after.

This only can deliver the soul from all doubts and
fears, inflame it with most ardent love, inspire it with
holy boldness, influence it to most cheerful obedience
and resignation to afflictive allotments, wing it with
holy longings after Christ and eternal glory, and make
it joyfully triumphant over the tyrant death, with
"Thanks be to God, who giveth us the victory, through
our Lord Jesus Christ." 1 Cor. 15 : 57. Does God love

his people in Christ with an everlasting love? does he will their salvation, and that they should clearly know and be comfortably assured of this? Most certainly; for he exhorts them to give all "diligence to the full assurance of hope." Heb. 6 : 11.

Jan. 22.—*He that acknowledgeth the Son, hath the Father also.* 1 John 2 : 23

If so, we cannot pay too much homage, nor ascribe too great glory to Christ. Did he receive from God the Father honor and glory, by this voice from the excellent glory, " This is my beloved Son, in whom I am well pleased?" 2 Peter 1 : 17. Is it the Father's will " that all men should honor the Son, even as they honor the Father?" Doth Christ say, " He that honoreth not the Son, honoreth not the Father that sent him?" John. 5 : 23. May we not then boldly say, with Paul, on another occasion, " As the truth of Christ is in me, no man shall stop me" of this glorying in Jesus as my Lord, my God. Yea, we will acknowledge him in his lowest form and meanest appearance; as the babe wrapped in swaddling-clothes, lying in a manger, a destitute, outcast infant, obscure and mean in his birth and parentage, working at a common ordinary employ, without form and comeliness, despised and rejected of men, a man of sorrows and acquainted with grief, mocked, derided, laughed to scorn, crowned with thorns, condemned and crucified as an accursed wretch unworthy to live, adjudged fit only to die in company with thieves and highwaymen on a gibbet: wholly to trust in this man, this God-man, Jesus of Nazareth, the Root and Offspring of David, this is " the faith of God's elect." This is the acknowledgment of the truth which is after godliness. This is the only " hope of eternal life, which God, who cannot lie, promised before the world began." Tit. 1 : 2.

This is "repentance to the acknowledging of the truth."
2 Tim. 2 : 25. Thus are simple, believing hearts "comforted, being knit together in love, unto all riches of the full assurance of understanding, to the acknowledgment of the mystery of God, and of the Father, and of Christ; in whom are hid all the treasures of wisdom and knowledge." Col. 2 : 2, 3.

In this rich mine of truth and consolation we are daily to dig for all wisdom, holiness, and happiness. In this acknowledgment of the Son thus saving us in his humble state, we have the Father's rich love and precious promises; and the Holy Spirit's power, influence, and witness. For he bears witness to, and takes of the things of Christ, and shows them to us. John 16 : 15. And thus we are made meet to be partakers of the heavenly inheritance. Be ever "giving thanks." Col. 1 : 12.

JAN. 23.—*Why art thou cast down, O my soul? and why art thou disquieted within me? Hope thou in God: for 1 shall yet praise him, who is the health of my countenance, and my God.* Psalm 42 : 11

We are not to expect the sunshine of joy all through this vale of tears. Comfortable frames and joyful feelings, though sweet and delightful, are not always most profitable. Were we ever on the mount of joy we should forget that we are strangers and pilgrims on earth, be for building tabernacles of rest in a polluted place, and cry out, with the highly-favored disciples, "It is good for us to be here;" but they knew not what they said. Luke 9 : 33. It is the glory of a christian to live by faith on Jesus, to judge of his love from the word of truth, more than by sense and feeling: yea, under dejection and disquiet of soul, to hope and trust in God, to check and rebuke one's self for doubts and diffidence, is the real exercise of faith. Faith supports the soul, and lifts it above the views of carnal reason and the sug-

gestions of sense. The believer is steadily to abide by
the word of truth, though in heaviness for a season; being persuaded that shortly he shall rejoice in, and praise
God even for this gloomy dispensation; concluding from
the word of God's grace and faithfulness, Jehovah Jesus
" is the health of my countenance, and my God." This
is the very joy of faith. Such was the sweet experience
of David, recorded in the 42d and 43d Psalms for our
instruction.

Disciple, it is well for thee to learn wisdom hereby.
The state of thy soul may vary; but the foundation of
God's love standeth sure, his promises cannot fail; the
word of truth, yea, the oath of Jehovah, are engaged for
the strong consolation of all " who have fled to Jesus
for refuge." Heb. 6 : 18. Thou mayest meet with many
things, from within and without, to cast down, distress,
and disquiet thee; but thou art called to look to Jesus,
not to stagger at the promises through unbelief; but,
like the father of the faithful, " against hope to believe
in hope ;" not to consider thine own corrupt nature, its
proneness to evil, its enmity to grace, so as to give up
thy hope. There is ever cause of humility, but no reason for casting away thy confidence in Jesus. Though
thou sinkest to hell, in the view of thy deserts, yet,
through the righteousness of Jesus, salvation is procured
for the hell-deserving. Encourage thy soul to hope in
him, so shalt thou glorify him. " I will bless the Lord
at all times, his praise shall continually be in my
mouth. My soul shall make her boast in the Lord."
Psalm 34 : 1, 2.

JAN. 24.—*For this thing I besought the Lord thrice, that it
might depart from me.* 2 Corinthians 12 : 8

Our Saviour represents God's own elect as crying
day and night to him. Luke 18 : 7. For sore tempta-

tions, soul-burdens, Satan's buffetings are peculiarly felt by them. Their crying under them is a proof of spiritual life; their crying to the Lord only is an evidence of the faith of God's elect; their entreaties to be delivered from them show the sanctified nature and holy disposition of their souls. Thus the Lord brings the graces of his children into exercise. His eyes are ever upon them, his ears open to their prayers, and his almighty power and grace sufficient to deliver them. But his time is best. It is his will that we should tell him of our trials and temptations; and after we have done this, "we have need of patience" to wait the fulfilment of his promise. This is our duty.

Paul prayed again and again; still the buffetings were continued, his mind was harassed, his soul distressed, the enemy triumphed, the Lord seemed as though he heard not. Prayer and patience must go hand in hand. Murmurings are the offspring of unbelief. Fretfulness arises from pride. To lie humble at the feet of Jesus is our wisdom. Never indulge one hard thought of our Saviour's will to make thee holy, or his power to make thee happy; though sin and Satan, like unwelcome visiters, daily intrude, appear in various shapes, attack from different quarters, and seem to gain upon thee in thought, word, or action. When inwardly discomposed by unholy tempers, and outwardly harassed by various temptations, poor souls are too ready to think the war will end in their destruction; that Jesus will never give complete victory. But he most assuredly will. In due time we shall reap, if we faint not. Let it suffice, that the triumphant Head in glory says to each of his militant members on earth, "My grace is sufficient for thee: for my strength is made perfect in weakness." This was the precious, humbling, joyful lesson Christ taught Paul; and which he will also make all his dear members learn. Importu nate praying, humble waiting, confident believing, comfortable hoping, are of the very life and essence of a christian. And let our besetting temptations and conflicting trials be what they may, it is our blessed privilege to write with the pen of faith, " Who or what shall separate us from the love of Christ ? Nay, in all things we are more than conquerors through him that loved us." Romans 8 : 35, 37.

> " Let me but hear my Saviour say,
> " Strength shall be equal to thy day ;
> " Then I rejoice in deep distress,
> " Leaning on all-sufficient grace."

JAN. 25.—*Jesus said unto him, Verily I say unto thee, To-day shalt thou be with me in paradise.* Luke 23 : 43

Unbelief, how great its power ! how strong its influence ! It would for ever blind all our eyes and harden all our hearts against Jesus and his grace ; but " he shall divide the spoil with the strong." The prophet's prediction is here clearly fulfilled, the sovereignty of grace fully displayed. Our Lord's doctrine is truly verified in these two thieves: " One shall be taken, the other left." Matt. 24 : 40. But doth our Lord bring sinners to glory without faith, repentance, and holiness ? Doth he leave his people to continue in their sin and rebellion ? No ; blessed be his name, Jesus is " exalted to be a Prince and a Saviour, for to give repentance and remission of sins." So he saves " his people from their sins." So he makes them happy in his love, by the secret power of the Spirit's inward operations. Who made these two companions in sin, these blasphemers of Jesus to differ ? Grace, sovereign, distinguishing, almighty grace did this wonderful work, " and it is marvellous in our eyes." How rapid its power ! how swift its course ! in one moment a railer against Jesus is changed to a believer in him; a proud rebel, to an humble suppliant; a self-justifying sinner, to a Christ-exalting saint; in a moment converted, pardoned, sanctified, and made meet for glory; to-day hell-deserving, to-day in paradise. Thus the thief believed with his heart unto righteousness, and made confession with his mouth unto salvation.

What hath grace done! what is it not able to effect! Sweetest encouragement to the vilest of sinners to look to Jesus: strongest assurance for the weakest believers to abide in him. "Lord Jesus, remember me," proceeds from grace in the heart of his members. "Thou shalt be with me in paradise" is the gracious answer. It was the grace of our Lord Jesus that saved this thief, this highwayman, and translated him from a cross on earth to a crown in glory. The most amiable character, the most upright person hath nothing else to look to, or trust in, but the cross of Christ alone for salvation. This is all our glorying. By the death of Jesus we are saved. Touched by the cross, we live. The Spirit which enables the soul to believe on Jesus, conforms it to him, makes it meet for the heavenly inheritance. Colossians 1 : 12.

JAN. 26.—*Let us therefore come boldly to the throne of grace, that we may obtain mercy, and find grace to help in every time of need.* Hebrews 4 : 16

Very few, comparatively, of the subjects of an earthly monarch are permitted free access to him. An honor this, too great to be common. King's courts are for the noble. The poor and destitute, the miserable and distressed have no admission there. But, ye poor, distressed subjects of the King of kings, it is not thus with you. Your King, though ever on a throne, where majesty and glory shine with brightest lustre, yet freely dispenses

grace and mercy to needy souls. Hither you are invited to come; yea more, to come boldly. Why? because you are "rich, and increased in goods, and have
need of nothing?" Nay, but because your King knows
that you are "poor and miserable, blind and naked" in
yourselves, with nothing to present to procure his favor or claim his acceptance of you. But he loves you,
has riches for your poverty, eye-salve for your blindness,
a garment for your nakedness, a robe for your rags, and
mercy for your misery; yea, a heaven of grace for
your hell of deserts.

Your Mediator with his blood, your High Priest with
his much incense, always intercedes. There can be no
period of your life but is a time of need; but who has
obtained all the mercy, who has found all the grace
which can be dispensed from his throne? Thou art still
a sinner, and wantest both mercy and grace; and as
thou findest thy want, thy need, hither thou mayest always repair with boldness, and ever expect a rich
supply. For God the Father is the fountain of grace
and mercy. Jesus thy Saviour is the treasurer. "All
fulness of grace dwells in him." The Spirit is the dispenser of mercy and grace. Why then, O soul, that
backwardness which too often besets thee? What privilege so great? What encouragement so strong?

"Come with boldness," yet with becoming awe and
reverence. Boldness of faith is grounded on something
without a man, on nothing in him; not on the fervent
heart of love, the bleeding heart of repentance, the
active life of obedience, the suffering mind of patience;
but faith fixes on Jesus, and the believer comes with an
empty heart and hand, to be filled with the free gifts
of grace. Sweetest encouragement from the Friend
of sinners! "Come unto me, all ye that labor and are
heavy laden," most blessed promise! "and I will give
you rest." Matt. 11:28.

Jan. 27.—*Unto you who believe, he is precious.* 1 Pet. 2 : 7

We are loved with precious love ; redeemed by precious blood ; comforted by precious promises ; justified by precious faith ; yea, righteousness, holiness, heaven, we have by union with a precious Jesus. Surely, then, "to them that believe he is precious." Say, ye sons of poverty, ye daughters of affliction, is this a time when friends grow cool and desert you? But in such a season to find a Friend who visited you in your distress, was ever saying kind things to you, ever doing all possible good for you ; when in prison sought you out and set you at liberty, when sick was your Physician and healed you, when naked clothed you, when in abject poverty made you rich ; and thus was always pleased when he could make you easy and happy : say, is not this a Friend of ten thousand? a Friend who sticketh closer than a brother? Is not such an one precious indeed?

All this, yea, infinitely more than all this, hath Jesus done for a poor wretched race of sinners. Therefore he is indeed to them a precious "Friend, who loveth at all times :" the precious "Brother, who is born for adversity." Prov. 17 : 17. "He is the same yesterday, to-day, and for ever." Precious in what he hath done *yesterday*—shed his blood for the guilty ; wrought out a righteousness to clothe the naked. *To-day* he is pleading our cause before the throne, where "he *ever* lives to save to the uttermost all them that come unto God by him." Heb. 7 : 25. He makes visits of love, sends kind tokens, refreshing manifestations, causing poor hearts to rejoice in him, filling them with peace and comfort from him. O he is inestimably precious in what he is doing, and in what he will do. For he will never leave one of his members till he has brought them all safe through a wicked world, given them victory over all sin, Satan, and death, and lodged them in

the arms of his embraces. O who can say how infi
nitely precious Jesus is to the saints above! This we
must die to know. Though now we know but in part,
and see but in part; yet from what we do see and
know by faith, we can say, "he is precious indeed."

However distressing our circumstances, yet he is
Immanuel, God with us. Are we sick of sin? He is
our Physician. Is sin our burden? He is our Deliverer.
Doth the law accuse and condemn us? He is the Lord
our righteousness. Do lust and corruption rebel? He
is our sanctification. Do the world, sin and Satan
threaten our destruction? He is Jesus, our salvation;
our all in all.

JAN. 28.—*My voice shalt thou hear in the morning, O Lord ; in
the morning will I direct my prayer unto thee, and will look
up.* Psalm 5 : 3

In the Lord we all live, move, and have our being ; it
is therefore the indispensable duty of all to call upon
the name of the Lord. But what is a duty from nature
and reason, is a rich privilege, an inestimable blessing
to the children of grace. The pouring out of the spirit
of grace and supplication is one of those spiritual
blessings wherewith we are blessed in Christ Jesus. In
the exercise of this, saints, in all ages, have experienced sweet fellowship with God, and have been indulged with those mercies they asked of him. "This
is the confidence that we have in Him, that, if we
ask any thing according to his will, he heareth us."
1 John 5 : 14.

Prayer seems to have been the first employ of David's heart. He began the day with it. So soon as his
eyes were favored with the morning light, he directed
them up unto the Lord. After his tongue had been
locked in silent sleep, the first sound of his voice

breathed an address to his God. Why is this holy
man's practice recorded? Doubtless for our instruction; .o remind us that it is sweet to begin the day
with God. Better to go from the throne of grace into
the business of life, than to delay approaching it till
worldly concerns have intruded on our minds. Wisest
to seek and serve our best Friend first. But, is it not
an affecting truth, that, though a throne of grace is
ever accessible, though believers may always approach
thereto in Christ, though we have the greatest encou-
ragements to draw nigh to God, though we have so
many strong corruptions and sinful passions ever ready
to break out, we are yet so often beset with backwardness to prayer? May we not justly charge most of our
sins and failings, and the breaking forth of our unholy
tempers, to the neglect of this duty? How ought we to
begin each day with seeking the power of the Spirit, to
enable us to mortify sin and live unto God! We complain of deadness and barrenness of soul; who can enliven and make us fruitful but our dear Lord, whom we
neglect to cry unto? If thine outward walk is a reproach, if the peace of thy mind is ruffled and dis-
turbed through want of peace and power from Jesus,
does not thy closet testify against thee as too much
neglected? May not this accusation be justly charged
upon us, "Ye have not, because ye ask not?" James
4:2. But our Beloved invites. His command is for
our blessing. "Ask, and ye shall receive, that your
joy may be full." John 16:24.

Jan. 29.—*Follow peace with all men, and holiness, without
which no man shall see the Lord.* Hebrews 12:14

"He that believeth shall be saved." This is the immutable decree of the God of truth. As without holiness no man shall see the Lord, so no man can be holy

without faith in Jesus. But this is the peculiar blessedness of every believer: he is "sanctified by faith which
is in Christ Jesus." Acts 26 : 18. All such are "called
to be saints," 1 Cor. 1 : 2 ; called to holiness of life and
conversation.

Gospel exhortations are suited to the spiritual state
of regenerate souls. They are the subjects of the
Prince of peace ; are at peace with God, through our
Lord Jesus Christ. As, agreeable to their character,
to the will of God, and for the peace of their own
minds, they are ever to study and endeavor to follow
peace with all men, consistent with faith and a good
conscience ; so, being holy members of the holy Jesus,
beloved children of a holy God, subjects of a holy Spirit, called by a holy Gospel, partakers of a holy faith,
heirs of a holy kingdom, they are all the way of their
journey thither to follow holiness. Partaking of the
root of holiness, by union with Jesus the fruits of holiness will be produced. Christ is the way wherein we
are to walk. Conformity to his image is the delight
of new-born souls. But we are subjects of a nature
which is averse to this. Still we know that holiness
and happiness are ever inseparable. Holiness is our
vocation, and is ever to be our constant aim ; not to recommend us to God to procure his favor, or as a condition of our acceptance in his sight ; but that we may
glorify him "who hath made us accepted in the Beloved."

Saints are not to indulge themselves on the bed of
sloth, dream of heaven, and vainly wish to cast themselves out of Delilah's lap of worldly pleasures and sinful gratifications, into Abraham's bosom of heavenly
joys. But we are studiously to avoid every thing which
is contrary to the nature of true holiness ; and ever
to be diligent in the use of those means which, through
the power of the Holy Spirit, may increase our love
of holiness, and cause us to abound in the practice of

it. True, we have innumerable enemies from within and without, to oppose our progress in holiness. So much the more need of diligence and activity. We know the delicious fruits of happiness grow only in the paths of holiness. The Lord's strength is for us. Great and precious promises are given us. All to encourage us "to serve him without fear, in holiness and righteousness before him, all the days of our life " Luke 1 : 74, 75.

Jan. 30.—*And now, Lord, what wait I for? my hope is in thee.*
Psalm 39 : 7

What a blessing is inward composure of mind! How delightful an exercise is waiting upon the Lord! What a profitable privilege is prayer! How happy that soul whose hope is in God! These are all sweet attendants upon, and promoted by the grace of faith in Christ Jesus. While that grows strong in the soul, we are lively and comfortable. Hence the disciples' petition, "Lord, increase our faith," is daily needful. Then it is well with the soul, when enabled to make this solemn appeal to its Saviour, "Thou, Lord, knowest what I long for, what I wait for, even the spiritual blessings of thy kingdom; to be more inwardly transformed into thine image, more perfectly obedient to thy will, and to obtain a more complete victory over my worst foes, sin, Satan, and the world."

Verily, the heavenly-instructed soul knows that all this is of God by Jesus Christ; and that the contrary to all this is from the lusts that dwell in him, and evils that surround him: therefore God alone is his hope. His hope is not in his graces, his feelings, his frames, his comforts, but in the God of all grace; not in the streams, but in the fountain; not in what he has received, but in the infinite fulness which is treasured up in Jesus for the needy. Hope of salvation in Jesus is our helmet. Faith guards the heart. Hope fortifies the head. Hence the christian lifts up his head in the day of battle, and in the hour of temptation. His head being thus armed, he dreads not Divine wrath, Satan's terrors, the law's threatenings.

Thou man of God, consult not thy carnal reason; consider not thy body, which is dead because of sin; but know that thy spirit is life, because of righteousness. Though the law is weak through the flesh, yet grace reigns; and through Gospel grace thou hast great and precious promises to encourage thee to hope confidently, and the omnipotent power of the Spirit to work in thee, to make thee go on cheerfully; while Jesus is the stay of thine heart, to uphold and strengthen thee. Fear not: only believe; greater is Jesus than all thine enemies. "Stronger is he who is for us, than all that are against us." Verily thou shalt not be disappointed of thy hope, seeing it is in the Lord. Where Jesus is the object of faith, and the anchor of hope is cast within the veil, the soul shall safely and comfortably weather out every storm, and assuredly obtain the haven of eternal rest. By faith we possess the promises. Hope expects the perfect fulfilment of them. In waiting, we renew our strength. Isaiah 40 : 31.

> "Wait on the Lord, ye trembling saints,
> "And keep your courage up;
> "He'll raise your spirit when it faints,
> "And far exceed your hope."

JAN. 31.—*Neither pray I for these alone, but for them also that shall believe on me through their word.* John 17 : 20

What a rich fund of comfort is here for every believer in the Lamb! His loving heart was not contracted, nor his eyes of compassion confined to the little flock now with him; but he looked forward in love, his bowels of tender mercy yearned over, and his innocent tongue pleaded in behalf of all the tender lambs of his flock, through all succeeding ages, in every period of time. Yea, ere they had a being in the world, or faith in their hearts, they had an interest in Jesus' prayers; for they were given to him by the Father. Methinks one hears some poor doubting member of Jesus saying, "Ah, if I was but sure my worthless name was written in the Lamb's book of life, if I could but know his heart of love was towards poor sinful me, that I was included in the happy catalogue of those Jesus prayed for, O how happy, how joyful should I be!" Here, thy Lord has answered thy request. Read it for the joy of thy heart and the establishment of thy soul in faith and love. Hast thou heard the apostolic truth, Salvation by Jesus Christ? Is it glad tidings to thy heart? Dost thou believe in Jesus Christ, as the only Saviour of the lost and guilty? as the only hope for thy, otherwise, hopeless soul? If so, verily thou hast as much reason to conclude Jesus prayed for thee, as if thy name were written at full length in this very petition. Jesus prays for all who shall believe on him through the apostle's word.

The whole of salvation is sure to all believers, even the weakest of all, from the covenant, from Jesus, from the Spirit, and from the oath and promises of God. Though there is a sea of corruption and sin in thy nature, a world of temptations around thee, legions of devils in battle-array against thy poor soul; yet as thou hast the faith of God's elect in thine heart, be it ever so weak, thou art possessed of a precious jewel, which is the inestimable gift of God's Holy Spirit. And verily, so sure as Jesus prayed this prayer on earth unto his Father, thou, even thou, wast in his all-seeing eye, hadst a place in his loving heart, and hast an interest in his finished salvation. That prayer, "Father, I will that they also, whom thou hast given me, be with me where I am, that they may behold my glory," verse 24, shall be answered, while you ascribe salvation to God and the Lamb through the happy ages of a never-ending eternity.

February

FEB. 1.—*I will lift up mine eyes unto the hills, from whence cometh my help.* Psalm 121 : 1

The most comforting subject to a spiritual mind, is "God in Christ reconciled to us, not imputing our trespasses unto us." The hills afford us a pleasing idea of Jesus. As they are parts of the same earth with the lowest valley; so Jesus was found in fashion as a man; took on him the same nature, and was in all things like unto his brethren, sin only excepted. Wherefore "God hath highly exalted him, and given him a name above every name;" Phil. 2 : 9; even the precious name, Jesus, the Saviour. We can never dwell too much upon the human form and humble appearance of him, while we entertain the most exalted ideas of his eternal power and godhead. "He bore our sins, and carried our sorrows;" all our help is laid upon him, all our hope is in him, and all our help cometh from him. And for the encouragement of faith, his word assures us of his love towards sinners, and his power to help them.

Soldiers of Christ, what is your chief business on earth, but to glorify God? what your daily work, but "to fight the good fight of faith, and lay hold on eternal life?" This is our calling: the light of another day is vouchsafed us. But whither can we turn our eyes, but enemies surround us on every side? Yea, from within as well as without. And can we experience safety, or walk in comfort, but while our eyes are up to Jesus? He is entered into heaven, "to appear in the presence of God for us." Hebrews 9 : 24. He says to us, "Look unto me, and be ye saved." Isaiah 45 : 22.

The sight of sin that dwelleth in us causeth dejection. Looking to our own righteousness and fancied excellence begets pride and vain confidence. The power and subtilty of that malicious spirit, "the prince of the power of the air," is enough to make one tremble. This present evil world, with its honors, profits, and pleasures, is exactly suited to our carnal nature. Who can withstand its smiles, renounce its carnal children, and bear their reproaches? who is proof against these potent adversaries? Verily, with all knowledge received, all grace communicated, all past experience enjoyed, we shall not be able to stand and maintain our ground, or persevere in comfort, if we are not continually lifting up our eyes and "looking to Jesus" as our only present help. For we are kept by his mighty power to salvation; but let us ever remember, it is through Christ-exalting faith. 1 Peter 1 : 5

FEB. 2.—*Thy word was unto me the joy and rejoicing of mine heart: for I am called by thy name, O Lord God of hosts.* Jeremiah 15 : 16

That is a sweet petition in the service of the church of England; "Grant, O Lord, that we may not only hear, read, mark, and learn, but inwardly digest the holy Scriptures." So soon as the Lord hath fulfilled this prayer upon any poor sinner, then Christ is the hope of his soul, he esteems the Scriptures as his daily food, and the doctrines of grace are the joy and rejoicing of his heart.

Glory to our loving Shepherd, he finds his sheep, scattered and starving upon the barren mountains, he leads them to green pastures of Gospel grace and love; there they feed, and lie down, beside the still waters of peace and salvation. And this heightens every comfort and improves every joy, even an inward testimony, "I am called by thy name, O Lord God of hosts."

How happy, when minister or disciple is able, in simplicity and godly sincerity, to make this appeal, "Thou hast called me!" Thou, Jehovah, who rulest over the armies of angels and all the heavenly host, thou hast condescended to make known thy name, thy grace, thy salvation to me, even wretched me. I hear thy voice, I know thy voice, I feel desires after thee, my heart thinks of thee with pleasure and delight, I find a hungering and thirsting within me, which nothing but thy blessed self can satisfy; I am grieved when I offend thee, happy only when thy love and presence are enjoyed, and am concerned that I enjoy them no more This is heaven below. Feeding upon the word of truth increases desires after Jesus, the object of faith. So the soul also becomes dead to the life of sense, the intrusions of sin, the allurements of the world, and the baits of Satan. Happy those in whom the word of Christ dwells richly in all wisdom! Happy those in whose hearts Christ dwells by faith! O soul, hast thou an appetite to feed upon the Bible, and digest it? Is it health and nourishment to thee? Then thou art blessed with the most exquisitely delicate taste. A poor sailor was lately cast away, lost his all, was almost naked. The first half-crown he got, he inquired where to make a purchase—of what, think you? O, what was dearest to his heart—a Bible. Blessed evidence of a christian! "Let the word of Christ dwell in you richly." Col. 3 : 16.

"The volume of my Father's grace
"Doth all my grief assuage:
"Here I behold my Saviour's face
"Almost in every page.

"O may thy counsels, mighty God,
  "My roving feet command;
"Nor I forsake the happy road
  "That leads to thy right hand."

FEB. 3.—*Ye are Christ's; and Christ is God's.* 1 Cor. 3 : 23

The apostle Paul searches heaven and earth, time and
eternity, to make up the christian's rich catalogue of
mercies. But, as though the utmost stretch of thought
of men or angels might omit some part of the believer's
treasure; and lest any thing should be found wanting
for support and comfort to any needy soul, he twice
repeats, "*All things* are yours." Believer, wouldst thou
know thy title? wouldst thou inquire, "Whence is it
that the Lord should consign such innumerable blessings, such infinitely rich mercies to us?" whereas one
thing we know, and feel daily, that we are sinners to this
very hour. And will not this prevent the right to possession, and the freedom of enjoyment? No: justice
and wisdom conspire to take away this, and every objection. The medium of communication is such, that
neither reason, law, nor equity can gainsay it.

Dwell on this point; look up to the Spirit of truth to
establish faith, strengthen hope, increase love, and promote joy. "Ye are Christ's," by special gift; his dear
purchase and his precious reward. We have all in him,
by rich love, peculiar grace, free gift, and precious promises. Precious faith is the blessed evidence of interest and proprietorship in this blessed inventory. But
how came faith? From hearing the word of God. From
whom came the word? By the Spirit of truth, who also
gives faith. Why is the Spirit given? Because Jesus
is glorified. Wherefore came Jesus, to seek and save
the lost? The Father loved us, and gave his Son for
us. Why did the Father love us? It was the good

pleasure of his will, according to which he chose us,
in Christ Jesus, before the foundation of the world;
predestinated us to the adoption of children, and blessed
us with all spiritual blessings in him. Eph. 1 : 3-5.
Hence, O believer, how clear thy title! how certain
thy possession!

"Christ is God's," God's beloved Son; so art thou
in him. Christ's is God's gift for thee, God's gift to
thee, and thou art given to him. Thou enjoyest all in
him, and receivest all from him. Canst thou ever want
food for faith, a source of love, a fountain of holiness,
or a spring of consolation? What have we done, or
what could we do, to get an interest in Christ, or procure a right to such heavenly treasures? Verily, we
have done enough to forfeit, but nothing to deserve them.
Know this and be humbled; consider this, and be joyful
in love: "All things are of God, who hath reconciled
us to himself by Jesus Christ." 2 Cor. 5 : 18. Improve
your blessed privileges, by walking worthy of the Lord.
Col. 1 : 10.

FEB. 4.—*Jesus said, One thing is needful.* Luke 10 : 42

The disposition and conduct of the sisters, Martha
and Mary, may suggest to our minds the different desires and actings of the flesh and spirit, of which every
christian is composed. The flesh is "careful and
troubled about many things:" it is ever restless and
uneasy, always in want, seldom satisfied, never truly
happy. But the spirit has chosen the good part, the
"one thing needful." It is truly wise in its choice,
quite satisfied in its object, and really happy in its
enjoyment.

Thus it is, while the christian is under the prevailing
influence of this one thing needful. One thing, the enjoyment of God, was our first parents' paradise. A thirst

after an enjoyment of two things,—the knowledge of evil as well as good,—caused all their wo, and made them miserable. And it is this knowledge of evil which keeps all their posterity in the sad circumstances into which they are fallen, till they are brought to know *the one thing needful.* What is this but the saving knowledge of God our Saviour? This was the great apostle's continual prayer, "That I may know him." Mary was happy in the enjoyment of this; for it our Lord himself commends her; calling it "that good part which shall not be taken away."

This one thing comprehends all wisdom, holiness, and happiness. To know Jesus, is to believe in him; to believe in him, is to love him; and to love him, is to keep his commandments. In every station, in all seasons, and under every circumstance, this one thing, this knowledge of Jesus, is ever needful, ever seasonable. Does the christian enjoy health? This knowledge joins to health of body, peace and joy of soul. Is he in sickness? To know Jesus is the richest cordial, the most reviving draught to his soul. Is he tempted? What consolation to know, Jesus was tempted in all things as we are, that he might succor the tempted. Doth sin distress? doth the law condemn? The soul that knows Jesus can boldly challenge, "Who shall lay any thing to the charge of God's elect?" He can confidently declare, "there is no condemnation to them who are in Christ Jesus." Does death, the king of terrors, affright him? By the knowledge of Jesus he is disarmed of his strength and sting, which is the law and sin. So that, O soul, thou mayst take up this triumphant challenge against the last enemy, "O death, where is thy sting? O grave, where is thy victory?" I have all things, and abound, in possessing this one thing: I have Christ my Saviour found, and I pray daily to be found in him. Phil. 3 : 9

FEB. 5.—*That repentance and remission of sins should be preached in his name among all nations.* Luke 24 : 47.

This is God's method of saving sinners by Jesus Christ. Those who know his preciousness, who have any regard to the glory of God and love for immortal souls, will make this the rule of their preaching; for this doctrine, where known and experienced in the heart, makes a true christian. Evangelical repentance flows from a seeing eye, a hearing ear, and an understanding heart, and is an evidence and effect of Gospel faith. To see the evil nature and dreadful effects of sin, as shown in the sufferings of Jesus; to hear the curses and condemnation of the law against sinners, its dreadful thunders and menaces in the conscience; to understand in the heart that nothing but the blood of Jesus could atone for the guilty, none but he could fulfil the perfect demands of a holy law for the unrighteous: this humbles the soul, cuts off false hopes, lays it low in self-abasement before Jehovah, and causes it to cry out, "I am the man, the sinner I, who am cursed by law, exposed to wrath, and deserve hell. I mourn without hope in myself. I hear of Jesus, the Saviour of sinners; I turn to him for hope and salvation. Sin has destroyed me. Jesus, save, or I perish."

This repentance Jesus is exalted to give. This makes a proud sinner humble. Remission of sins makes a poor sinner a happy saint. Hath Christ obtained remission of sins by his blood? Hath he commanded that this should be preached in his name? Is he exalted to give it? Has he brought the poor sinner, by his Spirit, to his feet to sue for it? And will he refuse to make that soul happy in the sense of it? Never, never let such a thought be indulged by any poor desponding sinner. We read no such hard lines in his word. We find no such dejecting views from his life and death. The doctrine he prescribed is a lively transcript of all that was in his loving heart.

Be assured, O soul, there shall be a performance of all things, that are promised of the Lord, to him that believeth. That same Jesus, who gives the soul the humbling view of itself, and by repentance to turn to him, will give it the joyful knowledge of himself, by the remission of sins through faith in his blood. Repentance and remission of sins are joined together in preaching; they can never be separated in the experience of the heart. So sure as repentance is given to any soul by the Spirit of Jesus, that soul is forgiven by God the Father, through the blood of Jesus. Eph. 1 : 7.

FEB. 6.—*Then shall we know, if we follow on to know the Lord: his going forth is prepared as the morning; and he shall come unto us as the rain, as the latter and former rain unto the earth.* Hosea 6 : 3.

Disciples enjoy sweet fellowship in the truth. Hence they mutually help and encourage each other's faith. Christ blesses them, and manifests himself to them in this way. So the disciples, after his crucifixion and death, resorted together and communed with each other; and Jesus, though unknown to them at first, joined their company, expounded the Scriptures, and opened their understandings; "and they said one to another, Did not our hearts burn within us as he talked with us by the way?" &c. Luke 24 : 32.

Thus disciples in the Old Testament church exhorted one another in faith. "We shall know, we shall follow on to know the Lord." So the words may be rendered. Those who know a little of Jesus' love, and are but just brought acquainted with his free grace and salvation, shall hold on their way. Knowledge, light, peace, and love shall increase to their souls, through that Spirit by whom they are regenerated and born again. Though at first they are but "babes in Christ, yet, through the milk of the word, they shall grow and increase with the increase of God." The going forth of Christ's love towards us is as the morning. At the dawn of day light is scarcely discernible, it seems opposed by surrounding darkness, yet gradually increases, till the sun gains its meridian. So "the path of the just shineth more and more unto the perfect day."

The sun never forsakes the earth, though, at seasons, its light and heat seem withdrawn in comfort and enjoyment. Thus is it with the Sun of righteousness. He shall also "come unto us as the rain," to refresh, enliven, and make our souls fruitful in knowledge, peace, love, and holiness; yea, as "the latter and former rain." In the land of Israel they had usually two rains in a year, one just after the seed was sown, the other when the corn was almost ripe, and the harvest at hand. Sometimes, just after the seed of eternal life is sown in the hearts of young converts, they are favored with happy refreshing seasons of love and joy. Others experience the most plentiful showers of heart-reviving love just as the sickle is to cut them down, that they may be gathered into the heavenly garner. Our Lord best knows what seasons to give, whether the storm of affliction, the rain of prosperity, or the sunshine of joy. Jesus "is a God of judgment: blessed are all they that wait for him." Isa. 30:18.

FEB. 7.—*The sacrifices of God are a broken spirit: a broken and a contrite heart, O God, thou wilt not despise.* Psalm 51:17

It is the wisdom and joy of disciples to see somewhat of Jesus in every page of the lively oracles. Then the word is searched with pleasure, studied with delight, and made exceedingly profitable to the soul. To this end, the sins and backslidings, humiliations and repentings, joys and experiences of saints of old are recorded. We see their deserts to be the lowest hell; but grace reigns. Though sin abounded in them, yet grace superabounded over them. But all is through Jesus: no mercy for sinful men, but through that blessed Mediator.

So he glorifies his name, and makes his power known to be "the same yesterday, to-day, and for ever," in saving his people from their sins. Though sin may blind the eyes to his love, and harden the heart against his fear, and the spirit become stout and rebellious for a season; yet see his amazing love, behold the effects of his almighty grace! A criminal, yet beloved David shall be arraigned, plead guilty, sue for mercy, and hope for pardon.

But, did a broken spirit and a contrite heart *entitle* him to this? Did he plead his present griefs and humiliations to *atone for* his past transgressions? No: alas, if he had no other hope than this, horror and black despair would have been the portion of his backsliding soul. God will not, doth not, cannot bestow pardon of sin till he makes the soul sensible of and sorry for sin. Nor will he ever despise, abhor, or reject broken-hearted, contrite souls. For his Spirit effects this in them. Though no plea can be founded on this, yet the soul is sweetly encouraged hereby to hope; here is an evidence that the Lord hath not given up such to a reprobate mind. He still works in them. They feel the effects. A sense of guilt is dreadful to be borne, and distressing to feel; therefore such will cry for deliverance, "Restore unto me the joys of thy salvation."

Our loving Lord breaks the heart for sin, though sin cannot break the covenant of his love, and shall not reign unto death. O soul, art thou mourning for thy sins? Remember Him on whom the iniquity of us all was laid. Look to him " who bore our sins in his own body on the tree, by whose stripes we are healed." A contrite spirit flies from the pleasures of sin, which are but for a season ; he cannot rest till former joys are restored ; he is also solicitous about his future walk, lest he fall again ; therefore cries, " Uphold me with thy free Spirit."

> " I cannot live without thy light,
> " Cast out and banished from thy sight:
> " Thine holy joys, my God, restore,
> " And guard me that I fall no more."

FEB. 8.—*The wicked is driven away in his wickedness; but the righteous hath hope in his death.* Proverbs 14 : 32.

" O how comfortable, in a dying hour, to look back upon a well-spent life," say many. But it is most comfortable, to "forget the things that are behind, to look forward, and press towards the mark, for the prize of our high calling of God in Christ Jesus," saith the christian. Phil. 3 : 14. What a delightful prospect, in a dying hour, to view a reconciled God, a glorified Jesus, and a kingdom prepared for us from the foundation of the world ! But, if we have not experienced a life of faith in Christ, and by the grace of God had our conversation in the world, a life of self-righteousness will only beget vain confidence, and delude the soul with false hopes, which will end in awful disappointment at death. But who are the wicked ? Verily, all who reject the faith of the Son of God, refuse to submit to his righteousness, hope in themselves, and trust to what they can do to make themselves righteous, and to make their peace with God. This is the very essence of wickedness All such are destitute of righteousness. Their eyes are blinded by sin, and their hearts hardened against the truth. Living and dying so, they shall be driven away from the comforts of the righteous in the awful hour of death. In the tremendous day of judgment they shall be driven away from the presence of Jesus, with, "Depart, ye cursed."

Who are the righteous? All who receive the gift of new-covenant love, the gift of righteousness, which cometh upon all the children of faith by one, Jesus Christ. Rom. 5 : 17. The righteous man is born again from above: he hath the mind of Christ, he loveth righteousness and hateth iniquity. The righteous hath hope in a God of justice, hope in a God of truth, hope in a God of faithfulness, because his hope standeth in God's own covenant grace and love, which makes sinners righteous in Christ. This hope shall never forsake the righteous: it animates him in life to love and obedience; it comforts him in death against fears of wrath and terrors of hell; it inspires him with joyful assurance of a crown of righteousness in life and immortality, according to the precious promises of God, through the righteousness of Jesus.

Well might that eminently faithful minister of Jesus, the late Rev. Mr. Hervey, so sweetly fall asleep with this hope in his heart, while his lips were warbling his dying song, "Precious salvation! precious salvation! O precious grace! precious promises! precious faith! precious hope! All flowing to poor sinners through the perfect righteousness and precious blood of the infinitely and eternally precious Jesus." Well might Paul sum up all our blessedness in that apostolic benediction, which includes all our hope: "The grace of the Lord Jesus Christ, and the love of God, and the communion of the Holy Ghost, be with you all. Amen." 2 Corinthians 13 : 14.

FEB. 9.—*The end of all things is at hand; be ye therefore sober, and watch unto prayer.* 1 Peter 4:7.

The word of grace and truth, like a judicious physician for the body, prescribes different kinds of recipes for the soul. Sometimes the bitter draught of affliction, at others the strengthening, comforting balsam of faith, with the restorative mixture of love; but at all times a necessary regimen, whereby to rule and govern our lives, so that our souls may prosper and be in health.

To use means, in faith, is our bounden duty. To neglect them is a contempt of the wise Prescriber, whereby we suffer loss and receive hurt to our souls. As faith binds the soul to Jesus in the sweet bands of love, so it produces a conformity to him in heart and life. As the Spirit enriches the soul with precious graces, so they are accompanied with his transforming influence. He ever directs to the word he inspired, that we may be taught to avoid all things contrary thereto, and also to practise those duties which have a tendency to strengthen the soul in persevering in truth and holiness.

An intemperate thirst after, and the inordinate indulgence of ourselves in the enjoyment of any of the good things of this life, sadly indispose the mind to spiritual concerns. This is contrary to the life of faith, interrupts sweet communion with the Father of spirits, deadens the heart to holy fellowship with Jesus, and opposes the comforting consolation of the blessed Spirit. Hence the soul finds great languor, deadness, and formality in its addresses at the throne of grace. Thy soul and mine are therefore called upon to consider, Time, how short! Eternity, how near! The Judge is at the door. All things are on the point of dissolution. We are to be expecting the certain messenger, to call us hence.

Since continuance here is so uncertain, all wordly enjoyments are so precarious, and all certainly perish in the using; what temperance, what sobriety of conduct becomes us! And this is certain, Jesus, with his much incense, is ever before the throne. It is a mercy-seat, sprinkled with his precious blood. From hence all grace is bestowed, all power given. O may we be concerned to watch continually against the motions of the enemy, the stirrings of pride and lust, watching in prayer for the power of the Spirit, watching after prayer for an answer of peace. And when is the time that this exercise may be omitted? Verily, not till faith is lost in sight, hope turned into enjoyment, and prayer lost in praise. O what a precious word is this from our Jesus! "Whatsoever ye shall ask in my name, that I will do." John 14: 13.

FEB. 10.—*Forasmuch as the children are partakers of flesh and blood, he also himself took part of the same; that through death he might destroy him that had the power of death, that is, the devil.* Hebrews 2: 14

We read of one who was so affected with the glory of the sun, that he thought he was born only to behold it. With what propriety may a christian judge of himself, that he is *born again* to behold the glory and delight himself in the daily contemplation of Jesus, the Sun of righteousness! Lord, thou shalt never stoop to that mean office of "washing my feet," said honest-hearted Peter. But what was that stoop of abasement, when Jesus was in flesh, compared to his taking flesh upon him? Be astonished, O heavens! rejoice, O children of faith! admire, and adore, what you can never fully comprehend: the Lord of Life and Glory in your nature, clothed with flesh and blood, a man of sorrows and acquainted with grief. See Jesus—consider Jesus; O dwell in contemplation on the humility of our Divine Redeemer, till it warms your heart with love. Say which is greatest, his love or his humility?

He took part with "the children." Such was Jacob's
delight in Benjamin, that "his life was bound up in the
lad's life." Gen. 44 : 30. The soul of Jonathan was so
knit to David, that "he loved him as his own soul."
1 Sam. 18 : 1. Verily, our life is bound up in the life
of Jesus. Truly, he hath loved us better than life. He
took our part against our invincible foes, sin, Satan, and
death. He hath conquered all—for whom? "The children;" by nature children of wrath, by practice rebels
against God. Yet, amazing grace! the objects of his
Father's love; hence given to Christ, to redeem and
save. They had interest in his love ere they had a being in the flesh. Therefore he prays for them as their
Mediator; he owns them, by that special mark which
the Holy Ghost puts upon each of them, in the day of
his power—faith. "I pray for them also which shall believe on me." John 17 : 20.

We may joyfully triumph, "If Jesus be for us, who
shall be against us?" Every believer may be sure of
victory. Faith in Jesus overcomes the world, disarms
death of its sting, which is sin; and of the strength of
sin, which is the law. By the blood of the Lamb, Satan is
overcome. Thus we are more than conquerors, through
Him who loved us. Christ gained the conquest, in our
nature, over Satan and death, by taking away that which
gave power to both over his children—sin. This he
effected by his own death. He died for sin. He rose to
justify. He lives to save. Thanks eternal for his
victory. 1 Cor. 15 : 57.

Feb. 11.—*In a little wrath I hid myself from thee for a
moment, but with everlasting kindness will I have mercy on
thee, saith the Lord thy Redeemer.* Isaiah 54 : 8

Love is ever open and communicative: it conceals
nothing from the object beloved which may profit or

comfort. "Shall I hide from Abraham that thing which I do?" saith the God of love, concerning his friend, Gen. 18 : 17. The Lamb saith of his followers, "Ye are my friends." Servants are not made acquainted with their masters' secrets; but friends are. Therefore saith the great Interpreter of covenant love, "All things that I have heard of my Father I have made known unto you." John, 15 : 15. He does not suffer his children to be chastised, but they shall be told of the Father's kindness, and mercy in it. Love is ever in his heart, though wrath may appear in his conduct.

The joy of creation is revived by the bright shining of the sun. When that is withdrawn, clouds, mists, and darkness gather. So when the Sun of righteousness hides himself from the soul, it seems a dark season of wrath. The mists of corruption rise, the thick fog of unbelief spreads, the gloom of dejection hangs heavy on the mind, and the prince of darkness is very busy at such a season: like Job's friends, he is a physician of no value, but a miserable comforter to the soul. Now all sense, nature, and feeling write bitter things against the poor sinner. The Father chastises, the Saviour hides himself, the law accuses, conscience condemns, sin terrifies, Satan threatens, but—Father, thy mercy never dies, thy love changes not. Therefore faith endures, and turns to love. "In a little wrath I hid myself." Little in comparison of thy deserts, O soul! little compared with the greatness of the love of thy God. Faith listens to the testimony of Jesus. The Lord thy Redeemer speaks: "My deserting thee is of the shortest duration, a moment, the twinkling of an eye;" as no space of time, compared to eternity. Then love vents itself and declares, "With everlasting kindness will I have mercy on thee."

The word of the Lord shall stand. His covenant is sure, his love unchangeable, his promises immutable

Hence the soul is excited to confidence, to assurance, full assurance; yea, the fullest assurance of a God of truth, though all present appearances seem against it Then hope dawns in the soul, and love to Jesus is quickened. Holy shame and godly sorrow for past follies fill the heart, while the Comforter inwardly testifies of Jesus. His love, how infinite! his person, how precious! his promises, how reviving! his presence, how joyful! Such is Jesus' love. "Weeping may endure for a night, (of desertion,) but joy cometh in the morning, (of his presence.) Psalm 30:5.

FEB. 12.—*Therefore with joy shall ye draw water out of the wells of salvation.* Isaiah 12:3

Why "therefore?" what had the church done to procure such an inestimable promise? O, the joyful day of her public espousal to Jesus is come; that day, that blessed day of power, when the loving bride claims her beloved Bridegroom, Jesus. Therefore she sings this joyful song, "Behold, God is my salvation: I will trust, and not be afraid. For the Lord Jehovah is my strength and my song; he also is become my salvation." The claims of the faith of poor sinners are well-pleasing in the sight of God. They honor his word, glorify him, and cause joy in heaven among the angels, while the humble claimants obtain the consolation thereof. "Them that honor me, I will honor," saith the Lord. "With joy shall ye draw water out of the wells of salvation."

But, this was not to be a transient fit of comfort, but an inexhaustible fountain of joy. Believers are to come daily and draw water with joy out of the wells of salvation. Jehovah, the Father, is "the fountain of living waters." Jerem. 2:13. Salvation takes its first spring from his everlasting love, is secured by his unalterable covenant and unchangeable promises. The Spirit and his grace are called "a well of water springing up to everlasting life." John 4 : 14. He shows poor sinners their want of Jesus, this living water, its freeness and sweetness; supplies them with the bucket of faith, to draw with joy, and drink with pleasure. This well of salvation by Jesus was opened in paradise ; its streams have run through every successive age of the church. Patriarchs, prophets, apostles, believers in all ages, have had their hearts made glad and their souls joyful hereby

The everlasting love of the Father, the rich grace of the Son, and the exuberant joy of the Holy Ghost compose these wells of salvation. Yet it is but one fountain of grace flowing from the unity of the Divine essence, and is communicated to us out of the fulness of the man Jesus. Hence we are invited by him, " O friends, O beloved, drink ! yea, drink abundantly." Song of Solomon 5 : 1. This fountain is ever free, full, and inexhaustible. Why, O why, then, are we not always joyful ? why do we ever complain for want of comfort ? This well is ever open, this fountain ever near. Why do we so much neglect, so often forsake this Fountain of living waters ? Where is our faith ? Why is that precious grace given us, but for use and exercise ? So shall we the more glorify the God of all consolation, be refreshed in our spirits and made fruitful in our lives, and our thirst after the perishing comforts of time and sense shall be allayed. For, saith Jesus, " Whosoever drinketh of the water that I shall give him, shall never thirst." John 4 : 14

Feb. 13.—*Commit thy way unto the Lord ; trust also in him, and he shall bring it to pass.* Psalm 37 : 5.

We are too apt to forget where we are, what we are called to, and whither we are going. When we take a survey of the present state of things, judge according to appearances, and see one event happen alike to all,

we are ready to ask, what advantage then hath the christian? or what profit is there to new-born believing
souls? Much every way. For unto them, chiefly, are
committed the lively oracles of God. The Bible is an
epistle of love. The tender affections of our loving
Father, the living and dying compassions of our gracious
Redeemer breathe in every page. Here we see the various conflicts and trials our brethren in the flesh were
exercised with; how they were supported under and
carried through all, safe to glory; and this by the very
same grace and power which are still our happy portion.
They, being dead, yet speak to us, animating and encouraging our hearts to be strong in the Lord and in
the power of his might. We see in them the inexpli-
cable mysteries of providence unveiled; and how, out
of the weakness of nature, they were made strong in
grace.

It is the glory of believers to take their views and
form their judgment from God's truth: to oppose nature,
sense, and feeling; to wait for the salvation of God;
to omit no appointed means, but to be diligent in the
ways of God, patiently submitting every issue to his
wisdom and goodness. This is the obedience of faith,
it is attended with the patience of hope, and the issue
is always determined in love. It is impossible it should
be otherwise. For it is the immutable decree of heaven:
"All things work together for good to them who love
God, to them who are the called according to his purpose." Rom. 8 : 28.

Committing our way to God unburdens the mind;
trusting our all to him makes the heart easy; relying
on him to bring our concerns to pass, makes the spirit
joyful. But when carnal reason is suffered to make its
report, then, with Jacob, we cry, "All these things are
against us." Hence fainting and drooping come from
fear, fear from doubting, doubting from unbelief, and un-

belief chiefly prevails through ignorance and inatten
tion to God's word of grace, covenant love, precious
promises, and solemn oath in Christ. Committing and
trusting is thy work—to bring to pass is the Lord's.
Beware of committing thy ways into his hand by prayer, and again taking them into thine own by diffidence.
"I will trust, and not be afraid." Isa. 12 : 2.

FEB. 14. —*Remember the word unto thy servant, upon which
thou hast caused me to hope.* Psalm 119 : 49.

It is not natural to us to hope in God's word : this
the power of God causeth us to do. Where there is true
knowledge of Jesus, the essential Word, there will be
a real esteem for the Scriptures, the written word of Je
hovah. The same Spirit that dwelt in Jesus, dictated
the truths concerning him; and the same Spirit testifies
of Jesus in the hearts of his children. By the word we
are favored with clear ideas, just conceptions, and encouraging views of the truths of grace and salvation.
Hence we have the firmest foundation, the strongest confidence, and fullest assurance to build our faith and hope
upon. Hence, also, we are emboldened to draw nigh
to a throne of grace, to plead our cause, present our distress, and claim with humble boldness a supply of all
our need.

When there is a death upon all comfortable and joyful
feelings, when all things around us wear a gloomy aspect, when conscience within writes bitter things against
us, the law works wrath, and its terrors make us afraid ;
and an insulting foe, to heighten distress and increase
our sorrows, stands over us with " There, there, so would
I have it !" in such a season, O it is life from the dead
to remember the infinitely transcendent love, victorious
toils, and triumphant conquests of Jesus over all things
for us ! How joyful to read that all the promises centre

in him, and that they are infallibly sure to all the seed, yea and amen, to the glory of God the Father! How establishing to hear such gracious words from the mouth of Jehovah, "I, even I, am he that blotteth out thy transgression for mine own sake, and will not remember thy sins!" Isa. 43:25. How powerfully alluring, how sweetly attracting to the affections, when love calls, "Put me in remembrance," plead with me; thou shalt not call in vain, I will hear, I will answer thee! Thus love, thus grace descends to the heart, thus it speaks by the word. Hence desires are kindled in the soul, blown into a flame, and ascend in fervent, earnest prayer and pleading to a faithful, promise-fulfilling God. Surely we can never enough prize God's word, never sufficiently adore the Holy Spirit, for the knowledge of Jesus by the word. And if the word of the Lord is our hope, we have eternal truth, everlasting love, infinite power, and unchangeable faithfulness engaged for us. What a special privilege is this, to have God's own word for our hope in him and plea before him! "Every word of God is pure; he is a shield unto them who put their trust in him." Prov. 30 : 5.

FEB. 15.—*He gave them their request; but sent leanness into their soul.* Psalm 106 : 15

When the sunshine of worldly ease, and a greater portion of the good things of this life than he was wont to enjoy, fell to the lot of that champion of Jesus, of blessed memory, Luther, it excited a holy fear and jealousy in his heart, which made him cry out, "Lord, I will not be put off with these things!" However pleasant and agreeable worldly prosperity may be to the flesh, yet indulging and pampering the body is destructive to the health of the soul. The body, without exercise, loses its strength and vigor. Afflictions are the exercise of the soul; though dreaded, because grievous to the flesh, they are yet profitable to the spirit; or else not one of God's dear children should know what a single trouble is; for they are all the allotments of covenant love. In our prayers we too often imitate James and John, " we know not what we ask." We ask amiss, and yet are ready to complain that the Lord doth not answer us according to our desire; though the very thing we asked would have proved as a serpent to bite and destroy us.

O what patience doth our God and Father exercise towards the froward dispositions of his dear but unto-ward children! It would be bad for the best of us, if we were our own providers. Let Peter have his request, and Jesus had not died: then Peter and every soul of man must have perished. It is our mercy, that the Lord sometimes answers prayer with denials; he most blesses us by denying our petitions. Saints long and pray to be entirely delivered from the body of sin; but though the Lord doth not take it away, yet he gives what is better, grace to subdue our corruptions, and withal sub-dues pride, and keeps the soul dependent upon himself, which is best of all. *Thy will, thy glory* should ever set bounds to our petitions. The health and prosperity of the immortal soul is infinitely to be preferred to the happiness of the perishing body. Gay clothing, with empty pockets, and a lean, starving body, is a distressed condition. But how much more deplorable, how awfully to be dreaded the state of many professors! They have got what they eagerly sought, the riches, honors, and pleasures of this world. But alas! their precious souls are lean and starving. Can the comforts of a perishing world compensate for the want of a sense of God's love, the reviving grace of our Lord Jesus, and the comfort-ing fellowship of the Holy Ghost? In all our petitions we should make the enjoyment of God our chief aim.

For he says, "Hearken diligently unto me, and eat ye
that which is good, and let your soul delight itself in
fatness." Isa. 55 : 2.

FEB. 16.—*Then opened he their understanding, that they might
understand the Scriptures.* Luke 24 : 45.

Though Jesus had captivated the heart, and drawn the
affections of his disciples to himself before his sufferings
and death, yet they had very little knowledge in the
mysteries of his kingdom, or of "the mystery of iniquity"
which worked in them. They were but weak in understanding the Holy Scriptures. Hence arose their diffidence and suspicions concerning him. He left them
scattered through fear and unbelief, and he finds them
full of unreasonable doubts and troubles. For this he
reproves them, "O fools, and slow of heart to believe
all that the prophets have spoken."

But amidst all their weakness and ignorance there
was a sweet and secret confidence in their hearts. Jesus
had apprehended them as prisoners of love, and they
were kept by an invisible power, that they might apprehend that for which also they were apprehended of
Christ. Though he made the hearts of two of his disciples "burn within them," yet there was more warmth
than light, a transient heat of affections, but not a settled
understanding of the Scriptures. Thus it is with many
of the lambs of the flock now. They have been taught
to call "Jesus Lord, by the Holy Ghost." They feel some
flashes of comfort, but they are oftener exercised with
doubts, fears, jealousies, and surmises. But as the Saviour hath loved and called them to himself, he will establish their hearts in faith. He not only warms the affections, but opens the understanding. Many mistake
here—not the fire of our passions is to govern us, but
our clear understanding of the Scriptures. By them our

faith is strengthened, our judgment established, our love increased, our hearts comforted, our holiness promoted. Thus Jesus honored the Scriptures. So he gave his first-resurrection-blessing to his weak disciples.

"Christ died for our sins, and rose again, according to the Scriptures." 1 Cor. 15 : 3, 4. His whole work on earth was to fulfil the Scriptures. So he honored them, and herein he has left disciples an example. Prize the word of truth, study it constantly, pray over it daily. By it the Spirit teacheth knowledge. The Scriptures are the sword of the Spirit: Satan will fly before them, because they testify of Jesus. Here then is an evidence of a true disciple. Jesus hath opened his understanding to understand the Scriptures. Has the Lord thus blessed thee ? Then thou seest Jesus to be the sum and substance of the Scriptures, therefore thou wilt esteem them as thy companion, guide, and familiar friend. "For whatsoever things were written aforetime, were written for our learning ; that we, through patience and comfort of the Scriptures, might have hope." Rom. 15 : 4.

Feb. 17.—*But grow in grace and in the knowledge of our Lord and Saviour Jesus Christ. To him be glory both now and for ever. Amen.* 2 Peter 3 : 18

Christian, know thy danger. Thou art ever liable to be led away by the error of the wicked one, to decline from the truth, and to fall away from thy steadfastness in the faith of Jesus. Exhortations warn of this: they tend to quicken stronger exercises of faith and love, as a remedy against this: yea, through the influences of the Spirit they cause new-born souls to increase with the increase of God: just as reviving showers of rain and warm influences of the sun cause the fruits of the earth to grow. It behoves us to consider this: to wrestle with the God of all grace, lest we grow faint in our

mind, our hands hang down, and our knees become feeble
—that we may become "strong in the grace which is in
Christ Jesus." Behold the inseparable connection between grace and Jesus, knowledge and growth. There
is no growth in grace but by the knowledge of Jesus
The more thou growest up in thy Head, Christ, the more
thou wilt grow out of hope in thyself, out of conceit with
thyself and with the self-righteous wicked.

To know and experience the grace of God in Christ
is the special mercy of poor sinners. To grow in the
faith of the truths of his grace and in the knowledge of
Christ's love, is our richest consolation, our highest joy.
Hast thou tasted that the Lord is gracious? In this consists thy present blessedness, peace, and joy. But alas!
what is thy knowledge and experience? but like a drop
of water to the vast ocean. Art thou hungering after
more grace, thirsting after greater knowledge of Jesus?
Verily thou shalt be filled, "filled with all the fulness
of God."

It is the nature of grace, the property of this knowledge, to create an insatiable thirst in the soul after
deeper experiences of it. Hence means of grace will be
diligently used, the Scriptures constantly searched, the
Gospel highly prized, the sincere milk of the word desired, and the influences of the Spirit implored. Why
all this? That the soul may grow in the faith and love
of Jesus; that the bud of grace may blossom and bear
ripe fruit to his glory. The smallest knowledge of Jesus
shall increase, till the believing babe in Christ comes "in
the unity of the faith and in the knowledge of the Son
of God to the measure of the stature of the fulness of
Christ." Pray mind the doxology in the text. Glory is
due to God only. But it is here ascribed to our Saviour.
Therefore we safely and comfortably conclude, He is
"over all, God blessed for ever. Amen." Rom. 9:5.

Feb. 18.—*God is faithful, by whom ye were called unto the fellowship of his Son Jesus Christ.* 1 Cor. 1 : 9

While we entertain thoughts of God out of Christ, it affords no comfort to hear of God's faithfulness. Nay, if we were not blind to our state as sinners, the thought would fill us with dread and horror. For how awful, how terrifying is this declaration from a faithful God, "I will by no means clear the guilty." Exodus 34 : 7. But we know "that the Lord our God, he is God, the faithful God, who keepeth covenant and mercy with them that love him and keep his commandments to a thousand generations." Deut. 7 : 9. O this is the life of poor sinful souls! this is the joy of their hearts. For whenever one reads of the covenant, it reminds of Jesus the Surety, the Mediator; of God in Christ, the God of love, our reconciled God and Father. We have no immediate access to the Father, but by his Son Jesus Christ. When called into fellowship, intercourse, familiarity, and sweet converse with Jesus by faith, then we have free access to the Father's throne of grace and his heart of love. We glory in his great and precious promises, and triumph in his declarations of faithfulness and truth.

The faithfulness of God is the foundation of all present grace, the security of future glory.

Many weak disciples are perplexed with dark and disturbing thoughts in this matter. Their hearts are not carried up to rest in the love of the Father, where all is serene and quiet; but they keep below, in the region of doubts and fears, storms and clouds. Their souls may be exercised, and often distressed; but they are safe, because called to the knowledge of, faith in, and fellowship with Christ, their Redeemer. This is by the love of the Father, through the power of the Spirit. And God is faithful to his covenant, to his Son, to his people, to his own word to them, and his work in them. "For whom he calls, them he glorifies." Faithful to support them under all present dejections of mind and sinking of spirits. Faithful to preserve them in all times of danger, and to give them living comforts in a dying hour

Now, O believer, thou art called to honor the faithfulness of thy God, by trusting in his word of truth, glorying in his promises of grace at all times. Yea, in thy darkest hours, when appearances are all against thee, then the Lord is for thee. "The Lord is faithful, who shall stablish you, and keep you from all evil." 2 Thess. 3 : 3. He is faithful to confirm you unto the end, that you may be blameless in the day of the Lord Jesus." 1 Cor. 1 : 8.

FEB. 19.—*If any man sin, we have an Advocate with the Father, Jesus Christ the righteous.* 1 John 2 : 1

In the glass of God's righteous law we see what an unholy and unrighteous thing sin is ; it is hateful in the eyes of a pure God ; has separated between God and the sinner, and tends to his eternal destruction. The Gospel in no wise renders sin less odious to God, less heinous in his sight ; far from it. Yea, rather, it paints sin in the blackest colors, and shows its deepest malignity by the gracious method of its atonement. View the holy Lamb suffering for sin on the cross ; see the streaming blood, and hear his bitter groans on account of sin ; and say, O believer, is sin a little matter, a trifling thing ?

Learn daily sin's evil, by its remedy ; sin's poison, by its antidote ; the hell it deserved, by the Person who redeemed. And ever, O my soul, ever hold fast this as a sacred truth, though God loves thy person in Christ, yet he hates thy sins ; though reconciled to thy soul through Him, yet he never can be reconciled to sin ; though at peace with thee, through the blood of the cross, yet ever at enmity against thy sins. Hence the beloved disciple declares, " These things write I unto you, little children, that ye sin not." Beware of sin as the worst evil, your most deadly foe ; strive against, oppose, resist it, in the power of the Spirit, as your greatest enemy, and most hateful to your best Friend.

But if any man sin, (for none are perfectly free from sin in their nature, nor exempt from it in their practice,) what then? must he lie down and despair? No : " We have an Advocate with the Father :" Jesus Christ pleads the cause of sinners, though he is not an advocate for sin ; for he is " the righteous." Therefore, he doth not deny the charge that we are sinners, he extenuates none of our sins, but owns every accusation brought against us by a perfect law and strict justice, with every aggravating circumstance which can be urged. But against all charged upon us, he pleads his own righteous work. Have his people sinned? his blood has atoned. Have they deserved the curse of the law? he has borne it for them. Have they deserved hell? he has opened the kingdom of heaven. Are they unrighteous? he has fulfilled the law for them, and clothes them with his perfect righteousness. Therefore he pleads, that sin may not be imputed to them ; but that pardon of sin and peace of conscience may be bestowed on them by the word and Spirit ; and that they may be sanctified in him, and glorified with him. Thus saith our dear Lord, " I will not leave you comfortless." John 14 : 18.

FEB. 20.—*Without controversy, great is the mystery of godliness : God was manifest in the flesh.* 1 Tim. 3 : 16.

The truths of the Gospel are, undoubtedly, great mysteries to carnal reason. We have, naturally, no idea of their existence ; but being plainly revealed by the Spirit of truth, they cease to be hid from our knowledge. They are no longer secret mysteries as to their matter, but plain and open truths to faith.

True, *the manner* of their existence is incomprehensible to reason, and will ever remain a mystery to us. Therefore the sons of natural pride and human ignorance reject and disbelieve them. But the children of wisdom and humility esteem the whole mystery of godliness, every Bible truth, as precious objects of their faith. Blessed be God, our comfort and salvation consist in believing, not in explaining.

What the Lord hath taught in his word, we receive as the food of our souls. This is our simple answer to the god of this world, and to the wise disputer of this age. We cannot *comprehend* how God dwelt in flesh, but we are fully assured he did. We have the fullest proof of it in his word; and his word is truth. And it is the very life of our souls, and the joy of our hearts, to believe our God. Why God dwelt in flesh, and the glorious ends he hath accomplished hereby, we know. Of this also we are perfectly assured. We believe it from the same infallible testimony. To the faith of this we have the inward witness of the Spirit also. God known in the flesh, beheld in human form, viewed in our nature, is the very essence of our faith; we now partake its blessings, and experience its comforts. Hence springs the assured pardon of all our sins, the acceptance of our persons, the sanctification of our souls, and sure and certain hope of eternal life and glory. All this is by free promise, according to the everlasting covenant of grace, to the glory of the ever-blessed Trinity, and to the comfort and salvation of us lost sinners. Thus saints are called into one body, by one Spirit: have " one hope, one Lord, one faith, one baptism, one atonement, one righteousness, one God and Father of all, who is above all, and through all, and in them all." Eph. 4 : 4–6.

FEB. 21.—*Behold, I see the heavens opened, and the Son of man standing on the right hand of God.* Acts 7 : 56

"Sufficient to the day is the evil thereof." As the trial and exercise of our day is, so shall our strength be. Saints shall have suffering grace for suffering times. Hours of great outward calamities often prove seasons of the greatest abounding of inward consolation. It is said, Stephen "fell asleep." What! under a shower of stones? Yes: the sweetest sleep he ever experienced. It was preceded by a supernatural sight of glory. He awoke in the full enjoyment of it. He suffered first for Jesus; he is the first who is favored with a view of the glorified Jesus in his kingdom.

How faithful is the Lord we serve! how great are his compassions! how reviving to the soul is the spiritual sight of him! Patriarchs, prophets, apostles, martyrs, and believers in all ages—the same Lord was the object of their faith; they were comforted by the same Spirit, whose blessed office is to glorify Jesus in the view of believing souls. True, "No man shall see me and live, saith the Lord." Exod. 33 : 20. Even highly favored Stephen saw not the essential glory of Jehovah, but through the medium of the man Jesus. Whether with his bodily sight, or "in the full vision of faith" and the Holy Ghost, he "saw the glory of God" in the person of the glorified Son of man—this fired his soul with heavenly joy, and inflamed his heart with holy transport.

Faith's views of Jesus have a transforming influence upon the soul. While he is beheld, love is communicated. Ascending hearts to Jesus are favored with descending love from Jesus. Love, received in the heart cheerfully, diffuses its sweet savor around us. It enlarges the feelings of compassion, and opens the mouth in prayer, even for its worst enemies. Thus Stephen prays for his very murderers. When for himself, he stands : when for them, he kneeled down. As though more importunate for them than for himself.

How precious is the sight of Jesus to those who believe ! how should our hearts long for clearer views of him ! As in his love, so in his person, he is wonderful. He appears in his human form before the throne. The same Man, who loved our persons and bore our sins, still lives and pleads our cause, as our triumphant Conqueror, in our nature, over all our enemies. Thus daily conceive of, look to, and embrace in the arms of faith, thy Lord and thy God. So mayest thou ever comfortably say, "Into thine hand I commit my spirit : thou hast redeemed me, O Lord God of truth." Psalm 31 : 5.

FEB. 22.—*Jesus said, This sickness is not unto death, but for the glory of God, that the Son of God might be glorified thereby.* John 11 : 4.

It frequently happens, that intervening occurrences seem to contradict the truths of God. Therefore, if we judge from sight and appearance, we shall be often deceived. God's word alone is the rule of faith. What he has declared shall certainly come to pass, however repugnant it may seem to carnal reason. Thus our Saviour declares of Lazarus, "This sickness is not unto death ;" yet he afterwards told his disciples plainly, "Lazarus is dead :" and Jesus found him in the grave where he had been laid four days. But he, who had power over death and the grave, knew his own intention of raising him up, for his Father's glory as well as glorifying himself. This was the great end of his coming into the world. Therefore, in the life and by the death of Jesus, glory redounds "to God in the highest, peace on earth, and good will to men."

Did Jesus love Lazarus ? did his compassionate eyes drop a tear of affection over his friend's grave ? O what an innumerable company of poor sinners did his loving eyes behold, who, like Lazarus, were not only to all appearance past hope, but actually "dead in trespasses and sins!" And he says of them also, "This sickness is not unto death." Eternal death shall not have the dominion over them; but he would get glory to God, and glorify himself, in quickening and raising all God's chosen, all his dearly beloved members.

On the death of Lazarus "Jesus wept: he groaned within himself;" and he cried to his Father. How must the heart of Lazarus be inflamed with love to his dear Lord, for giving him a second life! O believer! the raising of thy soul from a death of sin to a life of righteousness, cost thy Saviour not only a sigh, a tear, a groan, a prayer; but agonies, tortures beyond thought, sufferings beyond expression. His immaculate heart's blood he freely poured forth for our sins, to procure the life and to obtain the salvation of our souls. Canst thou think of this love without reflecting on thy misery? O hard heart! O cruel unbelief! How little affected with such love as none but a God could show! Is this thy case? Come then, that the Son of God may be yet more glorified in thee; bring thy hard heart to the feet of Jesus, and confess thy unbelief to him, with this humble cry, "Lord, I believe, help thou my unbelief." Mark 9: 24. "This is a faithful saying, and worthy of all acceptation, that Christ Jesus came into the world to save sinners." 1 Tim. 1: 15.

> "Come, happy souls, approach your God
> "With new, melodious songs;
> "Come, tender to almighty grace
> "The tribute of your tongues.
>
> "So strange, so boundless was the love
> "That pitied dying men,
> "The Father sent his equal Son
> "To give them life again."

FEB. 23.—*Seekest thou great things for thyself? Seek them not*
Jer. 45 : 5

The glorious company of the apostles, the goodly fellowship of the prophets, the noble army of martyrs, all
the members of the church of Christ in all ages, were
called to deny and mortify self. In this there is no difference. All are equally subjects of the same corrupt
nature; are men of like passions, and are therefore in
danger of self-seeking, and of their affections being attracted from Jesus to the alluring objects of this present evil world. Here is a very short chapter recording
the conduct of the prophet Baruch. On reading this we
may truly look within and around us, and cry, " Lord,
what is man ?" and with astonishment may add, " that
thou art mindful of him."

Yea, what is every Baruch, that is, every blessed man,
who bends the knee to Jesus and is renewed in the
spirit of his mind ? Alas! he is still of the earth, earthy,
prone to cleave to the dust, ready to seek great things
for himself from the objects of this world. One would
have thought, just at a time when the prophet had been
reading the dreadful roll, full of mourning, lamentation,
and woe which were shortly to come upon the kingdom,
that this would have entirely curbed every carnal desire
after selfish views and earthly glory. But no; the lusts
of the flesh can only be mortified by the power of the
Spirit. Jeremiah is sent with a kind warning and tender
prohibition to Baruch : "Is this a time for self-seeking,
instead of thy Master's glory ? What ! aspire after worldly honor and dignity in a time of threatened ruin ? Be
wise ; know thy station; act in character."

Here, O christian, see the picture of thy own corrupt
nature. Know thyself. Consider, thou also art in the
body. Remember, " in thy flesh dwelleth no good thing."
Though under threatened ruin and destruction, yet it will
lust after such things as are agreeable to its carnal state.

Never say with Hazael, "Am I a dog," that I should act thus and thus. Beware of the deceitful reasonings of the flesh. It ever has plausible pleas to urge for its gratification. Self-seeking is one of the lusts of the flesh. All views that arise from self, centre in self, and tend to please self, are contrary to fellowship in Jesus. If self is indulged, it will prove like a pampered steed, to run away with thy spirit from thy Beloved. What will it profit thee, if thou couldst gain the whole world, and lose, if not thy soul, yet sweet peace with God, communion with Jesus, and joyful fellowship of the Holy Ghost ? "Ye cannot serve God and mammon." Matt. 6 : 24.

FEB. 24.—*Let not your heart be troubled : ye believe in God, be-lieve also in me.* John, 14 : 1

Jesus comforted the heart of a sorrowful widow by restoring her dead son to life again. Could he not also, by the power of his Spirit, console the hearts of his dear disciples, without preaching outward rules and directions to them ? Yes, but he will be heard as our Prophet. Those disciples only who obey the word of his doctrine, shall enjoy the consolations of his love. Troubles are the common lot of God's dearest children ; "many are the afflictions of the righteous." They feel and groan under heart troubles, inward disquietudes, which carnal men are amazed to hear of, are utterly free from, and congratulate themselves that they are not troubled about.

Ah, this inward insensibility is a bad sign ! But the troubles of his people are the concern of Jesus. He has a remedy against them. He will give comfort under them. Believing in an absolute God will not do this For the glory of his majesty, the greatness of his power, the perfection of his justice, appear in dread array against us. We dare not think of God out of Christ, knowing ourselves to be poor sinners. Therefore says Jesus, "Believe also in me." Believe my humanity: that I became man for your sakes; died for your salvation; and rose again, in your nature, to pray for you. Remember the covenant that is established between the Father and me, on your account. When your poor hearts are troubled with finding you are still but "unprofitable servants," you see much cause for sorrow, mourn and complain that there are so many things amiss in you; that you do not believe so perfectly, love so devotedly, obey so cheerfully as you wish. Yet, ever remember I am your Mediator before the throne: you stand not in the Father's love for your work's sake; but he loves you, and is well pleased with you for my sake. Sorrow not as without hope; but believe in me, and be comforted. You have no sin but what my blood atoned for; you want no perfection but what my righteousness supplies; you stand in need of no holiness and conformity to me but what the Spirit bestows. Thus believe on me as your living Head; thus daily look on yourselves as my dear members; thus live on me, and glorify me, as your only Saviour.

This is to obey Christ's command. Thus is the troubled heart comforted. This is our sweetest privilege: let it be our daily employ. Shortly all our troubles shall end; for "we shall meet the Lord in the air; and be ever with the Lord. Wherefore comfort one another with these words." 1 Thess. 4: 17, 18.

FEB. 25.—*While the earth remaineth, seed-time and harvest, and cold and heat, and summer and winter, and day and night, shall not cease.* Gen. 8: 22.

"Godliness is profitable unto all things, having the promise of the life that now is, and of that which is to come." 1 Tim. 4: 8. By faith we receive the declarations of Jehovah, as the blessings of a father's love. The returning seasons, the revolving periods of time, declare the glory of our heavenly Father. While the christian meditates upon the innumerable blessings of time, and gratitude inspires his heart for them; yet, far nobler subjects demand the contemplation of his soul. Happy for us, when temporal blessings are enjoyed as covenant mercies, and are sanctified to us in Christ. We see and adore the sovereignty of God in appointing times and seasons. The immutability of his will is the law by which they are governed. When the fixed period shall come, all nature shall be reduced to its primitive no thingness. Time shall be swallowed up in a never-ending eternity. Happy souls, who are taught the displays of grace from the images of nature; who bow to the sovereignty of love, rejoice in the covenant of grace, and rest upon the immutability of God's purposes, and promises in Christ to poor sinners. Such are assured, that as in nature, so in grace, seed-time and harvest shall not fail to God's church and people, because of "his everlasting covenant, which is ordered in all things and sure."

There is a time for the immortal seed of the word to be sown in every elect soul. This is experienced by the seed striking root in conviction of sin, and its springing up in faith, desire, and love to Jesus. And because the Sun of righteousness ever lives, and shines upon his members, they shall most assuredly reap a harvest of eternal glory. Chilling cold and winter's blasts may succeed the summer of love and warmth of affection. Nights of darkness, from desertion, temptation, and affliction, may follow days of peace, joy, and consolation. These various seasons and changes will pass upon and be experienced by believing souls "while the earth remaineth"—so long as our earthly nature continues; but it is sentenced to dissolution. We must leave it on this side Jordan; then we shall see it no more, as an enemy,

for ever. But, in the presence of Jesus, the soul shall
have fulness of joy, and the body shall be raised a glorious body, to enjoy the pleasures which are at God's
right hand for evermore. There shall be no night of
darkness, no chill of affections, no winter of distress
This is now our sweet consolation; Christ saith, "Because I live, ye shall live also." John, 14 : 19. And
"when Christ our life shall appear, then shall we also
appear with him in glory." Col. 3 : 4.

FEB. 26.—*My soul cleaveth unto the dust: quicken thou me
according to thy word.* Psalm 119 : 25

One would dread that state, more than all others,
which St. Paul describes as "being past feeling." Eph.
4 : 19. True, there is this alleviation, such are insensible
of their deplorable condition. But, if the great trumpet
of the Gospel awakes not the soul, in this life, to spiritual
sense and feeling, verily, the loud archangel's trumpet
will rouse it, to hear its awful sentence, and feel its
dreadful doom at the last day. O what a miracle of
grace to be quickened, to know one's misery, feel one's
wants, believe the remedy, and cry for relief! This
blessed work is not from the will of the flesh. No man
can quicken his own soul. It is the sovereign work of
almighty power. It is equally ascribed to the loving
Father, redeeming Son, and sanctifying Spirit. John 5 :
21, and 6 : 63. Therefore, gracious souls, give all the
glory to the ever-blessed Trinity. Be clothed with
humility.

"I am come, that ye might have life," saith Jesus.
He quickeneth the dead in trespasses and sins; and then
they cry to him, to have life more abundantly. Here is
the wisdom of heaven-born souls; they deny themselves
the vain pleasures, carnal delights, and sensual gratifications of this world. They know these things oppose

the life, interrupt the peace, and damp the joy of their souls. Their only happiness centres in Jesus, and in life and love communicated from him. Therefore they study to avoid such things as are contrary to his mind and will. And as they too often find themselves cleaving to the dust, to the sensible, earthly, vain enjoyments of this world, this alarms them, it is a burden and grief to them. Hence they pour out their complaints to their beloved Lord, with "Master, let it not be thus. Quicken my drooping spirit. Enliven my declining heart. Cheer my languishing soul, according to the word of thy grace and the truth of thy promises." Here is the blessed confidence of faith. His word is our plea. By that we have assurance of being heard and answered. The precepts of his word teach us his will; and we cannot feel a want, but God's word promises to supply it. Therefore, that is the warrant of faith, a light to direct our feet; and is also our best directory for prayer. So Christ prays for all his, "Sanctify them through thy truth: thy word is truth." John 17: 17. Ever remember thy Lord's words, "It is the Spirit that quickeneth; the flesh profiteth nothing." John 6: 63.

> "My soul lies cleaving to the dust;
> "Lord, give me life divine:
> "From vain desires and every lust
> "Turn off these eyes of mine."

FEB. 27.—*When the enemy shall come in like a flood, the Spirit of the Lord shall lift up a standard against him.* Isa. 59: 19

When a poor sinner knows what human nature is, and sees his brethren and companions after the flesh "living without Christ and without God in the world;" making a mock at sin, and ridiculing his truths and ways; and finds his own heart touched with a holy, loving fear of the Lord, he is ready to cry out, Whence is this? He can only say, "Grace reigneth; the Sun of righteousness

hath risen upon me. So, Lord, it seemeth good in thy
sight. I have not deserved this. Thou hast spoken in
truth, and fulfilled in faithfulness. So thy word runs, so
thy Gospel is glorified, free as the sun, powerful as the
wind." Jehovah's *word* is his people's triumph. Here
are most absolute declarations for faith to fix upon, and
plead, in any hour of Satan's attack.

For, so sure as we fear the Lord, the enemy will oppose us. For, if he dare plead with the Saviour, " Shall
the prey be taken from the mighty, or the lawful captive
be delivered ?" Isa. 49 : 24. Verily, he will follow after
his once seized prey, and strive to regain his ransomed
captive ; yea, he will challenge the sinner as his property. But, is it not strange that the loving, almighty Saviour suffers the enemy to molest his dear children, and
strive to tear his peace and love from their hearts ? No :
it cannot be otherwise in our present state ; for we are
clothed with a nature " earthly, sensual, devilish," to
which Satan has easy access.

Humble souls have little reason to complain that they
have not known so great a degree of wrath, nor have
been terrified with such dreadful apprehensions of hell
and damnation as some others. O rather love and praise
Jesus if thy soul is brought to choose him in faith, and
follow him as thy Saviour and thy all, than wish to have
the enemy let loose upon thy soul. But if this is the
case, he shall not go beyond the length of his chain.
His power is thy Father's permission. He may terrify
with wrath, but it shall issue in love. Yea, though he
should, like a powerful deluge, come in and distress with
blasphemous thoughts, perplexing fears, and pronounce
hell and destruction to be thy doom, even then thou art
safe   The Saviour's power is thy shield. " The Spirit
of the Lord shall lift up a standard"—the Lamb on the
cross. In the faith of this, " resist the devil and he will
flee from you." James 4 : 7

FEB. 28.—*If thy presence go not with me, carry us not up hence.*
Exod. 33 : 15

Happy for us, if this were our address to the Lord in every enterprise ; how many distresses and difficulties should we avoid! how much more peaceful and comfortable should we be in our journey through life.

It is a blessed thing to have an especial eye to God's *presence* as well as to his providence. The Lord may permit his children to succeed in their schemes and undertakings, in the course of his providence, when he doth not accompany their souls with his favor and presence. Yea, believer, canst thou not see in many of thy ways wherein thou hast been permitted to go, that they have proved the very means of losing the sweet sense of thy Lord's presence ? Whatever outward profit or pleasure thou hast gained, verily thou must confess thou hast sustained an inward loss.

How doth it behove every disciple of Jesus to " consider his ways !" It is our wisdom daily to reflect : What is the tendency of my present pursuit ? what is my chief aim ? what can I expect from the end of it ? am I going to gratify the flesh, in pleasing diversions, in carnal delights ? Stop one moment. Consider. Canst thou expect the presence of thy God ? Canst thou lift up thy believing heart in prayer to Jesus to accompany thee ? Certainly, if it is not right to ask or expect his spiritual presence to go with thy soul, surely there it is unlawful for thee to go. If thou canst not pray in faith, canst thou go in faith ? O remember the love of thy Saviour, who died to redeem thee from this present evil world. Call to mind those joys and pleasures which are experienced from a sweet sense of his love and presence. Think now cutting to thy heart, how grieving to thy spirit, if, under any vain indulgence, thy Saviour should put this question, Disciple, " lovest thou me more than these " vanities ? Better for Peter to have been in his Lord's

presence with a cold body, than warming himself with
the high priest's officers and servants; for there he was
blown down by the breath of a damsel. Let his fall
warn thee of thy danger.

It is related of Satan, who had taken possession and
greatly terrified and distressed the soul of a christian,
that on his being asked how he dared to enter into a
child of God? he replied, "I found her on my own
ground, at the play-house; therefore I challenge her
as my servant." Whether the story be true or not,
the moral is good. Christians have no business on the
devil's ground. "Be thou an example of believers."
1 Tim. 4 : 12.

> "Not earth, nor all the sky
> "Can one delight afford,
> "No, not a drop of real joy,
> "Without thy presence, Lord."

[FEB. 29.—*Behold, the Lord God will come with a strong hand,
and his arm shall rule for him: behold, his reward is with
him, and his work before him.* Isaiah 40 : 10

What was foretold in prophecy is fulfilled in the faith
and experience of saints. Here are two notes of attention. "Behold;" it highly concerns us. Take special
notice.

When the Lord God, our Immanuel Jesus, came to
his temple, he found that beautiful building in sad disorder; his spiritual worship lost; and his house of
prayer turned into a den of thieves. Behold, with a
strong hand and out-stretched arm, with no weapon but
an insignificant scourge of small cords, he drove the multitude from the temple. Amazing miracle! The meek
Lamb is also "the Lion of the tribe of Judah." Thus he

came not only with a strong hand, but against the strong as some render it.

So, behold, he comes to take possession of the temple of his people's hearts. This temple he finds in most woful plight. All the powers of earth and hell are engaged against him. " The strong man armed keeps possession." But precious, powerful Jesus casts out Satan, enters by his love and rules by his Spirit where Satan reigned. But he comes not by power only, but by grace also ; behold, he brings his reward with him. The distressed soul he pardons ; the naked soul he clothes with the robe of his righteousness ; the hungry soul he feeds with good things ; he giveth such his flesh to eat and his blood to drink. Then, how do their hearts pant after Jesus ! how do they hunger and thirst after righteousness, and cry and pray, "Lord, increase our faith, that we may eat as thy friends, drink larger draughts as thy beloved, and be more abundantly satisfied with thy love !"

Thus our Lord Christ rewards his people with the fruits of his own toils and the blessings of his own finished work and salvation, even with righteousness, peace, and joy in the Holy Ghost. But, O Jesus, cries the poor sinner, " What a vile, sinful, carnal, earthly-minded wretch am I still by nature !" Fear not, saith Jesus, thou art called to look unto me. Behold, " my work is before me." Have I vanquished the powers of death and hell for thee, and can I not conquer sin in thee, and subdue thy flesh under thee ? Was his blood the price of thy soul and the atonement of thy sins ? Then must thou wait in faith for the total destruction of thy last enemies, sin and death, at his second coming. Then, in the triumph of thy soul, thou shalt joyfully proclaim the perfect victory of Jesus, and say, " Worthy is the Lamb that was slain." Rev. 5 : 12.]

March

MARCH 1.—*My son, give me thine heart.* PROV. 23 : 26

Many are the competitors for the heart of man. Though our dear Father and best Friend lovingly calls for the free-will offering of this precious jewel, yet we are foolishly inclined to give it to our worst enemies. This pleasing world, with all its gay scenes of happiness and joy, attracts our affections, enchants our minds, and bewitches our senses, so that we love it dearly, devote our hearts to it, and dread the very thoughts of leaving it.

"Thou shalt have no other God but me," saith Jehovah. We own the duty and decry the wickedness of worshipping an idol, though all the while we are serving the god of this world: he blinds our eyes and we see it not. The grace of God, though sovereign in its operations, yet acts not by force and compulsion, as upon mere machines, destroying the will and dragging men to heaven, as some in contempt please to assert. No, the service of our Lord is perfect freedom. He loves a cheerful giver. Glory to his grace, he opens the eyes of our understanding to know what is the hope of his calling, and what are the riches of his glory. Eph. 1 : 18 Then we see Jesus as our portion and treasure, and willingly and cheerfully devote our hearts to him. Is the miser's gold his god? does it captivate his heart and delight his soul? why so? Because he sees that in it which suits his disposition and excites his pleasure. So it is of every other idol suited to nature and sense. "Where the treasure is, there will the heart be also." Spiritual affections can only be happy from spiritual objects. The heart can only be happy in God, when cheerfully given up to him in faith and love. This is the very essence of vital godliness.

Our Father invites us to spiritual joys. "I know, my children, in your present state, clothed with flesh, you

nave many lovers which would rival me in your affec
tions, but cheerfully devote your heart to me. Let your
eyes be upon my ways. Consider my love to you. I
gave my beloved Son to die for you. My Spirit hath
called you to enjoy my love. It is my good pleasure to
give you a kingdom: therefore, in love to my glory and
for your comfort, I demand your heart as a free-will offering." O where is the faithful, grateful soul, but in ec-
stacy of love will cry out, Give, Lord, thy Spirit's power,
and command what thou wilt? For, mind, this giving
the heart to God is to be the daily work of thy life, because thou art his son, and a joint-heir of God with
Christ. Rom. 8 : 17.

MARCH 2.—*The Father himself loveth you.* John 16: 27.

The history of the life of sorrows, and death of shame,
the curse, and agony which Jesus sustained for sinners,
were this believed perfectly in the heart, would fill us
with the strongest affection, and inflame us with the most
fervent love. But, alas! all have reason to complain
for want of stronger faith and greater love to Christ.
O unbelief, what an enemy to love! Our love keeps
pace with our faith. As one grows stronger, the other
increases. But if faith grows weak, love declines. There
is no sinner, who *believes* the record of Jesus' love and
salvation as his only hope and confidence, whose *love*
is not, in some degree, drawn out to Jesus; for "faith
worketh by love." The soul in its first love, and for
a season, perhaps, thinks more of the love of Christ than
the love of the Father. It may be he considers that
what the Saviour did and suffered for sinners, was to
procure the love of the Father to them, and to appease
the fury of his wrath against them. But this is not right.
Let no disciple think so. For, saith the Saviour, " The
Father himself loveth you." Yea, he teacheth us the

love of the Father, as the only source and spring of his
coming in the flesh to save us; for "God so loved the
world, that he gave his only begotten Son, that whosoever believeth in him should not perish, but have everlasting life." John 3 : 16.

Hence it is plain, God the Father loves sinners, loves
them inexpressibly, with the greatest affection. For he
gave—whom? an angel? an archangel? myriads of the
heavenly host? No ; but one infinitely more dear to
him, his Son, his only begotten, his dearly beloved Son,
who lay in his bosom from all eternity, that we might
"believe on him, and live in him." So, the effect proves
the cause. It is plain, the love of the Father to his people was prior to the Son's coming into the world to save
them, or to their belief on Jesus. For, says he, "No
man can come unto me, except the Father draw him."
John 6 : 44. And because the Father "hath loved us
with an everlasting love, therefore with loving-kindness
he draws to Jesus." "Behold," O ye followers of the
Lamb, "what manner of love the Father hath bestowed
on us." 1 John 3 : 1. Trace his love to the fountain-head.
"Blessed be the God and Father of our Lord Jesus
Christ, who hath blessed us with all spiritual blessings
in heavenly places in Christ; according as he hath chosen us in him before the foundation of the world, that we
should be holy and without blame before him in love,
having predestinated us to the adoption of children, by
Christ, to himself." To what end? even "to the praise
of the glory of his grace, wherein he hath made us accepted in the Beloved." Eph. 1 : 6.

MARCH 3.—*I knew a man in Christ about fourteen years ago,
such an one caught up to the third heaven.* 2 Cor. 12 : 2

Visions, manifestations, raptures, and ecstasies of soul,
though even from God himself, (which there is ever good

reason to suspect, unless they sink the soul in humility, and excite such love to Jesus as is founded in knowledge, and productive of obedience,) are not to be gloried in. St. Paul says, it is not expedient for me to glory. I know the danger, I fear the evil of it, from the pride and treachery of my nature. It tends to exalt one above measure; and to make others think more highly of one than they ought to think. Therefore, glorying in these things is to be avoided. Indeed, the cause of truth may require it, and the glory of God may be promoted by it. Though, on these accounts, it may be expedient to glory; yet it is not expedient, for the christian's own sake, to do it. So Paul declared. Yet he did glory; for necessity compelled him.

Behold, admire, and imitate the humility of this great apostle, "I knew a man in Christ," &c. When he speaks of himself, it is as a poor sinner, under the most humbling, self-abasing views. Then it is I myself. Rom. 7. But here, lest ostentation should appear, he conceals himself under the character of another man. What a contrast is here between self-exalting principles and the grace of the Gospel! How widely different this from the notions which many professors entertain! For, if they can but give a tolerable account of some vision, revelation, or manifestation, which they suppose was from God, they conclude they know their sins are forgiven, and all is well. Perhaps this may have passed on them fourteen years ago, more or less. But what is their frame and temper now? what their pursuit and practice? If there is no present evidence of faith, hope, love, and obedience; but if, while sunk into carnality and the love of the world, they are yet strong in confidence that their sins are forgiven, and bold in hope of the safety of their state—surely such are blinded to the hope of the Gospel, through the spirit of this world. Satan transforms himself from a minister of darkness into an angel of light

Luther was wont to caution against the white devil as
well as the black one. By how many ways are we liable
to be deluded! How then doth it behove us to be on our
guard, searching the Scriptures and praying the Lord
to keep us! The apostle John's advice is ever needful,
"Beloved, believe not every spirit, but try the spirits
whether they are of God: because many false prophets
are gone out into the world." 1 John 4 : 1.

———————————

MARCH 4.—*These things have I written unto you that believe on
the name of the Son of God; that ye may know that ye have
eternal life, and that ye may believe on the name of the Son of
God.* 1 John 5 : 13.

Little Benjamin was as dear to his father Jacob as his
elder brethren. The child Samuel was as truly a priest
to the Lord as old Eli. So the feeblest lamb in the flock
of Christ, though ever so weak in faith and knowledge,
yet is as dear to the Father as the strongest believer,
loved with the same everlasting love, alike interested in
the salvation of Jesus, and as certainly an heir of eternal life. Many weak children are ready to own this; but
they doubt in their minds, and suspect in their hearts,
not happily knowing, nor being comfortably assured of
their own interest in the salvation of Jesus. There were
such in the apostles' days; therefore the Comforter inspires the beloved John to write to them. He condescends to notice their weakness of knowledge and comfort, because of the small degree of their faith; but yet
he speaks with the strongest assurance, and the boldest
confidence, of the truth of salvation by Jesus. That is
most certain. Eternal life is by Jesus only; and is sure
to every member of his. Do you believe in the name
of the Son of God, as the only Saviour of lost sinners?
This truth lies at the foundation of the hope of the Gos-

pel: when this is believed in the heart, that soul has the earnest of eternal life. By continuing to believe, it gains knowledge and assurance, as the fruits of faith. When the Spirit has bestowed the precious gift of faith, how weak soever the soul may be in the experience of comfort and joy; how much soever it may feel the work ings of carnal nature, unsanctified reason, and remaining unbelief, its sensible groanings and sorrowful complaints are evidences of the life of the soul, through the faith of Jesus. But is the poor soul always to abide in this weak, low, mourning state? No: that cannot be. Jesus will make his members happy in him. The Spirit who be- gets faith in the heart by the word, strengthens it also by the same truth. Faith comes by hearing the word, and is increased thereby. Therefore is Jesus and eter- nal life revealed. The apostles wrote, and ministers preach of this, that weak faith may be strengthened, strong faith increased; that knowledge may grow, and assurance be comfortably enjoyed; that believers may continue to believe, and persevere in believing, on the Son of God; who is "the Author and Finisher of our faith." Heb. 12 : 2.

MARCH 5.—*Whosoever believeth that Jesus is the Christ, is born of God.* 1 John 5:1

It is too common for many of God's dear children to perplex and distress their minds in seeking after marks and evidences of the new birth, expecting to find them outwardly in the flesh, instead of looking inwardly to the spirit. For the satisfaction and comfort of all such, the Holy Ghost hath laid down this inward evidence, faith in Jesus, as an incontestable mark of a new-born soul.

When Peter made that glorious confession, "Thou art Christ, the Son of the living God," Jesus replied, " Blessed art thou, Simon; for flesh and blood hath not

revealed it unto thee, but my Father who is in heaven."
Matt. 16 : 16, 17. All the powers of human nature and
reason, so far from teaching, are at enmity against this
soul-saving truth. No man can teach it his brother, so
as to cause his heart to receive and believe it. It is a
knowledge only revealed by the Spirit, received and believed by heaven-born souls, that the man Jesus is the
only Saviour, that he is the Anointed of God to the work
of saving lost sinners. The very devils know and confess
this, but without any hope of salvation hereby. But,
when any poor sinner is enabled to believe this in his
heart, it is a sure and blessed evidence of the love of the
Father and the power of the Holy Spirit. Then "he
hath the witness in himself that he is born of God." He
hath the mark and evidence of a child of God within
him. As the gift of Jesus is the fruit of God's everlasting love, so faith in Jesus is the fruit of his having died
for our sins, risen again for our justification, ascended
to the Father, and sent the Holy Ghost to testify of him.
This belief honors the God of truth, and glorifies the
God of grace, by receiving the record he has given of
his beloved Son Jesus. It is a holy faith; it dwells in
holy hearts, and produces holy fruits. Happy that
heart which has received this power and privilege to
become a son of God. The love of the holy Trinity is
upon such a soul. It is his privilege, like the happy
eunuch, "to go on his way rejoicing." It is his happiness ever to be "looking unto Jesus, the Author and
Finisher of our faith;" relying on Jesus, who is our
righteousness, (1 Cor. 1 : 30 ;) trusting in Jesus, who is
our hope, (1 Tim. 1 : 1 ;) rejoicing in Jesus, who is our
peace, (Eph. 2 : 14 ;) glorying in Jesus, who is our atonement, (Rom. 5 : 11 ;) and thus, as poor sinners, ever
"looking for the mercy of our Lord Jesus Christ unto
eternal life." Jude, 21.

MARCH 6.—*Jesus said, I thank thee, O Father, Lord of heaven and earth, because thou hast hid these things from the wise and prudent, and hast revealed them unto babes. Even so, Father: for so it seemed good in thy sight.* Matt. 11 : 25, 26.

The true ministers of Christ are greatly encouraged in their labors, knowing they serve that sovereign Lord who hath declared, "My word shall not return to me void, but it shall accomplish that which I please ; it shall prosper in the thing whereunto I sent it." Isa. 55 : 11. To some the Gospel is "a savor of life unto life ;" unto others, "of death unto death." To some Jesus is revealed ; to others the Gospel is hid. Nevertheless his ministers "are unto God a sweet savor of Christ, in them that are saved, and in them that perish." 2 Cor. 2 : 15.

What shall we say to these things ? shall we dare cavil against the sovereign dispensations of God, or arraign him at the bar of our weak judgments ? shall the potsherds of the earth contend with Jehovah and say, What doest thou ? Shall the pride of our carnal reason and the rebellion of our corrupt nature vent itself with "I will not allow it at all ; I cannot allow it to be just and righteous, that the Lord should act with sovereignty, give or withhold his special grace as it seemeth good unto him ?" St. Paul sharply reproves such daring speeches, "Nay but, O man, who art thou that repliest against God ?" It is plain that such walk not humbly ; they have not the mind of Christ. The Father's will was his joy ; Jehovah's purposes his delight ; and with sovereign dispensations Jesus most cheerfully acquiesced : "Even so, Father, for so it seemed good in thy sight." Herein he hath left us an example. This is beyond all other reasons we can assign for God's dealings both in grace and providence. Such sentiments show that we have been taught of God, are little in our own eyes, are as babes in our own judgment, and are submissive children to our Father's will.

A spiritual revelation of the hope of the Gospel is by the sovereign grace of the Holy Spirit, " who divideth to every man severally as he will." It ever begets humility of heart: Why me, Lord? creates amazement of soul: What am I? ever excites love and gratitude: Am I called to the faith of Jesus and the hope of salvation, while others of the wise and prudent of this world are left in the darkness, pride, and rebellion of their nature? O what shall I render unto the Lord? How fearful to offend, how studious to please, how joyful to glorify my God ought I to be from day to day! "looking unto Jesus, the Author and Finisher of our faith." Hebrews 12 : 2.

MARCH 7.—*Take heed to yourselves: If thy brother trespass against thee seven times in a day, and seven times in a day turn again to thee, saying, I repent; thou shalt forgive him.* Luke 17 : 3, 4

Mind this loving word. "Do thyself no harm." The least degree of malice, hatred, or revenge, is contrary to the genius of the Gospel, inconsistent with the character of a disciple of the meek and lowly Jesus. But our Master knows what is in man; that his members are composed of flesh as well as spirit, and therefore that they are liable to offend one against another, so as to hurt and injure each other in the peace of their minds and fellowship of their spirits. So also they cause the way of truth to be evil spoken of by the adversaries, who are glad at every advantage to cry out, "O these your saints! see how they bite and devour each other." Therefore "take heed to yourselves," saith the Head to his members. Watch against this evil. Offences will come. I teach you how to deport yourself under them.

Suppose thy brother trespass against thee, pity his weakness, pray for him by name to thy Father and his Father. Beware of angry resentment. If he aggravates his offence by frequent repetition, thou shalt in no wise hate thy brother; but as oft as he offends, if he as often "turn again to thee, saying, I repent; thou shalt forgive him." But are we not to forgive him until and unless he do turn and say, I repent? In one sense we ought; perhaps not in another. We must not, at our peril, entertain anger, or let the sun go down on our wrath, but in our hearts freely and fully forgive an offending brother. But what if he remains stubborn and persists in a spirit of bitterness? Even then we are to forgive him in our hearts, and be desirous of embracing him in love.

But may we not justly suspend declaring our forgiveness to him, until he turn and say, I repent? Herein have we not God's word and method as our example? Though God loves his people in Christ, and for his sake pardons their sins, yet until they actually turn to him and repent he doth not manifest his pardon and love to them. But let us ever remember, as God's thoughts of love are towards us before we turn to him, so our thoughts of love should be to our offending brethren ere they turn to us. Doth the Lord Jesus require us to forgive every repeated offence, even until seventy times seven, four hundred and ninety times daily? surely then he will magnify his love and display his mercy in pardoning the innumerable offences of all who turn to him. "Forgiving one another, even as God, for Christ's sake, hath forgiven you." Eph. 4 : 32.

MARCH 8.—*And I said, This is my infirmity.* Psalm 77 : 10

While in the body, we are in such an imperfect state as to be liable to various exercises of mind, through indwelling corruptions and the suggestions of Satan

Saints in all ages have experienced fluctuating frames. Like mariners on a tempestuous sea, at one time they seem to mount up to heaven, in comfort and joy; at another, they sink down, in apprehension, to the depths of hell; then, like persons at their wits' end, they express themselves in a very unreasonable manner. Doubt and uncertainty take place of knowledge and truth; unbelief seems to prevail against faith: and they are ready to call all in question; not only past sweet experiences of God's love to their souls, but the very existence of God's promises, faithfulness, and truth. And they write with the pen of inspiration (though not of the Spirit of truth, but of a lying spirit) many false and bitter things against themselves. " Wo is me, I am undone," saith Isaiah. " Wo is me," saith Jeremiah. " Without were fightings, within were fears," say the apostles. " I shall one day perish by the hand of Saul," saith David. And in this psalm hope seems to be, as it were, giving up the ghost, and with languid, faint accents, breathes, " Will the Lord cast off for ever? will he be favorable no more? is his mercy clean gone for ever? doth his promise fail for evermore? hath God forgotten to be gracious? hath he, in anger, shut up his tender mercies?"

So you see, O tossed, tempted, tried believer, this is the way saints in all ages have gone to glory. Thou hast thy lot with them now; soon thou also shalt be where they are. But O what a gloomy prospect, what soul-distressing views must that poor sinner have who lives upon his frames, whose hope springs from his own faithfulness, or who trusts to the exercise of his own grace, instead of the God of all grace, the blessed Jesus, " who is the same yesterday, to-day, and for ever!" How comforting! how heart-reviving to know that the Lord, " who sent redemption unto his people, will ever be mindful of his covenant, which standeth fast for ever!"

Psalm 111 : 5. Therefore the Holy Spirit stands engaged, in covenant contract, to execute his office as the Comforter. When he is pleased to revive the soul with the views of Jesus, his glorious work and finished salvation, Satan retires abashed : the believer returns to his right mind, takes shame to himself, and says, That I should ever doubt of thy love, call in question thy truth, and suspect thy faithfulness ; O my God, " this is my infirmity !"

> " In vain the tempter frights my soul,
>   " And breaks my peace in vain ;
> " One glimpse, dear Saviour, of thy face
>   " Revives my joys again."

MARCH 9.—*Wherefore, beloved, seeing that ye look for such things, be diligent that ye may be found of him in peace, without spot and blameless.* 2 Peter 3 : 14.

It is a most grand delusion to imagine that the doctrines of grace tend to lull the soul asleep in supine indolence or slothful stupidity. The believer hath not so learned Christ. Though he is saved by grace freely, yet he is called to " labor diligently." By faith he looks forward to the fulfilment of awful predictions and precious promises. Hence we are excited to daily diligence in the performance of duties, the use of means, and the exercise of graces.

Do we look for the burning of the earth, the elements, and all sublunary things ? do we expect to be inhabitants of new heavens and a new earth ? do we wait, and sometimes long for the coming of the Lamb, our loving Master and precious Saviour ? and shall we indulge carnal ease and spiritual sloth ? shall we not fear to be found of Jesus in such a state ?

Most true, " Jesus hath made peace for us by the blood of his cross " But shall we not be diligent to maintain

a lively sense of this sweet peace in our hearts? shall
we not labor after purity of heart? And how is this to
be expected, but by studiously avoiding those things
which tend to draw the heart and alienate the affections
from Jesus? If we lose sight of the Lamb, we lose the
sense of peace. If we look at the things which are seen,
this begets love to them, and increases anxious solici-
tude for them. And, alas! then they only pierce us
through with many sorrows. And most of all, when we
are in our right minds, do not our sorrows increase, if
we decrease in spiritual diligence, and grow in worldly-
mindedness.

Christian, though thou knowest it is God that giveth
thee power to get wealth, and his providence is engaged
to preserve thy body; yet this doth not cause thee to
abate thy diligence in thy worldly concerns; nor doth
it make thee careless to preserve thy body from harm,
and administer to it such things as are for its health.
Most happy is it for thee thus daily to watch over and
care for the peace and purity of thy soul. Jesus is thy
peace: by living on him peace is enjoyed. He is thy
Saviour: by looking to him thou shalt be kept from sin.
Thus, by maintaining fellowship with Christ, walking
with Christ, keeping up a free intercourse with Christ,
peace of mind and purity of heart are preserved. In this
way, verily, thou shalt be blameless. And be assured,
" the diligent soul shall be made fat." Prov. 13 : 4.

MARCH 10.—*We shall not find any occasion against this Daniel,
except we find it against him concerning the law of his God.*
Daniel 6 : 5.

Happy Daniel, to have such a testimony of thy con-
duct from the mouth of thine implacable enemies?
These men could allege nothing against this servant of
God, in regard to his outward life and conversation; for

he was a good subject, a quiet neighbor, just and honest
in his dealings. Though in an eminent station, yet, with
what contempt and scorn do they seem to speak of him!
This Daniel, this over-righteous fellow, who pretends to
be more religious than all the rest of his neighbors. As
it was in the beginning, so it is now, and ever will be;
he that is born after the flesh will persecute him that is
born after the Spirit. Gal. 4 : 29. What then? our enemies no sooner assault us with their tongues, but our
God takes our part. "If ye be reproached for the name
of Christ, blessed are ye; for the Spirit of glory and of
God resteth upon you." 1 Pet. 4 : 14.

But let every disciple see to it that he suffers as a
christian. Take heed that thy life and conduct be as
becometh the Gospel. It is a great blessing so to live
that carnal men can find no just occasion against our
moral conduct. This they are judges of. Their eyes
are upon us. They watch over us for evil. This ought
to make us very circumspect. Our religion they con-
temn. For this every follower of the Lamb is sure to
be hated for his Master's sake. Wo be unto us when
all men speak well of us, saith our Master. Luke 6 : 26.
They seek enough against us, as to our faith, hope, and
life. And some would as surely cast us into a den of
lions, as they did Daniel, were it practicable and permitted. Yet they could not deprive him of the love, presence, and protection of the Son of God. These make
every place a heaven of delight and joy. And when
hated of all men for his sake, he pronounces us blessed,
bids us rejoice, and hath left us an example, patiently to
follow his steps.

Christ's dying prayer, for his very murderers, was,
"Father, forgive them, for they know not what they do."
Ignorance of the truth is the cause of hatred and malice
against his servants. Hast not thou a heart to pity and
a tongue to pray for thy enemies? Here we may indulge

sweet revenge. These weapons we may always use
And how knowest thou but the most furious persecutor,
like Paul, may be a chosen vessel of God the Father,
redeemed by the blood of Jesus, and ere to-morrow's
sun the grace of the Holy Spirit may make him a humble penitent? "Who maketh thee to differ from another? or what hast thou that thou didst not receive?"
1 Corinthians 4 : 7.

MARCH 11.—*For Christ is entered into heaven itself, now to
appear in the presence of God for us.* Heb. 9 : 24

How highly was Zacharias honored! He heard the
Gospel of salvation from the mouth of an angel, who
said, "I am Gabriel, who stand in the presence of God,
and am sent unto thee, to show thee these glad tidings."
But we see the awful effects of unbelief. Though thus
beloved and honored of God, yet he was struck dumb
for a season. Luke 1 : 20. Though God most dearly
loves his people in Christ, yet he sees their sins, and
with fatherly affection chastises for them.

Do we not see something of our own case here? For
as faith inspires the heart and tongue with boldness, so
unbelief strikes us dumb. We cannot speak a word or
offer a plea for our poor souls, if faith lose sight of Jesus. But he never forgets us. Our souls are never neglected by him. The Lamb is in the midst of the throne
for us. In our nature, in the same human body which
was hanged on the tree, with the five pierced wounds of
his hands, his feet and precious side, he appears in the
presence of God. There, like some victorious conqueror, who has gloriously delivered his country from
the cruelty and rage of a merciless enemy, he glories
in the scars he received in the field of battle.

When Jesus wept over dead Lazarus, " See how he
loved him!" said the Jews. But when poor sinners

think of our dear Lord's wounds, crucifixion, agonies, and death, O what infinitely greater reason have we to say, See how he loved us ! see how he still loves us ! Notwithstanding all our base, unloving behavior to him, still, O soul-affecting truth ! still he appears before God for us ; he presents his once mangled body, he pleads his once bleeding wounds in our behalf, as the atoning sacrifice for our sins, for our salvation. Thus glorified, Jesus now appears in the presence of God for us ; as our Mediator and Lord, our precious Saviour, our affectionate Advocate and powerful Intercessor.

But saith the adversary, "This is a cunningly devised fable." "What profit is this to me ?" saith carnal reason, backed with unbelief. But the Spirit of truth bears witness to this, first, in type and figure under the law; and, now, in reality and substance in the Gospel. To this very end, that at any time, when sin burdens the conscience, when sorrow bows down the heart, doubts arise in the mind, and fears oppress the spirit, the poor sinner may with confidence thus consider Jesus, look unto him, and call upon him ; and find this to be the food of his faith and the support of his soul : for "if God be for us, who can be against us ?" Rom. 8 : 31.

MARCH 12.—*And she shall bring forth a son, and thou shalt call his name JESUS ; for he shall save his people from their sins.* Matthew 1 : 21

O precious birth! precious son! precious name ! The Holy Ghost brings consolation to the hearts of poor sinners from the belief of the manhood of Jesus. To this end he bears so particular witness in the word, of Christ's conception and birth. It is our happiness, at all times, to consider the Saviour as "Immanuel, God with us ;" Our Brother, "flesh of our flesh, and bone of our bone." Thus to conceive of Jesus is a sweet mystery, joyfully known to believing hearts.

The name of Jesus is above every name to us; it is "as precious ointment poured forth;" it diffuseth the sweet odor of the Father's everlasting love issuing in our eternal salvation. In the name of Jesus the whole Gospel lies hid. By his work he saves us. Here is no if, perhaps, or peradventure; but a positive declaration what he absolutely shall do. He shall save his people from the curse of the law, by being made a curse for them; from the wrath of God due to them, by suffering in their stead; from the punishment their sins deserve, by the atonement of his precious blood; from the guilt of sin in their conscience, by the sprinkling of his blood through faith; from the love and power of sin in their hearts, by his Spirit, regenerating and renewing them in the spirit of their minds. So that they are as perfectly saved in Jesus from all sin, as if they had never fallen into sin. And all this by no strength or desert of theirs. Here is blessed work for faith to glory in!

Whom does Jesus thus save? "His people:" all his people, of every kindred, nation, tribe, and tongue, even all that the Father hath given him. John 17 : 9. Who are partakers of this precious salvation? Every one who believes in Jesus. It is free for all who will come to him. All who do come, and trust in him, find he is JESUS, their salvation. O believer, here is the nature, the name, the work of thy precious Jesus to look to and live upon from day to day. It is thy mercy that salvation is his work, and he hath finished it. It is thy comfort to believe this daily. It is thy duty to give him all the glory. The more light thou receivest from the word and Spirit of truth, so much the more wilt thou see of thine own vile, sinful nature, and abhor thyself, even until thou receivest the end of thy faith, the salvation of thy soul. Then wilt thou eternally glory in ascribing all salvation, from first to last, to God and the Lamb. Revelation 7 : 10.

" How sweet the name of Jesus sounds
  " In a believer's ear;
" It soothes his sorrows, heals his wounds,
  " And drives away his fear.

" It makes the wounded spirit whole,
  " And calms the troubled breast;
" 'Tis manna to the hungry soul,
  " And to the weary rest."

MARCH 13.—*The ornament of a meek and quiet spirit, which is in the sight of God of great price.* 1 Pet. 3 : 4

Godly parents are delighted in their hearts if they see their dear children partakers of the grace of God. How joyful to hear those who are part of one's self inquire after Jesus and his salvation! Love and duty unite to constrain us to teach our little ones the knowledge of Jesus, and to instruct them in the ways of the Lord. And if the Spirit of grace is pleased to crown such endeavors with success, infinitely more precious is the adorning of grace to their immortal souls than all the gayety of dress to their perishing bodies.

As we over ours, so doth the Lord rejoice over all his dear children in Christ. He takes pleasure in their dress, which is the glorious robe of his Son's righteousness. Their ornaments, which are the graces of his Spirit, are delighting to his eyes. "He makes them all glorious within:" he loves his own image, which he hath formed by his Spirit, "in the hidden man of the heart." Both their inward graces and their outward fruits are an ornament to them; and are in the sight of their heavenly Father "of great price."

By daily fellowship with our God and Saviour we become more and more "conformed to his likeness." By close walking, constant communion, free conversing with Jesus, love is maintained in the heart; and a meek and quiet spirit ever accompanies love. Where the former is wanting, the declining of the latter is evident. As faith works by love, so love shows itself by meekness of spirit and quietness of behavior.

There is a sweet harmony in the graces of the Spirit. By faith the soul abides in Jesus and receives out of his fulness. By love the heart is made happy. And as Peter and John said to the beggar, What we have received of the Lord, that we give unto you; so the christian dispenses out of his heart love to his brethren and peace and quietness to all mankind. Love controls the boisterous passions of nature. Love constrains to meekness of temper and quietness of Spirit. We sadly mistake and are greatly deceived by our corrupt nature, carnal reason, and the subtlety of Satan, when we act with any other spirit and attempt to find an excuse for it. It is unbecoming our character, a disgrace to our profession, a dishonor to our Saviour, it grieves the Spirit, is a badge of Satan's livery, a fruit of the flesh, and is contrary to the Spirit. The wrath of man worketh not the righteousness of God, peace with men, nor the comfort of the soul. "Put on, as the elect of God, bowels of mercies, kindness, humbleness of mind, meekness, long-suffering." Col. 3 : 12.

MARCH 14.—*Because in him there is found some good thing towards the Lord God of Israel in the house of Jeroboam.* 1 Kings 14 : 13

Such was the testimony which the Lord gave, by his prophet, of young Abijah, the son of wicked Jeroboam. The father was branded, even to a proverb, for his abominable wickedness. Behold, the son is recorded by the Lord for his goodness; singled out from the whole house of his father, to be blessed of his God, and come to his grave in peace.

Children of grace often spring from the loins of ungodly parents. The offspring of godly parents often appear graceless. Grace is not hereditary: it is the sovereign gift of God. Parents may, and ought to give good instructions, but God only makes them successful. " Some good thing " would not have been found in young Abijah, if the Lord had not wrought it there. It was of the will of the Lord, or because the Lord was his father, as his name, *Abijah*, signifies. God's covenant children, though by nature children of wrath, and though in their " flesh dwells no good thing ;" yet through the grace of the Holy Spirit, " they are created anew in Christ Jesus, in righteousness and true holiness, unto good works ;" and after the inward man, " they delight in the law of God." " Some good thing " is found in them, which manifests itself in love, fear, and obedience to the Lord their God. The graces of the Holy Spirit in the hearts of believers, and the fruits of the Spirit in their lives, are evidences of God's covenant love to them, in Christ Jesus. God views the work of his new creation in the soul with delight; pronounces it good, and to his own glory records the graces of his people. What comes from God leads to him, and to his glory.

Thus we see " some good thing " found in the heart of Abijah, manifesting itself in the wicked house of Jeroboam, to the glory of Jehovah, the God of Israel. O how highly honored are some who are brought to devote themselves to God's glory and service in the morning of youth! while the Sun of righteousness doth not arise upon others till the sun of nature is near setting. Hath distinguishing grace made us to differ, as well from our former selves as from others? It is all from the love of the Father, through Jesus Christ, by the power of the Spirit. We have nothing whereof to glory in ourselves, nor over others; it is our duty to confess it with our lips, and manifest it in our lives. May it encourage us daily to walk in faith and love. "The just shall live by faith." Heb. 10 : 38.

MARCH 15.—*Verily thou art a God that hidest thyself, O God of Israel, the Saviour.* Isaiah. 45 : 15

Mourning under a sense of sin, and complaining of inbred corruptions, are consistent with true faith in Jesus and real rejoicing in his salvation. Sorrowing under the painful sense of an absent God has been the experience of blessed saints in all ages ; few, if any, have been exempt from it. And this is a sure evidence that they have felt his comforting presence, enjoyed the smiles of his love, and rejoiced in the light of his countenance. So the life and love of the soul are manifested. A christian is known by his sorrows as well as his joys. He sorrows after a godly sort. This the unregenerate are perfect strangers to.

But why should a God of love hide himself from his own dear children ? We may say, he is a Sovereign, and answer in the words of Elihu, "He giveth not account of any of his matters." Job 33 : 13. But it is most sweet to say with David, " continually, Let the Lord be magnified, who hath pleasure in the prosperity of his servants." Psalm 35 : 27. Therefore when God hides himself from the souls of his believing children, it is in wisdom, love, and faithfulness to them ; it is to advance his own glory and heighten the prosperity of their souls. But he never leaves himself without a witness in their hearts. For we see the church addresses him, even though he hideth himself. She sweetly applies to him as Jesus, the only Saviour, and utters her complaint before him, " Thou hidest thyself," and I am troubled. So the sun, withdrawing his genial warmth, makes vegetable nature droop and languish, and mourn in silent sadness. But the root is still alive, and it will, when the sun returns, bring forth its fruit in due season. Backward springs often produce the most plentiful harvest. So the Lord teaches his sovereignty, roots the soul in humility, prevents the growth of spiritual pride, reproves for a careless walk, chides for worldly-mindedness, causes great searchings of heart, imbitters sin, excites to holy mourning, calls forth earnest longings, restless seekings, and fervent praying. " Saw ye him whom my soul loveth ?" will be the restless inquiry of a loving, deserted heart. I cannot live without him : his presence is heaven, his absence hell. Soul, ever beware of questioning this precious declaration of thy unchanging God of truth and love : " In a little wrath I hid my face from thee for a moment ; but with everlasting kindness will I have mercy on thee, saith the Lord thy Redeemer." Isa. 54 : 8.

MARCH 16.—*And the counsel of peace shall be between them both.* Zech. 6 : 13

With what rapture and ecstasy of soul did good old Israel hear of his son Joseph ! Not only alive, but also governor of the land of Egypt. " It is enough," said he ; as though he could enjoy no more. How then ought our hearts to be filled with joy, and fired with transport, to hear that our Friend and Brother, Jesus, lives for evermore ; that " the government is upon his shoulders ;" that he is our King and Priest upon his throne ; that the counsel of peace is fixed and unalterably established between the Father and him, on our account ! Surely, if we believe this as verily as Jacob believed the report of his son, we shall also cry out, " It is enough," perfectly sufficient. More joyful news cannot be heard, more comfortable truth be believed, fuller evidence be desired, or stronger proofs be given, than are revealed of the covenant transactions of the adorable Trinity in behalf of sinners.

Here is " the Lord of hosts," and the " Man," who is
called the " Branch." And see we not the third Person
in the Divine Essence? For the establishing of faith, be
it ever remembered, though the Father and the Son only
are often mentioned in Scripture, yet the Lord, the
Spirit, in his office is evidently to be seen and clearly
known. For whatever is covenanted and agreed between
God the Father and Son, is manifested, revealed, and
enjoyed in the heart by the Spirit. We had never heard
of this blessed peace, had it not been by the Holy Ghost,
through the word of truth. Therefore " the Spirit
bears witness, because the Spirit is truth." 1 John 5 : 6.
Ever bear this in thy mind, disciple. As thou hadst not
known sin but by the law; so thou couldst have no
knowledge of peace but by the Gospel, through the
Spirit. He is the revealer, sealer, and applier of all
grace, peace, love, and holiness. " The love of the
Father is shed abroad in our hearts by the Holy Ghost."
" He shall testify of me," saith Jesus ; all my members
shall be taught of him: " He shall glorify me." John
16 : 14. Here is a peace established between heaven
and earth, between the righteous Lord and sinful man,
firm as a rock, durable as the ages of eternity. God the
Father is the Author of this peace. Jesus obtained it by
the blood of his cross. Rebels and traitors against God
are made the subjects of it. The Spirit begets faith,
and applies the peace of God, which passeth all understanding, to the soul. And though all in nature, sin, Satan, and the world are at war with us, still this is our
glory: Jesus " is our peace." Eph. 2 : 14.

MARCH 17.—*In the multitude of my thoughts within me, thy
comforts delight my soul.* Psalm 94 : 19.

Vain thoughts and carnal reasonings, like impertinent
visiters, often intrude upon the christian's mind. In this

depraved state it cannot be otherwise. Though born again of the Spirit, and our minds renewed by grace, still our old friends, our present foes, the world, the flesh, and the devil, will furnish us with various exercises from troublesome thoughts. That they do cause grief, are prayed against, and are resisted, are blessed evidences of a regenerate soul, which is also fed, delighted, and comforted with the precious truths of God's gracious word. Is this thy experience? then, praise thy Lord

There are frequent seasons when God's dear children are exercised with distressing, gloomy thoughts. Afflictions are painful and grievous to the flesh; then how naturally do murmuring and repining thoughts arise: "Are these the tokens of God's love? how can I, who am visited with sorrow, pain, and trouble, think the Lord loves me with the love of a tender father, or that I am his child?" The sight of our vile, polluted nature, sinful passions and affections, sinks and discourages us. A multitude of thoughts arise within: How can I have faith in Jesus, love to him, and delight in his ways, while I find so much in me contrary to his will and unconformed to his image? If the Lord hides his face, then these dejecting thoughts beset us: God is acting in wrath against us, his mercy is clean gone for ever. And with the church we complain, "The Lord hath forsaken me; my Lord hath forgotten me." Isa. 49 : 14.

This is all very natural. But how speaks the voice of grace? Most cheering to the harassed mind. "Many are the afflictions of the righteous, but the Lord delivereth out of them all." "As many as I love I rebuke and chasten." Rev. 3 : 19. "Can a woman forget her sucking child, that she should not have compassion on the son of her womb? Yea, she may forget, but I will not forget thee." Isa. 49 : 15. Jesus "receiveth sinners.' Luke 15 : 2. His "blood cleanseth from all sin." 1 John 1 : 7. God's immutable love, unchangeable covenant,

eternal truths, precious promises, and solemn oath, all
stand engaged for the safety and salvation of souls redeemed by Christ, who saith, He that believeth on me
shall never perish. John 3 : 15. Shall all the powers
of earth and hell make the God of truth a liar? The
Bible is the christian's charter. Study that and judge
of God's love, not by our circumstances or feelings, but
by his word and promises.

MARCH 18.—*Strait is the gate, and narrow is the way, which
leadeth unto life, and few there be that find it.* Matthew
7 : 14.

So Jesus taught. But teachers in every age have
taught a broad way and wide gate, and multitudes have
readily received their doctrine. This is an awful truth.
Therefore Jesus adds, "Beware of false prophets." It
is the sole prerogative of the King of saints to open a
gate and make a way to his own kingdom. Glory to
our God, who in sovereign grace and everlasting love
hath done this: and the Gospel proclaims, Welcome;
come who will; enter freely, without money and without price.

Jesus is the one strait gate of God's love, the only
way of righteousness. By him we enter into access with
God, stand perfectly justified and graciously accepted
before him. Jesus is the narrow way: by the blood of
his cross he hath made peace, and atoned for the sins
of transgressors by his one offering. Hence it is called
strait and narrow, because the only way to life is by one
Man, one righteousness, one atonement. Thus it is a gate
of love, a way of grace. Too strait a gate for blind men
to see; too narrow a way for proud, self-righteous, natural men to submit to walk in. Hence, "few there be
that find it."

But, most awful to think of, whoever takes any other

way, or seeks to enter by any other gate, goeth in the broad road to everlasting destruction. That he is bold and confident is no proof that he is right; but a melancholy sign that he is blind and deceived. For "the way of a fool is right in his own eyes." Prov 12 : 15. "There is a way which seemeth right unto a man, but the end thereof are the ways of death." Prov. 14 : 12. But whoever enters the kingdom by Jesus, feeds in the pastures of everlasting grace, truth, and love; drinks of the river of consolation, and shall be nourished up to eternal life. As a person who takes up his residence for life in a more delightful kingdom than that where he was born, and conforms to its laws and customs; so the believer is conformed to the laws, speaks the language of the New Jerusalem, and "hates the garment spotted with the flesh."

Thus the Holy Spirit leads the blind by the way they knew not, even by Christ, the right way to peace, love, holiness, happiness, eternal life, and salvation. Thus, to a "little flock it is the Father's good pleasure to give the kingdom." By his word he directs them; by his Spirit he guides them; by his love he comforts them; by afflictions he profits them; by conviction of sin he humbles them; by the prospects of hope he animates them. All this is to make them walk steadily in Christ, who is "the way, the truth, and the life." John 14 : 6.

MARCH 19.—*Let us hold fast the profession of our faith without wavering; for he is faithful that promised.* Hebrews 10 : 23

Poor christian! thy profession is envied by malicious devils; scorned and ridiculed by natural men; and is contrary to thy own carnal reason. Hence thou hast a combined force, of threefold alliance, in arms against thee, striving, by all means, to rob thee of thy hope.

Happy christian! who, like thy blessed Master, in the face of every adversary, hast "witnessed a good profession." 1 Tim. 6 : 13.

Here is a precious exhortation, backed with a most animating assertion. Attend to it. For thou must expect to be assaulted by the rage of devils, with scorn and contempt from wicked men, and often put to the stand by thy carnal reasonings. Here is thy duty: "Hold fast," in spite of all opposition.

But, what is the profession of our faith? even the revealed truths of God, which proclaim his grace and glory, and our salvation, by his beloved Son. We cannot give up one of these without suffering loss. All of them are precious in our eyes and dear to our hearts; and, therefore, must be held fast in faith. "It is written," is sufficient to silence every carnal argument, support our souls against every attack from men and devils. With this weapon thy blessed Master put Satan to flight. Thus defend thyself with this sword of the Spirit against every foe. Thus daily "hold fast thy profession. He is faithful that promised."

Why then should thy mind at any time waver, be agitated, or tossed to and fro? The foundation of God standeth sure. To confide in the word, promises, and oath of a faithful God, is the glory of thy soul, and glorifies him. Is Jesus thy profession? is all thy hope in him, and thy expectation from him, for pardon, righteousness, sanctification, wisdom, and eternal redemption? Then be careful for nothing but to please him, fear nothing but what may offend him. Look to him only, and be of good courage. Remember thy foes are his conquered enemies. When they oppose, attack, assault, it is to try thy faith, that thou mayst glorify him the more. Hast thou not the Lord's faithful word pledged for thy safety and salvation? Hast thou found peace of conscience, comfort of heart, joy of soul in Christ? Then cleave close to him, hold fast by him. Ever plead (not thy own, but) his faithfulness. Attend his sweet call from heaven above, to all his conflicting members below : "That which ye have already, hold fast till I come." Rev. 2 . 25 Ever remember thy Lord's words, He, and only he, that endureth to the end, shall be saved. Matt. 24 : 13.

MARCH 20.—*A new heart also will I give you, and a new spirit will I put within you : and I will take away the stony heart out of your flesh, and I will give you a heart of flesh.* Ezekiel 36 : 26.

What absolute declarations are here ! all display the sovereign will and almighty favor of a covenant God. As God's heart of love is towards his people in Christ, so his Spirit of power works in them, according to the counsel of his will. Hence they know, love, and serve him. By the blood of Jesus their sins are pardoned and their consciences cleansed from guilt. By the Spirit of Jesus they are inwardly sanctified from their filthiness and idols ; a new heart and a new spirit is put within them, and they are enabled to walk in his statutes and keep his judgments. Thus "all things are of God, who hath reconciled us unto himself by Jesus Christ." 2 Cor. 5 : 17, 18. "If any man be in Christ he is a new creature ; old things are passed away ; behold, all things are become new."

"A christian (as Luther says) is a new creature in a new world." He has a new heart, is under a new go vernment, serves a new Master, obeys new laws, is ac- tuated by new fears, influenced by new love, animated with new delights and new joys.

"Ah, (says a disciple,) this is sweet in theory and true in doctrine, but in experience I find and feel, to my grief, an old nature of sin and unbelief, and groan under a body of death " This also is very true ; yea, it is perfectly consistent with a state of regeneration. Saints of God in all ages have found it so. The Lord, in this very text, accounts for it: "I will take away the stony heart out of your flesh, and I will give you a heart of flesh." Naturally, thy heart is hard as a stone. Thou couldst neither feel sin, mourn for sin, nor be humbled under a sense of sin. But through the blood of Jesus, applied by the Spirit in believing the truth, thou hast a soft, tender, yielding heart, a heart of flesh, susceptible of impressions, looking to Jesus by faith, melted by love, and mourning for sin. Though the king's daughter, the Lamb's wife, is all glorious within, though her clothing is of wrought gold, yet she is unhappily allied to a base, wretched, churlish Nabal. Hence, though "thou hast no confidence in the flesh, and in it dwells no good thing;" yet thou dost delight in the law of God after the inward man; and hast continual cause of rejoicing (not in thyself, but) in Christ Jesus. Phil. 3 : 3.

MARCH 21.—*But I say unto you, Love your enemies, bless them that curse you, do good to them that hate you, and pray for them that despitefully use you, and persecute you.* Matthew 5 : 44

Love is the very badge and characteristic of a disciple of Jesus. Love is of God. All tempers and passions which are contrary to love "are earthly, sensual, and devilish." Let no disciple say, This is a hard saying, who can hear it? Nay, it is the command of thy loving Saviour; he practised it, he has left thee an example. To this end thou art born from above of the Spirit of love; and possessed with that "faith which worketh by love." Therefore, though hard and impossible it may seem to carnal reason and to flesh and blood, yet we are under the indispensable obligation to follow the steps and obey the commands of that Jesus who loved us, and died for us, though his enemies. He hath blessed us, prays for us, and does good unto us, though we have rebellious natures, which are at enmity and hatred against him. Never, never, till thine enemy's hatred and variance against thee exceed thine to thy Lord, art thou at liberty to dispense with this command. It is for the health and profit of thy soul. In keeping this command of love, verily there is a great reward of inward peace and consolation from the God of love. So shalt thou enjoy the witness of his Spirit, of thine adoption.

Tell thy Lord of thine enemies, and pray for them by name. Behold the blessed effects of love upon the heart of a most bitter and implacable foe in 1 Sam. 24. See how David, the man after God's own heart, acts; how his faith works by love. When his persecuting foe, Saul, was delivered into his hand, love would not suffer David to do him any hurt. Yea, love smote his heart for only cutting off the skirts of his robe. Hear the pathetic cry of the bloody-minded Saul; struck with astonishment and melted by love, " Is this thy voice," such thy con- duct to me, " my son David ; and he wept. Thou art more righteous than I; thou hast rewarded me good for evil : the Lord reward thee for it." Admire and imitate. Love is the weapon of our spiritual warfare ; by it thou art sure to prevail against and conquer every enemy. Therefore " if he hunger, feed him ; if he thirst, give him drink ; for in so doing thou shalt heap coals of fire upon his head." Thus strive to burn up his wrath and melt him into affection. But suppose it hath not this effect upon him : it shall turn to the peace and comfort of thy own soul. Thou shalt enjoy that peace and love which is in Christ Jesus. " Walk in love." Ephes. 5 : 2.

MARCH 22.—*Let us therefore fear, lest a promise being left us of entering into his rest, any of you should seem to come short of it.* Hebrews 4 : 1

Fear, without faith, enslaves the soul to wrath and bondage. Faith, without fear, tends to licentiousness. But a loving, filial fear of offending our heavenly Father and precious Saviour, ever accompanies the grace of faith in the heart.

Jesus is the rest of his people. This rest is by promise; and therefore it is sure to all his spiritual seed. They now enter into it and enjoy it by faith. But from awful instances of others falling away from the hope of Jesus, the apostles ever exercised a fear and godly jealousy over their beloved converts, lest any of them should even but seem to come short through unbelief. The Lord only knoweth who are his elect according to his covenant of grace. This did not lie open to the eyes even of his chosen apostles. It could only be made manifest by faith and its fruits. Hence they were continually exhorting disciples to give all diligence to make their calling and election sure; to work out their own salvation with fear and trembling; not with a suspicious fear of the love and faithfulness of a covenant God, but nothing doubting the finished work of Jesus' salvation, or the safety and security of every believer in him. These are truths of the greatest certainty, and are to be held with the strongest confidence. But the apostles would have them fear lest their own souls should at any time be captivated by the devices of Satan, enslaved by the snares of the world, allured by the lusts of the flesh and the pleasures of sense, and so kept from Jesus by the workings of unbelief, that their conduct should give sad evidence of their state : lest it should seem that they sought other lovers than Jesus, other rest than in him, other hope and other comforts besides those which the Gospel affords.

So the apostles were excited to a godly fear over their professing brethren. Blessed also art thou, disciple, who thus fearest continually. By this evangelical fear verily thou shalt be kept from departing from the Lord. Count not this fear legal, as though it tended to bondage; nay, but as a fruit of thy Father's love, a grace of the gospel-covenant: it is essential to the health of thy soul, as faith is to thy being a disciple of Jesus. "Be thou in the fear of the Lord all the day long." If, at any time, this fear be cast off, thou art that moment in danger of falling. But " in the fear of the Lord is strong confidence; and his children shall have a place of refuge." Prov. 14 : 26.

MARCH 23.—*I will not leave you comfortless.* John 14 : 18.

We are born into this world crying, live in it complaining, and go out of it sorrowing, as for any comfort it can yield us. Says Cardinal Wolsey when cast off by his king, "Had I served my God as faithfully as I have my prince, he would not have deserted me thus." The more we see of this world, the more we know of its folly and vanity. The more we enjoy of its smiles and friendship, so much the more sorrow and reluctance is there in leaving it. But with our heavenly Friend it is quite otherwise. "He never leaves nor forsakes: whom he loves, he loves unto the end." Nor will he ever leave us in a comfortless state of sorrow and dejection, like poor orphans cast upon a wide world of wo, without any loving heart to pity, or kind hand to relieve them. For, when all other comforts forsake us, still Jesus abides by us. His Spirit comforts us, by showing what he is to us, has done, is doing, and will do for us. The apostles had full experience of their gracious Lord's promise. "He comforteth us in all our tribulations." 2 Cor. 1 : 4. "In me ye shall have peace."

But why doth he assure us, "In the world ye shall have tribulation?" John 16 : 33. Truly, he loves us too well to suffer us to take up our rest in it. If, with Paul at Ephesus, "after the manner of men" we fight with beasts, (1 Cor. 15 : 32;) all this is to render the world more inhospitable, to make us loathe the husks of it, that we may feed more upon Christ, the bread of life.

Why is sin suffered to dwell in us, make us groan, and distress us? To make it more hateful to us, to put us out of conceit with ourselves and our own righteousness, and to endear Christ's atonement and righteousness to our souls, that all our comfort should spring from him.

Why is Satan suffered to harass and perplex us? That, as Christ's sheep, we may keep close to our Shepherd; or as frighted children keep near their father's protection and within the bounds of his habitation, so we may find the comfort of living near our Saviour.

Have we a weak, disordered body? Here is our comfort, "We faint not, for though our outward man perish, yet the inward man is renewed day by day." 2 Cor. 4 : 16. Thus our Lord comforts us by faith, and causes us to rejoice in hope of the glory of God; and to glory in tribulation, "knowing that tribulation worketh patience, patience experience, experience hope, and hope maketh not ashamed, because the love of God is shed abroad in our hearts by the Holy Ghost." Rom. 5 : 3-5.

MARCH 24.—*Likewise the Spirit also helpeth our infirmities.*
Romans 8 : 26

How reviving to the soul, how encouraging to the mind of a disciple, to hear the experience of his brethren and companions in the faith of Jesus! To this end the blessed Spirit hath caused the saints of old to leave on record his dealings of love with their souls. Thus is the word of God most valuable for our instruction, edification, and comfort. Let no follower of the Lamb think he is singular in feeling an insupportable pressure of infirmities. No; the children of God in all ages knew and felt the same. Whether prophets or apostles, none were perfectly free from inward distresses, temptations, fears, dejections, &c. all which arise from our still possessing a fallen nature. They are our burdens We cannot but feel them, and groan under them. O sad and dreadful fall which has so terribly maimed and bruised the royal offspring of God! Our infirmities daily preach to us our fall. Shortly we shall be perfectly freed from all. This is our glorious hope.

But, alas! how oft do present distress deject us, infirmities bow down our soul, faith grow languid, love decline, hope seem at the last gasp, just as if giving up the ghost! And indeed all would end in dejection and despair, if the Lord was entirely to forsake his new creation. But that never can be while the Father loves, the Lamb pleads, and the Spirit hath power to help Therefore when the Spirit sees the souls of his charge pressed above measure in themselves, and ready to sink under their burdens, he reaches forth a tender hand of assistance, helps against infirmities by enabling the soul to look to the adorable Jesus, to an everlasting covenant, to precious promises, to a reconciled God, and puts this sweet cry in the heart, Abba, Father. Then confidence revives, hope springs afresh, love is excited, the power of prayer breaks forth in the heart and ascends in sweet fervor from the soul. Whatever flesh and blood may allege to the contrary, infirmities are made profitable to the soul; or St. Paul never would have declared, "Most gladly therefore will I glory in my infirmities." Why? is there any good in them for which they should be desired? No; but "that the power of Christ may rest upon us." 2 Cor. 12 : 9. "Grieve not the Holy Spirit." Ephesians 4 : 30.

"Eternal Spirit! we confess
"And sing the wonders of thy grace;
"Thy power conveys our blessings down
"From God the Father and the Son.

"Enlightened by thy heavenly ray,
"Our shades and darkness turn to day:
"Thine inward teachings make us know
"Our danger and our refuge too."

MARCH 25.—*But this man, after he had offered one sacrifice
for sins, for ever sat down on the right hand of God.*
Hebrews 10 : 12

The cross of Christ is the christian's glory; but the
small share that Jesus hath in his affections is his shame.
Disciples do not love their Saviour as they ought. They
are slow of heart to believe his love to them and his
sufferings for them. How little are our hearts in meditation upon the labors of love, toils of sorrow, and agonies of soul which Christ in our nature sustained for us!

If a friendly arm is reached forth and snatches a mortal from the jaws of approaching death, how does it call
forth love to his kind deliverer! when he reflects on his
danger, how does it excite his gratitude! he cannot
think of his preserver but he remembers his mercy. But
where is our warm affection, our fervent love to that
precious Redeemer whose heart was a flame of love to
us, and who willingly offered himself as a sacrifice for
our sins? How was he straitened till this baptism was
accomplished! how did his soul long till it.was finished!

Alas! we think too little of our danger. We are too
prone to look on sin as of small moment, because the
sacrifice of Jesus is not constantly upon our hearts.
Disciple, dost thou not see cause of mourning for this,
and to pray daily for more heart-affecting views of Jesus by the Spirit! O the infinite value of this one sacri-

fice! Sin, how malignant its nature! how deep its stain! nothing but blood Divine could atone for it. How prevalent this one sacrifice! it hath for ever put away all our sins.

Behold the Man! gaze, wonder, adore, and love Jesus on the cross fully atoning for sin. This work being for ever done, behold this same Man for ever set down on the right hand of God. There he pleads the sinner's cause and presents the perfection of his sacrifice. What singular consolation this! A sense of sin is distressing to the converted soul. But O, when this one sacrifice, by this one Man, is beheld by the eye of faith, how does it revive the drooping heart, give peace to the troubled conscience, and excite joy in the sorrowful mind! Poor sinners have nothing else to look to for hope. Pardon and peace can be had from no other object. Of this we can never glory too much: nor can our confidence be too strong, our expectations too great, our triumphs in Jesus over sin, Satan, the law, and death, at any time unseasonable. These precious truths are our never-failing springs of consolation. If we "sin, we have an Advocate with the Father." 1 John 2 : 1. His blood "cleanseth from all sin." 1 John 1 : 7.

MARCH 26.—*Jesus said, Will ye also go away?* John 6 : 67

This is the voice of our Beloved and our Friend to his disciples. Our Captain keeps no pressed men in his service. All his subjects enter as volunteers. They are made willing to come to, believe on, and follow him in the day of his power. Force and compulsion act not on their ingenuous minds. But what they see in Jesus now, what they expect from him hereafter, endears him to their souls.

But daily observation furnishes instances of many who profess to own Christ and follow him for a season, but anon, through not understanding his doctrine, not seeing their own wretchedness, and not knowing his love, they are offended and forsake Christ, his truths and ways. They go back again to the world, the enjoyment of its pleasures, and seek to those who cry, Peace, peace Thus they make shipwreck of faith and a good conscience which they professed to have. They forsake their own mercies by going away from Christ, and are left to perish without hope or remedy.

But all who know Jesus in spirit and truth, he keeps from such folly. The sight of others falling off and leaving him is made of blessed use to them. It excites humility and gratitude, quickens holy jealousy and godly watchfulness. Such a tender expostulation, " Wilt thou also go away ?" kindles a spark of fire, and blows up a flame of love in the sinner's heart. As when a tender parent says to his dear child, Wilt thou go away and leave *me ?* How does it draw forth its affections, while it with eager embraces clings the faster to its parent. By this question our dear Saviour has often roused my sluggish heart, called forth a holy fear, and excited an earnest cry, "Lord, keep me. O never, never let me forsake thee !"

When the aged Polycarp was going to seal the truth with his blood, the pro-consul threatened death in various ways. He answered, "Why tarriest thou ? Bring forth what thou wilt ; we christians are fixed in our minds not to change from good to evil." He was promised liberty if he would reproach Christ. Full of love he replied, " Eighty-six years have I served my Lord, and he has never done me the least wrong ; how then can I blaspheme my King and my Saviour ?" How victorious is faith ! how powerful is love ! Lord, increase our faith ! inflame our love ! " To whom should we go ? Thou hast the words of eternal life. We believe and are sure that thou art Christ, the Son of the living God." John 6 : 68, 69.

MARCH 27.—*All Scripture is given by inspiration of God, and is profitable for doctrine, for reproof, for correction, for instruction in righteousness; that the man of God may be perfect, thoroughly furnished unto all good works.* 2 Tim. 3 : 16, 17

The poor sinner who writes this, being in a dangerous illness, was in a very dark and comfortless frame of mind for two days. The third day, light, peace and joy overspread his soul by these words being brought to his mind: "After two days he will revive us: in the third day he will raise us up, and we shall live in his sight." On this he called for a Bible. O how was his inexpressible joy increased when he read these words! Hosea 6 : 2. On being asked if he had done with the Bible? he answered with a flood of joyful tears, No: never, never shall I have done with that most blessed book till I change time for eternity." The Spirit of inspiration ever honors his own word of truth. All peace, comfort, and joy are derived from it through faith. We shall suffer no loss if we suspend judgment on comforts till we have tried them by this touchstone of truth. Be on your guard against the flatteries of false peace and the delusions of unscriptural joys.

Scripture truths are inspired of God; they are the objects of faith. By the knowledge of them the Spirit consoles the soul, lovingly reproves for and corrects what is amiss, profitably instructs in the fundamental truths of Jesus' righteousness unto justification of life, and the believer's obedience unto righteousness. No one doctrine of God's word should be slightly regarded. In this sense he that rejects one point of truth is guilty of all. This is to impeach the wisdom of the Spirit, as if he had made known any one needless or insignificant doctrine. This, instead of being doers of the word, is to judge and condemn the word.

Jesus is the sum and substance of the Scriptures. All
the promises are in him. All the doctrines of grace
lead to and centre in him. These are the furniture, of
faith, while Jesus is the chief object of the soul. So
disciples go on to perfection in knowledge, love, and
holiness; therefore we should prize the Scriptures as
our companion, consult it as our familiar friend, and
pray over it as our constant guide. To these ends all
Scripture is given of God. When thus received by us,
we shall also, like disciples of old, be "edified, and walk
in the fear of the Lord and in the comfort of the Holy
Ghost." Acts 9 : 31. Look, then, for all comfort from
belief of the Scriptures, and in Christ testified of in them.
For the Holy Ghost gives comfort in no other way.
He fills us "with all joy and peace in believing."
Romans 15 : 13.

> "Laden with guilt and full of fears,
> "I fly to thee, my Lord;
> "And not a glimpse of hope appears
> "But in thy written word.
>
> "The volume of my Father's grace
> "Does all my grief assuage:
> "Here I behold my Saviour's face
> "Almost in every page."

MARCH 28.—*We have not an High Priest who cannot be touched
with the feeling of our infirmities; but was in all points
tempted like as we are, yet without sin.* Heb. 4 : 15

"Without sin!" O that this were my happy state,
cries the sanctified soul. Verily, as sure as the word of
God is true, thou shalt soon enjoy this perfect freedom
from thy worst enemy. But thou must be content to
wait God's time and live in his way, that is by faith
upon thy best Friend, Jesus. Thy present blessedness
is to understand and rejoice in this great mystery, that
Christ, who knew no sin, was made sin for us. There-

fore by faith we glory, knowing that God looketh on us, blesseth us as righteous in Christ, and doth not impute sin unto us. As the Head is without sin, so are all the members, as viewed by God. And this is the evidence that we are born of the Spirit, and have the mind of Christ, that we hate all sin, long for entire deliverance from it, and aspire after full conformity to the image of God. But this we cannot enjoy in the body. We must first sleep in Jesus, ere we awake after his perfect likeness. Press towards the mark.

In the meantime we have a loving, sympathizing High Priest before the throne of God. This is our comfort That very human nature on which our sins were laid, and in which they were all expiated on earth, is now crowned with glory in heaven. This is most refreshing. Christ can as soon forget his own glory as any one of his suffering members. He feels for them. He is touched with the most tender concern and affection towards them. "He knows what sore temptations mean, for he has felt the same."

Temptations, even though most violent, cannot harm us. Nay, they do not defile us, unless we enter into them. Therefore they should not deject us. And need we ever be overcome by them? Doth not Jesus live? Have we not free and familiar access to him, as the glorified man, our Mediator? Is not all power in heaven and earth given unto him? Believest thou this, O soul? Think on his love at Calvary. Remember his resurrection at Bethany. Call to mind his tender love to, and affectionate care for his sheep, when worried by Saul. He called, "Why persecutest thou *me*?" Thou canst not hurt them but I feel it. He ever lives at the right hand of glory, to intercede for and save us poor sinners. And let thy distress be what it may, his loving advice suits it. "Call upon me in the day of trouble: I will deliver thee, and thou shalt glorify me." Psalm 50 : 15

MARCH 29.—*Now our Lord Jesus Christ himself, and God, even our Father, who hath loved us, and given us everlasting consolation and good hope through grace, comfort your hearts, and stablish you in every good word and work.* 2 Thess. 2 : 16, 17

We know "the remembrance of sin is grievous and the burden intolerable." A sight and sense of sin affects our conscience with sorrow and distress. Our hearts daily need to be comforted and established in every good word and work. But from whence shall we derive this? from striving to forget, palliate, or excuse our past sins? by promising to be more steadfast in God's truths and obedience to his will? Alas, he who truly knows his sinful nature, who is really acquainted with his own weakness and insufficiency to any good and his proneness to all evil, will not, cannot thus deceive his own soul, but will ingenuously confess his sins to God his Saviour, with all their aggravating circumstances, mourn over them with a godly sorrow, own his just deserts for them, and in faith look " to the Lamb of God who taketh away the sin of the world."

Here is our everlasting spring of consolation, which God hath given us : "the blood of Jesus Christ his Son cleanseth us from all sin." Here is our good hope: we are completely righteous, and perfectly accepted in God's beloved Son. Faith and hope are inseparable. We believe the truth as in Jesus; we hope daily for more and more of the consolations of it. In this grace, disciple of Jesus, never canst thou believe nor hope too much. Nay, is it not thy distress and heaviness that thy faith is weak, thy hope languid, and thy love cold? But why so? Not for want of a foundation for faith and hope; for " our Lord Jesus Christ himself, and God our Father, hath loved us,"—even us sinners of mankind. Such was the character of all those whom the apostle includes in the pronoun *us.* And as the consequence of this love, " he hath given us everlasting consolation."

Not the effect of time, not subject to mutability, but solid, perpetual, and eternal; founded in the everlasting covenant, established in everlasting righteousness, issuing in everlasting salvation, revealed in the everlasting Gospel, and applied by the everlasting Spirit. Consolation and comfort are enjoyed by stability in the good word of God, and in the good works of faith, "to the praise of the glory of God's grace." Eph. 1:6. "Be ye followers of God, as dear children." Eph. 5:1.

MARCH 30.—*This is the true God and eternal life. Keep yourselves from idols. Amen.* 1 John 5:20, 21

It is a common objection, with carnal men, against Christ's ministers and members, "You can preach and talk of nothing but Jesus." Truly, we consider him as the end of all our conversation. Heb. 13:7. Conscious of what he is to us, hath done for us and in us, verily, he is all in all to us. We know that the Son of God is come in our flesh. We are sure that by the blood of his cross he hath made an end of sin, finished transgression, made reconciliation for iniquity, and, by his holy life, hath brought in an everlasting righteousness. Daniel 9:24.

All this we poor sinners wanted. Nothing short of this could save us. Yea, eternal life we have in our wonderful Friend, the God-man, Christ Jesus. Blessed be his infinitely precious name, he hath given us understanding to know him. We desire to be eternally indebted to his name, his grace, his love; for we see our union to him, and feel our oneness with him. Marvel not, then, that we speak so highly of our Beloved; for if we should hold our peace, the very stones would cry out against us. Say, ye first-born sons of light, say, ye children of grace, of whom should we glory, if not of Jesus our "true God, and eternal life?" We disclaim

all other gods. We "know and believe that the Father
is in him, and he in the Father." John, 10 : 38. He
teacheth the Father's love in him to us, and sends the
Comforter, who proceeds from the Father, through him,
to shed his love abroad in our hearts.

But alas! how did we live before we knew Jesus, the
only true God? Truly, though we talked of God,
thought we knew, worshipped, and feared him, yet we
were all the while, like the rest of the whole world, "lying in wickedness," fast asleep in the arms of the wicked
one, were without Christ, "without God in the world,"
and consequently had no hope. Eph. 2 : 12.

How deluded are the wise and learned of this world
with their notions and worship of—an unknown God!
while little children are truly wise and best learned, who
know Jesus as their Lord and their God, and abide in
him. The truth of their faith, uprightness of their hearts,
and sincerity of their love, are best evidenced by keeping
themselves from the insnaring vanities and bewitching
idols of time and sense. "Adorning the doctrine of
God our Saviour in all things. Looking for that blessed
hope and glorious appearing of the great God, even our
Saviour Jesus Christ, who gave himself for us," &c.
Titus 2 : 10, 13.

> "Jesus, my God, I know his name,
>   "His name is all my trust;
> "Nor will he put my soul to shame,
>   "Nor let my hope be lost."

MARCH 31.—*O wretched man that I am! who shall deliver
me from the body of this death!* Romans 7 : 24.

Spiritual sense and feeling are peculiar to regenerate
souls While "dead in trespasses and sins," though
the law thunders its dreadful curses against us, we hear
not. Though by nature children of wrath and deserv-

ing hell, yet our danger we see not. Though our sins are gone over our heads, and like a sore burden are too heavy for us to bear, yet we feel them not. But when quickened we groan, being burdened with a body of sin, and pant after deliverance. This was the experience of holy Paul. Such the experience of saints in all ages.

But, thank God, though ever so deeply distressed, and greatly depressed with sin, yet we sorrow not as without hope. We are not ignorant of, but know our deliverer, Jesus Christ. None but he is able. He hath, he doth, he will deliver. He hath delivered from the curse of sin by his death. He doth deliver our conscience from the guilt and dominion of sin through faith. He will deliver us perfectly from the being of sin, when the body is "sown in dishonor to be raised in glory." The last enemy, death, is not yet destroyed. None are perfectly exempt from sin which brought death into the world. But present deliverance thou hast, O believer, and perfect deliverance thou dost pant after and long for.

Think not, that feeling a body of sin, (which, like thy natural body, consists of many parts and members,) groaning under it, breathing out ardent desires for deliverance, inscribing "wretched man" upon thyself, like a criminal compelled to carry a dead, putrified body; think not all this inconsistent with being blessed "with all spiritual blessings in Christ." No, thou art not singular. It was once the lot of all thy brethren, now perfect in glory. It is the lot of all thy companions in the faith and patience of Jesus on earth.

When Paul in spiritual ecstasy was caught up to the third heavens, he knew not whether he was in the body or not. He might then think he was perfect, entirely freed from his burden. But a little time convinced him to the contrary. We find him "as sorrowful, yet always rejoicing." 2 Cor. 6 : 10.

Blessed be our compassionate Saviour for his reviving

cordials of consolation. These cheer our drooping spirits under our burden. This favor no kind hand administered to him, when sinking under the ponderous load of our sins on the cross. O the joy of faith! Though sin is felt, grieved for, mourned over, yet "there is no condemnation to them that are in Christ Jesus" Romans 8 : 1.

April

APRIL 1.—*I press toward the mark for the prize of the high calling of God in Christ Jesus.* Phil. 3 : 14

By effectual vocation the soul is called from a death in sin to a life of righteousness. By spiritual illumination the most desirable objects are discerned. The faith of God's elect manifests itself to be an operative grace in the heart by the conduct of the life. Blessed Paul, though such a zealous champion for the sovereign operations of free grace, though so averse to the pride of man and the confidence of human righteousness, both in his writing and preaching, yet his life and exhortations are equally opposite to all licentious practices and unchristian sloth. He had a race to run, a prize to win, the end of his calling to attain.

Thus it is with all who are partakers of like precious faith. Folding the hands, sitting down contented, resting in ease and indolence may suffice when doctrines are only received as notions in the head. Truths may be assented to in the judgment, as dry speculations, so as to engage the tongue, without warming and influencing the heart and producing the fruits of holiness in the life. But the truth received in the love of it excites to activity

Says the christian, "I press forward," like a racer who considers the mark before him, turns his back upon the place he set out from, and is solicitous so to run that he may obtain the prize. Jesus is the christian's mark—he presses towards him; he is solicitous to enjoy much of Christ below; he longs for full enjoyment of him above. This is our glorious high calling. What can be put in competition with it? the world with all its sinful customs, vain pleasures, and carnal delights? No, we forsake these, and leave them behind us. We fear being entangled with the objects of time and sense, preferring Jesus above all. Earthly things grow more and more mean and contemptible to us. The more we see our all in Jesus, and expect all from him, so much the more we press towards him.

Hence means of grace are prized, ordinances attended, Christ's word is precious, the prize glorious. Thou man of God, ever exercise a godly jealousy of being brought into bondage to the world or the flesh. Remember how unfaithfully, how dishonorably thou actest when any object engages thy attention and rivals thy Saviour. "So run that you may obtain." 1 Cor. 9 : 24.

> " Dear Saviour, let thy beauties be
> " My soul's eternal food;
> " And grace command my heart away
> "From all created good."

APRIL 2.—*The Spirit itself beareth witness with our spirit, that we are the children of God.* Romans 8 : 16

These words dropt not from the pen of a saint, in a state of sinless perfection: nor is this heavenly blessing peculiar to Paul the apostle, but to Paul, " less than the least of all saints," and chief of sinners, as he owned himself to be. It has been enjoyed by sinners, through faith, in all ages; it is the common privilege of all christians. Well may we cry out in astonishment, "But will God in very deed dwell with men on the earth? Behold, heaven and the heaven of heavens cannot contain thee." 2 Chron. 6 : 18. Amazing condescension! "Lord, what is sinful, hell-deserving man, that thou shouldst visit him" with thy cheering presence?

Delightful to think of! There is a sweet relation subsisting between the High and Lofty One and miserable sinners. In Jesus they are united. The fulness of the Godhead and the misery and curse of our nature meet in him. From the head Jesus, the Spirit proceeds; and, like the oil on Aaron's head, descends to all the members. To their spirits he bears witness, agreeably to the word of their covenant relation, as adopted sons of God by faith in Christ.

Let no believer be distressed or deluded by the deceiving of others, so as to expect an outward vision, manifestation, or revelation that may be seen, heard, or felt by the outward senses. No; the Spirit bears witness *to our spirits*, not to our senses. Even as the law bears witness to the conscience, that we are sinners, and works wrath there; so the blessed Spirit bears witness to the mind, that we are the children of God by faith in Jesus; that "he died for our sins, and rose again for our justification;" that in him we are chosen, beloved, accepted, justified, pardoned, and shall be glorified with him. For, saith Jesus, "He shall glorify me; for he shall receive of mine, and shall show it unto you." John 16 : 14.

See, O believer, the riches of covenant grace! Admire and adore the wonderful love of the Trinity! Hast thou received the witness of the Spirit in the word through faith! Happy, highly favored art thou. Or art thou waiting and longing for the promise of the

Father, the joyful assurance of the Spirit, that thou art his? Such a blessing is not for any good naturally found in thee; but because Jesus intercedes before the throne. Therefore plead, in the assurance of faith, this promise, "Your heavenly Father will give the Holy Spirit to them that ask him." Luke, 11:13. "Ask in faith, nothing doubting." James 1:6.

APRIL 3.—*For what shall it profit a man, if he shall gain the whole world, and lose his own soul? Or what shall a man give in exchange for his soul?*—Mark 8:36, 37

Hast thou heard the voice of thy Beloved? art thou a willing disciple of a despised Master? But does the flesh shrink from, murmur, and reason against taking up the cross daily, " and suffering the loss of all things?" Listen, O soul, to the reasonings of Wisdom. Their dear Master here teaches the followers of the Lamb such reasoning and argument, drawn from the nature and fitness of things, as will, in a dying hour, and at the judgment-day, silence the tongue of every adversary. Ever use thy Master's weapon. Reason daily, O christian, upon thy spiritual gain, by the knowledge of Jesus. Study to look with contempt upon thy trifling, worldly loss. What is all the wisdom of this world, but folly? the righteousness of the whole world, but filthy rags? the hopes of a fallen world, but miserable delusion? the pleasures of a gay world, but vanity? the riches of the world, but deceitfulness? the honors of the world, but an empty sound? All these, though possessed and enjoyed, cannot profit the soul.

Nay rather, like Job's friends, they often prove only miserable comforters, distressing the mind, but can never bring comfort to the soul. Though often set by the enemy before our eyes, in the most conspicuous and advantageous light, as Satan tempted our Lord, yet is there any comparison between an eternal gain and a temporal loss? Verily, one moment's communion with Jesus by faith, infinitely transcends a life of threescore years and ten spent in all the glory and happiness this whole world can yield. O, this one word, "Thou fool, this night thy soul is required of thee," is a death-stroke to all worldly enjoyments.

What then can be placed in competition with an "exceeding and an eternal weight of glory?" How great is the worth of the soul! it is immortal. How rich the love of God! it is everlasting. How transcendent the love of Jesus! it passeth knowledge. How amazing the grace of the Holy Ghost! it proceeds from both. It is through his power any poor sinner is able to say: "What things were gain to me, those I count loss for Christ. Yea, doubtless, and I count all things but loss for the excellency of the knowledge of Christ Jesus my Lord—that I may win Christ and be found in him." Philippians 3 : 7–9.

> "When I survey the wond'rous cross
> "On which the Prince of glory died,
> "My richest gain I count but loss,
> "And pour contempt on all beside.
>
> "Were the whole realm of nature mine,
> "That were a present far too small;
> "Love so amazing, so divine,
> "Demands my soul, my life, my all."

APRIL 4.—*God forbid that I should glory, save in the cross of our Lord Jesus Christ, by whom the world is crucified unto me, and I unto the world.* Galatians 6 : 14.

Satan is very busy to hinder the christian's glorying in Jesus only. As an adversary to the truth, he objects by the men of the world, and it is frequently suggested to the believer's mind, "Jesus is ever, ever uppermost in your heart and tongue; you ascribe no glory to God the Father, and to the Holy Spirit." But this is vain and ignorant. For in our crucified Jesus we behold the great love of the Father. Our glorying in the cross of Christ alone, is by the grace and teaching of the Holy Spirit, whose office it is to testify of Jesus only, and of salvation by none other. So saith our Lord, " He shal. glorify me : for he shall receive of mine, and shall show it unto you." John 16 : 14.

God forbid that all the men upon earth, or devils in hell, all the temptations of our nature, or unbelief of our hearts, should corrupt our minds from the simplicity of Christ, or prevent our glorying in our ever dear, ever lovely and Divine Redeemer. He hung on the accursed tree with all our guilt, sin, and shame upon him. Was he ashamed to own our vile characters, or love our sinful persons? No. Shall we be ashamed to own and confess his innocent person, his glorious name, his gracious words, his accursed death, his perfect salvation? Surely then, the very stones would cry out against us.

" Whosoever shall be ashamed of me and my words, in this adulterous and sinful generation, of him shall the Son of man be ashamed when he cometh in the glory of his Father, and his holy angels." Mark 8 : 38. To expect salvation from no other, and all salvation from this man Jesus, this malefactor, as the Jews accounted him, as suffering, dying on the cross, a gibbet, a gallows : this is the very essence of the Gospel, the glory of God's grace, the wonder of angels, and the envy of devils; this the only hope of a poor humbled sinner, and the triumph of faith. Is this your glory?

Who can fully describe the blessedness of souls who glory only in Christ? As they find and feel new life from his cross, they experience a crucifixion and death to all legal hopes and vain confidence, in which a self-righteous world glory. From the cross of Jesus they view the world, with all its pomp and pleasures, riches and honor, glory and happiness, as accursed, sentenced, and devoted to destruction. Therefore as crucified persons, by the faith of Jesus, we die daily to the world "Christ is our life." Colossians 3:4

APRIL 5.—*And Hazael said, But what! is thy servant a dog that he should do this great thing?* 2 Kings 8:13

O the treachery of the human heart! both Scripture and experience prove this melancholy truth, that it is "deceitful above all things, and desperately wicked." Who can fathom the depths of its deceits? who can understand the mystery of iniquity which lies concealed in the nature of sinful man? Alas! presumptuous confidence that our nature is not so totally corrupt and abominable, too often deceives and betrays even God's children.

This wretch Hazael, who had premeditated rebellion and murder in his heart, yet starts at the prediction of such crimes which as yet had no real existence. Doubtless, he thought Elisha judged very hard of him. He could almost stare the prophet out of countenance. And, as though he charged him with degrading the dignity of his human nature, he demands whether he looked on him no better than a fierce, devouring dog, that he should commit such abominable wickedness? His very nature shuddered at the thought. But the history assures us, "lust had conceived, and it brought forth sin," which ended in the murder of his royal master. Hazael fully verified all the prophet's prediction.

Boast not of thyself, O christian! Say not I am a converted man, a believer in Jesus, not an ungodly wretch like this Hazael, therefore I shall not fall into that and the other sin. Be not high-minded, but fear. Thou standest not by thine own strength, but by faith. This grace **ever** leads out of self to its object, Christ. Flatter not

thyself that thy corrupt nature is in any wise better
than that of any other. Know there is no difference.
Deceive not thyself with conceits of perfection in the
flesh, or with the deluded dream, that the root of sin is
entirely destroyed in thy nature. Ever remember, " in
the flesh dwelleth no good thing;" therefore it is and
ever will be prone to do evil continually.

Happy for thee that thou art new-born, new-created
in the spirit of thy mind. It is thy privilege to live under the influence of grace and love. But still thy fallen
nature is ever the same; the old man is still alive;
there is the tinder of corruption, which may take fire
from the devil's sparks of temptation. What thou art
least suspecting, yea, when thou art most confident of
standing, thou mayest be in the greatest danger of falling. What thou fearest not to-day, to-morrow may
overcome thee. Think not more highly of thyself than
thou oughtest to think. "Be sober: watch unto prayer."
" God resisteth the proud; but giveth grace to the
humble." 1 Peter 5:5.

APRIL 6.—*Sanctify the Lord God in your hearts: and be ready
always to give an answer to every man that asketh you a reason
of the hope that is in you with meekness and fear.* 1 Peter
3:15.

When Christ the Lord God is the glory of the soul, it
is the soul's glory to sanctify him, and him only. How
joyful, to have one's heart detached from every other
object and hope, and its whole delight to glorify our
Saviour! How delightful to dwell on the wonders of his
love, the riches of his grace, the greatness of his sufferings, the fullness of his redemption, the perfection of his
righteousness, the prevalence of his intercession, and
all issuing in the eternal life of such vile, sinful wretches
as we.

Verily, under such views, most cheerfully does the

believer sanctify the Lord, Immanuel, in his heart.
Hence, how powerfully is his soul animated with holy
boldness against the fear of man! yea, inflamed with
love to the truth! how ready to give a reason of his
hope! Perhaps, through the warmth of his zeal and the
heat of his affections, he does not always act wisely
herein; and does what is forbidden by his Lord, "casting his pearls before swine." Hence he finds, as they
were ignorant of the worth of his jewels, they turn upon him with wrath. The apostle seems to guard against
this.

Christian, thou art to be always ready to answer, and
give a reason of thy hope. But to whom? Every man
that asks *with meekness and fear;* meek to receive instruction; fearing error; and desiring to know the truth,
as it is in Jesus. As the christian has freely received,
so it is his delight freely to give to others. He hopes
the Lord may make him the happy instrument of conviction, conversion, and edification to others. Far is it
from the nature of a christian "to eat his morsel
alone." While he imitates the meekness of the lamb in
his temper, the boldness of the lion is to accompany
his concern for God's glory and the cause of his truth.
Meek in speech; but not with timid fear to answer.

When God's truth is the subject, the strongest confidence and the greatest courage are our glory. What is
thy hope, O christian? Is it any other than that "mystery" of godliness, "Christ in you, the hope of glory?"
Col. 1: 27. Dost thou see such infinite charms, such
inestimable glory, in that despised Jesus who was hanged upon a tree as an accursed malefactor, that he is the
only hope of thy soul, the only glory of thy heart? O
blessed, highly favored art thou! Is it not thy joy to
say, "Come, hear, all ye who fear God, and I will declare what he hath done for my soul." Psalm 66: 16

APRIL 7.—*Now I know thou fearest God, seeing thou hast not withheld thy son, thine only son from me.*—Gen. 22 : 12

So spake Jesus to his friend of old. What! did not God know that Abraham feared him before this? Doubtless he did. But now in the exercise of faith and love he approved himself to God. He gave full evidence that God's commandments are not grievous; but that it was his joy and delight to obey his God. Lord, give what thou commandest, and command what thou wilt, is the breathing of faith and love! Thus was the faith of Abraham justified by its fruits.

Seest thou how his faith wrought by his works? And by works he gave full proof that he possessed the faith of God's elect. Thus he obtained this glorious testimony to his own soul, from the mouth of the Lord: Now I know that thou fearest God with a loving, filial fear. Thy faith worketh by love; it has influenced thy heart to this eminent act of cheerful, unreserved obedience to me. His faith consulted not flesh and blood, it surmounted carnal reason. The command of the Lord was the only rule of his conduct. He both sacrificed and enjoyed his Isaac. Thus saith Jesus to every believer, "Ye are my friends, if ye do whatsoever I command you." John 15 : 14. The Spirit of God, by St. James, styles him a "vain man," who thinks he has faith without works. James 2 : 20. For both his soul and his faith are dead.

It is our wisdom to know that justification in the sight of God, through the blood and righteousness of Jesus, is "perfect and entire, lacking nothing." This is received by faith only. But this belief cannot exist without its object, Jesus; therefore cannot be alone in the heart without love. Faith works by love, and love lives by faith. An inward faith manifests itself by obedience as an outward evidence. Thus the believer's works are manifest that they are wrought in God, and that the soul walks in the light of God's truth and love.

But, alas, how often is it true, amongst professors, as Paul said on another occasion, "Many are weak and sickly among you, and many sleep," through intoxicating draughts of the love of this world, and living after the flesh. Such have no inward testimony that they please God. They possess not joy and peace in believing. They give no outward evidence that they are married to the Lamb and live by faith on him. Examine thy own soul, O christian, whether thou art in the faith; prove thy own self. Knowest thou not thy own self, how that Jesus Christ is in thee, except thou be a reprobate? 2 Cor. 13 : 5.

APRIL 8.—*Learn of me, for I am meek and lowly in heart; and ye shall find rest to your souls.* Matthew 11 : 29

Thus, with tender affection, speaks Jesus our Prophet to the lambs of his flock. He well knows we stand in need of daily instruction from him. He teaches us in the truth, as we are able to bear it. He knows the weakness of our understandings. He is "touched with a feeling of our infirmities." Therefore, lest our poor hearts should at any time conceive thoughts of him contrary to his nature and office, he says, "I am meek and lowly in heart." You find you are poor sinners; ignorant of many truths; exercised with many conflicts, trials, and temptations : do not think of me only as "the High and Lofty One, who inhabiteth eternity," but as dwelling also with humble hearts. Look not on me as an austere master, a terrible lawgiver, a severe judge, who watches over you for evil, and is ever ready to take all advantages against you. No : I am your condescending, meek, and lowly Saviour; your loving Friend and kind Instructor; therefore come and listen to my words. "Learn of me."

What sweet encouragement is this! Art thou, O soul, tossed with temptations? harassed with corruptions? beset with sinful passions? Do these bring disquiet upon thy mind, distress to thy conscience, and prove a wearisome burden to thy spirits, so that thou dost not enjoy settled ease and rest. Remember thy Saviour's lowly character and kind advice. He hath an ear of grace for thy complaints, a heart of love to pity thee, a powerful arm to relieve thee. With sweet familiarity pour out thy heart to him. As a bosom friend tell him of thy sorrows, complaints, and fears. Always bear in mind his kind invitation, the loving meekness and lowliness of his heart, and the blessedness of his promise. He hath spoken it, and will he not bring it to pass? He hath said it, and will he not fulfil it? " Ye shall find rest to your souls;" such sweet tranquillity and inward composure as can be found in no object besides. Could the children of this world persuade us that there is no evil in their vain diversions and carnal delights; still, we know we cannot expect our Lord's presence, nor shall we find rest to our souls in all the delusive scenes of earth. No; but the more rest we find to our souls in Jesus, the more we are delighted with him; we become dead to all things that are contrary to spiritual peace and joy from him. "We who have believed do enter into rest;" and yet, we "labor to enter into rest." Hebrews 4 : 3, 11.

APRIL 9.—*Consider him who endured such contradiction of sinners against himself, lest ye be wearied and faint in your minds.* Hebrews 12:3

Come, christian, look up, look forward, and be of good courage. Though thy afflictions are many, and thy conflicts great; though weary *in*, yet be not weary *of* the ways of the Lord. Verily, in due time we shall reap an harvest of eternal felicity, after all our present toil and labor. Faint not. Continue to the end. Persevere in the work of faith, labor of love, and patience of hope. The battle is the Lord's. Thy foes are all conquered. Victory is obtained. The crown is held forth by thy conquering Lord. Press on.

But, alas! thou findest contradiction from every quarter; from within and from without. Numerous foes rise up against thee. Thy strength is small. Thy power weak. Most true! But know thy calling. Study thy privileges. Behold, thy Comforter holds forth a reviving cordial to thy drooping spirits. "Lest thou be weary and faint in thy mind," consider Jesus. Here is faith's mystery, the christian's triumph; hence derive fresh life and vigor to thy fainting mind.

Consider Jesus, in his Divine nature: thy covenant God; in his human nature, thy redeeming Brother; as God and man in one Christ, thy full salvation, thy almighty Saviour. Consider Jesus in his innocent life, enduring contradiction of sinners against himself on thy account; fulfilling all righteousness for thee; that thou mightest be perfectly righteous in him. Consider Jesus on the Cross, bearing thy sins amidst taunts and jeers, making atonement for thy transgressions. Consider Jesus entered into heaven, and appearing in the presence of God for us. Consider Jesus infinite in wisdom to know thy wants, infinite in love to sympathize with thee in all thy sorrows, infinite in power to support and strengthen under all. Consider what infinite riches of grace he has in glory to supply all thy need. O consider the fulness of grace that dwells in him for needy sinners. Live upon his fulness day by day, so as to receive out of his fulness grace for grace.

"Has the blood of martyrs proved the seed of the church?" Confident we are, the life and death, the blood and righteousness of Jesus are the life of our graces, the spring of our comforts, the support of our weary minds, and the only reviving cordials for our fainting spirits. Are we panting sinners at his footstool? Consider Christ makes us joyful before his throne now. Soon we shall be eternally happy in his presence. Imitate the father of the faithful. Be not weak in faith. Consider not thy own body, which is dead because of sin. Know the Spirit is life, because of the righteousness of Jesus. Rom. 8 : 10.

APRIL 10.—*And they laughed him to scorn.*   Matt. 9 : 24

Wonderful indeed is our Master in patience, meekness, love and goodness, under such insults. "When Herod saw Jesus, he was exceedingly glad. He desired to see him of a long season, for he hoped to see some miracle done by him." Miracles may satisfy curiosity. They do not of themselves convert the heart to the truth. This is plain. Herod saw in Jesus a most astonishing miracle. Behold, innocence itself arraigned and accused, death in its most cursed and ignominious form threatened. Amazing! Jesus stood mute: his tongue locked up in silence. His mighty arm, which could have dealt destruction at a blow, he suffered to be bound; himself to be set at nought, and in derision to be arrayed in a robe of mock royalty. Herod, though undesigned, gave him a token of his innocence; as Pilate, contrary to his intention, gave him a title, "This is the King of the Jews." Though requested to alter it, constrained to be inflexible, he replies, "What I have written I have written;" I will not revoke it.

See your calling. It is to confess and follow a once scorned, ridiculed Jesus. Never once dream of being excused from suffering with him. So surely as thou dost "witness a good profession" of faith in Jesus, and conformity to him, thou also shalt not escape laughter

and scorn from the world. Time was when we acted
as they do. Think of this and be humble. Glory be
to Him who taught us better. But what harm can this
do us? Harm! it is our greatest glory on earth.
"Such honor have all his saints." An honor angels
share not in. Sinners only are called thus to glorify
their Master. True, it is galling to the flesh. But
"they that are Christ's have crucified the flesh with its
affections and lusts." By the world's scorn pride is
mortified, while the soul is joyful; and the Spirit of
Christ and of glory rests upon us. The world may
laugh us to scorn, but Jesus smiles and approves. Shall
we be uneasy at this? No; our Master bids us rejoice,
and be exceeding glad. Thus, follow Christ and fear
not men. Formerly, it was a proverbial expression to
show an impossibility, "You may as soon turn a christian from Christ as do it." Steadfastness here is our
glory. In the things of God, said Luther, "I yield to
none." As God's calling is irrevocable, so let our confession of Christ be. Strive to imitate him in love and
patience. He has left us an example, that we should
follow his steps. 1 Peter 2 : 21.

APRIL 11.—*That no flesh should glory in his presence.*—*He that
glorieth, let him glory in the Lord.* 1 Cor. 1 : 29, 31

Humble, self-abased souls, who drink deep into self-
knowledge, whose eye of faith is to Christ, and to what
he is made of God to them, are as jealous of the pride
of the flesh as they are of its sinfulness. This is a safe
state. Such have little reason to murmur because
they do not experience those high flights and ravishing
ecstacies which appear to arise from nature and sense,
because they lead to glory in the righteousness of the
flesh. Flesh is proud, and prone to glory, even in the
presence of God. But faith in Jesus cuts off all glory-

ing in the flesh, as viewing all salvation out of ourselves in him. This is the very essence of the faith of God's elect. Yet, while in the flesh, we are daily exposed to the workings of pride, which darken the view of Jesus, and tend to self-exalting and self-glorying. What pains doth the loving Spirit take to humble us! He testifies of Jesus. He shows us, by line upon line and precept upon precept, by prophets and apostles, that in Jesus all his children are "justified, and shall glory." Isaiah 45 : 25.

Am I made wise unto salvation? Glory to Jesus. He is my wisdom. Am I righteous in the sight of God? Glory to Jesus. He is my righteousness; not obtained by my works, but by God's free gift. Am I sanctified? Glory to Jesus. It is through the faith of him, by the Spirit, that I have any drops from the fountain of Jesus' blood to wash away my guilt and to cleanse my soul. Have I faith, and hope of complete redemption from all misery to all happiness? Glory to Jesus. He is my redemption, he hath bought me, he hath conquered for me. In whom then should I glory, but in Jesus alone? In him all my wisdom, righteousness, sanctification, and redemption centre. "It pleased the Father, that in him all fulness should dwell." It pleases the Spirit to bear witness of and to glorify Jesus only.

Shall we glory in the fruits of the Spirit, as the foundation of hope and the cause of our acceptance with God? That were to deceive ourselves. The Holy Spirit produceth no fruits in us to this end. This is contrary to his office, inverts the economy of the covenant, makes faith void, and turns the eye of the soul to something within us, instead of Christ crucified for us. But by the Spirit, we glory in Christ alone. By faith in precious promises, we pray to be filled with "the fruits of righteousness, which are by Jesus Christ." To what end? That we should glory in the flesh because of these? No, but "to the glory and praise of God" Philippians 1 : 11.

APRIL 12.—*Gideon said, Alas, O Lord God! for I have seen an angel of the Lord face to face. The Lord said, Peace be unto thee ; fear not : thou shalt not die.* Judges 6 : 22, 23.

Jesus is "the same Lord over all, rich in mercy to all who call upon him." Rom. 10 : 12. There is no difference between Old Testament saints and New, in regard to the object of salvation, "Jesus the same yesterday, to-day, and for ever." Poor Gideon thought a sight of the Lord must surely be present death ; for saith the Lord, " There shall no man see me and live." Exod. 33 : 20. But the Lord appeared to him, as the Angel of the covenant, the Mediator, the Interposer. Not in terrible majesty and fiery wrath, to strike him dead ; but as the Saviour, the merciful One. This sight was attended with life to his soul and death to his fears. So Gideon found it, when he heard that ever-dear and most precious word, Peace.

This is ever the word of the Bridegroom to his church. His birth is ushered in with " Peace on earth." His dying legacy to his children is peace. Nothing but love dwells in his heart. Nought but peace is heard from his lips. This was his affectionate salutation to his beloved, though dejected disciples, when he first appeared to them after his sufferings and death. His tender heart well knew how troubled their poor minds were. Therefore, over and over, he repeats, " Peace be unto you." John 20 : 21.

As it was in the beginning, so it is now. Jesus silences guilty fears and perplexing doubts in disciples' hearts. Wo is me, saith the poor sinner, I am undone, I am unclean ; mine eyes have seen the Lord of hosts, in the purity and spirituality of his law, as a just God and a holy, a consuming fire; and who will by no means clear the guilty; I shall die. Fear not, saith Jesus to every such trembling, repenting, believing heart; thou shalt not die, but live. Neither shalt thou want my peace. Look unto me and be saved. Inwardly listen to my word. Treasure it up in thine heart. Wait in faith, for the sweet and still voice of my Spirit. I create the fruit of the lips, " Peace, peace to him that is afar off, and to him that is near, and I will heal them." Such shall not only hear Christ's voice, but feel his power. Their fears shall be taken away, and their sorrows removed. So shall their souls be joyful in him. Thus Jesus is precious to them. He delivers " them, who through fear of death were all their life-time subject to bondage." Heb. 2 : 15. "Having made peace for us through the blood of his cross." Col. 1 : 20.

APRIL 13.—*Marvel not that I said unto thee, Ye must be born again.* John 3 : 7

Spiritual doctrines ever appear foolishness to the judgment of worldly reason. Marvel not to find the wisdom of natural men ever crying out, "How can these things be?" and explaining away their spiritual meaning by corrupt reasonings. We are not to expect a total freedom from our own earthly objections. The old man is yet alive. The kingdom of his residence, the flesh, is at war against that kingdom into which the soul is spiritually born.

Many see clearly the nature of the doctrine of a new birth of the soul; and are convinced of the necessity of it, in order to see the kingdom of God; but how are they straitened, pained, and perplexed to know whether it be accomplished in them or not! And indeed, many have so unscripturally treated of the new birth, as sadly to puzzle and grievously distress simple hearts. Is it not

marvellous to find men gravely telling us how many
steps a dead sinner must take in order to get into this
new birth? The time when, many are uncertain of;
"for the kingdom of God cometh not with observation."
The manner how, none can explain; "for the things of
God knoweth no man, but the Spirit of God." But the
effects are visible and evident. As sense and motion are
the properties of natural life, so, when the soul is born
again of the Spirit, there is a sight of Jesus, a hearing
of his voice, the affections going out after him, believing
him to be the way, the truth, and the life.

Hence St. John lays down this infallible mark, "Whosoever believeth that Jesus is the Christ, is born of God."
1 John 5:1. This is a simple plain truth. Am I born
of God? This must be answered by inquiring, Do I
believe that Jesus is the Christ, the anointed Son of God
to the office of a Saviour for lost and perishing sinners?
Does this truth enter into my heart and mind? Is it received and believed as a matter which can only and
alone bring relief to my guilty conscience, peace to my
troubled mind, and hope to my dejected spirit? If so,
I do believe in Jesus; he is the object of my faith, and
the hope of my heart. I am born again; born of God:
born to see, to enter into, and enjoy the kingdom of
God. The evidence of this we get more and more
strongly and clearly settled in our conscience, as faith
grows and increases. For its fruits will be manifest and
abound, in seeing the pollution of sin, feeling its burden,
hating and resisting it; striving to maintain a holy fellowship with God the Father, and his Son Jesus, through
the Spirit. 1 John 1:7.

> "Who can describe the joys that rise
> "Through all the courts of paradise,
> "To see a prodigal return,
> "To see an heir of glory born?"

APRIL 14.—*The flesh lusteth against the Spirit.* Gal. 5:17

Christian experience fully proves this apostolic truth. Hence the children of God cannot do the things that they would. Nor have we any authority from God's word to conclude that this strife ever ceases, in any of the saints, till they get to glory; none are delivered from it while in the flesh. For, as the renewed soul, or spirit, loves to enjoy spiritual and heavenly objects, so the flesh, or unrenewed part, desires those objects it is naturally conversant with, and from which it derives its happiness. Here is thy conflict, O christian. Hence the necessity of thy Lord's command, Watch always. This is the use of the doctrine.

What woful effects have fulfilling the desires of the flesh produced in eminent saints! Thou standest by faith; be not high-minded, but fear. "When lust hath conceived, it bringeth forth sin. James 1:15. The commission of sin contracts fresh guilt. This is the malady of the soul. Hence the many symptoms attendant on guilt: terrors of conscience, accusations from the law, triumphs of Satan, dejection of soul, distance from God, backwardness to duty, coolness of affection to Jesus, neglect of the throne of grace. When poor souls have fallen, and are sensible of it, they feel the hurt they have received. Their hearts know the bitterness of it. Awful effects of fresh-contracted guilt! how much to be deplored! how carefully must we watch against it, how fervently pray to be kept from it.

But, whilst there is "a fountain opened for sin and uncleanness," whilst Christ's "blood cleanseth from all sin," whilst the glad tidings of the Gospel proclaim salvation by grace for the chief of sinners, there is no ground for indulging despair to any child of the God of love. Here is all encouragement—to what? To love living at a distance from Jesus, and in sin, because grace abounds? No godly soul can do this; for "the Spirit also lusteth against the flesh," and renews again to repentance.

Thus Luther says, "The more godly a man is, the more doth he feel this battle between the flesh and the spirit. Hereof cometh those lamentable complaints in the Psalms and other scriptures. It profiteth us very much to feel, sometimes, the wickedness of our nature and corruption of the flesh, that we may be waked and stirred up to call upon Christ. So a christian is made to see Jesus a wonderful Creator, who out of heaviness can make joy; of terror, comfort; of sin, righteousness; and of death, life. This is our ground and anchorhold, that Christ is our only and perfect righteousness."

APRIL 15.—*Blessed are the poor in spirit: for theirs is the kingdom of heaven.*   Matt. 5: 3

In the day of the Spirit's power, the lofty looks of man are humbled, the haughtiness of man is bowed down, and the Lord alone is exalted. Isa. 2: 11. Then a man's own righteousness, wherein he trusted, is seen as filthy rags. His strength, of which he boasted, is found to be perfect weakness: his heart, in which he gloried as good, he knows is deceitful and desperately wicked. Then he becomes, in his own eyes, a poor sinner. He knows his poverty. He feels his wretchedness. Thus, when Jesus alone is exalted in his sight, he becomes little and vile in his own eyes; then he is poor in spirit, a mere beggar, who must be wholly indebted to boundless grace and mercy.

Though he sees his state to be guilty, wretched, and desperate, yet he is blessed. Why so? merely because he sees and knows himself to be wretched, poor, miserable, blind and naked? Alas, this knowledge, like Job's friends, would prove but as a miserable comforter to his soul. He can no more trust in his known poverty and rags to entitle him to the kingdom, than in his fancied

robes and riches. But such are blessed, or happy, because the grace of the kingdom is in their hearts now,
and theirs is the kingdom of heaven in glory. Most
joyful consideration!

They are chosen to it by the love of the Father; they
are blessed in Christ with all spiritual blessings. And
as an evidence of this, the Holy Spirit bestows on them
wisdom and revelation in the knowledge of Jesus: he
enlightens the eyes of their understanding to know what
is the hope of their calling, and what is the riches of
the glory of his inheritance. Eph. 1: 17, 18. How un-
speakably blessed! How immensely rich are the poor
in spirit! Having nothing in themselves, yet possessing all things in Christ.

It is usual, in worldly commerce, where a person's
credit is not established, for him to value himself upon
the credit of some rich person; so he gains credit and
repute. Thus the poor sinner values himself upon the
riches of Christ for all acceptance in God's sight. Jesus
is our wisdom, righteousness, sanctification, and redemption. This is our daily rejoicing. Here, O soul, is thy
precious inventory! Read, and rejoice at thy riches.
"All things are yours;" ministers, the world, life, death,
things present, things to come—all are yours; for "ye
are Christ's, and Christ is God's." 1 Cor. 3: 23.

APRIL 16.—*He shall glorify me.* John 16: 14

The Gospel is suited to our indigent state and distressed circumstances. But we are averse to receive
it, in the love of it, because of our lofty spirit and pride
of heart. Any system that exalts and glorifies us in
our own eyes, and in the sight of others, we are, naturally, very fond of. This notion we do not easily part
with. To imagine ourselves possessed of some inherent good dispositions and amiable tempers, which put

us upon more respectable terms in the sight of God, and gain his favor—this we are apt to mistake for the work of the Spirit upon the heart. But, as this notion leads from the faith and hope of the Gospel, opposes the glory of Jesus, lays another foundation than him for hope, and tends to plume the creature with pride and vanity; we are taught to detest it, as the spirit of antichrist and delusion. For this God severely reproves his church of old: "Thou didst trust in thine own beauty, and playedst the harlot because of thy renown." Ezekiel 16 : 15.

But the Spirit, who effects the marriage union between the Lamb and his bride, does nothing upon the heart that it should trust in, to attract the affections from Jesus, or alienate the life from him. The Spirit shall glorify, not yourselves as the subject of his operations, but " he shall glorify me," saith Jesus, in your sight and affections. He shall bear witness to my person and offices, the relation I stand in to you; that justification is solely by my righteousness, atonement by my one sacrifice, and pardon of sin by my blood; that I am your Priest, ever before the throne, representing your persons and pleading your cause. So shall you find peace in me, live daily on me, and rejoice only in me.

Thus, while the Spirit exalts and glorifies Christ only, our hearts are comforted in truth, and sanctified in love, to his honor and service. Thus he makes Jesus precious to us; because we see the Father's love diffusing itself through his pierced heart to ours, by the Holy Ghost given to us. Hence we become alive in our spirits and affections to God? and dead to self-righteous, self-glorying views. We die daily to carnal lusts and corrupt affections, which we know tend to dishonor our dear Lord, are contrary to his will, degrade our souls, and rob us of heart-felt communion with him. The more Jesus is thus glorified, and we abide in him, so much the more are we enabled to bring forth the fruits of the Spirit to his praise and glory. "As many as are led by the Spirit of God, they are the sons of God." Romans 8 : 14.

APRIL 17.—*Fear not, thou worm Jacob.*   Isaiah, 41 : 14

In the light of truth, and teaching of the Spirit, every believer in Jesus loses sight of the once-fancied dignity of his human nature, and sinks, in the view of himself, to the meanest reptile. Probably the church in Isaiah's days had been, considering her weak, helpless state, surrounded with trials and difficulties ; exposed continually to the power of enemies on every side ; in great danger of being trodden under foot and crushed to death ; and had been laying her case before the Lord, confessing, "I am a worm and no man." Psalm 22 : 6. Well, the Lord condescends to reply to such humble souls, Though as mean in thine own eyes, and as despicable in the sight of others, as a poor, base, insignificant, crawling worm of the earth ; yet thou art precious in my sight. Though thou hast no power in thyself to resist enemies ; no strength to support thyself under afflictions and distresses ; though Satan threatens, troubles bow thee down, corruptions rage, and all the combined force of earth and hell is enraged against thee, yet, "Fear not, thou worm," saith the Lord.

Soldier of Jesus, "Fear not." This is thy Captain's word of command. Scarcely any phrase so frequently occurs in the word of God as this. Consider it as an antidote against all desponding, doubting, and dejection Thou canst never fall into any exercise, be under any temptations, be visited by any afflictions, come into any straits or difficulties, but what the power of God can support thee under, and bring thee safely through. Consult not human probability ; judge not according to appearances ; say not, " Worm as I am, I shall surely be crushed." Nay, but is any thing too hard for God ? He saith, "I will help thee," I will succor, I will support thee, I will strengthen thee ; my grace is sufficient for thee. Can a God of truth promise in vain ? Will a God of love ever fail to assist ? Doth not a God of wisdom know when to deliver ? Suffice it, we have his promise. That engages his truth, and demands our faith to honor him.

"I am with thee," saith the Saviour. He is present, though, perhaps, thou thinkest otherwise, and feelest not his comfortable presence. Thy most secret sigh, as well as every distress, lies open to his view. The crafty designs of thy subtle foe, and all his vile stratagems, are without a covering before thy Lord. Terrify and distress thee he may ; but prevail over thy soul he shall not. For He that keepeth Israel neither slumbereth nor sleepeth. He is ever watchful to guard and powerful to keep. And he says, "No weapon that is formed against thee shall prosper ; and every tongue that shall rise against thee in judgment thou shalt condemn." Isaiah 54 : 17.

APRIL 18.—*Be careful for nothing ; but in every thing by prayer and supplication with thanksgiving let your requests be made known unto God.* Phil. 4 : 6

All anxious cares, which torture and distress the mind, arise from unbelief, are contrary to our profession, dishonorable to our God, and injurious to our peace and comfort. Therefore they are forbidden by the Gospel of grace, in love to the children of God. But, believer, thou hast not so learned Christ, as to pass away a life of careless indolence and thoughtless inactivity. No : vigilance, industry, and fervency of spirit ever become thee. " Not slothful in business," but " fervent in spirit, serving the Lord."

Careful and diligent we are to be, in the use of all means in our power, both to procure the subsistence and welfare of the body, and also to preserve the liveliness and vigor of the soul. Careful and diligent, yet, without care that brings disquietude and distress. As to the things of this life, it is sufficient to answer all our anxiety and silence our every fear and doubt, " Your heavenly Father," saith Jesus, " knoweth that you have need of them." He feeds the birds. Will he suffer his children to starve ? Thou shalt have all things needful for life and godliness. If such a sinner as I may speak of himself, under worldly losses and disappointments, I have thought, "Well, though I have not what I expected, I can very well go to heaven without it." This consideration, thanks to my dear Saviour, hath often brought a heaven of contentment in a world of disap pointment.

As to spiritual blessings, " He that spared not his own Son, but delivered him up for us all, how shall he not with him also freely give us all things ?" The Father, who hath " blessed us with all spiritual blessings in Christ Jesus," will hand them down to us by his Holy Spirit, in number, weight, and measure, just as his wisdom sees best. And it is our wisdom to be content and thankful. Here is encouragement for faith, prayer, and praise.

And canst thou look within, without, around, above, and see no cause for thanksgiving ? O christian, are not what thou hast in hand, and in hope, the free gifts of the grace of thy God ? Call to mind his mercies, to excite gratitude. Reflect on his promises, to quicken prayer. Under all thy trials, distresses, sorrows, fears, doubts, and difficulties, here is sweet encouragement to speak them out freely and familiarly unto God. Hear

and rejoice; He " is able to do exceeding abundantly
above all that we ask or think." Eph. 3: 20.

APRIL 19.—*My grace is sufficient for thee; for my strength is
made perfect in thy weakness.* 2 Cor. 12:9

Spiritual conflicts with the enemy of souls are the lot
of all God's children. Holy Paul was hereby under
deep and afflicting distress. Satan, the adversary, assaulted him very powerfully. He groaned under it; he
frequently besought Jesus, that this grievous and painful messenger of Satan might depart from him, that his
conflict might be at an end. How does the enemy distress God's children! The hearts of such only know
the bitterness thereof. But is the Captain of their salvation regardless of them? Is he deaf to their prayers
when they call on him? No; he ever hears, he always
answers in love.

But did the Lord grant his dear servant's request? No:
then the design of love would not have been answered.
Paul was in danger of being " exalted above measure:"
this was to be prevented. He was " to glory in infirmities:" this was to be effected. Satan's design was for
his evil: Jesus makes it work for good. But that he
might not faint in the combat, this comfortable answer
is given, "My grace is sufficient for thee; for my
strength is made perfect in weakness." Let it suffice,
my love and favor are ever towards you; my almighty
strength is engaged to preserve you. Though you are
weakness itself, to withstand such an enemy; yet my
almighty strength shall uphold you; in this you shall
conquer.

Here is the strongest assurance for the confidence of
faith, and the most solid ground for the rejoicing of
hope—the grace and love of Jesus opposed to the malice
and hatred of Satan; the strength of Jehovah triumphing in and made illustriously glorious through our

weakness. O what an ever-loving, all-sufficient, omnipotent Lord is Jehovah Jesus! The Lord whom thou servest, believer, knows every distress and conflict of thy soul. He will strengthen thee in, support thee under, and bring thee safe through, all thy exercises and troubles. Thou shalt lose nothing in the furnace but the dross of nature's pride and corruption, and the vanity of self-glorying, self-sufficiency, and self-righteousness. The Spirit will teach thee to profit in humility and self-diffidence, to glory in and exalt the Lord Jesus more and more. Sweet and encouraging is that promise to God's people in general; strong and comforting is God's declaration to Paul in particular, "Fear not, for I am with thee; be not dismayed, for I am thy God: I will strengthen thee; yea, I will help thee; yea, I will uphold thee with the right hand of my righteousness." Isa. 41 : 10.

APRIL 20.—*Judge not according to the appearance, but judge righteous judgment.* John 7 : 24

By acting contrary to this advice of our great prophet, the children of God often bring sorrow upon themselves "My feet were almost gone; my steps had well nigh slipped," said the Psalmist. Why? what was the cause? Alas! alas! he had been looking at the outward appearance of the wicked; how happy, gay, and joyful they seemed. So that corrupt nature and carnal reason had erected a tribunal in opposition to faith and truth. "Verily," says he, "I have cleansed my heart in vain." But he was soon undeceived, and brought to "judge righteous judgment" from the records of truth in the sanctuary of his God. Psalm 73.

Professors of old had a severe check for thus judging: "Your words have been stout against me, saith the Lord. Ye have said, It is vain to serve God." Mal. 3. "Ye call the proud," that is, self-righteous, but disobe-

dient persons, whom I resist and abhor, "happy."
Christian, beware of judging of men. Be cautious of
determining of matters by appearances. They are very
deceitful. Judge of no man's state by appearances.
Evil actions we may condemn. Good actions we should
applaud. But to judge and determine the eternal state
of any by appearances, we have no authority. It was
a judicious speech of St. Austin, "If I see a wicked
man die, shall I say he is gone to hell? I dare not
Shall I say he is gone to heaven? I cannot."

How awful were the falls of David and Peter! To
what dreadful lengths of cruel persecution against
Christ, his truth and members, did Paul run! Yet, how
did the rich grace of our God triumph in their repentance and salvation! Therefore, believer, even as to
thine own eternal state, judge not from present sense
and appearance, though all things seem against thee.
Oppose not thy feelings to God's truth, love, grace,
promises and oath in Christ. For they all point to
sinners, lost and perishing sinners. Whatever else thou
hast lost, a sense of sin is with thee. True, sayest thou,
and a dreadful sense it is. I also know it : I have fellowship with thee in the same sorrowful truth. But
still " this is a faithful saying, and worthy of all acceptation, that Christ Jesus came into the world to save
sinners." Is there a doubt in thy heart, a fear in thy
mind, a sin upon thy conscience, but he is able to relieve and cleanse thee from? "Be not faithless, but
believing," saith thy Lord. John 20 : 27.

APRIL 21.—*We know, if our earthly house of this tabernacle
were dissolved, we have a building of God, a house not made
with hands, eternal in the heavens.* 2 Cor. 5 : 1

It is the grand device of the arch-deceiver, Satan, to
represent the religion of Jesus as tending only to melan-

choly, gloom, and sadness. But daily experience proves the reverse. ' For, under a sense of a weak, disordered body; from views of its approaching dissolution; with thoughts of its being shortly committed to the silent grave—except the christian, who can put on an air of composure, joy, and delight? Who has such cause for continual felicity as he who knows his lease of his present house is well nigh expired, that shortly it is to be pulled down, but who, through the kindness and love of his heavenly Father, has a free grant of his eternal inheritance given him, "a house not made with hands?" What comfort must it yield him, to know the nature of the purchase; the certainty of its being obtained; the price fully paid; the deeds signed and sealed; the conveyance legally made; his trustee Jesus. actually in possession; yea, and "the earnest of his inheritance" in his heart "by the Holy Ghost given unto him!"

O the inexpressible joy of this knowledge! All this we know assuredly by faith. Come, my brother mortal, is thy house like mine, feeble, and just ready to fall? O let us daily be looking, by faith, from Pisgah's top to the promised inheritance. Let us daily consider our approaching dissolution, that our hearts may more and more love and live with our dear Saviour, who hath told us, I go to prepare a place for you; I will come again and receive you to myself; where I am, there shall you be also. John 14 : 2, 3.

Vain and trifling is all this perishing world has to offer, compared with the glory which shall shortly be revealed in us. Yea, not to be set in competition with the grace that is now upon us. And what can deprive such an heir of his inheritance? Shall sin? No; that is fully atoned by the blood of Jesus. Shall the world? No; he hath victory over that by the faith of Jesus. Shall Satan? No; "the God of peace will bruise Satan under his feet shortly." Rom. 16 : 20. Shall the corruptions of his nature and the workings of unbelief? These may distress and make him groan, may deject with doubts, but, through grace, shall not prevail against him. "Sin shall not have dominion over you, for ye are under grace." Rom. 4 : 14. "Kept by the power of God, through faith, unto salvation." 1 Pet. 1 : 5.

APRIL 22.—*They who feared the Lord, spake often one to another : the Lord hearkened, and heard it.* Mal. 3 : 16.

The tongue, though but a little member, yet is capable of being employed to the best services or worst purposes. He is a perfect man who offends not in word. He is a man after God's own heart who prays daily, "Let the words of my mouth and the meditation of my heart be acceptable in thy sight, O Lord." Psalm 19 : 14. "By thy words thou shalt be justified, and by thy words thou shalt be condemned." Matt. 12 : 37. Most weighty considerations! Let us take heed that we offend not with our tongue. But, most encouraging assurance, our God hearkens to his dear children when they converse together about his kingdom and glory, and our peace, edification, and holiness. Yea, more; O condescending love! "a book of remembrance was written before him, of them who feared the Lord and thought upon his name."

Is such kind notice taken of our converse? then what emulation ought to fire us, that our tongues may edify and provoke each other to love and good works! What shame to christians, that they too often meet and talk, and their poor hearts are neither edified, warmed, nor comforted! Why is this? Truly the end of their conversation, "Jesus, the same yesterday, to-day, and for ever," was not considered. He is always most worthy to be uppermost in our hearts and tongues. This, like a live coal from the altar, is the only fire to make cold hearts glow with love, and warm hearts burn with affection. The best news of the day, the fittest subject for conversation, is the rich, free, sovereign grace of our God; the love of Christ; the glad tidings of the Gospel; the joyful news of salvation finished by Jesus. This we are going fully to enjoy.

What then should we talk of by the way but this? O disciple, dost thou find a dull frame and a sad heart? and therefore, sayest, I am unfit to converse of these things? This is, really, like staying from the fire because cold, or abstaining from food because hungry. Consider the conduct of the disciples. Jesus drew near to them, and asks, "What manner of communications are these that ye have one to another, as ye walk, and are sad?" Luke 24 : 17. Though they had lost sight of Jesus, though their hearts were sad about it, yet they refrained not talking and communing about him. And he soon made their hearts burn within them.

APRIL 23.—*No man having put his hand to the plough, and looking back, is fit for the kingdom of God.*—Luke 9 : 62

The eye, though a little member, is yet, perhaps, of all the senses, the greatest inlet to temptation. The first motion to sin entered by seeing. Eve saw the fruit was good and pleasant to the eye. Looking begat longing. So lust was conceived and brought forth sin. Sin, when it was finished, brought forth death upon her and all her posterity. When Satan tempted Jesus, he began the attack by presenting to his view the kingdoms of the world and the glory thereof. Seeing this, we have reason with Job to make a covenant with our eyes; and with David to pray daily, "Turn away mine eyes from beholding vanity." No state more awful, than to set out in the best cause and turn back to the worst enemy. The end of such is dreadful. Most deplorable, to turn from following Jesus, and make shipwreck of faith and a good conscience!

Whether it be minister or disciple who hath put his hand to the gospel plough, if his eye is attracted and his heart allured after "the lust of the flesh, the lust of the eye, and the pride of life," these will render him unfit for the kingdom of God. For these are as contrary to the spirit of Christ and his kingdom, as heaven to hell. No man can serve two such opposite masters.

If thou hast chosen Jesus for thy portion and thy all, why look back to the world? What contempt doth such conduct pour upon him! The heart is not whole with him. It speaks loudly, as if there was something desirable in Christ and his ways; but not enough to win the heart and engage the affections entirely, and make the mind completely happy. "If any man draw back, my soul," saith the Lord, "shall have no pleasure in him." And, verily, such a soul can have no pleasure in God. Whither will he fly, to what refuge betake himself, in the hour of calamity and day of distress? A forsaken Jesus, a slighted Gospel and neglected salvation, will wound the conscience with the keenest sting.

See to it, O professor. Watch over thy lustful eye. It is ever looking back to and longing after more from this world. Beware of thy deceitful heart, lest it turn from Christ to the world. If so, thou wilt soon let go the gospel plough, and yet find earthly pleas for thy conduct. Many barren professors have ever a reason (such as it is) at their tongue's end, for their covetous, worldly-minded spirit. Yet, like Lot's wife, they look to Sodom, and are monuments of God's displeasure. "But, beloved, we are persuaded better things of you, and things that accompany salvation, though we thus speak." Heb. 6 : 9.

APRIL 24.—*Search the Scriptures ; for in them ye think ye have eternal life ; and they are they which testify of me.* John 5 : 39

It was an excellent reply of a christian lady to a scoffing infidel, who ridiculed the Scriptures, and asked, What proof she could give of the truth of holy writ? "Yourself, sir," she said, "is one. For it is written, 'There shall come in the last days scoffers, walking after their own lusts.'" 2 Pet. 3 : 3. Even Satan, when he tempted our Lord, though he dared to pervert, yet he never once attempted to deny holy Scripture to be the truth of God.

Shame to professors who are ignorant of God's word! For Jesus and eternal life are revealed therein. Even devils, who have no hope from the Scriptures, seem well versed in them. But, may not Jonadab's question to Amnon be put even to some of God's children, "Why art thou, being a king's son, lean from day to day?" 2 Sam. 13 : 4. Leanness of soul comes on many through neglecting the nourishing truths of God's word. It is the rich feast of the Father's love. By it the soul is fed and nourished up to eternal life. Verily, when we lose our appetite for the Scriptures, and they are not savory food to us, our souls become sickly and languish.

"They testify of me," saith Jesus. Is not that word enough? what so sweetly, so powerfully engaging to the soul, as when something of our dear Saviour is to be learned from every page? The more we are acquainted with his precious person, his amazing love, his wonderful humility, his astonishing sufferings, and his finished work on earth; so much the more will he be endeared to our hearts. We shall prize the word that testifies of him, and the Spirit who glorifies him. We shall think of him, love him, live upon him, live to him, long to be with him, from day to day. So we shall beguile all our troubles and trials below. Our hearts will be simple and happy. Our conversation and conduct will be more like the meek Lamb of God. Thus shall we grow as Pharaoh's "kine, fat-fleshed and well-favored," while we feed in God's meadow. Gen. 41: 18. If we neglect the Scriptures, that testify of Jesus, no marvel we enjoy not the comfort of the Spirit's witness of him.

Says Luther, " Let the Lord take me out of life this hour, or when it pleaseth him, I leave this behind me. I will own Jesus Christ for my Lord and my God. This I have not only out of the Scriptures, but by manifold experience also ; for the name of Jesus hath often helped and comforted me when no creature could." " Holy Scriptures are able to make us wise unto salvation, through faith which is in Christ Jesus." 2 Tim. 3 : 15

> " Great God! mine eyes with pleasure look
> " On the dear volume of thy book ;
> " There my Redeemer's face I see,
> " And read his name who died for me."

APRIL 25.—*Ye are come to Jesus the Mediator of the new covenant, and to the blood of sprinkling.*   Heb. 12 : 24

When, from zeal and affection for their beloved Master, the disciples would have called fire from heaven, " he rebuked them, saying, Ye know not what manner of spirit ye are of." In young disciples there is often much zeal, which is not according to knowledge. They know but little from what evils they are called, and to what privileges they are come. It behoves all to be diligent in reading, hearing, and studying the truths of Jesus. So the Spirit makes wise heads and joyful hearts.

To learn something of Jesus, from the law, the types and figures, the prophecies, promises, and the Gospel, is the chief concern of sincere souls. So their hearts are daily more and more established in faith ; and they know more assuredly that they are really come to Jesus.

When we read of Moses sprinkling the peop e, and crying out, "Behold the blood of the covenant," (Exod. 24 : 8,) this reminds us of the pardon of sin by the precious blood of the dear Lamb ; and how the sprinkling of this blood purifies the heart from sin, and the conscience from guilt, by faith.

The acceptable sacrifice of Abel, by which he "obtained witness that he was righteous," brings to our mind the most excellent sacrifice of our beloved Saviour. This speaks righteousness, peace, love, and salvation to our souls. This silences all guilty fears. This revives and comforts drooping, trembling hearts, knowing that Jesus, our Mediator, is ever before the throne. This gives boldness, and confidence of access to God, and freedom of heart, to draw nigh to, love him, and rejoice in him.

Whatever our various conditions or circumstances are, our only wisdom and comfort lies in simply commending all to Jesus, knowing that we are come to him, and live comfortably by daily coming to him. Is sin our sorrow, grief, and burden ? Jesus has a plea for it. He does not extenuate or excuse it : nor should we, but confess it with all its aggravations. His blood speaks before the throne. The Spirit bears witness to it. When the voice of sin and terror is heard in thy conscience, Christ's blood speaks pardon from God, freedom from condemnation, peace of conscience, joy of heart, and a hope full of immortality, happy to have come to Jesus ; and joyful to believe in him as our Mediator O how full of the richest consolation is this declaration ! "If we confess our sins, God is faithful and just to forgive us our sins, and to cleanse us from all unrighteousness." 1 John 1 : 9

APRIL 26.—*Jesus said unto Peter, Wherefore didst thou doubt!*
Matthew 14 : 31

The best of men are but men at the best. The most
eminent saints of God have experienced doubting, fearful frames, as well as believing, joyful ones. We have
many instances of this in the bold and courageous Peter.
Now, at the command of his Master, we behold him
walking safely on the surface of the great deep. Here
he honoured his Master's word, was very safe and comfortable, while he believed his power. To see Peter
walking upon the liquid ocean is not more beyond the
power of reason to comprehend and account for, than to
see a poor sinner comfortably living and walking by
faith on the Son of God, in spite of all the raging waves
of unbelief, *and the corruptions of his nature.*

But as it was with Peter, so is it often with the believer. The workings of Peter's natural senses, the
suggestions of his carnal reason, opposed the actings of
his faith : he heard the roaring winds, he saw the boisterous waves, he considered the bulk and weight of
his body : reason assures him fluid water cannot support him ; faith fails ; he doubts, he fears, he sinks. So
the poor sinner, who hath heard the inviting voice of
Jesus and obeyed the word of his grace to believe on
him, walks sweetly and comfortably for a season. But
anon, corruptions, like the surging billows, lift up their
threatening heads ; temptations, like the stormy wind,
blow violently upon him ; the thunderings of a fiery
law are heard ; he thinks incensed justice pursues
him, and that the face of Majesty looks stern upon him.
Hence he reasons upon what he is, what he has done,
and what he may expect ; and all in nature, sense, and
his own feelings, is against him. O, then, he doubts,
and sinks.

But when he reflects, Jesus is above all, he is mighty
to save ; then, seeing all hope in him, and none beside

him, he cries, "Lord, save, or I perish." This is right
Our Saviour loves to hear his poor disciples cry to him.
He is near them, and, as Peter was, they are always
within the reach of his arm. He loves their persons,
approves their crying; but reproves their doubting.
Wherefore didst thou doubt? Though thy sins have
reached to heaven, yet my blood is before the throne.
Who shall lay any thing to thy charge? It is God that
justifieth; who shall condemn thee? I have died; what
shall destroy thee, seeing I am able to save to the
uttermost?—Verily, O Jesus, to the poor and needy in
their distress thou art a refuge from the storm. Isa
25 : 4.

> " What though the hosts of death and hell
> " All armed against me stood,
> " Why should their terrors shake my soul?
> " My refuge is my God."

APRIL 27.—*If ye know these things, happy are ye if ye do them*
John 13 : 17

Jesus is a Prophet to teach, a Priest to atone, and a
King to reign, by love, in the hearts of all his subjects.
So every christian receives him. Faith in him begets
an ear of love to his doctrine, and a heart of obedience
to his commands. Let no one call evangelical obedience legal bondage. For every precept that dropt
from the mouth of Jesus flows from love to us. When
he saith, "Do this;" it is for thy happiness, O soul.
" Avoid that;" love is careful of thee. " Do thyself no
harm;" this it is pleasant to the renewed soul to hear,
his happiness to obey. Faith in Jesus makes all things
easy. " His commandments are not grievous." To
know them is our privilege; to do them our delight.
Knowledge without practice is vain.

Say, O christian, is not this thy experience? Art
thou not happy in doing the will of Jesus, who died for

our sins? Art thou not delighted in obeying Him who hath made peace between God and thy soul? Art thou not joyful in glorifying thy Father, by bringing forth the fruits of righteousness which are by Jesus Christ? Verily, "in keeping thy commandments," O Lord, "there is great reward," of grace, in peace and happiness of soul now; and hereafter such shall hear that joyful sentence from our loving Saviour, "Come, ye blessed of my Father, inherit the kingdom prepared for you from the foundation of the world." Matt. 25 : 34. Then shall the works of the righteous be proclaimed by the Judge. They are called to inherit the kingdom. Why? Because blessed of God the Father with all spiritual blessings in Christ Jesus. Hence the kingdom was prepared for them before the foundation of the world.

But it constitutes no part of the believer's happiness to do any work whatsoever whereby to entitle himself to the favor of God, or to make the work of salvation more effectual than it is made by the blood and righteousness of the Son of God. No, this is to be rejected as the vilest slavery, the worst of drudgery; contrary to faith, inconsistent with christian love, and derogatory to the salvation of Jesus. Luther was wont to say, "If picking up a straw would save me, (by my own merit,) I would not do it. It would be an act of unbelief of my dear Lord's salvation. But being already saved by Jesus, through his grace, I would go through fire and water to obey his commands." Where Jesus is the life of the soul, this will be manifest in obedience to his commands. "Blessed is the man who delighteth greatly in his commandments." Psalm 112 : 1

"I hear thy word with love,
"And I would fain obey:
"Send thy good Spirit from above,
"To guide me, lest I stray."

APRIL 28.—*Many there be who say of my soul, There is no help for him in God. Selah.* Psalm 3 : 2

Had David's foes said of him, He deserves no help from God, he would readily have owned this as a great truth. As God's children are comforted by the truth, so the enemy advances lies to distress them. When he attacks their faith and comfort, he boldly impeaches the love and faithfulness of their God.

"No help for me in God!" O my soul, wilt thou listen to this suggestion? Canst thou indulge such a thought one moment? Art thou beset with distress of soul, and surrounded with troubles and difficulties? art thou singing a melancholy note? "Selah," saith David: pause, consider this; lift up thy mind to attend, how dishonorable to thy God, how destructive to thy faith, peace, love, and holiness is this! Know the voice of thy enemy. Hear the voice of thy Saviour. His word is adapted to thy circumstances, however distressing or desperate. "Thou hast destroyed thyself!" What is added? Perish in thine own misdoings? No: for almighty love proclaims its own triumph; "In me is thine help." Hosea 13 : 9.

"Man is born to trouble as the sparks fly upward." When born again, he finds more enemies and troubles than ever. A sinful nature burdens him. Carnal lusts perplex him. Satan tempts and accuses him. Unbelief besets and dejects him; but, most joyful truth, God is his dear Father, Jesus his precious Saviour, the Holy Spirit his Comforter. Where should the poor sinner look? To whom should the distressed, afflicted soul go? Happy for him, when, with David, he goes with child-like simplicity, and tells his sorrowful complaints to his dear Saviour: "Lord, how are they increased that trouble me! Many rise up against me." They say of my soul, "There is no help for me in God."

The Saviour loves to hear his members' complaints

He delights to redress them. Thus, when driven from all hope and help from within and without, then they honor him in faith and prayer. As when a little child is affrighted with lying stories it flies to the arms of its father for safety, tells him of its fears, and thus its little heart gets ease. So David found it. His experienced heart cries out, "Thou, O Lord, art a shield for me; my glory, and the lifter up of my head. Salvation belongeth unto the Lord; thy blessing is upon thy people." Thus, though a mournful complaint ushers in this Psalm, yet it concludes in the joy and triumph of faith. "Weeping may endure for a night, yet joy cometh in the morning." Psalm 30 : 5.

> "What though the hosts of death and hell,
>   "All armed against me stood;
> "Terrors no more shall shake my soul,
>   "My refuge is my God."

APRIL 29.—Blessed are they who hunger and thirst after righteousness; for they shall be filled. Matthew 5 : 6.

To thirst after happiness is natural; to seek it from wrong objects is natural; to desire to escape a hell of misery and enjoy a place of happiness is equally natural. If this may be called salvation, all men wish to be saved. The most wicked may wish to die the death of the righteous, and that their last end may be like his. This every man may desire as a rational, intelligent being. And many are striving to make themselves righteous in order to be saved. But to desire salvation in God's way, to hunger and thirst after Christ and his righteousness, is peculiar to the quickened only. The dead hunger not. Spiritual appetites spring from spiritual life.

To know ourselves to be miserable sinners, destitute of righteousness; to believe Christ has obtained it for us, and to hunger and thirst after it: this lies at the foundation of true godliness ; this enters into the very essence of our religion. Such self-emptied, hungry and thirsty souls are blessed ; for they shall be filled : filled with all the blessings of Jesus' everlasting righteousness, acceptance with God, pardon of sin, and peace from God ; filled with the fruits of righteousness which are by Jesus Christ, with all the graces of God's Spirit on earth, and with all the fulness of God in glory. " This is the heritage of my servants, and their righteousness is of me," saith our Lord. Isa. 54 : 17. " The skies pour down righteousness," the faithful open their hearts and receive it. Isa. 45 : 8.

O what delightful fellowship and intercourse subsist between heaven and earth, hungry souls and righteous Jesus ! Says Bishop Hall, " If Jesus had not said, ' Blessed are those who hunger,' I know not what could keep weak christians from despair. Many times all I can do is to find and complain, I want Jesus : I wish to enjoy him. Now this is my stay : he in mercy esteems us, not by having, but by desiring. There never was a soul that perished, longing after grace. O blessed hunger, that always ends in fulness ! I am sorry I can but hunger, yet would not be full, for the blessing is promised to the hungry." As truly as Christ wrought out righteousness for sinful man, all thirsty souls who come to him shall be filled with righteousness. For he fills "the hungry with good things," while he sends the rich (the self-righteous) empty away. Luke 1 : 53.

APRIL 30.—*There is therefore now no condemnation to them which are in Christ Jesus.* Romans, 8 : 1

Burkitt observes, " This chapter is a summary of evangelical duty, and a magazine of christian comfort ; it begins with no condemnation to believers, and ends with no separation from the love of God." It is natural to conceive that if we had never sinned there would be no condemnation against us; but that being sinners, and naturally under the condemning sentence of God's holy law, there is yet *no* condemnation to us, this our carnal reason cannot conceive, and therefore opposes it. But it is God's truth and the joy of faith.

This unfolds the great mystery, that we are one with Christ; viewed, beloved, and chosen in him. This gloriously displays the attributes of Jehovah's justice and holiness; while it shows a full and ample discharge to all Christ's members, from all condemnation by his righteous law. Therefore that blessed name Jesus " is above every name" to us. In this and every other matter of salvation, every believer's knee will bow to him, and his heart confess that Christ is all in all. Rich privilege to be in Christ Jesus! Unspeakable happiness to be freed from all condemnation! Blessed effects of covenant-union with Christ! Joyful experience of the grace of faith in him! To have such a knowledge, and pass such a judgment upon thy soul, O christian, is just and right. It is thy duty and privilege at all times. Practise it.

As to Jesus, how readest thou? "The Lord hath laid upon him the iniquity of us all." Isa. 53:6. Christ "bore our sins in his own body on the tree." 1 Pet. 2:24. "Christ suffered, the just for the unjust." 1 Pet. 3:18. "We have redemption through his blood, the forgiveness of sins. He was made sin for us who knew no sin." Can we read all this without singing a triumphant challenge, Who then " shall lay any thing to the charge of God's elect?" Shall God that justifieth? No. "Who is he that condemneth? It is Christ that died, yea rather, that is risen again, who is even at the right hand of God, who also maketh intercession for us." Rom. 8:33, 34. Here is the glorious triumph of faith. Thou art " carnal, sold under sin." Rom. 7:14. In thy flesh dwelleth no good thing; though thou hast no reason for confidence in the flesh, thou hast always abundant cause to rejoice in Christ Jesus; for in him thou art perfectly righteous, in him for ever freed from all condemnation. O believer, thou art called ever to rejoice in this liberty, and to manifest it by walking "not after the flesh, but after the Spirit."

May

MAY 1.—*Thus saith the Lord God, Behold, I lay in Zion for a foundation a stone, a tried stone, a precious corner-stone, a sure foundation: he that believeth shall not make haste.* Isaiah 28:16

A day is coming when every man's work shall be tried. The foundation of the Lord standeth sure. But every other foundation shall be destroyed. He who is built on Christ and derives all his hopes of life and salvation from him, is safe in time and to all eternity. Before men begin to build they draw a plan; and every wise builder looks carefully to the foundation; for on this depends the safety of the superstructure.

The plan of salvation was drawn in the eternal counsel. It is founded in the love of the Father; effected by the obedience and sufferings of his Son. Hence what was contrived in infinite wisdom above, is laid as a sure foundation in the church below, by the love and power of the Spirit, the Comforter. It is his peculiar office to lay this foundation in Zion, and to manifest and make known to the prophets and apostles, teachers and saints, that Jesus is the only foundation; as a stone for strength; a tried stone, approved of by the Father, and by his children in all ages; a precious corner-stone; the ornament and beauty, as well as strength and security, of the whole church. Precious is Christ in all his offices to them that believe : a sure foundation ; sure to all the seed ; certain to all the purposes of their salvation. And, as the Lord the Spirit lays this foundation in the church in the truth of doctrine, so also in the faith and experience of all redeemed souls.

What the word speaks of Jesus, that we prove and find him to be. This is our mercy. "He that believeth shall not make haste." He shall possess such serenity and composure of mind, that he shall not be frightened, in times of distress and calamity, to quit his confidence ; not be ashamed of his hope in the Lord. Being well satisfied that Jesus reigns, that the government of his church is upon his shoulders, and the residue of the Spirit with him ; he will, by faith, patiently wait and quietly hope for the fulfilment of every promise. Sin and Satan shall not overcome him. In the awful hour of death he shall not be confounded, because his heart standeth fast, believing in the Lord. And when Jesus his Friend appears, he shall stand forth with boldness ; and shall find an abundant entrance into the presence of God and the Lamb, to live, and love, and reign in glory for ever and ever. "Ye are built upon the foundation of the apostles and prophets, Jesus Christ being the chief corner-stone." Eph. 2 : 20.

MAY 2.—*But the Comforter, who is the Holy Ghost, whom the Father will send in my name, he shall teach you all things, and bring all things to your remembrance, whatsoever I have said unto you.* John 14 : 26

Our blessed Lord here gives us the clearest discovery of the ever-glorious three persons in covenant for our salvation. In this knowledge lies all our hope. From this belief springs all our comfort. In the love of this is our heaven upon earth. For the knowledge, belief, and love of this truth, we are wholly indebted to the Comforter. He teaches all things; not by a new revelation; but he graciously instructs and comforts us by the same light of truth and love which beamed in the first promise, and which shone brighter and brighter in prophecies, types, and shadows, until the substance, Jesus, was come. Then the canon of revealed truth was completed by the apostles, under the teaching of the Holy Ghost. The substance of which is, what Jesus spake, did, and suffered on our account, as our substitute, and for our salvation.

It is the peculiar office of the Spirit to glorify Jesus and to sanctify us. This he does by the word of truth: teaching us the Father's electing love in Jesus, and directing our eyes to him, as of God made to us "wisdom, righteousness, sanctification, and redemption." Let no man deceive us with expectations of new revelations from heaven, or new truths to comfort us; but ever hear Paul, "Though we, or an angel from heaven, preach any other Gospel unto you than that ye have received, let him be accursed." Gal. 1:8.

Let us prize and study the Gospel. In and by that the Spirit teaches and comforts. In everlasting love, and the most ancient truth, he establishes us. We are poor sinners from day to day. We feel many things in and around us to deject and distress us. When we remember what sin hath done to us, brought on us, and exposed us to, we are in fears and doubts what will become of us. But the Comforter brings to our minds the transcendantly rich love of Jesus; what he undertook, spake, and did in life, suffered in death, and still lives to plead for, before the throne, in our behalf. O the heartfelt joy of this! He relieves our minds, and refreshes our spirits by the knowledge of the truth. So he teaches us self-despair, animates us to go on in the path of holi-

ness, and fortifies us to withstand all that is against us.
"Grieve not the Holy Spirit of God, whereby ye are
sealed unto the day of redemption." Ephes. 4 : 30.

MAY 3.—*Therefore, brethren, we are debtors, not to the flesh, to*
live after the flesh. Romans 8 : 12

Christianity teaches us to owe no man any thing. He
is prudent who keeps his accounts clear, and knows to
whom he is indebted. He is grateful, who owns favors
with just sentiments. If this be necessary and com-
mendable in the economy of this short life, how much
more so in things spiritual and eternal! How wise, how
just to render to all their dues! If we are debtors to
the flesh, let us serve that; but if to the Lord, it is our
duty and privilege to serve him.

What owest thou, O christian, to the flesh? verily,
neither suit nor service. But, alas! thou hast obeyed
its sinful motions, gratified its corrupt desires; and what
hast thou reaped but shame and sorrow? These are the
only fruits that sin and folly bear. The flesh, with its
sinful affections, is at enmity to thy God, and at war
against thy soul. Willingly to give place to such an
enemy, to live after the desires of the flesh, will most
assuredly weaken thy confidence in Jesus, and bring
death upon thy peace and comfort. Yea, "if ye live
after the flesh ye shall die." Lord, strengthen us daily
to deny its demands and mortify its lusts! for we are
not debtors to the flesh, but to the Spirit. Debtors, in
an immense sum of love and gratitude. Time can never
discharge it. We shall be paying this debt through a
never-ending eternity.

The Gospel is no licentious doctrine. True, it sets at
liberty, but it is from the most galling yoke, and most
servile drudgery to sin. But yet it binds the soul, in
sweetest bands of grateful service and loving obedience,

to Jesus, the best of Masters. What owest thou to the
Spirit, O christian? write upon thy heart, "Even all
my present peace, all my future hopes." For he it is
who convinced thee of sin, revealed the love of God in
Christ, gave thee power to believe, and grace to repent. He fills thee with joy and peace in believing
He bears witness with thy spirit, and assures of thine
adoption to be a child of God; teaching thee to mortify
the deeds of the flesh, to love thy Saviour, and live to
his glory.

And canst thou deliberately grieve this blessed inha
bitant, this loving Comforter, by yielding service to thy
inbred enemy? O with what fire of indignation, with
what warmth of affection, doth Joseph cry out under
the solicitations of a strong temptation, How can I do
this great wickedness? and what?—sin against the best
of masters? against my own soul? no, but against the
Lord my God? Genesis 39:9.

MAY 4.—*Casting all your care upon him; for he careth for
you.* 1 Peter 5:7

We are called to confess Jesus in a day when the
fury and rage of persecution are restrained. Bonds and
imprisonments do not await us. Yet we must not think
to be exempt from trials and difficulties of various
kinds. Our adversary is not dead. The corruptions of
our hearts are alive, and daily fight against us. The
love of Jesus is ever accompanied with the world's hatred. His people are not mere stoics. Such opposition is a trial to them. Sometimes it may be their lot,
like the disciples, to be in the midst of a sea of troubles, tossed with the waves of difficulty; the wind of
providence appearing contrary; and, to the eye of nature and sense, Jesus seems asleep to their sorrows, as
though his kind love to them and tender care over

them were suspended. Here is the trial of our faith. But this grace never consults nature and appearances; it looks through all, to the everlasting love and almighty power of Jesus; knowing he can save from the uttermost depth of distress, and raise to the extremest height of comfort.

Thus triumphs the church under all her tribulations: "I will look unto the Lord; I will wait for the God of my salvation: my God will hear me. Rejoice not against me, O mine enemy: when I fall, I shall arise; when I sit in darkness, the Lord shall be a light unto me." Micah 7:7, 8. Sweet confession of faith, under most discouraging views. For, while the Lord cares for us, what can harm us? While we cast our every care on him, we obey his will, honor his word, and he fills our hearts with peace. How composed did the three children of faith stand before the wrathful monarch? How easy their minds, under the dreadful threatening of a fiery furnace! How calm their reply! "O king, we are not careful to answer thee in this matter." The Lord careth for us. We cast all our care upon him.

Ever judge of Jesus' care for sinners by his love to them. Ever remember, while we were enemies his blood atoned for our sins. Can we believe his love to us, and doubt his care for us? O how unreasonable is unbelief! But, if we had no corruptions to conflict with, no troubles to exercise us, no burdens to bow us down, no cares to beset us, no fears to attend us, a great part of God's word would be useless. As we are not to expect total freedom from these, the exhortations of the word are suited to our state, and direct to a loving Friend, whose kind invitation under every distress is, "Come unto me." Matt. 11:28.

MAY 5.—*The work of righteousness shall be peace; and the effect of righteousness quietness and assurance for ever.* Isaiah 32:17

The light of this day assures us the sun is risen upon the earth. Here is not a more evident truth in nature than this in reason, that righteousness once lost can never be regained by all that sinful man can do. Consequently, no peace can subsist between a holy, righteous God, and guilty, unrighteous man. "There is no peace, saith my God, to the wicked."

But who are the wicked? Even all who, through unbelief, reject the truth as it is in Jesus. It is the essence of wickedness to oppose a righteous God, go about to establish our own inherent righteousness, and not submit to the righteousness of Christ. Hence the conscience is defiled with guilt, the heart impure, and the life unholy. Yet pride blinds men's eyes, and self-righteousness deludes their hearts with a false peace. For as there is but one atonement by which guilty sinners are pardoned, so there is but one righteousness, even Christ's perfect righteousness, by which alone unrighteous sinners are made righteous in God's sight. He accepts no other. His law is honored by no other. The Scriptures reveal no other. Faith receives no other. The Spirit bears witness to no other. Sinners have no other to stand in before God, and enjoy peace with him. But possessing this righteousness by faith, we enjoy a peace which passeth all understanding.

There are many things from a sinful nature, Satan, and the law, to disquiet our minds daily. But the blessed effect of Jesus' righteousness is, quietness to the conscience. This comforting thought, my Father hath accepted me through the righteousness which my glorious Redeemer wrought out for me, quiets my mind. I am satisfied. I can seek no better. I dare trust in no other.

And this righteousness is presented with the **clearest** evidence, the strongest confidence, the fullest assurance. The triumphs of Jesus' resurrection proclaim its acceptance with God. The Spirit testifies of it in the word, and gives assurance of salvation by it in believing hearts. Hence the holy boldness and happy rejoicing of faith before a righteous God. David's address to Jesus is, "My mouth shall show forth thy righteousness and thy salvation all the day. I will make mention of thy righteousness, even of thine only." Psalm 71 : 15, 16. As there is but one faith, so saints in all ages had but one object to look to for righteousness, even Jesus Therefore, with holy Paul, we pray that we may be found in Christ, not having our own righteousness. Philippians 3 : 9.

MAY 6.—*All things are lawful unto me, but all things are not expedient.* 1 Corinthians 6 : 12.

The constraints of love and the jealousy of fear sweetly unite in believing hearts. Where the faith of Jesus prevails love constrains. It holds and keeps us in our station and duty. What cheerfulness and activity of soul do we experience when we can say with the church, Jesus' " banner over me was love?" Song 2 : 4. Then how sweetly do we judge and determine our conduct by the law of Christ, which is love! This excites a godly fear lest we should allow ourselves a latitude in things indifferent, to the wounding of our souls or injuring our brethren. Though all things, of an indifferent nature, which are innocent in themselves, are lawful to us, yet the cause and interest of our dear Saviour, and the good and edifying of his beloved members, should be ever near our hearts, and make us consider their expediency.

How narrow is the path of duty ! yet is it pleasant **to**

the faithful. For Jesus hath strewed it with the fragrant fruits of peace, love, and comfort. Peace from God, and with our brethren. Love to God and one another While we walk according to this rule, we bring glory to God, who hath called us by Christ to glory; and will also, assuredly, glorify us together with himself. What circumspection becomes us in our daily walk that we give none offence; neither to the Jew, nor to the Gentile, nor to the church of God.

The eyes not only of God, angels, and devils are upon us; but the eyes of men also, our brethren, and our opposers. Did the Rechabites wholly abstain from wine because Jonadab commanded, " Ye shall drink no wine ?" Did the Lord honor their obedience in this indifferent thing with his approbation ? Jer. 35. How much more will Jesus honor his disciples, who, with an eye to his glory and his members' good, abstain from things that are not expedient ! Thou free-man of the Lord, with a holy resolution, assert thy dignity. I will not be brought under the power of any thing contrary to the love of Jesus. Happy is he who seeketh not to please himself, but profit others. How then can those answer to the Lord Christ, their own souls, and their brethren, who indulge themselves at card-tables, play-houses, &c. and say, " These are indifferent things; I see no harm in them ?" Is this following " after the things which make for peace, and wherewith one may edify another ? Happy is he that condemneth not himself in that thing which he alloweth." Rom. 14 : 19, 22.

MAY 7.—*What doest thou here, Elijah ?* 1 Kings 19 : 13

Prophets, as well as God's people, may be found where they ought not to be. Elijah had now taken up his residence in a cave in the wilderness. What work could he do for his Master here ? what glory bring to

his name in a barren mountain? Here were no lambs of
God's flock to be gathered; no sheep of Christ's pas-
ture to be fed; no torn sheep to be healed, and nour
ished by his word and doctrine. It seems as if he
thought all his work was at an end; his zeal quite de-
cayed; and in a fit of fear, unbelief, and despondency,
he retreated from public opposition to the dreary mansions of a mountainous cave, for rest and quiet. But the
Lord followed him; calls him to new work; endues
him with fresh strength; and animates him with the
pleasing assurance that he had seven thousand faithful
servants yet in Israel: for poor Elijah thought he was
left alone.

See the effect of judging according to appearances.
Carnal reason is a bad judge in spiritual things. The
wisdom of the flesh is contrary to the wisdom of God.
Beware of your frames, O disciples. If on the mount,
in the sunshine of comfort, be not vain and confident,
with "I shall never fall." If in the gloomy vale, where
light and joy are obscured, be not dejected. "The
Lord reigneth. Rejoice in him." Though clouds and
darkness are round thy God and Saviour, yet "righteousness and judgment are the habitation of his
throne." Psalm 97.

Above all, beware of thy conduct. Fly not to places
of sinful vanity and earthly pleasures. These can never
profit thy soul. Nay, if dark and uncomfortable, thou
wilt be darker and more uncomfortable. This is a farther
remove from the Saviour's love and presence. What
canst thou expect but this cutting reproof, this keen
interrogation, "*What doest thou here?*" Was Elijah reproved for being in a barren wilderness? how canst
thou answer it to thy loving Saviour for being found on
worse than barren ground; where the alluring baits of
sin, the poisonous weeds of Satan, grow in abundance
to poison and destroy unstable souls? Hear the call

of thy beloved Lord. "Depart ye, depart ye, this is not your rest." Know your glorious privilege ? "Ye are the temple of the living God; God dwells in you and walks in you." Listen to his voice. "Come out from among them, and be ye separate; and I will receive you; will be a Father unto you; ye shall be my sons and daughters, saith the Lord Almighty." 2. Cor. 6 : 17, 18.

MAY 8.—*Let us lay aside every weight, and the sin which doth so easily beset us.* Heb. 12 : 1

Christian, thou art called to run a race. The eyes of innumerable spectators are upon thee. The powers of many enemies are against thee. But fear not. In the strength of Jesus, through the power of faith, thou shalt obtain the prize; even the salvation of thy soul. It is thy wisdom to know thy foes, and guard against them : to know thine own vileness and weakness, and look to thy Friend for power.

Thou hast a heavy burden, which hinders thy running with alacrity and delight; this, in the exercise of faith, thou must lay aside; therefore "put off the old man with his deeds." This, through the Spirit, is to be thy daily work. Every sin is a weight, and as such is to be laid aside. "The body of sin" is a sore burden, therefore to be put off. But thou hast a besetting sin. Thine own conscience best knows its name and nature. This thou art called to lay aside. In the nature of all men there is one sin, a master sin, the source and spring of every other sin, which even believers are not exempt from; but it is ready, at all times, easily to beset them. It is that monster of iniquity, unbelief.

"Faith is the substance of things hoped for, and the evidence of things not seen." Heb. 11 : 1. In this chapter we see what glory is given to God, and what wonders were wrought by faith. It is the nature of unbelief to

deny the substance of what is hoped for, and to oppose
the evidence of invisible realities. It tends to make
faint hearts, weak knees, and feeble hands. It stops us
from running our race. And we should give up, and
give over all, but that Jesus prays for us; and we are
endued with power from on high. But, glory to him,
he does pray for us, therefore our faith fails not: we
are strengthened by the Spirit's might in the inner man
to endure unto the end.

Yet, shame to us, instead of laying aside this sin,
how often do we treat it as a bosom friend! How frequently consult it as a sweet counsellor! especially
when its arguments are backed by its constant companion, carnal reason. But, being assured the matter
of our faith is the word of truth; the author and finisher
of our faith, Jesus; we are not called to answer cavils
from carnal reason; nor to silence unbelief by explaining the mysteries of godliness; but to lay it aside; put
it off as David did Saul's armor; put it away as men do
childish things; and run with patience the race set before us, "looking unto Jesus."

> " By glimmering hopes and gloomy fears
>   " We trace the sacred road;
> " Through dismal deeps and dangerous snares
>   " We make our way to God.
>
> " See the kind angels at the gates,
>   " Inviting us to come!
> " There Jesus, the forerunner, waits
>   " To welcome travelers home."

MAY 9.—*That I may know him.* Phil. 3 : 10

" There are three things that are never satisfied, yea,
four say not, It is enough." Prov. 30 : 15. This is true
of the fire of love, when kindled in believing hearts.
It burns with insatiable desire towards Jesus. Amazing!
Had Paul so long known, loved, and preached a crucified,

risen Saviour, and yet now desires to know him? Yes.
Such is the nature of faith, that like riches to a miser,
the more they increase the more the desires of his heart
increase after them. His wants are greater than his
possessions.

So the living members of precious Christ see such
inexhaustible treasures in him, their living Head, and
such numerous wants in themselves, that their hearts
are ever crying after, looking to and longing for more
of his presence, blessings and comforts in knowledge
and experience. And, like a chaste virgin espoused to
an affectionate lover, her heart will never be completely
satisfied till she is brought into the nearest relation,
when she takes up her abode and enjoys the presence
of the object of her love. Lovers of Christ can never
be satisfied with any other but him; nor will they be
fully satisfied, nor perfectly happy, till they are for ever
present with their ever-loving Lord.

But the knowledge of Him, even now, creates a paradise of peace, a heaven of love and holiness in the soul.
Hence there is a godly jealousy in espoused souls, lest
other objects should steal upon their affections. If at
any time their eyes have been turned from the Lord,
there is a holy shame; they blush at their folly and cry,
O that I may know Him who rests in his constant love
to me a poor sinner. In this consists the life and joy
of the heart, to know that Jesus hath made peace for
us by the blood of his cross; that he hath wrought out
a robe of righteousness, by the obedience of his life, to
adorn us; and that he ever lives to pray for us: yea,
daily, constantly to know him, as dwelling in my heart
by faith, ever present with me, to the joy of my mind
and to the peace of my conscience.

And truly, beloved, if we are not kept thus knowing
Jesus, looking to and feeding upon him continually in
our heart by faith, we shall know and feel that other

things will creep in, and sadly distress our mind. The voice of the law will be heard in our conscience, backed by Satan's injections, and we shall find anguish of spirit and bitterness of soul. But sweetly abiding in the knowledge of Jesus, by faith, we manfully stand our ground, and courageously conquer and triumph. So shall "grace and peace be multiplied through the knowledge of God, and our Saviour Jesus Christ." 2 Pet. 1 : 2.

MAY 10.—*Work out your own salvation with fear and trembling.*
Philippians 2 : 12

Salvation, from first to last, is all of grace : not of works. Rom. 11 : 6. It was planned in the covenant of grace. It is finished by the grace of Christ. The moment we believe on him, salvation is ours.

Why are we called to work it out ? Consider, salvation implies deliverance from dangers and enemies. We are surrounded with these without, as well as within. The legality of our spirits, pride of our natures, lusts of our flesh, rebellion of our wills, self-righteousness of our hearts, worldly-mindedness of our desires, carnality of our affections, turbulency of our passions, and unbelief, the offspring of all ; say, are not these like a legion of enemies to our salvation ? Is not Satan ever working, by means of all these, to bring us into dangers and distress, if by any means he may prevent our peaceably possessing and eternally enjoying salvation ?

Judge then, O believer, is there not necessity for working out thy deliverance from their force and fraud ? Is there not constant need for faith to work by love ; striving against sin ; resisting Satan ; mortifying the flesh ; perfecting holiness ; thus producing fruitfulness in good works ? The commands of thy God make the work of faith, the labor of love, and the patience of hope necessary. The Gospel requires, love constrains to be much in prayer, meditation, searching the Scriptures, and all holy ordinances. And to encourage to this, ever remember, it is "God who worketh in us both to will and to do." Be strong, for I am with you, saith the Lord of Hosts. Haggai 2:4.

Does thy happiness consist in enjoying the full assurance of this salvation? then "work it out with fear and trembling." Fear to think of establishing thy works and duties, as thy righteousness, to procure God's favor. Tremble to entertain any hope of salvation but by the atoning blood and perfect righteousness of Jesus; any way of access to God but through his mediation. Fear and tremble, above all, after thou hast done all, to think I am perfect. Know thou art still "an unprofitable servant." Tremble at the thought that thy might, power, faithfulness, procure for thee salvation. Fear ever to ascribe any glory to thyself. "Whoso looketh into the perfect law of liberty, and continueth therein, he being not a forgetful hearer, but a doer of the work, this man shall be blessed in his deed." James 1:25.

MAY 11.—*Let your light so shine before men, that they may see your good works, and glorify your Father which is in heaven.* Matt. 5:16

Can sinful man, a worm of the earth, a creature of a day, glorify the infinitely great and eternally glorious Jehovah? Yes: such honor, such exalted honor have all his saints. For his glory they were created at first. For his glory they are created anew in Christ. He commands all his members to this, as their bounden duty; the Spirit enables to it, as their greatest privilege. The Father accepts, is well pleased with, and declares himself glorified by, the praises of his children. Psalm 50:23.

Did Samuel consent to Saul's request, "Honor me

now, I pray thee, before the elders of my people;" 1 Sam 15 : 30, and canst thou, O Son of the Most High, ever need a motive, or want an argument to glorify thy Father before men? It is to be the chief work of thy life. In this work, as Moses said to Pharaoh, so thy Deliverer saith to thee, "not an hoof is to be left behind." With all thou hast and art, thou art to glorify thy Lord.

For thou hast only one thing but what thou hast received from thy Lord : this is sin. By this thou dishonorest God. By every thing contrary to this God is glorified. Happy souls, who study God's word as the rule of their conduct, consider the enjoyment of God in Christ their greatest felicity, and direct all their views to his glory. Thus, when the light of Jesus shines into the heart, it beams forth its evidence and glory in the outward life and conversation. When the light of truth is accompanied by the warmth of love and the obedience of faith, men will see we have been with Jesus : that we not only have light in our heads, but love and zeal for God's glory in our hearts. The former may acquire honor to ourselves of being good talkers for God ; but the latter, only, can prove that we live uprightly, as his obedient children ; that we are his " peculiar people, by being zealous of good works ;" that we really are concerned for his glory—have it at heart ; that we love not only in word, but also in deed and in truth. The genuine language of a converted soul is that of Paul, "Lord, what wouldst thou have me to do?" It is the burden of a faithful, loving heart, that it does so little for the glory of God, and it ever longs to glorify him more. While the light of truth is our glory, and the love of truth our happiness, we shall study to "adorn the doctrine of God our Saviour in all things." Titus 2 : 10.

May 12.—*Grieve not the Holy Spirit of God.* Eph. 4 : 30

How affectionate and condescending is this address of the great God and our Saviour to his children! Paul writes to Philemon, " Though I might be bold to enjoin thee that which is convenient; yet, for love's sake, I rather beseech thee." So, with infinitely higher authoʻ rity, the Lord might command with terror, instead ot beseeching with love. Astonishing expression! " Grieve not the Holy Spirit of God." Hast thou been, canst thou, O believer, be guilty in this matter ? It is easy to conceive that we may grieve our own spirits, and the spirits of good men, by our sin and folly; but to think of grieving the Spirit of God, is enough to make us cry out in amazement, What mystery of love is this!

But verily, so dear are God's children to him, that as, in love to us, he took our nature; so, in condescension to our weak capacities, he borrows language from nature, and assumes to himself passions like ours: for he was in all things like unto us, but without sin. So it is said, God delights in the prosperity of his people, he rejoiceth over them to do them good. But when, through sin and folly, they hurt their own souls, Jesus is touched with a feeling of our infirmities; his Spirit is grieved at our conduct.

Who can tell in how many ways christians do this ? Inwardly, by giving way to unbelief; by low, unworthy thoughts of Jesus, his blood, righteousness, and salva- tion; his mediation and intercession, of whom the Spirit is the glorifier : so also, by indulging vain, carnal, sinful thoughts. Outwardly, by neglecting the Gospel of grace; not walking closely with Jesus by faith; not conforming to his will in our lives and conversation.

And experience wofully convinceth, that when the Holy Spirit is grieved the soul is distressed. We never send the Spirit grieved to heaven, but he leaves our spirits grieved on earth. He is our Comforter. By him believers are sealed unto the day of redemption. Though we are sealed by him as the Lord's own possession, yet if he leaves us to ourselves, the view of Jesus is obscured to us, and his comforts withheld from us. Then natural fears, legal terrors and desponding doubts seize on us, and evil spirits rejoice over us, with "There, there, so would we have it." Though he never becomes the spirit of bondage to us, yet he leaves us to the bondage of our own legal spirits. What reason have we to pray daily, Cleanse us, O Jesus, from our secret faults; and let not, O Spirit, presumptuous sins get the dominion over me! Psalm 19 : 12, 13.

> " The Spirit, like a peaceful dove,
> " Flies from the realms of noise and strife ;
> " Why should we vex and grieve his love,
> " Who seals our souls to heavenly life ?"

MAY 13.—*I rejoice at thy word, as one that findeth great spoil.*
Psalm 119 : 162

The saints of God in all ages were taught by the same Spirit, looked for the same salvation, and were comforted by the same truths of God's word. Hence the word is so precious to them; for it causes their souls to rejoice. Thus it is of the written word of the Lord, which makes known his everlasting, loving designs to sinners of mankind.

This also is true of the essential, divine and uncreated WORD, the Lord Jesus. He, in person, manifested God's thoughts of love, as words declare what is in the mind. Jesus lay in the bosom of the Father from eternity. He has revealed the Father's eternal love to us. He who findeth Jesus, will rejoice indeed. With joy says Philip, " We have found him of whom Moses in the law and the prophets did write." John, 1 : 45.

Hath a conqueror cause for rejoicing who hath obtained a complete victory over and is enriching himself

with the spoils of a wealthy enemy? how much greater
has the christian daily from the word of the Lord!
Alas! the joy of the one is but momentary and uncertain. What he hath gained in war to-day, he may be
deprived of to-morrow. But joy through the victory of
Jesus, and the spoils the christian reaps from his word,
are durable and eternal. The victory of Christ Jesus is
the christian's spoil. Here he beholds sin subdued, death
conquered, Satan vanquished, hell overcome, and a
crown of eternal life and glory, which shall be enjoyed.

In the written word of the Spirit are given unto us
"exceeding great and precious promises." In the essential Word Jesus "all the promises are yea and Amen
to the glory of God." By the former we understand
"what is the hope of our calling, and what the riches
of the glory of our inheritance in the saints." By union
with Jesus and faith in him, we obtain the happy assurance that all things are ours. "Whether the world,
life, death, things present, or things to come, all are
yours, and ye are Christ's, and Christ is God's." 1 Corinthians 3 : 22, 23. And "nothing shall be able to separate from the love of God, which is in Christ Jesus."
Romans 8 : 39.

Blessed be God for the word of his grace, the Bible;
and for his unspeakable gift, Jesus. Here is thy treasure, O christian: where should thy heart be, but in
meditation and delight herein daily? For thou canst
get spiritual joy from no object but Christ set before
thee in the Gospel. The clearer thou seest salvation by
him, the stronger will be thy faith in him. "Rejoice in
the Lord alway." Phil. 4 : 4.

> "How doth thy word my heart engage!
> "How well employ my tongue!
> "And in my tiresome pilgrimage
> "Yields me a heavenly song."

MAY 14.—*This same Jesus, which is taken up from you into heaven, shall so come in like manner as ye have seen him go into heaven.* Acts 1 : 11

The parting of dear friends is grievous and affecting, but sorrow is alleviated by the hope of meeting again. O the joy of meeting our dear friends in glory who are gone before! But what will heighten all will be the sight and enjoyment of our best Friend and dearest Saviour. The disciples were looking steadfastly tc heaven after their dear Master, ascending to glory, when they received this assurance. They saw his human form, the same dear man, their beloved companion, with whom they had so often ate and drank, taken sweet counsel, and who was lately crucified, dead, and buried— this very man Jesus, they saw ascend. The Son of God came from heaven ; assumed a body of flesh and blood ; lived in it on earth, and, having " finished the work his Father gave him to do," he took the same body with him to glory. This same Jesus shall so come again in like manner. Every eye shall see him in the last day in his human form.

Thus, in all the transactions of Jesus, we behold by faith the MAN. View him in his birth, an outcast babe in poverty. In advanced years, "a man of sorrows and acquainted with grief, despised and rejected of men." He died as another man ; yea, an accursed death, as a malefactor. He rose and ascended with a human body like our own. Such, believer, was thy Saviour, a man like unto thyself in all things, but without sin. And having perfectly expiated and atoned for all our sins, he is now at the right hand of God, the glorified man still, in human form pleading our cause.

God is in Christ. Thou canst not come to the Deity but through the humanity of Jesus. Mind that. How sweet and encouraging this to faith, that our Saviour, our Brother, our Friend, is in our nature before the throne? "He ever lives; he is able to save." And canst thou ever doubt either his love or willingness? O, remember Calvary! think of his agony and blood-shedding there. Canst thou want a proof of his love, poor sinner? If thou, whilst an enemy, wast redeemed and reconciled to God by his blood, how much more, being reconciled, shalt thou be saved by his life! It is thy happiness to be ever looking upon and unto Jesus, as the Man and Mediator by whom thou comest to God: be looking for him, to see him in his glorified form. "He shall come again in like manner;" "to be glorified in his saints, and to be admired in all them who believe." 2 Thess. 1 : 10.

MAY 15.—*Draw nigh to God, and he will draw nigh to you.*
James 4:8

How sweetly is the children's duty and the Father's promise united! the latter is a most powerful encouragement to the former. Though we were "sometime afar off, yet being made nigh by the blood of Jesus," we are exhorted to draw nigh to God in prayer and full assurance of faith; "faithful is He who hath promised," he will draw nigh to, and bless us. To live near God is our heaven below: to experience a distance from him our misery.

We cannot draw nigh to God but in the way he has drawn nigh to us; this is in the humanity of his Son. In all approaches to God, consider this. Jesus, and God in him, is the object of our faith. All other objects drawn nigh to, will leave the soul in a painful sense of distance from the true God and real comfort. Happy, only happy canst thou be, whilst daily living in close communion and near fellowship with God thy Saviour. While the terrors of the law drive legal spirits to duty, to fulfil terms of acceptance; evangelical promises ever sweetly constrain, and encourage to every duty, those who "are not under the law, but under grace."

To live in neglect of duty and God's ordinances, is licentiousness; but, to be fervent in spirit, serving the Lord, is christian liberty: here is our mercy, we have a sure way of access; by Jesus we draw nigh; in him God and man meet; the Holy Spirit is our strength; "praying in the Holy Ghost." As it is the office of Christ to intercede *for* us, so the Holy Ghost intercedes *in* us. As an advocate within, he enables us to plead, in faith, what Jesus is to us, and hath done for us. So we speak with confidence to our dear Father: the Spirit helps in prayer, as a nurse does a little child that is unable to go of itself; or, as a weak, decrepit person is upheld by the arm.

Here is our word of promise, "God will draw nigh to you." This is our happiness below, our heaven on earth, to have access to the God of mercies; and for the Father of all consolations to draw nigh to us. Not merely to draw nigh to duty, but to God in duty; to find and feel the special presence and blessing of the Lord. Without this, loving hearts cannot be satisfied. Communion with God, finding nearness of spirit, delightful intercourse with God, and receiving inward peace and love from him; O, this is the glory of the life of faith, and draws us from, and makes us dead to all things beside. When God, and Christ, and heaven are within, all without becomes truly mean and despicable in comparison. "It is good for me to draw near to God." Ps. 73:28.

MAY 16.—*I am crucified with Christ: nevertheless I live; yet not I, but Christ liveth in me: and the life which I live in the flesh I live by the faith of the Son of God, who loved me, and gave himself for me.*—Gal. 2 : 20

The state of a Christian is a seeming paradox. No

marvel the things of God are foolishness to natural men,
and that they account us fools for Christ. For the truths
of God, as well as the life of his children, appear absurd
to them. But the life of Jesus is made manifest in our
flesh. 2 Cor. 4 : 11. Hence he saith, "If any man will
come after me, let him deny himself;" Matt. 16 : 24;
deny the pride of his own righteousness, the corrupt
lusts of his sinful flesh, and own me as his life, and follow me as his Lord, in the regeneration. This crucifixion
of nature is death to every hope but Jesus. This life of
faith on him consists in peace, love, holiness, and joy.
This springs from love, excites love, and is nourished
by love. So we enjoy heaven below. This is heaven
above insured to us.

Blessed life! happy believer, to feel Christ living in
thee, to live on him by faith. Envy you, ye sons of
folly and vanity, we do not. Join with you in your
carnal delights we cannot; joys infinitely superior are
ours. Pity you, indeed we do. Nor with you, ye sons
of the bond-woman, can we live on our works and
duties, derive life from terms we fulfil, as if for so much
work we earn so much wages. Our God owes us nothing; yet, astonishing grace! he gave his Son freely,
"that we might live through him," though wretched,
guilty, damnable creatures by nature and practice: of
this we are bold and confident. This truth bears the
Divine impress. The Lord hath confirmed it with an
oath. Here to admit the least doubt is base and unreasonable. The life of faith springs from truth itself,
and is as contrary to doubting as to sensuality; yet,
while in the flesh, it will be opposed by both.

But is every believer in Jesus assured, with Paul,
"Christ loved *me*, and gave himself for *me?*" No:
though this knowledge is essential to the comfort of
our souls, yet not to the being of faith in the heart; nor
is it the object of faith; yet it is the joyful privilege of

every believer, and as such, is earnestly to be coveted, and all diligence should be given to attain it. We are loved with the same love ; saved by the same truth ; the same faith given us by the same Spirit which Paul had, and to the same end, to make us holy and happy. And the Comforter, who testifies of Jesus in the word, will sooner or later also bear witness to the heart, and fill the soul with the comforts of faith and the joy of assurance. Every faithful soul, abiding in the Lamb, shall rejoice to say, The Spirit itself beareth witness with my spirit that I am a child of God. Romans 8 : 16.

MAY 17.—*Remember Lot's wife.* Luke 17 : 32

It may do us much good, it can do no harm, to call to mind the judgments of our God. Hence we may learn from others' harm to be more wise and wary. If we see professors fall away, it teaches us to take heed : it tends to lay us low in humility at the feet of Jesus ; and excites gratitude and love in our hearts, and makes us cry out in astonishment, Why are we not fallen ? How are we kept ? " Glory to grace !"

O believer, ever remember, thou standest by faith. " Be not high-minded, but fear :" fear to look back, with a wishful eye, to the sinful vanities of a carnal world. Remember Lot's wife. What of her ? She loitered behind her husband. So, soul, if thou dost loiter, and not keep close with Jesus, thou wilt be in danger. " She looked back from behind him." Here was an act of folly, in thinking, as she was behind Lot, her looking back would not be seen ; of unbelief, in not steadfastly crediting God's word ; and of disobedience, in looking back to Sodom, contrary to his word. O soul, forget not that Jesus sees the looks of thy heart to this perishing world. He sees the unbelief of thy heart when thou lookest to any thing but him for happiness. He will

punish disobedience to his command, "Follow me."
"She became a pillar of salt." Gen. 19 : 26. A lasting monument of God's judgment. Though we never
saw this pillar of salt, yet we may see such every day.
How many seem to turn their backs upon the world
and escape to Jesus, but they look back again to it.
Looking begets longing. Their feet are again entangled
in its snares; their hearts bewitched with its smiles;
they are hugged to death in the world's embraces; and
become as a monument of God's judgment upon their
conduct.

It is supposed Lot's wife retained her natural shape
in this pillar. So, in such professors, there may be all
the appearance of the form of religion, while the spirit, life, and power of it are extinct in their souls.
Their hearts are as cold and dead to God as Lot's
wife was, when she became a pillar of salt, to the
things of this life.

The eye is a great inlet to temptation. Saints have
wofully experienced this. David did. He saw; then
he longed after enjoyment. O believer, Jesus is thy
only object. Here looking may beget love and longing,
without danger of harm ; yea, with the greatest certainty
of good to thy soul. Thou hast escaped for thy life.
"Look not behind thee." "Press toward the mark for
the prize of thy high calling of God in Christ." Philippians 3 : 14.

MAY 18.—*Knowing that of the Lord ye shall receive the reward of the inheritance: for ye serve the Lord Christ.* Colossians 3 : 24

Saving knowledge is accompanied with humility, and
is productive of love to Jesus and delight in his service.
To desire to know more of the truth, in order to gain
greater measures of love, and more cheerful conformity

to him, is praise-worthy. For "whoso looketh into the perfect law of liberty, and continueth therein, he being not a forgetful hearer, but a doer of the work, this man shall be blessed in his deed." James 1 : 25.

Christian, thou art not called to dream over dry disquisitions and subtle refinements, merely to fill thy brain with nice speculations; but to have thy heart warmed with love, thy practice influenced to obedience, as well as thy judgment established in truth. Remember thy calling. Study thy reward. Glory in being a servant of Jesus: his work is pleasant, his service perfect freedom, his wages infinitely great reward in thy work, reward for thy work, and an eternal inheritance when thy short day's work is ended. And all of the rich favor and free grace of the Lord Christ.

Shall the pleasures of sin, which are but for a season; the vile drudgery of Satan, which is miserable bondage; the alluring smiles of a perishing world: shall these be placed in competition with the service of Jesus? "Knowing that we serve the Lord Christ." O how does this sweeten duty, and make every path delightful! Canst thou hesitate one moment, when the question is, "Choose you this day whom you will serve," Christ or Satan? No; verily thou canst not, if so be thou hast tasted of the infinitely rich grace of the eternally precious Christ.

Hath he bought us with his blood? redeemed us to God? wrought out a righteousness to clothe and adorn us? and prepared mansions in heaven to receive us? And shall our conduct be contrary to our profession? our practice not conformable to our judgment? or our walk inconsistent with our faith? Where then is the proof that we serve the Lord Christ? What evidence that we know the Lord, are interested in, or may expect the reward of his inheritance? We may well cry out, Wo to our wretched sinful nature, which is contrary to Jesus, and is ever opposing his truth, ways, and love. Shame to us, that we love him no more and serve him no better. Blessed be Jesus Christ for the gift of his Spirit. O that through his sanctifying and sin-mortifying operations we may be, in love, wholly devoted to the service of him, who in mercy wholly devoted himself for our salvation. "Ye are not your own." 1 Cor. 6 : 19.

MAY 19.—*The law was given by Moses, but grace and truth came by Jesus Christ.* John 1 : 17

It is natural to us all to say of the moral law, as the king of Israel of faithful Micaiah, "I hate him, for he doth not prophesy good concerning me, but evil." 1 Kings 22 : 8. True, God's holy law yields no comfort, hope, or peace to any sinner. Yet believers in Jesus cannot hate the moral law. It is a transcript of our Father's mind and will; his good gift; and answers most valuable ends and purposes to us. We know sin by the law, as we know Christ by the Gospel.

Though the law was given by Moses, a meek prophet, yet it is full of wrath, condemnation, and curses; yea, denounces damnation to every transgressor. Yet why hate the law? That is not the cause of all these evils, but our violations of its holy, just, and righteous precepts. Here fix thy hatred: here it is just. Believer, the law is thy friend, it shows thee thy duty, cuts off all legal hopes, all trust in thy own righteousness, razes every false foundation. The trumpet sounds its alarm louder and louder. The voice of words is shriller and shriller, and will ever be terrible in its sound to thy conscience, except thou art under that grace and truth which came by Jesus Christ.

Behold and admire the transcendant excellencies of Jesus, "full of grace and truth." Grace, even the free favor of God to sinners, came by Jesus Christ: truth, in every accomplishment of the ceremonial, in perfect fulfilment of every righteous demand which the moral law could exact. Here is our wisdom, to oppose Jesus' life and death to every righteous demand, terrible threatening, and dreadful curse of the law. As our husband, all debts, dues, and demands he for ever satisfied. He came, not to destroy the law, but to fulfil it. Matt. 5 : 17.

Says the immortal Hervey, "Jesus is the author of our faith and former of our graces. In his unpolluted life we see the path, in his meritorious death the price, and in his triumphant resurrection the proof of bliss and immortality. If we offend, and fall seven times a day, he is the Lord our peace. If depraved, and our best deeds unworthy, he is the Lord our righteousness. If brutish in heavenly knowledge, he is the Lord our wisdom: his word dispels the shades, his Spirit scatters the intellectual gloom, his eye looks our darkness into day In short, we are nothing, and Christ is all. Worse than defective in ourselves, we are complete in him. We act by strength, and glory in a righteousness not our own." All is of faith, by grace. Rom. 4 : 16.

MAY 20.—*Master, carest thou not that we perish?* Mark 4 : 38.

Saints in all ages have experienced that their extremity of distress has been God's opportunity to deliver. So these disciples found it. They were in the most imminent danger and the greatest fears. Their vehement cry bespeaks it. "Jesus was asleep." We believe in our Saviour, as a man like unto ourselves—we adore him as the sovereign Lord, whose "eyes are over the righteous, and his ears ever open to their prayer." 1 Pet. 3 : 12. Of this we have the clearest evidence and fullest proof. Jesus awakes as a man; and with the power and sovereignty of Jehovah rebukes the boisterous wind; and says to the raging waves, "Peace, be still;" and instantly all nature obeys its Creator, all is hushed into a profound calm.

While others are pleased with the feats of a Cæsar, or the conquests of an Alexander; may it be our constant delight to meditate upon the wonderful works of our God-man and blessed Saviour. Transporting, to know this awful God is ours, our Jesus, and our Friend!

But art thou not ready, O believer, sometimes to say, "My Lord hath forsaken, and my God hath forgotten me?" It seems as though he cares not, even though I perish. I am in the wide ocean of difficulty and distress. Corruptions rage; temptations assault; fiery darts of the enemy fly thick around me; I groan under the sense of a hard heart and an absent God." Hear the voice of thy Lord, "O thou afflicted, tossed with tempest, and not comforted;—for a small moment I have forsaken thee, but with great mercies will I gather thee." Isa. 54 : 7, 11. Judge not of God's love by thy sense and feeling; but by his word of truth, the stability of his promises, and the security of his oath. He may be battering down thy life of sense, to make thee strong in faith, strong in the Lord, and in the power of his might.

These disciples, though in a terrible storm, were safe, because Jesus was in the ship, though asleep. So is every disciple where Jesus dwells in the heart by faith. The affection of God's love never ceases, though storms surround us, and the comfort of love may seem asleep. And as with these disciples, so shall it be, O christian; thou shalt find thy loving Saviour ever near to hear, and almighty to deliver thee. God's moment is thy mercy. In the deeps of distress are God's wonders known. "In the mount of the Lord," "Jehovah-jireh," "it shall be seen." What saith thy Lord? "Call upon me in time of trouble, and I will deliver thee, and thou shalt glorify me." It is the joy of faith to reply, "Thou shalt compass me about with songs of deliverance Psalm 32 : 7.

MAY 21.—*Go, tell his disciples, and Peter, that he goeth befor you into Galilee: there shall ye see him.* Mark 16 : 7

How different is the Gospel from the law. One is a voice of condemnation, terror, and wrath; the other speaks grace, peace, and love. When God's children only murmured for water, even meek Moses is in wrath, and calls them "rebels." Here the disciples had acted most basely and ungratefully to their loving Saviour; for they added sorrow to his distress when they all forsook him and fled; and Peter above all the rest; for, as if Jesus was the most abandoned wretch, Peter, with oaths and curses denied that he knew him.

What could they expect, but that his first message should be, Go tell those apostate rebels I am risen from the dead; they shall receive their just deserts; vengeance is mine, I will repay them? Be astonished, O heavens! Hear, wonder, and love, O ye backsliding children; devils are not permitted to terrify, but angels commissioned to comfort them. "Tell his disciples;" amazing! Disciples still! How unworthy the very name!

Yet more, lest his message should prove a dagger to poor Peter's heart, and he should write these bitter things against himself: "I am no disciple. Though all the rest forsook and fled from Jesus, yet not one of them sinned with so high a hand as I. I not only forsook him, fled from him, but denied him with oaths, cursed and swore that I knew him not. Wo is me; the Lord told me Satan had desired to have me; so it must be." No, no, Peter, thy Lord "having loved his own which were in the world, he loved them unto the end."

"Not all that sin or hell can say
"Can turn his heart, his love away."

Peter's name is in the commission of comfort. Did he sin above the rest? Yet grace superabounds, therefore he is particularized above the rest. "He goeth before you to Galilee; there shall ye see him."

But for this comfortable message poor Peter would have dreaded to see Jesus. He is gone before to glory; there shall we see him. But for the comfortable message we have had from him of his love and salvation, we might dread to see him. But who shall set bounds to his love? Will any trembling disciple say, "The Lord hath forsaken, my Lord hath forgotten me?" True, thou mayst deserve it; but he deals not with thee after that manner: though a sinner, a backsliding, hell-deserving sinner, the chief of sinners, yet still his name is Jesus, his nature is love. It is the joy of his heart, and the work of his life, "to save to the uttermost all who come unto God by him, seeing he ever liveth to make intercession for them." Hebrews 7 : 25.

MAY 22.—*Rejoice in the Lord alway; and again I say, Rejoice*
Phil. 4 : 4

"He that is of a merry heart hath a continual feast. Prov. 15 : 15. Every believer in Christ hath a continual feast; therefore has always reason to be of a merry heart. When he is not, he lives below his privilege, and forgets his loving Lord's command. Though we daily find enemies to our spiritual joy, yet none can destroy our ground of rejoicing. That is fixed as a rock; permanent as the mountains; and standeth fast for ever and ever. Paul gives us, from experience, this as the christian's motto, "As sorrowful, yet always rejoicing." Though with him daily crying out, "O wretched man that I am," according to the flesh; yet thou hast the same reason always to thank God and rejoice in Jesus as Paul had. Though, in thyself, cause for mourning and humiliation, yet continual matter of joy and rejoicing in the Lord Jesus.

Christian, here is thy wisdom, to understand aright and act suitably to thy character: " as having nothing " in nature ; " yet possessing all things" by grace : being united to Jesus, in whom all fulness dwells ; and " blessed with all spiritual blessings " by God the Father in him. It is therefore our sweet privilege always to re joice in Christ. We experience that believing views of Jesus cause rejoicing in him, *in* the Lord. Mind that little word *in*. The exercise of faith is ever to be on thy Lord. All cause of spiritual joy is in Jesus.

The word to us is, Believe and be joyful. If we search the Scriptures, which testify of Jesus; if we dwell much in meditation on his person, offices, blood, righteousness, intercession, we shall perceive never-failing springs of joy. Day by day be looking and praying, O soul, that through the Spirit thou mayst see and maintain a comfortable knowledge and settled assurance of thy own interest in Jesus, and salvation by him. O this will cause thee to rejoice indeed, with joy unspeakable and full of glory ! So that, even though outward things put on a gloomy appearance, yet shall we be like the steadfast prophet : "Although the fig-tree shall not blossom, neither shall fruit be in the vines ; the labor of the olive shall fail, and the fields shall yield no meat ; the flock shall be cut off from the fold, and there shall be no herd in the stalls—" what then ? does he hang down his head like a bulrush ? does joy of heart forsake him ? No. Says he, " yet I will rejoice in the Lord, I will joy in the God of *my* salvation." Habak. 3 : 17, 18.

> " Then let our joys abound,
> " And every tear be dry ;
> " We're marching through Immanuel's ground
> " To fairer worlds on high."

MAY 23.--*What doth it profit, though a man say he hath faith,*
and have not works? Can faith save him ?   James 2 : 14.

Many of God's dear children are often in doubt and
perplexity lest their faith should not be the faith of
God's elect. This may arise through the weakness of
their understanding in the word of truth ; and because,
as yet, faith doth not bring forth its fruits of joy and
assurance. But sooner or later the Holy Ghost will
make this matter clear and satisfactory to their hearts,
in believing.

But the soundness of our faith is least of all suspected
by us while in a state of nature. For we all think, are
very confident, have not the least doubt, but say, " we
have faith ;" true faith : but this is a weed which grows
wild in nature's field.   This is the faith here spoken of,
which all the world rest in who know not the Son of
God. All men have not faith, the faith of God's elect.
If we say we have faith, what doth it profit ? If it
brings no glory to God, no good to men, it only de-
ccives the soul.

" Can faith save him ?" What disputes and conten-
tions hath this question raised ! Some have even set
the apostle James at variance with the apostle Paul ;
as though the former contended for salvation by works
against the latter. " Can faith save him ?" a question,
equal to an assertion. It cannot. The supply of one
word here puts the matter beyond all dispute. Can *such*
a faith save him ?   No : it is impossible.

But dost thou, O christian, think thy faith, though
accompanied with good works, can save thee by its inherent excellence ? Verily, no more than thy repentance
or thy love : these are alike gifts of grace by Jesus
Christ. Given, not to rival him in the heart ; nor share
with him in the glory of salvation ; but to honor him,
and comfort his members. We are not saved *for* faith,
but through faith. Yet faith is a precious grace. It

endears a precious Saviour to the heart, and " works by love."

But faith doth not *procure* God's love, obtain his favor, make atonement for sins, work out a righteousness to justify, nor merit the power of the Spirit to sanctify. All this is enjoyed in believing, but not procured by faith. Faith, like the Baptist's voice, cries in the soul, " Behold the Lamb of God." By faith, we honor God's word, look to his everlasting love, rely on Christ, mourn over our sin, abhor ourselves, and repent as in dust and ashes. Peace, love, joy, and all inward fruits, as well as outward fruitfulness in every good word and work, are produced by the Holy Spirit, through the life and vigor of faith. It concerns us daily to pray, " Lord, increase our faith!" Luke 17:5.

MAY 24.—*For she said within herself, If I may but touch his garment, I shall be whole.* Matthew 9:21

The case of this poor woman was quite desperate. Many painful operations she had undergone, in hope of a cure. Her money was all spent in procuring remedies. Her disorder grew worse and worse. All human hope and help failed. Death seemed to approach her with great speed. But, strange thought! " If I may but touch the garment " of that man surrounded by yonder crowd, I shall certainly be healed. Surprising to think of, a cure from a touch! a touch not of his person, but his garment! How can nature and reason account for this?

Had she consulted flesh and blood, surely she would have concluded, this suggestion is only mere fancy, and will end in delusion. Had she consulted eminent physicians or learned pharisees about her thoughts, doubtless they would have pronounced Jesus a deceiver, her an enthusiast, and advised proper remedies to her as a

lunatic   But the Holy Spirit had, inwardly, made Christ
known unto her. She saw somewhat of his glory. Her
mind was disposed towards him. She believed in her
heart his power to heal her. She speaks within herself
her thoughts concerning him. She came with trembling
feet ; touched him with a fearful heart ; but departed
with triumph.

How secret are the operations of the Spirit in working faith in the hearts of sinners ! " No man can come
unto me, (saith Jesus,) except the Father draw him."
John 6 : 44. A sight of Christ is of special grace. The
first thought of help and hope in Jesus for sinners is
from the word of truth, and by the power of the Spirit.
The soul soon evidences itself to have " the faith of
God's elect ;" for, under a sight and sense of its desperate state and ruined condition, it speaks within itself of
going to Jesus, and him only, for pardon and salvation.

Yet the poor heart is often exercised with an *if ; if*
I did but believe in him, *if* I may but touch him, *if* I did
but feel in myself that I was healed of my sin and
plague, O how I should rejoice ! Well, though the soul
is opposed by a crowd of difficulties, yet will it not be
satisfied till it breaks through all earthly opposition and
finds peace in Jesus ; till it hears the voice of its Beloved speaking pardon and comfort by his word. When,
like Isaiah, the soul cries, " Wo is me, I am undone," it
cannot rest till with him also, a live coal from the altar
of Jesus' love is laid upon his mouth, and his language
is changed to "I am saved by Jesus." For " lo, this hath
touched thy lips, and thy sin is purged." Isa. 6 : 7.

MAY 25.—*A friend loveth at all times, and a brother is born
for adversity.* Prov. 17 : 17.

We have a striking instance of genuine and uninter-
rupted friendship which mutually subsisted between

David and Jonathan. How affecting is that pathetic, mournful exclamation of David, when friendship's sweet bands were dissolved in death! "I am distressed for thee, my brother Jonathan: very pleasant hast thou been unto me: thy love to me was wonderful, passing the love of women." 2 Sam. 1:26. Who can read this plaintive note without sympathy?

But though their love and friendship never abated in the dark scenes of adversity, but was alike at all times, death put a period to its existence. Natural friendship extends not beyond the confines of the grave. But we have a Friend who ever lives and always loves. The most exalted friendship, compared to his, diminishes in glory as the light of the brighest star when the sun appears. Is not Jesus this Friend who loveth at all times? Yea, before time commenced his love existed to his church. Every member was loved by him, and given to him of the Father. When he saw them polluted in their blood, defiled with sin, and loathsome in their persons; yet, (O wonderful!) that was the time of love; he passed by, his eye saw, his heart loved, and his lips said, Live.

Dost thou live by faith on the Son of God? This is the effect of love, known and manifested. But, dost thou find daily that thou art a poor sinner? and art therefore grieved, and thinkest thou shalt weary out the love of thy Friend? No; that cannot be, he loveth at all times. Jesus is the "Brother born for adversity," to comfort in and support under it. Now thou art in an adverse state. The world, the flesh, and the devil are against thee. But thy Friend is above, engaged for thee. He is stronger than all. Though in dangers oft, yet always safe. Jesus was born to suffer adversity for his brethren. A friend, and a brother, makes one's sorrows and sufferings his own. So did Jesus. Our sins were his, he "bore them in his own body." "He hath borne our grefs and carried our sorrows."

And did he love before time! Does he love at all times? Then what shall separate from his love? "In all things we are more than conquerors, through him who loved us." As Jesus' power is equal to his love, death, which parts the dearest friends, and dissolves the sweetest friendships below, shall introduce us to the nearest enjoyment of Him, our best Friend and glorified Redeemer above: for he says, "Father, I will that they whom thou hast given me, be with me where I am." John 17:24.

MAY 26.—*Behold what manner of love the Father hath bestowed upon us, that we should be called the sons of God.* 1 John 3:1

If a poor, insolvent debtor, who sees no hope but to end his miserable life in a loathsome jail, is yet unexpectedly called to hear the will of a loving friend, whereby an ample provision is bequeathed him, fully to satisfy all his wants; how must this rejoice his heart! How in the ecstasy of his mind would he be ready to call upon every one around him to behold the delightful testament!

This is but a faint view of the inestimable riches of glory and honor bequeathed to ruined sinners by New Testament love, ratified and sealed by the blood of Jesus. Upon a view of this, how should we be filled with wonder, fired with ecstasy, and our transported hearts should not keep silence! Angels, see and admire! saints, behold and adore the marvellously great, the inexpressibly glorious, the wonderfully discriminating love of the Father of Jesus! Amazing to tell! comforting to believe! transporting to feel! love, the love of God the Father, hath made its way to sinful man; flows through the heart of a crucified Jesus;

hath reached my poor heart. What terms have we fulfilled, what conditions have we performed to procure this invaluable blessing? O, the very question startles the gracious soul! He rejects the thought of his own merits with abhorrence; and cries, "Pride, thou busy foe, begone." All, all is freely given, richly bestowed.

And am I, vile and unworthy as I am, the called, the real son of God by adoption, through the faith of Jesus? O thou heavenly Paraclete, thou divine Sanctifier, influence, daily influence my heart, my tongue, my life, to glorify my Father, my Saviour, my God! Though I have done nothing to procure this inestimable privilege, yet, enjoying this rich grace, love and gratitude demand corresponding fruits; a holy walk, worthy of the vocation wherewith I am called.

Hence, assuredly, will spring another evidence of God's children; therefore "the world knoweth us not, because it knew him not." Though our dear Saviour "went about doing good;" yet even this could not gain him the approbation and esteem of the world Never let disciples expect to be above their Master. The more we follow Jesus, and are conformed to him, as obedient children, the stronger evidence shall we probably have of the world's enmity, as well as of our Father's love. Let us rejoice to follow Jesus, and be glad to imitate him; to do good, though we suffer evil. "Be blameless and harmless, as the sons of God." Philippians 2:15.

> "Behold what wondrous grace
> "The Father hath bestowed
> "On sinners of a mortal race,
> "To call them sons of God."

MAY 27.—*Go back again: for what have I done to thee?* 1 Kings 19:20

Astonishing! that the simple act of Elijah casting

his mantle upon Elisha, should cause him to leave oxen and plough, parents and habitation, to run after a stranger! Doubtless there is a mystery of the Spirit under the history of the letter. The outward act of Elijah could not effect this, unless the inward power of the Lord had accompanied it. So Peter might have cast his net, and toiled all his days, ere he had taken a fish with a piece of money in its mouth, unless the Lord Jesus had effected this.

Elijah's passing by Elisha, and casting his mantle upon him, and the effect that followed, is a striking resemblance of the Lord, strong in power and wonderful in grace, passing by us poor sinners and casting his mantle of love over us. Call to mind, disciple, endeavor daily to remember that time of love, when thy precious Saviour passed by, saw thee polluted in thy blood, immersed in busy care, when worldly hopes and carnal delights engrossed thy whole concern. No eye, no, not thine own, pitied thy precious, immortal soul; thou didst neither see its misery nor fear thy danger. But, saith thy Saviour, "When I passed by thee and looked upon thee, behold thy time was a time of love." Ezek. 16:8. O the mighty charm of Divine love! How is the heart attracted and drawn after Jesus, as Elisha to Elijah! So says the smitten soul to Jesus, "I will follow thee." And, like him, its affections are drawn from worldly objects, and it acts like the woman of Samaria: when she found the Messiah she forgot her errand, and left her water-pot behind.

"What manner of man is this," said the disciples in astonishment, "that even the winds and the sea obey him!" Surely we may cry out in admiration with St John, "What manner of love is this!" What a mighty God is Jesus, that the power of his love attracts our stubborn hearts to follow him! Admire the power and adore the freeness of Jesus' love. It found us ere we sought it. Little did Elisha think, when ploughing, of being called to be the Lord's prophet. Ah! what was thy employ when Jesus first cast his mantle over thee? Perhaps, like Saul, sinning with a high hand; employed in the devil's drudgery; in open rebellion against a loving Saviour; and yet priding thyself in the filthy rags of thine own righteousness. This is the joy and rejoicing of faith where God casts the mantle of his love; he clothes that soul with the robe of his Son's righteousness. So, grace reigns by Jesus Christ unto eternal life. Romans 5 : 21.

MAY 28.—*We look not at the things which are seen, but at the things which are not seen: for the things which are seen are temporal; but the things which are not seen are eternal.* 2 Corinthians 4 : 18.

The faith of the Gospel stamps vanity upon the righteousness, glory, and happiness of every object short of Jesus. When the soul beholds the King in his glory, it pours contempt upon all things beside. All the transient objects of time and sense die in esteem while the crucified Saviour is in view. He is our greatest gain, our chief glory. Far, infinitely beyond all the reasonings of vain philosophy, is the christian's sight by faith, to reconcile his mind to afflictions, endue with patience, and give victory over them. Thus Moses " endured, seeing Him who is invisible." Heb. 11 : 27.

Though the eye of nature hath not seen, nor the uncircumcised ear heard, nor can the carnal heart conceive the spiritual things of God's covenant, Jesus' incarnation and the Spirit's revelation; yet the enlightened, heaven-born soul, sees these things in open vision by the eye of faith. To look at them is our chief delight and joy, to obtain clearer views of them our daily study, to converse and be more familiar with them our chief happiness, our heaven begun on earth. A strange mystery to himself and to the carnal world is the believing soul. To prove and converse with an unseen Saviour, look to invisible objects, derive all happiness from things that are not seen: no marvel that there is so great opposition from fallen nature and carnal reason against such a life.

Ever remember with humility and thankfulness our dear Saviour saith, " Unto you it is given to know the mystery of the kingdom of God." Mark 4:11. " These things are hid from the wise and prudent." O disciple, whilst thou dost adore the Father's love, rejoice in the Son's grace, remember thou art wholly indebted for all this rich discovery to the Divine Spirit. Give him equal glory. Grieve not the Spirit, who is the glorifier of Jesus, by looking to any other object for righteousness, peace, and happiness.

Is Christ thy all? Are the unseen things of his kingdom thy portion? Be a chaste virgin to thy Lord. " Where thy treasure is, there let thy heart be also." Happy for thee to find with Paul, " I die daily." I am dying to the world, while living in it. I find and feel many pains and disorders in my frail body, as sure forebodings of hastening dissolution. I know perfectly that the day of the Lord is coming, that each breath I draw brings nearer this solemn advent. What then should I look to? on what place my affections, but on things above, where Christ is? Col. 3:1.

MAY 29.—*My God shall supply all your need, according to his riches in glory, by Christ Jesus.* Phil. 4:19

Paul, though an eminent saint and a great apostle, was yet a man of like passions, a poor sinner, even as others. Yet with what amazing boldness and confidence he speaks of what his God shall do! Though he had

never been admitted into the counsels of the glorious
Trinity, yet the Holy Spirit had well instructed him in
the covenant transactions of Jehovah. He well knew
the nature of the everlasting covenant; that it was
"ordered in all things" in infinite wisdom and eternal
love; that all the graces and blessings contained in it
are sure to all the heirs of promise. As soon might a
God of truth prove false, a God of faithfulness be unjust,
as any one of his promises in Jesus to his people fail.

Such is the security of the covenant; such the confidence of faith. God the Father is the fountain, the
Son the treasury, and the Spirit the dispenser of all
grace. Believers' needs are God's concern. They shall
have a rich supply for all their wants. The value of their
supplies is enhanced to the highest degree. Not only
riches, but riches in glory; glorious riches. For they
receive all from glory; and all comes to them through
the glorified man Jesus Christ. He is their "Friend
who loveth at all times; their Brother born for adversity." In the hour of our distresses, and time of our need,
we too often forget that we have such a God and Saviour
to trust in and call upon. Instead of looking to the
throne of grace, alas, we pore over our own corruptions.
Here we are sure to find nothing but misery, poverty,
and sin.

Is there such an inexhaustible fund of riches in Christ?
Is it for the poor and needy? Dishonorable thought
of Jesus, ever to imagine that he is an unconcerned
spectator of our wants; or that he will withhold when
we need! Nay, he knows how to "have compassion."
He is touched with a tender sympathy, a feeling sense
of our infirmities. Heb. 4:15. "Trust in him at all
times; ye people, pour out your hearts before him:
God is a refuge for us." Psalm 62:8. And he adds,
"Selah:" as if he had said, consider this well; spread
it before your minds; it is of the greatest importance.

"Lord, help our unbelief." Lord, quicken us to pray always, and not faint. Yea, also to praise thee for thy declarations of love and promises of grace to us poor needy sinners. "Pray without ceasing." 1 Thess. 5 : 17

> " In vain the world accosts my ear,
> " And tempts my heart anew ;
> " I cannot buy your bliss so dear,
> " Nor part with heaven for you."

MAY 30.—*He is our peace.* Eph. 2 : 14

When Jehu came to take possession of the crown of Israel, Jezebel put this (as she thought) cutting question, "Had Zimri *peace* who slew his master ?" 2 Kings 9 : 31. As Jehu was called and anointed to be king of israel, according to the word of the Lord, so is every christian called and anointed by the word and Spirit to the kingdom of Jesus. He "hath made us kings and priests unto God and his Father ; to him be glory," &c. Rev. 1 : 6

But ere we take possession of our crown in glory, we must expect many severe and aggravating questions from the mouth of the adversary on earth. Verily, he hath great reason to urge the most cruel treatment, and charge upon us the vilest behavior to our Master, Jesus. That bloody deed of crucifying the Lord of life and glory was caused by our sins. Not a transgression a disciple of Jesus commits but the precious blood of his Master was spilt for.

The life of sin, and love of sin, is in our nature, and the law of sin in our members. And while we are daily exposed to sin in our practice, Satan, like a powerful Assyrian army, will invade us, and attack the peace of our souls. What can we do ! If we deny his charge, and " say we have no sin, we deceive ourselves, and the truth is not in us." Acknowledge his accusations we must. All in nature, reason, and conscience unite to witness against us.

But shall this destroy the comfort of our minds, the hope of our souls, and the peace of our hearts? If so, how small our knowledge! how feeble our faith! how weak our hearts in the grace which is in Christ Jesus! All the powers of darkness, all the curses of the law, all the accusations of sin,—blessed, for ever blessed be the grace of our God,—cannot, shall not, overthrow this soul-comforting, Christ-exalting, love-exciting truth; this man, even Jesus, who was born in Bethlehem, and died at Calvary, he is our peace.

He hath made peace by the blood of his cross. Col. 1 : 20. The everlasting Gospel proclaims it; the eternal law of love confirms it; by faith we receive the joyful news of it; by the Spirit our souls are made to enjoy it; by the word the blessed Spirit stirs up our pure minds, by exhortations and examples, to look unto Jesus. Look away from every other hope. Turn from every other object. His name, his nature, his offices, his work, all speak peace to poor, guilty, self-condemned souls, whose only hope is Jesus. "The work of (Jesus') righteousness shall be peace; and the effect of (his) righteousness quietness and assurance for ever." Isa. 32 : 17.

MAY 31.—*This is the record, that God hath given to us eternal life, and this life is in his Son. He that hath the Son hath life.* 1 John 5 : 11, 12

Sovereign power permits man to fall. Guilt fills the wretched pair with dread, and cuts off all hope in God, all claim upon him. Hence our first parents "fled from the presence of the Lord, and hid themselves." Sovereign love interposed, and the poor, guilty, trembling partners in wo were called before the offended, justly-provoked Lord. Was it to behold him clothed with vengeance? to hear their sentence of eternal doom to destruction? to see hell opened to receive them? No. Be astonished, O heavens! rejoice, ye apostate children of hell-deserving parents! They heard a record of what was transacted in the eternal court and council of heaven, published on earth. This, instead of wrath, brought mercy; instead of wo, blessing; instead of eternal death, everlasting life; instead of a hell of misery, a heaven of happiness to their trembling hearts.

Fallen man sought not to meet God, to sue for pardon and entreat for grace, but fled his presence. But the Lord follows sinful man, with love in his heart to proclaim the joyful news of eternal life as the free gift of unmerited grace and mercy, in and by the Seed of the woman, Jesus Christ. Glorious record of love! Blessed testimony of life! Joyful tidings of grace! Hast thou heard, known, and believed this record? "Praise the Lord, O my soul, and all that is within me, praise his holy name." Behold and admire the wisdom as well as the love of thy God. In this rejoice always. Be humble continually. Life, eternal life, is given us. This life is in God's beloved Son. "Our life is hid with Christ in God."

O, if Jesus dwells in our hearts by faith, we have God's beloved Son, we have eternal life. The report of this is joyful to our ears. The enjoyment of this enters our hearts, creates a present heaven, and fills us with joyful hopes of future glory. We have the strongest confidence, the fullest assurance to animate our souls. Because I live, saith the Head, ye (my members) shall live also. John 14:19. God hath given us eternal life. He is faithful. He will not revoke his own precious free gift. Jesus hath overcome every enemy and opposer that might prevent our enjoyment of eternal life. The Holy Spirit hath effected such a union to Jesus as can never be broken. We are joined unto the Lord, and are one spirit. 1 Cor. 6:17.

June

JUNE 1.—*Hide not thy face from me ; put not thy servant away in anger: thou hast been my help ; leave me not, neither forsake me, O God of my salvation.* Psalm 27 : 9

"Love never faileth." It ever works in believing hearts towards its beloved object. It cannot bear distance from Christ. The thought is grievous and painful. The dread of it makes the soul plead, fills the mouth with arguments, lest the heart should lose the sweet sense and comfort of his love. His presence is heaven ; his absence hell. His smiles create joy ; his frowns gloom and sorrow.

When the heart feels the withdrawing of God and the light of his countenance, it cannot but be restless and uneasy. For we experience christianity to be more than a name, its doctrines more than mere speculations to fill the head or amuse the thoughts : in its ordinances, more is enjoyed than a dull and formal attendance on them. It is a life of love. It consists in knowing and enjoying the God of truth, faithfulness, and love, in his ordinances. Therefore a loving soul most of all fears the anger of its loving Father. It dreads to be put away in displeasure, though but for a moment. To be left to ourselves, O this calls up cries and tears, and urges us to plead hard with our dear Saviour.

"Thou hast been my help." Past experiences of thy love and power are remembered, and pleaded for present help and future hope. God's precious promises of faithfulness and truth are beheld as "fitly spoken, like apples of gold in pictures of silver." Prov. 25 : 11. Past love cannot be forgotten. Past mercies are recalled.

"Forsake me not." Why ? Because "thou art the God of my salvation." To whom should we go, but to thee, O Jesus ? Thou hast the words of eternal life. Forsake not the work of thine own hands ; the soul, for whom thou didst toil, suffer, bleed, and die. There is salvation in thee, and in no other. I have found it so. Arise, O Sun of righteousness, scatter the clouds of darkness, the mists of sin, and the fogs of unbelief. Recall my wandering steps. Revive my drooping spirit. Bring near thy salvation in present peace and love.

Such are the pleadings of loving hearts, springing from the faith which worketh by love. It ever hath God in Christ for its object, his faithfulness and truth its support, his promises its pleas, his glory its aim, and the comforting sense of his love its portion and heaven. "Whom have I in heaven but thee? and there is none upon earth that I desire besides thee." Psalm 73 : 25.

JUNE 2.—*Wait on the Lord: be of good courage, and he shall strengthen thine heart: wait, I say, on the Lord.* Psalm 27 : 14

"Be of good courage!" Alas, how can one be so, when all sense and feeling dishearten the mind and deject the soul? Lively frames in duty, sweet enlargements of heart, heavenly transports of joy, delightful ecstasies of faith, rapturous tastes of love, all, all, like Noah's dove, have taken their flight; and I fear, says the drooping soul, never, never more to return. Truly, like Hezekiah, "I mourn as a dove; mine eyes fail with looking upward: O Lord, I am oppressed, undertake for me." Isaiah 38 : 14. Still saith the Comforter, by his word, "Be of good courage." Remember thy calling. It is to live by faith, honor thy Lord, and be obedient to his word. Thou hast the sentence of death in thyself, that thou shouldst not trust in thyself, lest thine heart depart from thy Lord. Not frames and feelings, but God's love and promises in Christ to sinners, are the foundation of hope. These are abundantly sufficient to inspire the soul with courage, yea, with good courage, to go on in the ways of the Lord.

Steadfast faith cleaves to Jesus, abides by the truth, perseveres in dutiful obedience. Shall these ever be suspended for want of lively frames and joyful feelings? How would this prove that we walk by faith, and that our eye is single to Christ's glory? Nay, we should then serve him only according to the changes of sense and passion, rather than by the uniform, consistent obedience of faith.

The Lord's word is our rule of duty. His promises are our support. His grace is sufficient for us. His strength is made perfect in our weakness. If our hearts are weak, that we cannot run with alacrity the way of God's commandments as we desire, so much more reason have we to wait on the Lord for the "times of refreshing from his presence." For "he giveth power to the faint, and to them that have no might he increaseth strength." Isaiah 40 : 29. "Wait, I say, on the Lord." David repeats the injunction, with a holy fervor, to his own soul and others. God has promised; expect fulfilment. Here is the exercise of faith, trust in the Lord Christ for what we stand in need of; of hope, expecting to receive all from him; of patience, waiting continually upon him. Most precious promise! "They that wait upon the Lord shall renew their strength, they shall mount up with wings as eagles, they shall run and not be weary, walk and not faint." Isaiah 40 : 31.

JUNE 3.- *Now faith is the substance of things hoped for, the evidence of things not seen.* Hebrews 11 : 1.

Happiness, that inestimable jewel, every man is in search after. But to seek it from objects unseen and invisible to our natural sense, is a downright paradox, and will be ever condemned as the greatest absurdity, in the judgment of depraved sense and carnal reason. In the knowledge, love, and enjoyment of God, true happiness alone consists. The only living and true God hath revealed himself in Christ. This is the christian's God. He knows no other. It is a blessed truth of God's word. By faith this subsists in his mind, and is the evidence that his soul is new-born.

From this faith, " That God was in Christ, reconciling the world to himself," O what an extensive prospect hath hope! God in Christ; the promises all in Christ: he that believeth is in Christ. Christ dwelleth in his heart by faith. All the blessings of time, all the glories of eternity are sure, by the yea and amen of God, to such believing souls.

Shall any bold emissary from Satan demand, " What right hast thou to the inheritance of this good land?" Abraham's sons have Abraham's plea. It is mine by promise. By faith I sojourn in it. God's promise is faith's claim. What he has spoken is the ground or subsistence of hope. But may not other witnesses declare against the christian? Yea, doubtless, many; from the old man, sin remaining in us; from the flesh, Satan, and the law. But the first is under sentence of death, his witness is not valid. Satan is a liar from the beginning, therefore deserves no credit. The evidence of the law is superseded by the promise. For the law, which was 430 years after the covenant confirmed by God in Christ, cannot disannul it, to make the promise of none effect. Gal. 3 : 17.

But, blessed be our Lord, though he suffers us to be attacked by many adversaries, he leaves not himself without evidence in our hearts. Though each of us cannot say, I know I am a child of God; yet the weakest believer hath the evidence of truth; the witness in himself of the reality and certainty of invisible objects, " things not seen," the eternal covenant of grace and peace, the finished work of Jesus, and the glories of an eternal world. And, amidst opposition from every quarter, here is full proof of the inward subsistence of spiritual and invisible objects, in our desires for stronger faith in them and clearer knowledge and enjoyment of them. " To every one that hath shall be given, and he shall have abundance." Matthew 25 : 29

JUNE 4.—*The word of God, which effectually worketh also in you that believe.* 1 Thess. 2: 13

A proclamation of grace from an earthly king has reduced the most desperate and hardened rebels to lay down their arms and promise true allegiance. But, though the word of God is a proclamation of grace, glad tidings of pardon ; though replete with the most tender expostulations, and the most endearing invitations ; yet, so great is our perverseness, so daring our obstinacy, that, if left to ourselves, we should remain deaf to every call, and continue hardened in our rebellion against the most high God till we fell victims to his justly deserved wrath. For unbelief shuts up every avenue of the soul against the light, truth, peace, and love of the word of God. But, O amazing love ! lie in the dust, O my soul ! adore the power of our all-conquering Saviour. The gracious Spirit makes gracious words effectual. Hence faith esteems every portion of the Gospel as the food, life, and joy of the soul. By the Spirit's agency the word begets faith ; and then works effectually in believing hearts.

They speak unadvisedly, who call the word of God a dead letter. Indeed, Paul saith, " the letter killeth." But this can never prove God's word to be dead. That which is dead itself cannot kill. We should distinguish between the letter of the law, which killeth all flesh, and the Gospel of grace, that worketh life and salvation in all who believe. When we read the word of God, we should never consider it distinct from the essential and personal Word, Jesus. He is emphatically styled " The Word of God." Rev. 19 : 13. He who executed all the purposes of the word of truth, works effectually in the hearts of the children of faith.

Hence the once despised and lightly esteemed Nazarene is known, believed in, and loved, as most precious, the chief among ten thousand ; yea, as altogether lovely. God's precious promises in him, once wholly disregarded, are now richly prized. They are beheld as sweetly ranged and profusely scattered through every page of the lively oracles. The Spirit's holy gifts and sanctifying graces are pleaded as God's blessed charter of free grace. All his sovereign edicts, and absolute declarations of grace and salvation, instead of being proudly cavilled against, are bowed down to with humility. In the word of our King there is power. Sin and Satan are dethroned in the heart, and Jesus rules and reigns in the soul. Thus the word of God is quick and powerful. Thus it works effectually to salvation. Faith cometh by hearing, and hearing by the word of God. Rom. 10 : 17.

> " This is the word of truth and love
> " Sent to the nations from above;
> " Jehovah here resolves to show
> " What his almighty grace can do.
>
> " May but this grace my soul renew,
> " Let sinners gaze and hate me too;
> "The word that saves me does engage
> " A sure defence from all their rage."

JUNE 5.—*For me to live is Christ, and to die is gain.* Phil. 1 : 21.

O happy soul, who can thus say with Paul, in life, in death, Christ is my gain. Verily, if thou believest in Christ, thou mayst. Thou hast the same right and reason as he had. Paul was a sinner, even as thou art ; but Christ was all his gain. So he is to all who believe in

him. Come, christian, let us state our loss and gain, and
see the sum total to-day.

In ourselves, as to righteousness before God, peace
with him, love to him, hope in him, power to please
him, enjoyment of him, as the life of our souls, we are
lost, yea, our souls are all lost. We are all bankrupt
sinners; insolvent debtors to law and justice; and deserve the prison of hell. Awful loss!

What is our gain? Inestimable riches! nothing less
than Christ and his precious salvation. Is his dear
name enrolled in our hearts? Can we read Jesus there?
then we have perfect righteousness, full acceptance, free
access, love from, peace with, hope of enjoying, yea,
present fellowship with God. We are his children in
Christ. All that he has is ours. His every attribute is
engaged for us. His Spirit is ours, to make us holy and
happy, and lead us to eternal felicity.

"But," says one, "I am put to a stand in my reckon-
ing; though Christ is my gain, yet I have not lost my
burden. Sin is still alive in me." Stop not, O soul.
Reckon on. Though we have sin, and feel sin raging
and rebelling, yet, in Christ, we have gained a sacrifice
for it, and redemption from it. He hath put away sin
from us, and the wrath due to us from the justice of
God. So it stands upon record in the court of heaven.
The Holy Ghost is witness of it to us on earth. Record this in the court of conscience. Faith can show a
discharge from the guilt of sin and the curse of the law;
therefore "reckon yourselves to be dead indeed unto
sin." "Dead indeed!" how emphatic! yes, dead to sin;
and as much alive to God in Christ as though we had
never sinned. "For," O precious words! "the law of
the Spirit of life in Christ Jesus hath made us free from
the law of sin and death." Romans 8:2.

Thus, in Christ, we gain a perfect victory over sin
and the law. But sin will destroy our mortal bodies:

.et it. This is all it can do. It cannot hurt our immortal souls. For, thanks be to God, we have victory over death. Christ is our gain in death. We shall lose nothing by it but sin and sorrow; we shall gain eternal glory. "We shall be ever with the Lord." "I count all things but loss, for the excellency of the knowledge of Christ Jesus my Lord." Philippians 3:8.

JUNE 6.—*Behold, he cometh with clouds, and every eye shall see him.* Revelation 1:7

With what ardor of heart may every believer cry out, "Blessed be God, every hour brings nearer the solemn advent, the glorious appearing of the great God and our Saviour Jesus! Now is our salvation nearer than when we first believed. Come, thou once despised Nazarene, thou once crucified Saviour."

He shall come. He will come quickly, and be seen in his human form. Shall we not see those wounds and scars in his body, the tokens of his inestimable love, and the perfect victory of his cross for us poor sinners? How joyful in the exercise of faith, the fervor of love, the expectation of hope, is this contemplation! This quells the fears of nature, mortifies its lusts, subdues its corruption. To this end we are born again of the Spirit, that we should enjoy the visions of faith, see Jesus, live by faith on him, have fellowship with him in the sufferings of his cross, and long for his appearing in glory. Then shall we share with him in the glories of his kingdom. "He shall come to be glorified in his saints, and admired in all them that believe." Believe steadfastly; hope constantly; obey cheerfully.

Whence then our dejection of mind, our fear of death, our unwillingness "to be absent from the body and present with the Lord?" Truly, all this ariseth from the mystery of iniquity which worketh in us. But

it is our wisdom to oppose this by the mystery of faith
Never venture to think of your own dying, without considering the death of Jesus. Look not at your own
sins, without looking at the blood of Jesus. Think not
of his appearing as a Judge, without remembering him
as our precious Saviour. Dwell not on the glory and
majesty of his eternal power and Godhead, without reflecting on his humble form, his manhood state. Conceive not of him as a King and Lawgiver, without considering him as a Priest to atone for our sin, an Advocate to plead our cause, and our Forerunner entered
into the heavens for us.

Thus shall we daily prove that we are more than conquerors over every foe that opposeth the holiness and
comfort of our souls, through Jesus, who loved us.
"Behold, he cometh!" O joyful day! most desirable
sight! Then our sorrows, our fears shall for ever cease.
Then our eyes shall see our dearest Friend: and our
foes, that we this day find and feel, we shall see no
more for ever. "To them that look for him, shall he
appear the second time, without sin unto salvation."
Lift up your heads with joy, for your redemption draw-
eth nigh. Luke 21:28.

JUNE 7.—*Thou shalt guide me with thy counsel, and afterward
receive me to glory.* Psalm 73:24

That is a precious caution, "Judge not according to the
appearance." John 7:24. The apostle Paul reproves
saints, "Do ye look on things after the outward appearance?" 2 Cor. 10:7. Through this, saints in all ages
have puzzled their minds, distressed their souls, and
have been tempted to hard thoughts of their God
They have not "judged righteous judgment," in respect
to carnal men and the dispensations of God's providence to them. So we see Job greatly exercised, Job

21 : 7, and Asaph, in this Psalm. But, after the cloud of carnal reasoning and unbelief passed over their minds, the sun of glory and truth shone again with splendor upon them: then faith put forth its lively exercises and sweet appropriations of God. " O my God and Saviour, I see thy ways to man are just ! Righteous art thou, O Lord. Thou art my God, I will love thee. Thou shalt guide me by thy counsel."

As the Lord is often said to make a covenant with his people, when only renewing his old covenant of grace and love in Christ Jesus; so faith frequently makes a fresh choice of, claim to, and glory in the Lord Jesus. "My counsel shall stand, and I will do all my pleasure," saith the Lord. Isaiah 46 : 10. Amen, saith the believing heart. By thy word and Spirit guide me continually. I cannot guide myself. Jesus, be thou my guide, my companion, and my familiar friend.

Blessed christian ! though in Paul's case, (Acts 27 : 20) when neither sun nor stars appeared for many days—when no small tempest is upon thee, and all hope of being saved seems taken away ; yet Jesus is at the helm. Thy vessel shall ride out every storm. He will guide thee safe to the haven of glory.

Some seem so taken up with prying into the secret purposes and inscrutable depths of God's decrees, that they take no heed to their steps; but are like the philosopher who was so intent in observing the starry heavens, that, being careless of his walk, he fell into a ditch. Not God's secret purposes, but his revealed truths, are the object of our faith; "his word is a light to our feet." By that he counsels and directs us. His gracious Spirit leads and guides us in the paths of peace and holiness. Regenerate souls love God's word, the way of holiness, and long for glory. In this the children of God are manifest God will receive all such to glory. "As many as are led by the Spirit of God, they are the sons of God" Romans 8: 14.

JUNE 8.—*Giving thanks to the Father, who hath made us meet to be partakers of the inheritance of the saints in light.* Col. 1: 12

Too many of God's dear children seem to abound more in complaining of what they find and feel in themselves, than in praising God for what he hath done for and in them. Why is this? They do not live enough in their own kingdom, consider their privileges, nor dwell upon the rich love of God their Father to them, the free grace of Jesus *for* them, and the work of the Comforter *in* them. But, from a sense of their corruptions, the devices of Satan, and an apprehension of the spirituality of the law, they cannot think themselves made meet for God's kingdom; therefore they do not praise God for it.

Say, O ye children of the Most High, is this right? What! because you find sin abound in you, will you not give praise that grace doth much more abound to you, and in you also? Consider, God the Father hath made us meet. Who? Us, vile sinners. How? by taking away the being of all sin in us? No: no more than by taking us out of the body. If we never have meetness for glory till all sin is perfectly destroyed in us, we shall never begin the work of praise till we get to glory. But praise is a present work, for what God hath already done in us.

God hath delivered us from the power of darkness. The prince of darkness no more blinds our eyes to the evil of sin, the curse of the law, the glory of God, the face of Jesus, and the preciousness of his salvation. For God "hath translated us into the kingdom of his dear Son." We are out of the kingdom of nature, sin, pride, and unbelief. We live under the spiritual reign of Jesus. Therefore we possess the graces of this kingdom : faith in and love to the King of saints, and "to all the saints" who confess the Son of God, and salvation by him only.

Is sin our burden ? Christ our life of holiness ! Is holiness the desire of our souls ? Have we light, life, faith, love, holiness ? Then God hath made us meet for his glory. Nay, we do enjoy him now. We have fellowship with the Father, and his Son Jesus Christ. Therefore we are now to give him thanks. We shall never have any other meetness for heaven on earth ; though greater degrees of this may be experienced. O my soul, art thou no longer in the darkness of sin ; Satan's slave ; under the curse of the law ; blinded by pride to the charms of Jesus ; tied and bound by the chains of unbelief ; an enemy to God's grace, his truth, and his people ? "O Lord, my God, I will exalt thee, I will praise thy name ; for thou hast done wonderful things." Isaiah 25 : 1.

JUNE 9.—*I had fainted, unless I had believed to see the goodness of the Lord in the land of the living.* Psalm 27 : 13

In times of sore distress and affliction, whether in soul or body, saints are taught many sweet lessons. Chastenings from the Lord are all in love. By them our God teaches the soul to profit. "No chastening for the present is joyous, but grievous." In the dark night of sufferings, christians sigh out many a doleful strain. Sometimes, according to all appearances, from nature, sense, feeling, and the judgment of reason, they are ready to cry out, "All things are against me." Hence their courage sinks ; their hopes and their hearts fail them ; and they are ready to faint.

But they have an invisible Friend always near them. He supports them by his power under all their trials and conflicts, revives their spirits with the consolations of his word; and when he brings them out of their troubles, then how sweetly do they sing of him! How many a joyful psalm, what a rich treasury of experience, are we favored with from the pen of David dipt in the ink of affliction! how sweetly does he indite to the glory of his God, and the comfort of his Father's children in after ages! He believed, therefore he spake. Unless he had believed he had fainted.

O what a soul-supporting grace is faith! It will support when all things else fail. Why so? because it looks to the word, and trusts in an almighty, faithful, covenant-keeping God. Faith consults not flesh and blood, but the word of grace and truth. By faith we endure every fight of affliction, every onset of the enemy, seeing Him who is invisible. As faith is the support of the soul, God's word is the warrant of faith, and Jesus the object, author, strength, and finisher of faith.

Thy faith shall not fail, saith Jesus to Peter, "I have prayed for thee." It failed not as an abiding principle in the heart unto salvation, though it did in the confession of his lips. While the precious Head is praying above, the dear members shall be kept believing below. Though, through the enemy's power and the corruptions and rebellions of the flesh, poor souls may speak unadvisedly with their lips, as David did, (Psalm 116: 10, 11,) "I was greatly afflicted, I said in my haste, all men are liars." But in their right mind they give all glory to God, confess his goodness, and take shame to themselves for such base declarations; and, from their own experience, give sweet advice to their brethren. "I had fainted unless I had believed." Therefore "wait thou on the Lord; be of good courage, and he shall strengthen thine heart: wait, I say, on the Lord." Psalm 27: 14

JUNE 10.—*By the grace of God I am what I am.* 1 Cor. 15 : 10

It would be one great means of preventing our complaints and murmurings, if our hearts were more in meditation upon what we once were, what we still are, and what we deserve. Such was the conduct of the once persecuting, but afterwards Jesus-exalting Paul. The same grace that reached his heart, has been displayed through the many revolving periods down to this day, and effects the same blessed work on poor sinners now. Thou, therefore, O disciple of Jesus, hast the same cause as Paul had, daily to sing of rich, free, distinguishing grace, the eternal love and mercy of God to thy soul, in Christ Jesus.

Grace shines with resplendent lustre in the person of Jesus ; and operates with matchless power in the hearts of his members. It triumphs over all the rebellious motives, carnal workings, and perverse obstinacy of proud nature. Publicans and harlots are often raised and beautified by grace, while self-righteous Pharisees are left buried in the ruins of nature.

Hell-deserving soul! what hast thou to boast of? wherein canst thou glory? Art thou converted to Jesus? Ever know the cause. Study daily to give all the glory where only it is due, even to the boundless mercy of thy God. Wilt thou ever open thy mouth as to thy obedience, thy works of righteousness, by which thou hast obtained the prize? Ever know Jesus hath done all this. Hence grace freely flowed to thee. In the height of thy rebellion, in the depth of thy destruction, the voice of eternal love spoke to thy soul. The power of almighty grace challenged thee as its blood-bought purchase; seized thee as its lawful captive ; and snatched thee as a brand from the fire of destruction.

O wondrous love! Should not amazement strike thy heart, and the fire of love and gratitude ever burn in

thy soul? What shall we say to these things? Truly
grace, that dwelt in God's heart from eternity, hath
reached thy heart in time. Therefore art thou turned to
Jesus by repentance, and hast remission of sins through
faith in his blood. This is given, by the exalted Prince
of grace and peace, to thine heart. Hast thou love to
holiness and hatred to sin? This is contrary to nature,
and is given through the grace of the Spirit. "By the
grace of God I am *what* I am," is the confession of
saints on earth. By the grace of God I am *where* I am,
is the triumphant song of saints in heaven. For " where
sin abounded, grace did much more abound." Rom. 5 : 20

" 'Tis from mere mercy of our God
" That all our hopes begin :
" 'Tis by the water and the blood
" Our souls are washed from sin."

JUNE 11.—*Fear not, little flock; it is your Father's good pleasure to give you the kingdom.* Luke 12 : 32

When sinners are converted, they become little in
their own eyes, and they see but few, comparatively,
who follow the Lamb. Their former friends turn enemies. Their former hopes are cut off. They know
their own strength is perfect weakness; and they feel
the burden of a body of sin and death. Hence they are
often exercised with anxious cares and distressing fears.
Their Saviour knows this; therefore speaks to them in
love, forbids their fears, and administers the most reviving consolation.

Ye children, consider your dignity as adopted sons of
God. Call to mind your honorable state : heirs of a
kingdom, heirs of God the King of kings, and joint-heirs
with Jesus Christ, though, at present, ye are in a state
of exile. The world know you not. Your kindred
after the flesh may despise you. Carnal professors may

revile and persecute you. Satan is enraged to tempt and accuse you. Yea, and your worst foes are most nearly allied to you: the flesh, with its corruptions and lusts, sin and unbelief.

Yet, saith the Head in glory, to his conflicting members on earth, "Fear not." Why? what consideration can dispel the anxious fears, and alleviate the distressing doubts of drooping disciples? Verily, the good pleasure of their Father; the eternal purposes of his grace; the immutable designs of his love. A kingdom is prepared for you. Earth, with all its power; sin, with all its malignity; hell, with all its rage and malice, shall never deprive you of your Father's love. O disciple, how does this heighten the mercy, and secure the inheritance! It is a free gift by Jesus Christ.

Poor soul, thou art fearing about thy interest in the kingdom of glory. Verily thou canst find nothing in thyself to give thee the least right to it. But thy Saviour plainly assures thee, it is of "thy Father's good pleasure." What power can avert that? Hast thou a heart to seek the kingdom? dost thou believe in and follow the Lamb? dost thou see *that* in Jesus which attracts thy affections? is the desire of thy soul after him, and to the remembrance of his name? Then hath the glory of this kingdom shined upon thine heart by the Spirit. No marvel that sin is thy grief and burden, while Jesus is the delight and hope of thy soul. The Father's gift is sure: and so is the way also; it is by Jesus. And "through much tribulation thou (and all the heirs) must enter into the kingdom." Acts 14:22.

JUNE 12.—*And that, knowing the time, that now it is high time to awake out of sleep: for now is our salvation nearer than when we believed.* Rom. 13:11

It is an affecting but a real truth, that wise virgins are apt to slumber and sleep, as well as foolish. Through the pressures of a body of sin and death, and the opiates of worldly ease and self-indulgence, they sometimes fall into a drowsy state and a dull frame of soul. Hence they lose their former delight in religious duties and spiritual exercises. Their love to God and their brethren grows cold ; their zeal for Christ's glory and his precious truth declines. The enemy takes great advantages against them, and would triumph in their entire destruction. But "He that keepeth Israel neither slumbers nor sleeps." Will the loving father suffer his dear children to sleep in their beds till devoured by raging flames ? If we, being evil, have such love for our children, how infinitely greater is our heavenly Father's love ? Therefore he alarms and awakens souls to duty and watchfulness.

Thus Paul, his faithful watchman, lifts up his voice of warning, cries the hour, and reproves disciples as acting unbecomingly : it being both unreasonable and unseasonable for those who know the time of day, to indulge sloth and heaviness. It is high time to awake out of sleep. Come, christian, look about thee, look up. The Saviour reigns. It is broad day. See the sun shining ; nay, just in its meridian. Thou art near thy journey's end, in sight of thy Father's house. Thy Lord is coming to meet thee. What ! wilt thou sleep on and take thy rest ? The Spirit says to thee, "Now is thy salvation nearer than when thou didst first believe." The Lord is at hand. "Let thy moderation, in care for the things of this life, be known unto all men."

Why grasping so much of perishing things ? Thou canst not hold them long. Off hands, before death makes thee quit thy hold. Think for what thou art spiritua.ly born, to what thou art called, and of what thou art soon to take possession. Verily, if thy soul is broad awake, thou seest things as they really are. Time, with all its toys and pleasures, how short ! Eternity, with all its rich glories and inestimable blessings, how long! Jesus, with all his preciousness in his adorable person and finished salvation, the best object of thy hope, love, peace, and joy. For shame, sleep not when the delightful presence and heavenly fellowship of such a Friend may be enjoyed! If the sense of this be lost by sleep, resolve with the church, I will not give sleep to mine eyes until I find the Lord. Psalm 132 : 4, 5

JUNE 13.—*Watch ye, stand fast in the faith, quit you like men, be strong.* 1 Cor. 16 : 13

Believers in the Lord Jesus partake now of his ever-lasting salvation. No enemy can deprive them of the full enjoyment of it in glory; because "they are kept by the mighty power of God." But we are daily to consider that it is "through faith." 1 Pet. 1 : 5. Do we believe in the atonement of Jesus' blood? do we rely on the perfection of his righteousness? Why so? Because the word of the Lord is the warrant for our faith. Hence, O soul, exhortations from the same word to duty are equally binding on thy life and practice. The same Lord who has saved us from our enemies, calls us to watch against them. Jesus, who is gone to prepare a place for us in glory, directs us how to demean ourselves in the way to it. Christian soldiers, shall we neglect the commands of the Captain of our salvation, when his glory and the peace and comfort of our own souls are equally concerned? Surely not.

Through watchfulness many evils are prevented, many blessings enjoyed. When a christian is off his guard, or asleep when he should watch, how is he exposed to attacks, and liable to fall by temptations of the enemy! It is for our good that the Lord commands it as our duty. It is through his power that hereby the good soldier of Jesus is enabled to stand fast in the profession, power, and comfort of faith. It was Paul's joy in the view of death, that he had "kept the faith." 2 Tim. 4 : 7.

Would you enjoy the same comfort? strive, in the strength of the Lord, to follow his example. Check the risings of unbelief. Oppose the workings of carnal reason Resist steadfastly in the faith the subtle devices of Satan This is our duty and wisdom. So shall we quit ourselves like men of valor; like victorious saints of old, who overcame every enemy "through the blood of the Lamb."

Droop not, O believer, thy strength is the Lord's omnipotence. Lift up thy head with boldness, thine enemies are vanquished by thy conquering Redeemer. Be strong. Look out of thyself. Look to the Strong for strength. Look unto Jesus continually. Rely only on the power of his might hourly. His arm is not shortened. The reliance of faith engages his power. The cry of faith obtains victory. There is an open and effectual door by which thou shalt enter into glory; but thou must fight thy way through. Consider daily, this is our motto, "More than conquerors through Jesus who hath loved us." Rom. 8 : 37. "Be strong in the grace that is in Christ Jesus." 2 Tim. 2 : 1.

JUNE 14.—*Blessed are the pure in heart; for they shall see God.* Matthew 5 : 8

Every institution of purification, under the law, referred to Jesus, the purifier of his people. Old Testament saints received inward purity of heart from the same fountain, Jesus; and through the same means, faith in him. Without this inward purity of heart, " without holiness, no man shall see the Lord." When Jesus comes to his temple, even the hearts of his people, he " sits as a refiner and purifier " Sinners are the objects of his

love. Sin is the accursed thing his soul hates. From this he purifies them. In purity and holiness his soul delights: with this he blesses his disciples. He then pronounces them blessed. He tells them wherein their happiness consists: Blessed are you whose hearts are pure; blessed are your eyes, for they shall see God.

"Who can bring a clean thing out of an unclean? Not one" of fallen Adam's race. Job 14 : 4. Such power belongs to God only. Man in no degree effects it. Yet every believing, regenerate man, is the blessed subject of purity and holiness of heart. No glory is due to him; but holy, blessed effects flow from it, to God his Saviour's glory, to his present felicity, and to his eternal comfort and joy. To thy shame, disciple, thou knowest, that being a child of an apostate, sinful parent, sin naturally was the only delight of thine heart.

It is thy present blessedness to be a child of the holy God, a member of the holy Jesus, a subject of the Holy Spirit's new-creating influence, and a partaker of holy faith. Hence it is natural to thy new-born heart to love holiness, as agreeable to the perfections of thy God and Saviour, and as suitable to thy present state of blessedness in Christ.

Whence those sighs and sorrows at finding the Canaanites still in the land? whence those groans and prayers because sin dwelleth in the flesh? whence those importunate cries and longing requests to Jesus, for total victory and perfect freedom from this troublesome inmate? whence that holy joy and sweet complacency in bringing forth "the fruits of holiness?" These are indubitable evidences that thou art united to a holy Jesus, that thy heart is purified by faith, that thou hast a heart cleansed from sin by Christ's blood. A new heart and a right spirit are put within thee Thou dost see God in Christ now as thy covenant God. Thou hast received covenant blessings from him. Rejoice in him. Shortly thou shalt see him, and enjoy him to all eternity in his kingdom and glory.

JUNE 15.—*And Mary hath chosen that good part, which shall not be taken away from her.* Luke 10 : 42

What the Lord said of Aaron's rod, is true of the hearts of all his people : " The man's rod, whom I shall choose, shall blossom." Numb. 17 : 5. To see a dead, withered stick, cut off from the root, bring forth blossoms, is a miracle in nature. So, when the soul of a once dead sinner shoots forth the blossoms of affection to Jesus, and chooses him as its portion and happiness, and brings forth fruits of holiness, this is a miracle of grace.

The love of Jesus to his people was not only conceived in his heart from eternity, but was manifested on earth in his life and death. So, when our hearts are made acquainted with this love, it cannot be hid. When Jesus is chosen as our treasure, our affections cleave to him, we follow him, our delight is to hear his voice, to sit at his feet, and attend upon the gracious words which drop from his lips. Blessed be his name, he indulges his people now in real, spiritual communion with him, though we enjoy not his bodily presence. This is our heaven upon earth. But it differs from the heaven of glory in that here many things interrupt our constant enjoyment of Jesus ; Satan envies it ; the flesh lusteth against it ; the world, with its profits and pleasures, allures us from it. And, indeed, the poor heart is oft-times ready to fear, I shall lose the grace and salvation of Jesus. Though, like Mary, the soul hath chosen the good part in time, yet it sometimes doubts of the enjoyment of its portion in a blissful eternity. But " He is faithful that promised."

But had not Martha also a part in this one thing need

ful? Doubtless. But still she was over careful, and too much cumbered about other things. This our Lord reproves. The same grace which was effectual in Mary's heart, influences the heart of every disciple to the same choice; therefore, what Jesus said to her in the days of his flesh, is written by his Spirit for our consolation and establishment in faith and love. Mary displayed the greatness of her soul in being satisfied with no object short of Jesus, and the humility of her heart in sitting at his feet. Poor, doubting, fearing believer, thy choice of Jesus is the effect of God's choosing thee in Jesus; therefore thy good part, thy happy choice, shall never be taken from thee; but thou shalt soon hear the voice of thy Beloved, saying, "Come up hither." "Where I am, there shall my servants be. If any man serve me, him will my Father honor." John 12: 26.

> "The soul that seeks me shall obtain
> "Immortal wealth and heavenly gain;
> "Immortal life is his reward,
> "Life and the favor of his Lord."

JUNE 16.—*Truly our fellowship is with the Father, and with his Son Jesus Christ.* 1 John 1: 3

"Can two walk together, except they be agreed?" Amos, 3: 3. No. There can be no sweet communion, no comfortable fellowship between God and man, except they be agreed. See then, this fellowship is enjoyed by faith; for by faith we are brought into agreement with God. Consider how the glorious Three concur to make our souls thus happy. It pleased God the Father that all fulness should dwell in his Son. He displays all his grace and glory, in the man Jesus, for the sinner's salvation. Hence he saith, "This is my beloved Son, in whom I am well pleased; hear ye him."

But we are averse to agree with God, and to hear Je-

sus. We prefer fellowship with the unfruitful works of
darkness, and having the devil rule over us, to fellowship with God in Christ. But the Spirit loves us with the
same love as the Father and the Son; he takes the
scales of ignorance from our eyes, and the veil of unbelief from our hearts; and then we fall in love with
Christ's precious person. Seeing our sin and misery,
we gladly hear and joyfully receive Jesus to be our Saviour. Then we come to the exact point where the Father meets and embraces us; even in his Son Jesus. He
saith to us, My beloved sons, all I have is yours. We say
to him, O our loving Father! all we are is thine.

And just as children of one family have sweet communion, loving intercourse, and agreeable fellowship
with each other, and with their common parents; so
have we with our heavenly Father and our blessed Redeemer. He speaks to us; we hear and obey. We pray
to him; he hears and answers. We have fellowship in
the Father's love, in the Son's salvation, through the
Spirit's grace. O what wonder of love is this! sinners,
of a mortal race, enjoy fellowship with the high and
lofty One who inhabits eternity. This is our highest
felicity below. Here we admire, adore, and love. Angels behold it with wonder and joy.

But this fills with envy and fires with rage infernal
spirits. Though Satan knows not our sweet fellowship,
yet he sees we hate fellowship with him in unfruitful
works of darkness. Hence he is our adversary. And all
the world he would stir up to implacable enmity against
us. But faith is our victory. As this fellowship is begun in faith, the Holy Spirit will maintain it below, till
we come to the full enjoyment of God and the Lamb
above. "Let us hold fast the profession of our faith
without wavering, for he is faithful that promised."
Heb. 10 : 23

ᴶUNE 17.—*Charity shall cover the multitude of sins.* 1 Pet. 4 : 8

Many have awfully deceived their precious souls by a sad perversion of these words. For they suppose that being charitable to the poor will cover the multitude of their sins from the sight of a sin-avenging God. Most fatal mistake! Hence, from such a vain, unscriptural notion, they are encouraged in their sinful practices. It is thy mercy, believer, to be delivered from such delusion by the truth as it is in Jesus. To atone for sin was his blessed work. He hath done it effectually by shedding his precious blood. And every believer in Jesus is the only blessed man whose sins are covered by his all-perfect righteousness. Here is the true source and spring of charity, or rather love, love to God and man. "We love God, because he first loved us;" (1 John 4 : 19;) and through the faith of this we obey his commandment, "Love one another."

Of this charity, or love, the most excellent things are spoken in 1 Cor. 13. It is in the heart of every believer. Love influences to put the best construction upon the behavior of others; to hide their faults with a veil of charity; to cast a mantle of kindness over their failings. Like the painter who drew the picture of Alexander with his finger on the scar in his face; so love would hide the scars and blemishes, and cover the sins of others.

Love sees no faults. See it exemplified in that most illustrious exemplar of charity, Jesus, in his deep and distressing agonies and conflicts in the garden, when one would have thought his dear disciples could not be so regardless of his sufferings, so deaf to his request, as not to watch with him one hour. But, instead of this, they indulged themselves with sleep. Here love covered this fault : "The spirit is willing." Love speaks what is right. Love finds an excuse for what is wrong, "The flesh is weak." And when the same most blessed pattern of love hung expiring in the greatest agonies on the cross, yet, amidst all the taunts and jeers of his enemies and murderers, love vented itself with his expiring breath, "Father, forgive them;" adding this as a veil or covering, "for they know not what they do."

Thus hath Jesus left us an example. He hath given us a new commandment, "Love one another." May the Spirit of love keep alive this heavenly temper, and blow up every spark into a fervent flame, that all men may know his disciples by this badge of charity or love, and be forced to confess, "See how these christians love one another." "Love is of God." 1 John 4 : 7

> " Love suffers long with patient eye,
> " Nor is provoked in haste ;
> " She lets the present injury die,
> " And long forgets the past.
>
> " Malice and rage, those fires of hell,
> " She quenches with her tongue ;
> " Hopes, and believes, and thinks no ill,
> " Though she endure the wrong."

JUNE 18.—*Wherefore he is able to save to the uttermost all who come unto God by him, seeing he ever liveth to make intercession for them.* Heb. 7 : 25

When the strong blasts of temptations blow; the swelling waves of corruption lift up their heads ; malicious Satan casts his fiery darts ; the thunders of Sinai roar; the law threatens wrath and destruction; carnal reason pleads ; unbelief pronounces hopeless despair on them ; happy for believers to take up the language of faith expressed by God's children of old, "We are not careful to answer in this matter : our God whom we serve is able to deliver us ; and he will deliver us." Dan. 3 : 16, 17. Admirable faith and fortitude ! A shining example of Old Testament saints, worthy to be imitated by New Testament disciples. Such a conduct yields ease to the mind and peace to the conscience; while it confesses Jesus the only Saviour, it gives him the glory due to his name. And verily, according to their faith, so it was. They were saved to the uttermost. Though cast into the fiery furnace, they had the presence of Jesus; and he delivered them out of it unhurt.

Who can prescribe bounds to the salvation of Jesus? He saves according to his ability. Who can limit that which extends " to the uttermost?" Thou comer to God by Jesus, think not sin too strong in thee for Jesus to save thee from it. He is almighty to save, even " to the uttermost." Art thou not willing thus to be saved? Verily, faith longs for it, love desires it, hope expects it. Stagger not through unbelief. Our object of faith is a once crucified Jesus, an ever-living, interceding Man and Mediator, and who is also the omnipotent God. Is any thing too hard for the Lord? Why then should sin hold thee one moment under its power? why should it at all distress thy mind? Nay, it could not, but for thy unbelief.

Is not the strength of Jesus the most powerful encouragement for poor sinners to come to God continually? A throne of grace is ever open. A God of love seated on it. Jesus ever lives, and always prays. A salvation to the uttermost perfection is promised, and the infinitely powerful Jehovah able to effect it. Coming to God by Jesus—O this is a sweet mystery for faith to feed upon, and be nourished and strengthened by! We are confident of access; perfectly sure of acceptance by Jesus. We are not left to perhaps, or peradventure, because it is not founded upon ourselves, what we have done, or can do, but upon the eternal life, everlasting love, and unchangeable priesthood of Jesus. " The just shall live by faith." Heb. 10 : 38.

JUNE 19.—*Put ye on the Lord Jesus Christ.* Romans 13 : 14

Man is an active being. Happiness is his pursuit " Who will show me any good?" his continual inquiry— to seek it from wrong objects his constant practice Hence, naturally, we are ever restless and uneasy. The new-born soul only has found the centre of true felicity, real good, and permanent happiness, in the knowledge and enjoyment of his Saviour! Here paradise is regained; a heaven of bliss restored to his soul.

It is the peculiar glory of the Gospel that it ever presents a precious object to our mind, even Christ, from whom alone we derive peace of conscience, joy of heart, and transport of soul. Is there, believer, a day in the year, an hour in the day wherein thou wouldst pray to be excused from putting on the Lord Jesus Christ, as the perfection of thy nature and the adorning of thy soul? surely not.

As one made alive from the dead, the Holy Ghost, by the word, stirs up thy " pure mind by way of remembrance." Thou art not called to dream over dry, heathenish lectures of morality; nor, from philosophic rules, to acquire this and the other habit of virtue; neither art thou left to licentious liberty, to make provision for the flesh, to fulfil the lusts thereof. But it is to be the daily exercise of thy believing mind to " put on the Lord Jesus Christ," as the essence of every virtue; for in this consists all thy present comfort and holiness. And by this thou wilt become dead to all the pleasing, inviting objects that stand so thick around thee, to beguile thy mind and draw thy heart from its best Friend.

The miser calls his gold his own, it is his god. Hence he exercises all his affections upon it, and derives all his happiness from it. The man of pleasure is in continual search after the enjoyment of new delights from the gay surrounding objects of a perishing world. Infinitely greater blessings are christians called to. O believer, Jesus is thine.

In the exercise of thy mind and the affections of thy soul, put on thy Lord continually, as thy righteousness, strength, riches, pleasure, honour, thy glory, and thy all. Oppose Christ to all the pleasures of the world; to all the delights of sense; and every scene of vanity. Put on Christ in thy conscience; there plead the atonement of his precious blood, against the guilt of sin; the perfection of his righteousness, to every demand of the law; the prevalency of his intercession, against all thy fears; the freeness and fulness of his promises, against all thy doubts. Boldly withstand every accusation from Satan with, Christ hath died, yea, rather, is risen again; and ever lives to make intercession for us· " Who is he that condemneth?" Rom. 8 : 34.

JUNE 20.—*The end of all things is at hand: be ye therefore sober, and watch unto prayer.* 1 Peter 4 : 7

Yesterday we were born. To-day we live. To-morrow we die. The sum total of human life is justly calculated by the hoary-headed patriarch Jacob, " Few and evil have the days of the years of my life been." Gen. 47 : 9. A truth this that lies level with the common observation and judgment of all men; but is admitted into the regenerate heart and conscience only, with the importance it possesses, so as suitably to affect the mind and influence the conduct. Hence the absolute necessity of divine faith; the continual need of exercising our meditations upon the certain approaching dissolution of all things.

It is thus we learn to die daily to the perishing objects of time and sense; and to live like ourselves, immortal inhabitants of " a city that hath foundations, whose builder and maker is God." To live and lean upon our beloved Jesus, as the stay of our soul and the strength of our hope, is true happiness. While all things below perish in the using, invisible realities ripen in prospect, and most powerfully engage our affections, because they are durable and eternal.

Hence the believer is excited to watchfulness, that he may stand; to prayer, that he may be kept; and to sobriety, that he may persevere. Thou knowest, that the sin of open vice and excess is great; but know also, that the cares, riches, pleasures, and honors of this world as really intoxicate the mind as outward, gross sins do the body. What need, what daily need hast thou to watch constantly, be sober continually, and pray alway! Pride is contrary to sobriety of judgment of thyself. Lust and intemperance are inconsistent with the soundness of thy faith, the stability of thy hope, and the exercise of thy love. These are ever at hand to beset thee. Say, therefore, when canst thou dispense with a watchful frame of spirit? when intermit prayer and humble dependence on thy God; sweet exercise of watching unto prayer for divine power; in prayer, for sweet enlargements; after prayer, for a gracious answer from our Lord?

Ever may this just reflection be on thy mind, when tempted or inclined to cast in thy lot with the carnal, and to indulge thyself in attending the bewitching scenes of sin, folly and vanity, Am I now acting like one who knows the end of all things is at hand? do I conduct as one in his right mind? am I watching unto prayer? can I desire, pray for, and expect the sense of Jesus' love and presence to be with me? Remember thy calling: it is to love and live upon an unseen Jesus; and to act as daily expecting to receive the end of thy faith, the salvation of thy soul   1 Peter 1: 9.

JUNE 21.—*But thanks be to God, who giveth us the victory through our Lord Jesus Christ.* 1 Cor. 15: 57

Death, though conquered and disarmed of its strength and sting by our victorious Lord, so that it cannot destroy or even wound or hurt the soul of any one of his dear members, is yet an enemy, a formidable, disagreeable enemy to nature. When left to our natural conceptions, death appears to us with the grim visage of "the king of terrors." We cannot get rid of our fears; nor are we able to make him put on a more amiable aspect. But when, in the simplicity of little children, we go to our heavenly Father, and tell him how we are affrighted and terrified at the thought and approach of this dreadful enemy, he drives away our fears and terrors, and relieves our minds.

But how does our affectionate Father effect this? By telling us that we are perfect and sinless, and therefore have overcome death, shall never die, have nothing to fear, as death cannot hurt us? No. Though we are sinners in ourselves, and as such must die; though we are without strength to grapple with and subdue this powerful enemy; and though our bodies must fall victims to his stroke, yet, "praise the Lord, O my soul; praise him, all his saints;" he giveth us the victory. He puts songs of triumph into our hearts and lips; not for what we have done, but our Father refers us to the glorious achievements of our Redeemer and Lord. He hath obtained a perfect conquest for all the children of his Father's family; and victory is not only proclaimed, but given. Jesus is the unspeakable gift of the Father's love; victory over death is given through him: faith to believe it in the heart, and triumph over it in the conscience, is his free gift also. Thus the Spirit testifies of and glorifies Jesus. Thus his members rejoice in the truth, and are comforted by the truth.

Death was brought into the world by the father of

lies. He is vanquished and destroyed by Jesus, who is essentially the truth. "The soul that sinneth shall die."

"Die man, or justice must."

The man Jesus, the sinner's Surety, fell a sacrifice to this truth. Hence truth is fulfilled in his death. Justice is satisfied. Death disarmed of its sting, which is sin. Jesus hath "put away sin, by the sacrifice of himself." Heb. 9 : 26. And the strength of sin, which is the law, Jesus hath perfectly fulfilled in his life for us. He hath fully answered all its demands. By him all its accusations are silenced. Precious Christ! Happy believer! What harm can the most fierce, poisonous monster do thee when it has lost its sting and is without strength? Most precious truth! Death is yours. 1 Cor. 3 : 22.

"Now to the God of victory
"Immortal thanks be paid;
"Who makes us conquerors while we die,
"Through Christ our living Head."

JUNE 22.—*Then shall the King say unto them on his right hand, Come, ye blessed of my Father, inherit the kingdom prepared for you from the foundation of the world.* Matt. 25 : 34

We have a joyful word to our hearts now: "*Come, let us reason together, saith the Lord : though your sins be as scarlet, they shall be white as snow ; though they be red like crimson, they shall be as wool.*" Isa. 1 : 18. There is another precious word from Jesus to our souls, "*Come* unto me, all ye that labor and are heavy laden, and I will give you rest." But this last *Come,* from the lips of our King in the day of judgment, will be the most joyful, crowning word of all! Every soul who has tasted his love on earth, shall then drink his fill at the fountain-head, in a blissful, never-ending eternity of glory.

"Ye blessed of my Father;" beloved from eternity,

and blessed to eternity. Chosen in me; blessed in me with all spiritual blessings. I was given to you. I sought you, and gathered you to myself in time. Now come, live and reign with me for ever in my kingdom. Is not the thought of this enough to make us wish to break through the walls of our prison, the body? Pause, O soul! call together all thy faculties; rather, O Divine Spirit, realize the view, bring near the solemn, joyful day to our minds. Give us, even now, to dwell on it with rapture of affection and ardor of love.

"Inherit the kingdom prepared for you:" not bought by your good works; not purchased by your well-doings; not obtained by your faithfulness; but the free gift of my Father's love and good pleasure; richly prepared by his free grace and bounty, purposely reserved for you. Come ye all. Not one of my little flock shall be rejected; there is a mansion for each of you. Ere you had a being, or time commenced, the kingdom was established, the heirs chosen, places prepared. I visited you on earth; so that you loved me, though you saw me not. I invisibly wrought in your hearts, and drew them out in love to myself, my cause, and my brethren; so you approved yourselves my disciples, by following my example. Come ye, enter, possess, enjoy what you were born for, born again to be meet for. O methinks it strikes one's heart with heavenly joy to conceive of the loud hosannas and shoutings, (O that we may catch the heavenly flame,) "Salvation to our God, who sitteth upon the throne, and unto the Lamb." "Unto Him that loved us, and washed us from our sins in his own blood, and hath made us kings and priests unto God and his Father; to him be glory and dominion for ever and ever. Amen." Rev. 1:5, 6.

> "Now to the Lord, that makes us know
> "The wonders of his dying love,
> "Be humble honors paid below,
> "And strains of nobler praise above."

JUNE 23.—*Things that accompany salvation.* Hebrews 6:9

Mary mistook Christ for the gardener. John 20:15. We are very apt to mistake our graces for our Saviour. Some put their faith in the place of Christ's righteousness, as if we were justified by our faith, and not by the righteousness of Christ. But hereby the glory of Christ is eclipsed. The sinner's eye is turned from the Saviour to himself. His trust is placed in his graces instead of Christ. He mistakes the things which accompany salvation, for salvation itself.

What are the things which accompany salvation? Naturally, we have none of them. We have only the things which accompany damnation. We never work them in ourselves. They are the train of graces which attend the King of saints. The Saviour brings them with himself into the saved sinner's heart.

They are the graces of his Spirit: *Faith* in Jesus, as a redeeming, justifying, sanctifying Saviour. *Repentance* towards God, as receiving and pardoning sinners in Christ: hatred of sin, and turning from sin to Christ. *Hope*, which is an anchor of the soul, keeping it steady in the expectation of what the word promises and faith believes. *Love* to God, excited by his love to us in Christ. *Peace* with God, through our Lord Jesus Christ. *Joy* in God, having now received the atonement by faith. *Heavenly-mindedness*, by living on Jesus. *Deadness to sin*, by the body of Christ. Deadness to the world, being crucified with Christ. Living to holiness, being alive unto God through Jesus Christ. Love to our brethren and fellow-sinners, having passed from death to life. And add to all the rest, constant dissatisfaction with ourselves, seeing we still are miserable sinners, imperfect creatures, unprofitable servants.

We look on nothing within us as our title to glory, but look wholly and solely to Jesus. These graces we receive out of his fulness. These are evidences of inte-

rest in him, make us meet for heaven, and accompany
salvation. For we have fellowship with God and his
Son Jesus Christ. Paul was persuaded of these things
concerning his christian brethren. See then the glorious
nature of christianity. The faith of the Gospel and the
hope of salvation are not empty notions. But " whom
God justified, them he also glorified." Rom. 8 : 30.
Those whom he adorns with the glorious robe of Christ's
righteousness, he makes glorious with the graces of his
Spirit. "What God hath joined together let not man put
asunder." Matt. 19 : 6.

JUNE 24.—*To this man will I look, even to him that is poor, and
of a contrite spirit, and trembleth at my word.* Isa. 66 : 2

The Lord, whose throne is in the highest heaven and
whose footstool is the earth, here inquires after a place
of residence and rest. As though about to quit his
throne, he looks to man. Behold he tabernacles in man.
He makes the human nature his temple. Hence he
"looks" to his brethren in the flesh, however poor,
miserable, and distressed. As his look of love is towards
them, so he brings them to look for mercy from him.

But we are all naturally too rich in our own eyes to
be indebted to his grace, too stubborn of spirit to bow
to his sceptre, and too stout-hearted to hearken to his
voice and submit to his righteousness. Well, glory to
the Lord, he has mercy for rebels as well as heaven for
saints; yea, of stubborn rebels he makes humble saints:
" The day of the Lord of hosts shall be upon every one
that is proud and lofty, and upon every one that is lifted
up, and he shall be brought low." Isa. 2 : 12.

O soul, dost thou see thy poverty, infinitely in debt
to law and justice, and liable to be cast into the prison
of hell! Give glory to the Lord. The day of the Lord
is upon thee; the light of truth has shined into thee;

and as though there was not another man upon the earth, the Lord looks to thee, even to thee, thou poor sinner.

Thou sayest I abhor myself, I tremble to look at myself, I am so poor, so miserable, and so wretched. Surely the Lord must turn away his eyes from me with loathing and abhorrence. No, " To this man will I look," saith the Lord. Yes, saith the humble soul, If I had but "a contrite spirit," if I did but tremble at God's word, I might think so, I should hope so ; but I can see nothing in myself why the Lord should look upon me and love me. I tremble to be found in myself.

O, if the Lord had not looked on thee as he did on Peter, thou wouldst never have had such a contrite spirit, nor such a trembling heart. Jesus beholds and loves his image there. He was once a poor man as thou art. He had not where to recline his weary head, or to find comfort for his sorrowful soul, but in and from the loving breast of his dear Father. That is thy case ; instead of being a proud Pharisee, why art thou a poor sinner ? Instead of making a mock at sin, why is thy heart broken for sin ? Instead of despising the Lord's word, why dost thou tremble to be found out of Christ ? All, all is because the Lord looks to thee. O look, look unto him and be saved from all thy doubts and fears ! Thy poverty and contrition are not the grounds, but are blessed evidences of salvation. Our Lord assures us, "Blessed are the poor in spirit, for theirs is the kingdom of heaven." Matt. 5 : 3.

JUNE 25.—*In whom also, after that ye believed, ye were sealed with that Holy Spirit of promise.* Eph. 1 : 13

Some consider this sealing as the highest assurance, which but few obtain. Others, as a state of perfection in holiness, and entire freedom from the being of sin, which indeed no one enjoys in this life. But it is plain the apostle means nothing more than what all believers in common are favored with. *In believing* ye were sealed, says the learned Mr. Hervey. That is, as soon as ye received the truth in the love of it, ye were sealed by the Spirit as the children of God, by faith in Christ Jesus.

Consider *what is implied* in being sealed. The use of a seal is to make an impression of its contents. Sealing an instrument is making it valid, and acknowledging it as our act and deed. The heart of a believing sinner, melted by the word and Spirit of God, is the subject of this sealing. The contents of this seal is *grace* and *truth*, which came by Jesus Christ. John 1 : 17. This is sealed upon the heart by the act and deed of the Holy Spirit. This impress of salvation by the grace and truth of the Son of God, is made so deep and lasting on the believing heart, that time with all its changes, sin with all its malignity, the world with all its charms and frowns, and Satan with all his power and fraud can never, never efface it. It will remain as the impress of the seal on the wax. It answers to the revelation of Jesus made in the word, as the impressed wax to the seal. Such a sealed heart is God's jewel. He has distinguished it as his own. It will receive no other impression but from the broad seal of heaven, salvation by the blood and righteousness of the Son of God *only*. Now, is this seal upon your heart? Do you reject with abhorrence every other hope? Do you believe in, look to, and trust Jesus for all your salvation? Rejoice : you are sealed. For, consider further,

All believers are sealed. The sealer is the Spirit of *promise*. He is alike promised to all the believing members of Christ. They are heirs of promise. They have fled to Jesus for refuge, and laid hold of him as their hope : and nothing but consolation, yea, strong consolation awaits them from the God of promise. He is the

Holy Spirit. By this sealing he impresses the heart
with the love of Christ, of truth, and of holiness. And
he hereby fulfils our Lord's prayer for his members,
" Sanctify them through thy truth." John 17 : 17.

Therefore, though in heaviness through manifold
temptations; though in dejection from many enemies,
let not go your confidence of faith. Count not yourself
an unbeliever. Think not yourself under the curse of
the law. Deny not the Spirit's work. For if you believe
on Jesus in your heart, " ye are sealed unto the day
of redemption." Eph. 4 : 30.

JUNE 26.—*Lord, remember me when thou comest into thy
kingdom.* Luke 23 : 42

When Joseph had interpreted the chief butler's dream,
how pathetically does he plead with him! " Think of me
when it shall be well with thee." Gen. 40 : 14. But alas!
such is the base ingratitude of man, that all was in vain.
When restored to his dignity at court he thought no
more of poor Joseph in prison. Exalted stations raise
the mind above feeling for the distressed. But it is not
so with the King of kings. He is ever the friend of poor
sinners. He remembers us in our low estate. Behold,
for us he hangs on the accursed tree between two accursed sinners. One was taken, the other left. See your
own state in both.

Behold in one the marvellous power of the Lord's
sovereign grace. Here is a reviler of Jesus changed
into a suppliant to him. There was no alteration in any
outward circumstances. All things continued just the
same. Christ hung, to all appearance, as a mere man
dying at his side. What then caused the change in him?
O hide your heads and blush at the proud notions of
your own righteousness! fall down and adore distinguishing grace. One malefactor is left to himself, and

expires blaspheming Jesus : the other dies believing in him and praying to him. He was snatched, by grace, from the gates of death and hell, as a brand which our Saviour would not suffer to be burned. Now, do you see your nature to be as wicked and your state as desperate as this thief's ? then you will be humbled. Do you see that nothing but the same grace of Christ can save you ? then you will exalt the free grace of Christ.

See *the effects* of this grace. He owns the justness of his sentence, reproves his fellow-criminal, and proclaims the innocence of Christ. O fall down and own that the sentence of the law which curses you for sin is just. Repel the pride and self-righteousness of your heart. Exalt the love and grace of our Saviour.

Hear *his prayer*. "LORD, though thou diest as an ignominious man, yet thou art the Lord of life and glory. *Remember me.* There is no Saviour but thee, no salvation but by thee. I am a hopeless, helpless sinner ; unless thou save me, I must be damned eternally. Thou art a King. Thou hast a kingdom. O bring my soul into it !" Now, have you just the same plea this thief had ? Have you no other ? Do you desire no better ? Do you expect salvation from the same Saviour, on the very same terms ? Then you are taught by the same Spirit, have the same faith in, and shall soon be in glory with the same Lord, who " is rich " in mercy " unto all who call on him." Rom. 10 : 12.

JUNE 27.—*If any man have not the Spirit of Christ, he is none of his.* Rom. 8 : 9

This is one of the most awful truths in the Bible. He who hath not the Spirit of Christ, doth not know Christ, will not believe on him, cannot love him. Then that dreadful sentence stands against him and, living and dying so, will certainly fall upon him—" If any man love

not the Lord Jesus Christ, let him be anathema, maran
atha," that is, under the most dreadful curse, till the
Lord cometh to execute the severest vengeance of it.
1 Cor. 16 : 22. Jesus, Master, save us from this. Holy
Spirit, rather let us be destitute of every blessing than
want love to Christ. O shed a Saviour's love abroad in
our hearts, and that shall kindle ours.

What is it to have the Spirit of Christ? How may
we know that we have the Spirit of Christ? Consider
the appellation here given—the Spirit of CHRIST. This
will greatly help us to solve these questions. You may
perceive the spirit of a man by his temper and conduct.
The men of this world have the spirit of this world.
Their walk and conduct show it. They set their affections on the world, seek all their happiness in it, and expect all their comfort from its riches, honors and pleasures. So it is with us all by nature. We have not the
Spirit of Christ. But when the fulness of time comes,
according to his covenant engagements with God the
Father and God the Son, God the Spirit is pleased to
visit our souls. Then he opens our eyes to see both
our own sin and misery, and to behold the righteousness and happiness there is in Christ. He enables us to
believe in Christ, to delight in the things of Christ, and
cry out, None but Christ, none but Christ be my portion
in time and to eternity.

Have we a sigh in our hearts after Christ to be our
wisdom, righteousness, sanctification, and redemption?
This is the Spirit of Christ. Do we groan under a body
of sin and death, and cry out, Oh wretched that we are,
who shall deliver us? Do we thank God for Jesus Christ
as the only Saviour, justifier and deliverer? Then we
have the Spirit of Christ. Can we come to a throne of
grace, seeing ourselves miserable sinners, yet believing
that "the blood of Jesus Christ cleanseth from all sin,"
and the righteousness of Christ justifies from all con-

demnation, and therefore cry, God be merciful to me a
sinner; Jesus, save me or I perish? This is from the
faith of Christ. This is the prayer of faith The Spirit
of Christ has inspired it. We have the Spirit of Christ.
Do we delight to hear of Christ, to have fellowship with
Christ, to live upon Christ, to walk with Christ, and to
have the power of Christ's grace subdue the power of
sin in our hearts, lips, and lives? Then verily we have
the Spirit of Christ. "The flesh lusteth against the Spirit, and the Spirit against the flesh, so that ye cannot do
the things that ye would." Gal. 5 : 17.

JUNE 28.—*Jesus said, my mother and my brethren are these who
hear the word of God and do it.* Luke 8 : 21.

Looking at things which are not seen keeps the soul
from fainting and invigorates it to every holy duty. Do
I believe Christ now thinks of me and is this moment
pleading my cause in heaven? how then can I live
estranged from him on earth? "True," replies one, "if
I did but know that Christ loved me." How do you
expect to know it? Do you believe he loved his mother
and his brethren after the flesh? It cannot be doubted.
See then how near and dear to Christ, in a spiritual
sense, are all who hear the word of God and do it. They
are no less intimately allied to him by faith, and in
spirit, than his mother and his brethren were by blood.

To hear the word of God implies, to have such an
understanding of it, faith in it, hope from it, and love to
it, as to cause our souls to delight in God, and our affections to cleave unto him. Paul speaks of tasting the
good word of God. Heb. 6 : 5. There is a precious
savor in the word. To hear it is to have a spiritual
relish for it. Just as food is savory to the palate, so is
the word of God to the soul.

The word testifies of the word; the letter of the

word, of the spirit of the word: the written word, of the essential Word: even the Lord Jesus. In the word God speaks of Christ, by Christ, and of himself in Christ. Therefore to hear the word of God, is to receive Christ into the heart by faith, to know the Father's love in him, and to expect full and final salvation by him.

There is also a still and small voice, in which our beloved speaks internally the words of his Gospel. He says, "My sheep hear my voice." We know the voice of our Shepherd. It is the delight of our souls to hear him. Is this all? Do we only hear? Blessed be God, we are *born again* by the word of God. 1 Pet. 1 : 23. Therefore we not only hear the word of God, but do it. What is implied in this? That God's precepts are regarded by us as well as his promises. The one being fulfilled in us, causes the other to be dear to us. In one word, where there is a heart to hear the word of God, there is a desire to do the will of God. These are inseparable.

Let us not deceive ourselves. "This is his commandment, that we should believe on the name of his Son Jesus Christ, and love one another." 1 John 3 : 23. In believing we have everlasting life. John 6 : 40. In believing we enjoy the blessings of it. 2 Cor. 6 : 6. In doing the will of God we evidence that we are born of God. 1 John 2 : 17. O may "the word of Christ dwell in us richly, in all wisdom." Col. 3 : 16.

JUNE 29.—*The kingdom of heaven suffereth violence, and the violent take it by force.* Matthew 11 : 12

We say, hunger will break through stone walls. Desperate circumstances make men violent. Thus it is with a convinced sinner. He sees himself in the city of destruction. And Moses has set his house on fire about his ears, as Bunyan says in his Pilgrim's Progress. Now, he cannot think of God, sin, death, judgment, heaven and hell, with an air of indifference. No; he is awake. He sees their importance. His soul is alive. He feels the weight of them. He finds sin has destroyed him. The law terrifies him. Death stares him in the face Judgment alarms him. He trembles to see "hell moved from beneath" to receive him. Now his morality and fancied good works do not avail. He hungers after righteousness. His apprehensions of wrath make him violent. His hunger is keen. He besieges the kingdom of God with earnest prayer. He forces his way through every opposition. He breaks through every wall of obstruction with, "O give me Christ, or I perish. Give me his blood to pardon me, his righteousness to justify me, or I am lost for ever." This is fleeing for refuge. This is like one escaping for his life from dreadful flames and devouring fire. This is being violent. Such take the kingdom of God by force.

Though by grace we are brought into the kingdom of God, and enjoy pardon of sin and peace with God through our Lord Jesus Christ; yet the Lord forbid that we should so lose our conviction of divine truth as to have done with holy force and violence. Soldiers of Christ, to arms. What! think of laying down your arms and folding your hands to sleep on an enemy's ground, when all around are up in arms against you? There is enough yet before you to alarm you and to call up your violence. Sin is within you. Satan is plotting against you. The world would ensnare you. Death and judgment approach you. "The day of the Lord will come as a thief in the night, in which the heavens shall pass away with a great noise, and the elements shall melt with fervent heat, the earth also, and the works that are therein, shall be burnt up." O, dream not over dry doctrines and empty speculations, so as to be proof against the force of these solemn events, and to lose your holy violence. For " seeing that all these things shall be dissolved, what manner of persons ought we to be in all holy conversation and godliness, looking for the coming of the day of the Lord." 2 Pet. 3 : 11, 12.

JUNE 30.—*We having the same spirit of faith, according as it is written, I believed, therefore have I spoken : we also believe, and therefore speak.* 2 Cor. 4 : 13

We should greatly admire these phrases, "according as it is written," "according to the Scriptures." If our faith is not founded upon these, and agreeable to them, it is only a delusion. "The *same* spirit of faith." With whom? Paul ever has his eye upon Christ. He refers to Psalm 116 ; where Christ speaks by the mouth of David. But what need had Christ of faith? Never forget that he was *perfect man*, like unto us: as such, all the graces of the Spirit dwelt in him : *Faith* in his Father's promise. *Hope* in his love. *Delight* in his law. *Zeal* for his glory. Holy fear and reverence of his name. You see the whole chain of graces in that passage, "Who in the days of his flesh, when he had offered up prayers and supplications, with strong crying and tears, unto Him who was able to save him from death, and was heard in that he feared." Heb. 5 : 7. Here is faith in the ability of God, hope in him, prayer to him, fear of him, &c. This is joyful to consider : there is not a grace in us but what was in Christ our Head, and flows to us from him.

"The *spirit* of faith." It is a spiritual gift. It is a lively grace. It is not a dead notion in the head, but it brings the enjoyment of God into the heart. If we share in the graces of Christ on earth, we shall surely enjoy his kingdom in glory.

See the genuine *effects* of faith. We believe, and therefore *speak*. Faith in the heart opens the lips. We shall speak to God the Father, as to *our Father*, with the holy boldness and loving confidence of children. We shall delight to draw near to him, to tell him of our sorrows, our enemies, our sins, yea, of all that is in our hearts. For like as a father pitieth his children, so the Lord pitieth them that fear him. Psalm 103 : 13. *For* the glory of God, we shall speak of his everlasting love, the freeness of his sovereign grace, and the riches of his abundant mercy in giving his Son to be our Saviour. We shall speak of his Son's redemption of us from all sin: the glory of his righteousness in justifying us from all condemnation ; and everlastingly saving us from sin to holiness, from hell to heaven. We shall speak to the glory of the Spirit, of quickening our dead souls and making us happy in the Father's love and the Son's salvation. Such is the spirit of faith. Lord, help our unbelief. Lord, increase our faith.

July

JULY 1.—*I have blotted out as a thick cloud thy transgressions, and as a cloud thy sins ; return unto me, for I have redeemed thee.* Isa. 44 : 22

Thus of miserable sinners God makes happy saints. Here is the work of each divine person in the everglorious Trinity. God the Father blots out sins in the court of heaven: God the Son by his atonement on the cross: and God the Spirit in the court of a sinner's conscience. Believe and enjoy the comfort of this. "Now the God of hope fill us with all joy and peace in believing," and make us to "abound in hope, through the power of the Holy Ghost." Rom. 15 : 13.

When the dear women came unto the sepulchre to see our Lord, they said, Who shall roll away the stone from the door? Mark 16 : 3. But behold it was done. So a poor broken-hearted sinner says, "This thick, black, impenetrable cloud of my sins intercepts from my soul the light of God's countenance; it prevents the comforting rays of the Sun of righteousness from shining into my soul. O, who can disperse it? None but God." Behold he hath done it, and he assures us of it. Look within and be humble, look up and be joyful. Did you think a storm of divine wrath and terrible vengeance was gathering over your guilty head? Behold, love speaks, grace proclaims, mercy declares, I have dispersed the cloud : I have blotted out thy sins.

Grace superabounds over all the aboundings of sin. A deluge of pardoning love, mercy and grace washes away all thy transgressions. They are all dispersed like a cloud driven away by the sun. What! all this rich love, mercy and grace to such a hell-deserving sinner as I am? and that too without any deserts of mine? Yes, all is of rich love, free grace and sovereign mercy.

But behold the end of this. It is to attach thy heart to a sin-pardoning Lord. For he says, "Return unto me." O, nothing attracts the gracious heart from sin, the world and vanity, to the Lord, like free and full declarations of Gospel grace and pardoning love. O my soul, return from thy backsliding ways, thy unbelieving thoughts, thy jealousies and suspicions of thy Lord's love, unto him. For "I have redeemed thee." Look on thy sins, see thyself redeemed from them by blood divine. Look to heaven; see it purchased for thee, and secured by thy Redeemer's righteousness. Now glory in being and living like a son of God and a joint heir with Christ. O may his blood make all serene within. May that purge our conscience from all dead works to serve the living God. Heb. 9 : 14.

JULY 2.—*Is not this the carpenter's son?* Matt. 13 : 55

"Such indignity I cannot bear: such insult is intolerable." Ah! who, what art thou who speakest thus? Thou proud worm of earth, look unto Jesus. See, the King of kings, the Son of God becomes a man, the son of a carpenter; yea more, himself a carpenter, the son of Mary. Mark 6 : 3. Mark his condescension; hence learn humility. Behold his treatment and contempt. Learn patience and submission. Astonishing mystery! Let reason bow and faith adore.

Sinner, behold with joy and wonder, thy God in flesh. Born under that curse for sin, " in the sweat of thy brow thou shalt eat thy bread," Gen. 3 : 19, He follows an ordinary occupation. O ye great and mighty, who are above trade, and despise those who follow it, saved ye must be by this carpenter's son, or perish everlastingly. He is the one and only object of hope and salvation He is God and man in one Christ. One, not by conversion of the godhead into flesh, but by taking to himself our nature.

Well might Isaiah style him WONDERFUL. Chap. 9 : 6. He is so, both as God and as man, and as God and man in one Christ, wonderful in love, sufferings and power to save sinners. Wonderful in his humility, for he made himself of no reputation, and took on him the form of a servant. The Jews were "astonished at him, and said, Whence hath this man this wisdom, and these mighty works?" Yet they were offended in him, because of the meanness of his birth, parentage and education. Such is the folly of judging of Christ by sight and sense.

" Blessed is he (says Christ) who shall not be offended in me." Matt. 11 : 6. It is the blessed nature and peculiar office of faith, to pierce through the mean appearance of the humanity, and to see the godhead of Christ. Here is the sure evidence of our calling; though he is "to the Jews a stumbling-block and to the Greeks foolishness," yet he is "to them who are *called*, Christ the power of God, and the wisdom of God." 1 Corinthians 1 : 23, 24.

Now do you see salvation finished by the power and according to the wisdom of God by this carpenter's son? humble as he appeared in the eyes of others, do you see such matchless beauty, such divine glory shine in his person and works, as to say, "My Lord and my God?" O beware of looking on this as a common call. Know it is of special, peculiar, distinguishing grace. Give glory to the Holy Spirit for it. Rejoice at the condescension of thy Lord : love him for it : all was for thy salvation. Rejoice in him; though to the eye of sense humble and obscure, yet he is "able to save unto the uttermost all who come unto God by him." Heb. 7 : 25

JULY 3.—*Comfort ye, comfort ye my people, saith your God*
Isaiah 40 : 1

Who are the people of God? I am of that number, says one, "for I feel my heart to be full of comfort." It may be so. Then this text is not for thee. But it will do thee no harm to examine into the nature of thy comforts, their tendency, and how thou camest by them.

Saith another, "I am sure I cannot think myself one of the people of God." Why not? "Because, instead of the comforts of God's children, I have continual sorrow and conflicts, am oppressed by Satan, harassed with temptations, groan under a body of sin and death, and tremble lest, after all, I shall perish in my sins through unbelief." Thou art the very person, one of the happy number of the Lord's people, of whom he here speaks. He describes his people as poor and afflicted who trust in his name. Zeph. 3 : 12.

What is his holy and blessed will concerning you?

It is that you should be comforted. He knows your sorrows. He sees you want comfort. He therefore commands it to be administered unto you. This is a commission peculiarly directed to the Lord's ministers. I am not honored with that high calling; yet the Lord may graciously condescend to administer comfort by means of one so weak and unworthy as I am. For Paul says to private christians, "*Comfort one another* with these words." 1 Thess. 4:18. Therefore it is our duty. The Lord succeed us in it.

Mind then, thou poor sorrowful sinner, who art afflicted, tossed with tempest and not comforted; behold, thy Lord is mindful of thee. Take notice of the love of his heart, the tender compassion with which he speaks concerning thee: "*Comfort, comfort.*" Thou hast sorrow upon sorrow in thyself. Here is comfort upon comfort from thy Lord. He is the God of all consolation. Nay, look not within to find any cause why thy Lord should have such love to thee, or concern for thee. The cause lies in his own loving heart. He freely gave his Son for thee, he freely promises his Spirit to thee, he commands comfort to be spoken to thee.

Now, wilt thou go and indulge thy besetting sin of unbelief, and say after all this, "My Lord careth not for me, he hath forgotten to be gracious unto me?" O, rather bring tnat bosom sin of unbelief to thy Lord; beg of him to slay its power, that it dishonor him no more by disbelieving his precious word: for he saith, "Can a woman forget her sucking child, that she should not have compassion upon the son of her womb? Yea, they may forget, yet will I not forget thee." Isa. 49:15.

July 4.—*O death, where is thy sting? O grave, where is thy victory?* 1 Cor. 15:55

Says a celebrated poet, "All men think all men mor-

tal but themselves." True, there is a natural propensity
in us so to think; but new-born souls not only know
that they are mortal, but in the exercise of grace they
can indulge the thoughts of death with pleasing reflec-
tions. For death is not only a conquered enemy by the
Captain of our salvation; but he is also enumerated in
the catalogue of our blessings: "DEATH is yours:"
yours to deliver you from all sin, sorrow and temptation;
yours to introduce you into the presence of your God
and Saviour, and into the enjoyment of all the glory and
blessedness of his kingdom.

But death has a sting and the grave a victory: this
sting is sin: and what gives strength to sin and victory
over the sinner, is the law: that darts the sting into us,
and so fixes it in us, that, for any thing we can do, we
must feel its poisonous sting to all eternity. But, "Who
is this that cometh from Edom with dyed garments from
Bozrah? This, who is glorious in his apparel, travelling
in the greatness of his strength?" He answers, "I that
speak in righteousness, mighty to save." Isaiah, 63 : 1.
It is that glorious warrior, our almighty conqueror, Jesus,
who has disarmed death of his sting and obtained a
complete victory over the grave.

Do you ask, what is this to us? Truly we can draw
no comfort from it unless we believe in him and look
upon his victories as obtained for us: thus viewing our
triumphant, risen, ascended Saviour, we shall be enabled
in the confidence of faith to say, "O death, where is thy
sting?" Thou hast lost it in the flesh of Christ; by his
death he hath taken it from thee; through death he hath
destroyed him who had the power of death, that is the
devil; and delivers them who, through fear of death,
were all their life-time subject to bondage. Hebrews
2 : 14, 15.

Art thou in bondage through fear? Who holds thee

under it? Thy worst enemy, the devil. By what means? Unbelief: because thou dost not believe thy best friend, thy dear Redeemer. Dost thou say, I would believe, but cannot? what! canst thou not believe thy Lord? He says to all thy doubts, "*I speak in righteousness:*" I have wrought out and brought in an everlasting righteousness, to clothe your naked soul, and to make you stand before the throne of God perfect and entire, lacking nothing. Believe this, and triumph over sin and death. "*Mighty to save*"—can the power of sin, death and hell withstand my might? "Look unto me and be saved" from thy bondage and fear. Receive his word: rejoice in the comfort of it: Christ hath fulfilled it; "O death, I will be thy plagues; O grave, I will be thy destruction." Hosea 13 : 14.

JULY 5.—*If in this life only we have hope in Christ, we are of all men most miserable.* 1 Cor. 15 : 19

Here is a supposition, and a consequence drawn from it. Consider, this *hope in Christ*. It is not common to all men; it is a precious grace of the Holy Spirit; it springs from faith in Christ; it looks to the promises in Christ, and is nourished and supported by them. It is a *lively hope*, we are "begotten again to it, according to the abundant mercy of God our Father, by the resurrection of Jesus Christ from the dead." 1 Peter 1 : 3. By it we are made to differ from all other men, who, though they may talk of hope in God, yet have no hope, but are without Christ and without God in the world. Ephesians 2 : 12. Here is the proof of it: "Every man who hath this hope in him purifieth himself, even as he is pure." 1 John 3 : 3. Mind, Christ is the object of this hope, it is IN, or ON Christ. The man who is the subject of it purifies himself. How? By the blood of Christ, and by the grace of Christ. From what? From all sin:

from the love of this world: from its pomp and vanities. He lives not in them; he walks not after them; he hates them; he despises them. Hope in Christ springs up in his heart; this kills the love of the world in him.

What is it to have hope *in this life only?* It is to have our prospect bounded by the narrow limits of time: to take up with the joys and pleasures of the present world; to set our affections on them, and seek all our happiness in them, without looking and longing for the invisible glories of a better world.

Why then are we " of all men the most miserable ?" Because being new creatures in Christ, we have a new and spiritual nature in him and from him, we have communion and fellowship with him; and therefore cannot enjoy the pleasures, honors and riches of this world as other men do: we are " crucified to the world." Galatians 6 : 14. We are also often called to encounter the malice, hatred, and persecution of the men of the world for our hope in Christ. And we are miserable from the burden of a body of sin, which others feel not : from the fiery darts of Satan, which he aims not at others ; the workings of unbelief, which others feel not; that we ever offend the Lord, which others care not for: that we cannot perfectly and perseveringly obey his will in all things, about which others concern not themselves; that ever the Lord hides his face from our souls, which others know nothing of. From these, and innumerable other things, christians, as mere men of the world, may be " of all men most miserable." But, O blessed hope in Christ, " He is our hope." 1 Tim. 1 : 1. While Jesus lives our hope lives. Time with all its changes cannot frustrate it : death with all its terrors cannot destroy it: eternity with all its glories will be the end and fruition of it.

JULY 6.—*The wrath of God is revealed from heaven against all ungodliness and unrighteousness of men.* Rom. 1 : 18

One sin ruined the whole race of Adam; it brought curse and wrath upon every soul of man. Every man that ever lived, that now lives, and that ever shall live upon the earth, is by nature a child of wrath, and the wrath of God is revealed from heaven against his sin; not one soul excepted. How is this wrath revealed?

It was revealed at the giving the holy law at Mount Sinai. Exod. 19. There the Lord revealed all the terrors and glory of his majesty, as the most holy, sin-hating God. O, think of the mount that burned with fire, the blackness, darkness, and tempest; the awful sound of the trumpet: the terrible voice of words, which they who heard, entreated that they should not be spoken any more; and so terrible was the sight, that even Moses said, "I exceedingly fear and quake." Heb. 12 : 21. O think of this, and think not what is called the least sin to be small; for it has lighted up the fire of God's wrath.

See the wrath of God revealed in drowning the old world; in burning Sodom and Gomorrah; in the destruction of Korah; and in his judgments upon the ungodly in all ages. "God is angry with the wicked every day." Psalm 7 : 11. The fire of his wrath and indignation ever smokes against all sin. Remember this and be watchful.

Reflect on the wrath of God revealed from heaven, in the sufferings of his beloved Son for the sins of his people. See the sin-atoning, curse-sustaining Lamb of God on the cross. There see what sin is; there view the indignation of God against it, and the awful vengeance he executed upon it. O my soul, think of thy Saviour's inconceivable suffering for sin. Here see the exceeding sinfulness of sin; view its crimson dye in the

purple gore of the Son of God. Ever think of this, love
the Lamb, and strive against all sin.

The wrath of God is revealed against sin even in his
own children. He hates their sins. Beware of any
doctrine that makes light of sin ; or which would represent that God has not the same abhorrence of sin, indignation and wrath against sin in his own children as
in others. Do not hold the truth in unrighteousness ;
never think of reconciling a holy God to sin.

The wrath of God is revealed in the conscience of
his people. By the law is the knowledge of sin. Rom.
3 : 20. And the law worketh wrath. Rom. 4 : 15. It fills
the mind with terrible apprehensions of the wrath of
God, and a fearful looking for of his judgment and
fiery indignation against sin.

Bless Jesus that his blood cleanseth from all sin ; and
remember the awful day when God will "take vengeance on them who obey not the Gospel of Jesus
Christ." 2 Thess. 1 : 8.

July 7.—*Let us search and try our ways, and turn again to
the Lord.* Lam. 3 : 40

The book containing these words is justly styled, THE
LAMENTATIONS. The dear children of God were now in
captivity and deep distress. Jeremiah most pathetically
enumerates and laments their great calamities. We
shall never get out of this book of Lamentations while
in the body. We daily see cause for lamentation on one
account and another ; and indeed if we did not, it would
be a sad sign that our eyes are blinded by self-righteous
pride, or our hearts hardened through the deceitfulness
of sin. "As sorrowing, yet always rejoicing," is the
christian's motto. Times of calamity and seasons of
distress call for self-examination and soul-searching.
This will keep down murmuring and complaining.

"Let us *search*," look and inquire for something that may support and comfort us, and teach us to improve our distress. Soul, let thy circumstances be what they may, thy Lord's advice is ever seasonable : "Search the Scriptures." Why? They testify of ME. John 5 : 39. Christ is the head of the covenant : in him the Father loves us : through him his love flows to us. Afflictions flow from covenant love, and shall answer covenant purposes. The Scriptures are written for our comfort There we find that we have the common lot and inheritance with all saints.

Let us *try our ways* by that standard of justice and perfection, the law of God. O how will this make the sense of sin abound in our eyes! Is the law of God holy? our ways are unholy. Is the law spiritual? we are carnal, sold under sin. Is the law just? our ways are unjust. Is the law good? in us, that is, in our flesh, dwells no good. What must we do? Must we sit down in melancholy, give up all hope, and write despair upon our hearts? No, blessed be God ; though sin has destroyed us, there is salvation in the Lord for us.

Let us *turn again to the Lord :* such is the acting of a gracious heart : having once tasted that the Lord is gracious, and known the precious love of Christ, it cannot be happy in sin ; it cannot bear to live at a distance from the Lord, its life and love. Believing that all our iniquities were laid upon Christ, that he bore them in his own body on the tree, it cannot rest till it again finds pardon in his blood, the peace of God, and joy in the Holy Ghost. Bless the Lord, O my soul, for that gracious word, "Return, ye backsliding children, and I will heal your backslidings." Jer. 3 : 22.

> "Sin and the pow'rs of hell
> "Persuade me to despair;
> "Lord, make me know thy cov'nant well,
> "That I may 'scape the snare."

JULY 8.—*Godly sorrow worketh repentance to salvation, not to be repented of.* 2 Cor. 7 : 10

By setting forth the curses of the law and the terrors of hell, a sinner's conscience may be made to tremble under the dread of damnation; he may be said to repent. Judas thus " repented himself," and said, " I have sinned." He might be sorry for it; his sin might make his heart ache and fill his soul with horrors; but here was no *godly* sorrow; God was not in his heart; here was no repentance unto salvation; this was out of his sight; his repentance was unto damnation; for " he went out and hanged himself." Matt. 27 : 5. Natural fears and legal terrors may excite sorrow without the grace of repentance.

What then is godly sorrow? It springs from God, it is excited by the views of God, it is directed to God, and arises in the heart on account of God. With David the soul cries, " Against *thee only* have I sinned." Psalm 51 : 4. The heart is pierced to the very quick with anguish for having sinned against a God in Christ, a sin-pardoning, a soul-comforting, a most affectionate Father. This is the sorrow of faith; it is grateful to God.

Again, it *worketh repentance:* it causes the soul to change its mind and its conduct. Its *mind:* sin and Satan had deceived it; it foolishly fancied there were some sweet charms in sin that could make it quite happy; but it now feels the wormwood and gall of it; it looks at its sin, and looks at its Saviour, and cries, O my Lord and my God, could I ever be so mad as to turn from thee to sin? I lament my folly; Jesus, pardon me. Its *conduct:* godly sorrow causes the soul to turn away from sin with loathing and detestation, and to turn to the Lord with humble faith, holy hope, ardent desire, and earnest cry, " Cast me not away from thy presence; take not thy Holy Spirit from me; restore to me the joy of thy salvation." Psalm 51 : 11, 12. Though sin has made me miserable, yet thou, and thou only canst make me happy.

This repentance is " unto salvation :" it brings the soul to Jesus. There is salvation in him, and in no other. Acts 4 : 12.

This repentance is " not to be repented of." O my soul, canst thou ever change thy mind concerning the precious salvation of Jesus, by repentance unto life from a godly sorrow for sin ? Beware then of those " fools" who " make a mock at sin;" Prov. 14 : 9; of those who deride godly sorrow for sin, and laugh at all repentance as downright legality. " Except ye repent," says Jesus, " ye shall all perish." Luke 13 : 3.

> " 'Twas for my sins my dearest Lord
> " Hung on the cursed tree,
> " And groan'd away a dying life
> " For thee, my soul, for thee.
>
> " Whilst with a melting broken heart
> " My murder'd Lord I view,
> " I'll raise revenge against my sins,
> " And slay the murd'rers too."

JULY 9.—*The grace of God that bringeth salvation hath appeared to all men.* Titus 2 : 11

Here are three blessed and glorious truths : they demand the constant attention of our minds ; they tend to sink into the deepest humility of heart, to excite the greatest joy of spirit, and to inspire the most ardent love and gratitude of soul.

Salvation : this was the counsel of heaven ; the work of the Son of God : the wonder of angels ; the envy of devils, and the glory of apostate, rebellious sinners ; sinners who are born with enmity of heart, rebellion of will, and hatred of affections against God, and who have manifested the enmity of their mind by wicked works; the rebellion of their will, by taking arms against the Lord; and the hatred of their affections, by refusing to lay them down and submit unto him : O that precious word, full of wonder, grace and love, " God commendeth his love towards us, in that while we were yet sinners, Christ died for us—when we were enemies, we were reconciled to God by the death of his Son." Rom. 5 : 8–10. This is a salvation worthy a God of infinite love to bestow; here is a Saviour worthy to be received with all readiness of mind, to be embraced with the most cordial affection, and to be gloried in as the richest blessing, by lost, hopeless, ruined sinners.

This salvation is *brought to us;* the news of it is sounded in our ears; the report of it is daily made to us; it is displayed and set before us in all its glory, richness, freeness and fulness, in the Gospel, that we may receive it and enjoy it, take it as our own, and rejoice in the salvation of our God.

It is brought to us by *the grace of God* which hath appeared. Where? In the person of the Son of his love, and in the Gospel of his grace : there the grace of God appears; there the salvation of Jehovah shines forth and is made manifest to all men; to all sorts of men, Jews and Gentiles. Therefore it is revealed, as a free and full salvation, worthy of ALL acceptation, free from all limitation and restriction.

Paul speaks of " knowing the grace of God in truth." Col. 1 : 6. This is done when any poor sinner receives and believes the Gospel : it then becomes the power of God to salvation to that poor sinner's soul : he then knows the free favor of God in Christ Jesus : Christ is all his salvation and all his desire : the Holy Spirit, who hath convinced him of sin, and enlightened him to see Gospel truths and Gospel grace, will comfort him by them. Hath the grace of God thus appeared to thee?

Hath it brought salvation to thy soul? Dost thou believe the Gospel? Then take heed of mixing any righteousness of thy own with thy faith and hope in the grace of God and salvation of Jesus! for this were to degrade both, and bring thy soul into bondage to the law of works.

JULY 10.—*His name shall be called—Counsellor.* Isa. 9 : 6

Litigious spirits are fond of law. Paul absolutely forbids the brethren of Christ going to law one with another. 1 Cor. 6. Among other reasons, this is the greatest : they are concerned in a suit which will last their whole lives, and which requires all their time and attention. Though their cause has been tried again and again; though they have gained cause after cause; yet their adversary continues as litigious as ever; he is continually accusing them and preferring fresh bills of indictment against them; he sets the world upon us; he stirs up the flesh in us; he brings heinous charges against us; he is the accuser of the brethren before God, and to our own consciences, night and day. Rev. 12 : 10.

Have you heard nothing from Satan, your adversary and accuser, this day? If you have, be not dejected; let him accuse, and do his worst; it is our unspeakable comfort that we have a wonderful Counsellor : he pleads our cause before the throne of justice above; he pleads within us in the court of conscience : he counsels and advises us by his word and Spirit; his true and righteous pleadings for us shall prevail over all Satan's accusations against us. Would you wish your cause in better hands? Never attempt to take it out of his : continually consult him : leave all to him : for consider :

Jesus in the eternal counsel voluntarily, unsought and

unasked, stood forth and engaged to be our Counsellor;
as a generous counsellor in court, seeing the poverty of
an arraigned prisoner, freely, without money or price,
undertakes to plead his cause. O wonderful love! O
kind compassion!

He is a *wonderful* counsellor; for though law and justice condemn, yet he obtains an acquittal in court for all
his clients. Most wonderful in his plea. Not our innocence, sincerity, goodness—no; he owns our guilt
and vileness; he pleads his own work for us; the blood
he shed for our sins; his obedience unto the law for our
justification; and his sufferings for our salvation. *Justice* says, I am satisfied, I forgive them. *Truth* records
the sentence. *Mercy* declares, I will save them.

O wonderful Counsellor! It is sinners, none but sinners thou pleadest for: for this my soul loves thee. God
be merciful to me a sinner! This is ever my plea. I
take it up. Lord, show me from law and justice that
thou art just, whilst thou justifiest the ungodly. Desperate as my case is, may I ever flee to thee, and ever
consult thee: "Thou hast the words of eternal life."
John 6: 68.

JULY 11.—*Men ought always to pray, and not to faint.*
Luke 18:1

Then there can be no room for despair; for prayer
exports wants and imports blessings. But our dear Lord
knows there is in us all, at times, a backwardness to
prayer; this he would remove: it arises from fainting; this he would prevent; therefore he opposes praying to fainting, for fainting prevents praying. Have you
not found it so? When weary and faint in your mind,
when your spirits are oppressed, your frame low and
languid, you have thought this is not a time for prayer—
yea, but it is: pray *always*. Now sigh out the burden

of your heart and the sorrows of your spirit: now, though in broken accents, breathe your complaints into your Father's ear: now cry to Him who loveth you and careth for you with the love and care of the most tender and affectionate father.

What makes us faint? Do troubles and afflictions? Here is a reviving cordial: "Call upon me in the day of trouble, I will deliver thee, and thou shalt glorify me." Psalm 1:15. Does a body of sin and death? Here is a supporting promise: "Whosoever shall call upon the name of the Lord Jesus, shall be saved." Rom. 10:13. Do we faint because we have called and prayed again and again to the Lord against any besetting sin, prevailing temptation, rebellious lust, or evil temper, and yet the Lord has not given victory over it? Still, says the Lord, pray *always*—persevere; be importunate; faint not; remember that blessed word, "my time is not yet come: but your time is always ready." John 7:6. "Watch and pray, that ye enter not into temptation." Matt. 26:41. Note the difference between being tempted and entering into temptation.

We are assured that in due time we shall reap, if we faint not Gal. 6:9. Do we find the spirit willing, but the flesh weak? and because of our coldness, deadness, and languor in prayer, do we faint? You cannot pray as you would: you think your prayers are irksome to God; and therefore do you faint and are ready to give over praying? Look at David; he begins to pray in a very heartless, hopeless way, "How long wilt thou forget me, O Lord? for ever?" but see how he concludes: he breaks out in full vigor of soul, "I will sing unto the Lord, because he hath dealt bountifully with me." Psalm 13:6. Above all, look to Jesus, who ever lives to pray for you: look for his Spirit to help your infirmities. Rom. 8:26.

JULY 12.—*Now abideth hope.* 1 Cor. 13:13

Gospel faith and christian hope are twin graces in the heart; they are inseparable. Faith exists not without hope; hope has no being without faith. Such as a man's faith is, such is his hope: they both flow from God's word, as light and heat from the sun. Take away the word spoken, and faith has no being. Without a promise made, hope has no existence. Faith receives and takes possession of Christ, as set forth in the word. Hope expects all promised blessings, comforts, and joys in him, with him, and from him, according to the word: "the word of God liveth and abideth for ever." 1 Pet 1:23.

Jesus, who is the essential Word, "is our hope." 1 Tim. 1:1. He is the cause of our hope, the object of our hope, and the life of our hope. Therefore our hope abideth: yea, though all in nature fails, all in sense forsakes us, and all as to outward appearances are against us; though Satan raises storms and tempests; though corruptions rage and foam, and lift up their boisterous waves; though like Paul we are in the great deep, and see neither sun nor stars for a season, yet hope abideth, for Jesus, the object of hope, lives.

The grace of hope cannot perish: it is an anchor to the soul: it keeps it sure and steady. Why? Because it is not cast within us, but without us. What a foolish mariner would he be who should think his vessel would ride safe and steady against wind and tide because he had an anchor on board! Just as foolish are those professors who cast the anchor of hope within themselves, on their own graces, inherent righteousness, as it is called, &c. Why, as the sea phrase is, the anchor will come home; it will not hold the vessel; there is no ground for it to fasten in: but the christian's hope "entereth into that within the vail;" Heb. 6:19; into heaven itself; it fixes and fastens upon Jesus, who has entered into heaven *for us*.

As by faith we receive the atonement of Christ for our sins, and trust in his righteousness for our justification, so hope looks for and expects the heart-reviving, soul-sanctifying comforts of this from the Holy Spirit in time, and all the glory and blessedness which Jesus hath by his life and death obtained for us in an endless eternity. Faith has to do with things invisible to sense. God's truth is the foundation of faith; faith keeps hope in lively exercise, "looking for that blessed hope and glorious appearing of the great God and our Saviour Jesus Christ." Tit. 2:13.

JULY 13.—*Ye were sometimes darkness, but now are ye light in the Lord: walk as children of light.* Eph. 5:8

Natural persons raised from indigence to opulence do not love to hear of their pedigree; they see not the hand of the Lord in it; what detracts from their person and merit hurts them: but disciples of Christ love to hear of, love to look back upon what they were by nature, that they may ascribe fresh praise to the Lord, who of his mere grace "raised their poor souls out of the dust, and lifted their needy souls from the dung-hill, and has set them with the princes of his people." Psalm 113:7, 8.

We are here reminded, "Ye were"—what? dark, having some glimmering light of God, his truths, his ways? Nay more, darkness itself; blind to them, as if totally deprived of sight; ignorant of them as a beast; as dark about them as we should be about natural objects without the sun. We walked in darkness and knew not that we were in the high road to hell. But *now*, O wonder of grace! ye are—what? enlightened by the Lord? have light from the Lord? Yes, this is true.

But more, we have "light *in* the Lord," like the angel which John saw standing in the sun. Rev. 19 : 17. We have not only the light of life, but we are *in* Christ, who is the Sun of righteousness and the light of the world. Here we see our Father's glory shining in the face of Christ; feel his love in him; behold his grace and truth which came by him; enjoy precious promises in him; know the glorious doctrines taught by him: all which lead to him and centre in him.

Hence we look down upon the world with contempt, upon sin with abhorrence, upon Satan with defiance, upon carnal men with pity, and up to our Lord with love and praise ; for " we have an unction from him, and know all things." 1 John 2 : 20. His truths are our delight: "His commandments are not grievous." 1 John 5 : 3. Here is all comprised in one word, *walk as children of the light*.

But how shall I know I am a child of light ? Strange question ! As if a person with his eyes open at mid-day were to ask, how do I know I see ? But if you do not enjoy the comfort of light it is because you do not walk as a child of light ; there are many such. No marvel they are unhappy professors. Paul wept on account of such. See them described : " They mind earthly things." Phil. 3 : 19. They have a tongue for Christ, but the world has their heart. Beware of such ; refrain from them ; for " if we say that we have fellowship with Christ, and walk in darkness, we lie, and do not the truth : but if we walk in the light, as he is in the light, we have fellowship one with another," and " the blood of Jesus Christ his Son cleanseth us from all sin." 1 John 1 : 6, 7.

JULY 14.—*Where two or three are gathered together in my name, there am I in the midst of them.* Matt. 18 : 20

Our hope and comfort rise or fall according to our

conceptions of what Christ is in himself, and what he is to us. Attend to this: you will find this true in your experience. Therefore it is of no small moment whether you believe Christ to be " God over all," or only a mere man: nay, it is of the utmost importance; it enters into the very life, peace, and joy of your soul. He here puts this beyond a doubt. None but God is at one and the same time in more places than one; but Christ declares, Wherever my disciples " are gathered together in my name, there am I :" therefore Christ is the omnipresent God; this is the joy of our faith; this the glory of our souls: and it should be our grand concern to bring this into experience and practice.

Remember, " the eyes of the Lord are in every place, beholding the evil and the good." Prov. 15 : 3. O soul, what have you to do at places devoted to sin and vanity? Know the eyes of the Lord are there: if he sees you there he will surely make you smart for it.

Our Lord delights in the assembly of his disciples in his name, even if but two or three, and no matter where. O let this call up your attention to his name; let this reprove professors that they do not always meet in Christ's name, speak to each other more of his glorious person and precious salvation; this is the way to be helpers of each other's faith, hope and love in the Lord. Be ashamed of yourselves, ye professors who can talk fluently of the things of the world, but are dumb when Jesus is the theme. What! can you go day after day without calling your family together to speak a word of Jesus to them and to Jesus for them? O, of what seasons of peace, comfort, and heavenly-mindedness do you deprive yourselves! The presence of a king makes a court: the King of kings makes a court, a temple in your houses, yea, in your hearts, when you assemble in his name.

Let this precious word encourage you: " There AM I

in the midst of them." Have you not found it so ? The most unworthy of all has. There AM I, as though Christ was first there waiting for us. Can his presence be with us without shedding his light, life, liberty, and power among us ? No, no more than the sun can shine in its meridian without shedding upon us light and heat.

Remember, " two or three " are within the compass of the promise : not angels, not sinless men, but poor miserable sinners Christ delights to be in the midst of O love and praise our dear Lord for his marvellous condescension and this precious declaration : study more and more to improve it, to build up each others souls in him, and to glorify his precious name. See his affectionate notice of such, Mal. 3 : 16, 17.

JULY 15.—*The Lord thy God in the midst of thee is mighty : he will save, he will rejoice over thee with joy.* Zeph. 3 : 17.

A truly gracious heart is restless and unhappy when it experiences distance from the Lord : those who are alive to God cannot rest without enjoying his presence ; they will draw nigh to him, praying him, " Draw nigh to my soul and say, I am thy salvation." That precious word lives and abides in our heart : " Now in Christ Jesus " we poor sinners, " who in times past were far off " from God, " are made nigh by the blood of Christ." Eph. 2 : 13. Hence we are called upon, " Sing, shout, be glad, rejoice with all the heart." Yea, thou God-fearing, soul-trembling sinner, even thee the Lord has in his eye, and speaks from the love of his heart, " Fear thou not, let not thine hands be slack." Zeph. 3 : 16. Dread not thy mighty, thy many enemies ; put on courage ; lift up the hands which hang down ; take hold of thy Lord's word ; for,

The Lord thy God in the midst of thee is mighty : the might of the Lord his God was in the midst of the

heart of the young David when he went to fight the
Philistine giant. Hence you hear not one word of himself, of his own might and power, but "The Lord will
deliver now; I come forth in the name of the Lord:"
so Paul, "I can do all things, through Christ, who
strengtheneth me." Phil. 4: 13. Now here is the nature and work of faith: when Christ dwells in our hearts
by faith, self-confidence is destroyed: says the soul, I
am weak and helpless; I am not sufficient of myself to
think any thing as of myself, but my sufficiency is of
God. 2 Cor. 3: 5. This language is a proof that the
Lord is in the midst of that soul: he has proved that he
is mighty in it by "casting down imaginations and
every high thing that exalteth itself against the knowledge of God, and bringing into captivity every thought
to the obedience of Christ." 2 Cor. 10: 5. His mighty
salvation is begun in that heart; it has no cause for de
jection; for,

He will save: you believe the Lord's might; he is
able to save; his word declares this, and his work
proves his willingness: exercise your faith upon his
will to save you both from all your fears and all your
foes; cast your all upon *the will* of Jesus; for,

He will rejoice over thee with joy: it was his joy to
bleed and die in agony and blood for thee; it is his joy
that thou comest and criest to him as a lost sinner for
salvation: he will rejoice in his work for thee, his grace
in thee, and his salvation of thee. O, well mayest thou
be called on, "Rejoice in the Lord alway, and again, I
say, rejoice." Phil. 4: 4.

JULY 16.—*That he should gather together in one, the childrer.
of God who were scattered abroad.* John 11: 52

These words are like Samson's riddle, which **some**
read thus: "Food came from the devourer, and **sweet-**

ness from that which is violent or fierce." Judges 14 :
14. Caiaphas the high priest, though a devourer of Jesus, yet holds forth precious food : though violent and
fierce against Christ, yet he delivers sweet truth. Truth
is truth, though from the tongue of an enemy : yea, it is
a double confirmation of truth. If Christ is preached
let us rejoice, though even by bad men and from bad
principles. The Holy Ghost causes this wicked high-
priest to prophecy of Jesus. By these words the Holy
Spirit plainly instructs us in the following precious
truths : O that we may receive them in love !

Though the whole world is become guilty before God,
yet he has his people who are here called *the children
of God :* they were not so by nature, but children of
wrath, even as others : but God " predestinated them unto the adoption of children, by Jesus Christ, to himself,
according to the good pleasure of his will." Eph. 1 : 5.
Simply to believe this is to bow to the will of God : to
object to it is to cavil against God's good pleasure as
well as his mercy.

These children are all *scattered abroad :* every one of
them is turned to his own way of sin and folly ; they
delight in their distance from God ; they hate the knowledge of God, and are at enmity against his law : they
say unto God, depart, depart, we desire not the knowledge of thee : they sport themselves in their own delusions ; they would fill up the measure of iniquity till
their souls drop into hell : but,

They are to be *gathered together in* ONE : O the amazing mercy ! O the astonishing grace of this ! Christ is
this blessed ONE : he, like a good shepherd, gathers his
poor, scattered, lost sheep into himself : " unto him
shall the gathering of the people be." Gen. 49 : 10. "He
gathereth the outcasts." Isa. 56 : 8. They were given to
him of the Father. John 17: 12. Now are you deeply
concerned to know, what all the world care nothing

about, whether you are a child of God ? Here it is come
to a point. Has Christ gathered you ? Has he called
you by the grace of his word and by the power of his
Spirit to come to him ? Have you seen misery and destruction in yourself, and mercy and salvation in Christ ?
Can you say from your heart, Jesus, save me or I perish ?
If so, you are surely gathered by Christ : you are really
a child of God by faith in Christ : let sin, Satan, and
unbelief ever so much object against it, doubt not of it.
Here are two little words, worth the study of your whole
life, IN ONE : O, ever meditate upon the glory and blessedness of being *one in and with Christ Jesus*

JULY 17.—*Thou God seest me.* Gen. 16 : 13

" Why sayest thou," O trembling sinner, " My way is
hid from the Lord and my judgment is passed over from
my God ?" The Lord here asks thy reason and reproaches thy speech. Isa. 40 : 27. Look at Hagar, and
be ashamed of the unbelieving surmises of thy heart.
She was left to suffer sore distresses ; her mistress
treats her cruelly : she flees to a solitary wilderness :
here was no eye to pity, no hand to relieve, no friend
to comfort her ; but the God of providence follows
her—the angel of the Lord, rather the Lord, the angel,
the messenger of the covenant, the Lord Jesus the Saviour ; he found her, called her by name, inquires the
cause of her distress, and bids her return to her mistress. Hagar knew her Saviour : she sets up a memo-
rial of his sympathizing love for her and care over her :
she called the name of the LORD, who spake unto her,
Thou God seest me.

O, how much is implied in this ? In every distress
remember this for thy comfort, and in every perplexity
think of this for thy support, " Thou God seest me."
Let this be the daily watchword of thy soul. It implies

what the church says, "I was in his eyes as one who found favor," or peace. Song 8:10. "Therefore the eyes of the Lord are upon me, and his ears are open unto my prayers." 1 Pet. 3:12. His loving eyes looked upon me, pitied me when I was polluted in my blood, called me to enjoy his favor and his peace.

Am I in a wilderness of perplexity? Do I find no one who can comfort me? Do I think I have deserted the Lord, and therefore he hath deserted my soul? Still remember, "*Thou God seest me.*" He sees the sorrows, marks the sighs, and hears the complaints of thy laboring breast with an eye of sympathy and a heart of love; our great High Priest is most tenderly "touched with a feeling of our infirmities." Heb. 4:15. Therefore he searches after and follows us with this tender and compassionate call, "Return again to me." Jer. 3:1. "Come unto ME" ye weary and heavy laden, I will give rest and refreshment to your souls. Matt. 11:28.

Is there sorrow in our hearts for the folly of our ways, and this cry in our souls, "Oh that it was with me as in months that are past? This is because the Lord sees us in mercy, comes after us in love, and has not given us up in wrath: and what says he? I have seen his ways, and I will—what? O the riches of grace! "I will heal him." Isa. 57:18. *Thou God seest me:* O may I always live as seeing thee by the eye of faith; live in thy service, walk in thy fear unto thy glory.

JULY 18.—*The rod of the wicked shall not rest upon the lot of the righteous, lest the righteous put forth their hands unto iniquity.* Psalm 125:3

How shall we draw the line between the righteous and the wicked? How shall we distinguish them, seeing they are both alike the subjects of a wicked nature, derived from sinning Adam their father? The Holy

Ghost does this: he sets a mark upon the righteous, by which they are essentially distinguished from the wicked, in the first verse of this Psalm: *they trust in the Lord.* The wicked trust in themselves that they are righteous, trust in their own power to make and keep themselves so, and hope for God's favor and heaven, because they are so: they trust in their own wisdom to guide them through life, and to their own goodness to make them happy in death. The righteous are stript of their own righteousness: they are convinced of sin: they are poor, hopeless, desperate, and wretched in themselves. (Do you see your own picture here?) They trust in the Lord Jesus for righteousness to justify and entitle them to heaven; to cleanse them from sin: for wisdom to guide, power to support, grace to sanctify, and love to bring them to glory.

Now these two classes of persons are diverse from each other: the face of one is towards heaven, of the other towards hell. They are of two seeds, there is enmity put between them: the wicked have always a rod for the back of the righteous. Ay, and for wise and gracious ends the Lord often permits them to use it for a season; yet he will not suffer it to rest there long. Wicked Saul was a scourge to righteous David, so was blaspheming Sennacherib to good Hezekiah; and says the church, " Thou hast caused men to ride over our heads." Psalm 66 : 12. Yet David came to the throne. Hezekiah and his people were unhurt by the Assyrians: and the church says, " We went through fire and water, but thou broughtest us into the wealthy place."

Here is a reason why our Lord will not suffer the rod of the wicked to rest on the righteous: " lest he put forth his hand unto iniquity." We never suffer judgment, but mercy is in it: our troubles are dealt out to us by the hand of love: mercy is mixed with them all The Lord knows the righteous is but frail: he remembers he is but dust, and liable to sin: he is wise to prevent this. When oppression and trials from the wicked bring us low and make us cry to the Lord, then we honor his grace and his power, his truth and his love, by the affiance of our heart: "He will fulfil the desires of them that fear him, he also will hear their cry and will save them." Psalm 145 : 19.

JULY 19.—*O visit me with thy salvation.* Psalm 106 : 4.

There is no good obtained by paying trifling visits and receiving trifling visiters: the soul that is alive to God will be unwilling thus to sacrifice time : Christ hath redeemed us from our vain conversation. 1 Peter 1 : 18. Our grand business is to be contemplating, glorying in, and talking of his righteousness and his salvation all the day long: this was David's practice; if we followed it more, we too should say with him, " My lips shall greatly rejoice, and my soul which thou hast redeemed." Psalm 71 : 23. As our joy in Christ increases, vain impertinent acquaintances forsake us. Here is the cry of a convinced sinner, of a truly gracious heart; *O visit me with thy salvation:* this is a blessed frame of soul; Lord, help us to consider it, and animate us to live to thee. Here is spiritual sight and spiritual feeling. What is a christian without these? Truly sunk into a state of dead formality.

Here is spiritual *sight:* the poor sinner sees himself totally ruined, and that he must be eternally miserable, for any thing he can do to save himself: sin has destroyed him, and the law of God curses him; but he sees that Christ has perfectly fulfilled the law, suffered its curse, and eternally satisfied Divine justice. Thus is salvation finished: in the firm belief of this he cries, Visit ME, even me, a desperate sinner in myself, with the joys of thy salvation. O Jesus, I cannot be content with hearing of salvation, with seeing it is for sinners, with believing it is everlastingly finished for them, without tasting the joys and feeding upon the comforts of it in my own soul.

Here also is spiritual *feeling*. Laugh on, deride as you please, ye giddy multitude, the joys and sorrows of living souls. We feel the bitter of our misery as sinners we groan, being burdened with a body of sin and death; we cry out, Oh wretched that we are, who shall deliver us? But, blessed be God, "We do *know* and *feel* that there is none other name under heaven given to men, in whom and through whom we may receive health and salvation, but only the name of our Lord Jesus Christ:" this is the sweet feeling of faith; therefore in faith we cry, Visit ME, miserable ME, with thy salvation, Lord Jesus; make me feel the peace of God, which passeth all understanding; O shed abroad in my heart the love of God. The Lord keep our souls in this believing, praying, tender, loving frame below, till we come to full fruition above, rejoicing that we are made "wise unto salvation." 2 Timothy 3 : 15.

JULY 20.—*Know ye not your own selves, how that Jesus Christ is in you, except ye be reprobates?* 2 Cor. 13 : 5

Happy for ministers, when their mission from Christ is called in question, to appeal to their people's hearts to prove that Christ hath spoken to them. Happy for christians, to examine, prove, and know themselves, and to find Christ in them. Ignorance of ourselves lies at the bottom of error and self-deceit. Lord, help us deeply to consider this important question.

"Know ye not *your own selves?*" Come, you who are ready to judge ministers, find fault with them, and call their gifts and graces in question: look at home: know yourselves; be not puffed up: consider yourselves;

be humble. Your hearts are "deceitful above all things, and desperately wicked;" your nature is totally corrupt: in your flesh dwells no good thing! its motions are to bring forth fruit unto death: they tend continually unto sin. Know, that there is no difference in your nature from that of the most vile and abandoned sinner upon the face of the earth. If left to yourselves, there is not the most atrocious sin but you might commit; there is not a hell in which others are eternally suffering for sin, but what you justly deserve and would fall into: for your sinful nature is as reprobate, corrupt and adulterate as others, even as the most vile; yea, and your state is also by nature as bad as others, even *children of wrath*. Know ye not your own selves? Has the Spirit of truth made you thus acquainted with yourselves? Be not afraid to see and know the very worst of yourself. For,

Know ye not that "*Jesus Christ is in you*, except ye be reprobates?" Blessed distinction! In this the elect differ from the reprobate; the former have Christ in them; the latter reject Christ, and are without any true knowledge of him, faith in him, and love to him. What is implied in Christ's being in us? His dwelling in our hearts by faith: a clear knowledge of him, cordially receiving him, heartily believing on him, steadfastly cleaving to him, constantly abiding in him, steadily looking to him as he is revealed in the word, the righteousness of sinners, the atonement of the guilty, justification for the ungodly, and the Saviour of the hopeless, helpless, and desperate. Therefore, He is precious to us, as being suitable for us in his glorious person and all his blessed offices; hence our hearts go after him, our affections are placed on him, and it is the desire and delight of our souls to honor, serve and obey him: thus self-knowledge and the knowledge of Christ are the very criterion of salvation. O that we may sink into the depths of humility by the one, and rise to the heights of comfort, peace and joy by the other: so shall we prove that we have true christian experience of the love and grace of Christ.

July 21.—*Only believe.* Mark 5:36

A short answer to a case of great distress: a simple recipe from the greatest Physician: a grand catholicon, or universal remedy that suits all cases, states and circumstances, and is seasonable at all times. Look at this history: look to the Author of faith to profit by it. Here is a ruler falls at Christ's feet, beseeching help for his daughter at the point of death: Jesus went with him: before he arrives at the house news is brought that the child is dead: the Lord of life and death forbids the father's fears: *be not afraid;* he encourages his hope: *only believe.* Fears are natural to sinners; faith expels them. Christ restores her to life: joyful news for us.

Here is precious encouragement for our faith in every application to Christ: a marvellous display of his great love, ready will, and almighty power to help and relieve us: he not only restores at the last gasp, but when life is departed recalls it. If your soul is alive to God, you have experienced this: it was dead in sin: Christ quickened you: now he is your life; how are you to walk and enjoy the comfort of this? Only believe. How many hearts burn with indignation against this doctrine? How many taunt us, "O, you are all for faith, nothing but faith, only believe!" True, we are all for Christ, nothing but Christ, only Christ; and we can enjoy him only by believing: he reproves our slowness of heart to believe as our greatest folly. Luke 24:25. All our comfort flows from faith; all our misery from unbelief.

Bring this to a point. Are we groaning under the burden of inbred sin, vexed with sore temptations? Do we feel the accusations of conscience, fear the terrors of a broken law, see the drawn sword of justice in the hand of a sin-avenging God, and tremble at the solemn thoughts of death and judgment? Under all this, what can bring relief to our conscience, hope to our mind, and peace to our soul? *Only believe* that Christ hath redeemed, justified, and will eternally glorify us: this is death to our fears and life to our joys. Again, how is the life of holiness maintained? *Only believe* that walking in fellowship with Christ infinitely exceeds all the pleasures of sin, the joys of sense, and the happiness of the world. Faith elevates the soul above all this, and causes it to look down with a holy contempt upon it. Faith enjoys Christ, that is heaven in the heart. In this steadfast faith we are to resist Satan, 1 Pet. 5 : 9, and "overcome the world." 1 John 5 : 4.

JULY 22.—*Whosoever liveth and believeth in me shall never die, believest thou this?*   John 11 : 26

In a state of declining strength and dejection of spirits, and in consideration of the near approach of death, these precious words of our dear Lord were brought to my mind; and were as a comforting, reviving draught to my spirits. Lord, I bless thee for them. O, my soul, dwell on them.

Am I a sinner born to die? Is death the wages of sin? Must these eyes which now read these precious sayings be soon closed by death? Must the hand which now directs this pen be shortly stiff in death? Yet dost thou, my Lord, say, living and believing in thee, I "shall never die?" Dost thou ask me, "Believest thou this?" Lord, thou who knowest all things, knowest that by thy grace I can say, THOU ART THE SON OF GOD : thou hast fulfilled thine own promise, "O death, I will be thy plague; O grave, I will be thy destruction." Hosea,

13 : 14. "Death is swallowed up in victory." 1 Cor. 15 : 54. "Shall never die:" death has lost his form; he is changed from a substance into a shadow. Psalm 23 : 4. Only children and fools are afraid of a shadow.

Glory to thee, my Lord, that I am a man in understanding, and by thee am made "wise unto salvation." Death has lost both his sting and his strength; sin is atoned; the law is fulfilled: I believe in thee, O Jesus, who hast done both for the victory; it is mine; I have it in possession; thy word cannot fail; thou hast said, I "shall never die." The terrors of death are changed into the sweet composure of sleep. I shall soon fall into this precious rest, sleep in thee; thou shalt soon wipe away all tears from mine eyes; I shall awake with thee, and sin and sorrow shall be no more for ever. O, well mayest thou ask, "Believest thou this?" For in the faith of this consists all my comfort, which results in loving thee and glorifying thee in life and in death.

"Faith works by love:" it works by the Father's everlasting love, in giving his holy Son to be our Saviour: it works by the precious love of Thee, thou sin-atoning, law-fulfilling, justice-satisfying, death-conquering Son of God: it works by the love of Thee, thou soul-renewing, faith-begetting, sin-subduing Spirit of holiness and truth. This is the vital principle of love, from which faith springs, upon which it lives, and by which it works: here faith is all in all; for it brings Christ and all his victories into the heart, puts death and every enemy under our feet, silences all Satan's accusations and all legal condemnations. "This is the victory, even our faith." 1 John 5 : 4.

JULY 23.—*Beloved, if our heart condemn us not, then have we confidence towards God.* 1 John 3 : 21

A text misapplied is like a bone out of joint, which puts the body to pain: this text may have such an effect upon the soul; for, what poor sinner is there upon earth but his heart must condemn him for coming short of God's glory and perfect obedience to his holy law? Must he therefore give up his "confidence towards God?" This evidently was not the apostle's design: this would effectually destroy love to God, and take away the comfort of faith, that "there is no condemnation to them who are in Christ Jesus." Rom. 8: 1. What means he then? Plainly to establish our heart in the faith of God's love to us in Christ, and from this love experienced in the heart, to awaken love to our brethren in Christ; for the context shows that this is the scope of the passage. This also is an experienced truth, that if faith and love abate, our hearts condemn us and our confidence towards God grows weak: in proportion to our lively faith and warm love, confidence towards God is strong.

As to *faith:* the apostle calls on us, 1 John 3: 1, "Behold what manner of love the Father hath bestowed upon us, that we should be called the sons of God." Now, are you beholding, believing and living upon this stupendous love of God in Christ? Are you dwelling upon it? Does it engage your attention? Does it captivate your affections? Does it swallow up the low, inordinate love of the world? If not, your heart will condemn you; your confidence in God will abate; you will not delight in him with the affection of a child, nor draw nigh to him with joyful gladness, as to your loving Father.

So of *love:* it is of love to the brethren of Christ the apostle is here treating: lively faith in Christ ever begets warm love to our brethren; then we have strong confidence towards God, that he is our loving Father and we his obedient children; but if love be wanting, our hearts will smite and reproach us and confidence in God forsake us.

See hence, that all our comforts spring from our confidence towards God, and all our distress from our hearts condemning us for want of faith and love. O let us cry to the blessed Spirit to enable us to live more upon love, the matchless, everlasting, unchangeable love of God to us in Christ Jesus. Let us be thankful that he has given us feeling hearts, which are not like the wicked, hardened by the deceitfulness of sin; but are tender, to feel the least condemnation; and when our hearts condemn us, let us flee to our great High Priest, who is touched with a feeling of our infirmities. Heb. 4 : 15.

JULY 24.—*Wherefore let him that thinketh he standeth take heed lest he fall.* 1 Cor. 10 : 12

Formal professors of his name are called the Lord's people, as well as those who are possessors of his love : the former for want of love to God have no zeal for his glory : hence they are careless of their walk, and are liable to fall from the height of a towering profession into the bottomless pit of perdition. Possessors of God's love are also liable to fall into many things which may wound their souls, bring distress into their consciences, a dishonor on the name and Gospel of Christ, and give enemies an occasion to blaspheme that worthy name by which they are called.

O christians, see to your standing : you are called upon as you love your dear Saviour, as you value the peace of God and the comfort of your souls, to "take heed lest you fall." Be not high-minded, but fear : you stand by faith. The dreadful falls of others are here set before us for ensamples, types or patterns of the awful judgment of God against sin, and as a warning to us to beware that we fall not as they did.

They fell into *idolatry :* O beware of sacrificing your

precious time and attention to heathenish vanities. Any thing that takes your heart from God is an idol. Mixing with the wicked and profane, to partake of their carnal joys, is a species of idolatry. You as much as say I cannot find complete happiness in God, therefore I seek it here. " Covetousness is idolatry." Col. 3 : 5. A covetous man seeks that in his gold which can only be enjoyed in God: be sure the anger of the Lord will smoke against such.

They " tempted Christ :" O beware how you distrust the grace, power, and faithfulness of Christ to keep you and comfort you, so as to withdraw your faith in him, hope in him, and prayer to him : or tempt him, by presuming on his power to keep you in the midst of snares and temptations, while you wilfully run into them.

They " murmured :" O watch against a spirit of dissatisfaction with the dispensations of providence and the displays of grace : the pride of our nature is prone to find fault with both. What caused all this? They " lusted after evil things :" this is the source and spring of every sin : "When lust hath conceived, it bringeth forth sin, and sin when it is finished, bringeth forth death." James 1 : 15. What is the sovereign antidote against all this? Standing in and walking by the faith of the Son of God: this brings fellowship with God. Hence lust is killed in the heart, that it cannot break out into sin in the life : "Be ye therefore sober, and watch unto prayer." 1 Peter 4 : 7.

JULY 25.—*Make me to hear joy and gladness, that the bones which thou hast broken may rejoice.* Psalm 51 : 8

Of all the curses of sin, may the Lord deliver us from Antinomian licentiousness, which consists in being so hardened by the deceitfulness of sin, as to make light of it. Though David had been awfully licentious in his

practice, yet we see the grace of the saint shine forth
in his brokenness of heart, sorrow of soul, and contrition
of spirit for his sins.

Never quote David's dreadful fall, without his deep,
heart-broken sorrow and repentance: never think of
one without the other; lest you think slightly of the
most cursed evil of all evils, wilful sin against a gracious God. O who can tell the horrors of soul and
terrors of conscience David felt when he uttered these
words! Consider them, O my soul: the Lord make sin
more dreadful to thy view, and hateful in thy sight.

Spiritual joy and gladness of soul in the Lord had
forsaken him: what had the gratifying of his accursed
passions brought upon him! A guilty conscience, a
heavy heart, and a disconsolate soul: the spirit of peace
and joy was grieved at his conduct, and withdrawn
from his soul: Satan, the tempter, was now his accuser:
the ghost of URIAH appeared to his mind; the thought
of Bathsheba brought hell into his conscience: all within was terror: all around distress, and all above horror:
but the Lord had not given him up to a reprobate mind;
he convinced him of sin, and, by grace, broke his heart
for it. Hence, "behold he prayeth:" O, was it possible
to recall the accursed lust and bloody deed, he would
rather have parted with his crown and kingdom than
ever have been guilty of them. What would he not
now give to hear the joy of pardon from God, to make
glad his soul?

He complains of "broken bones." Who can describe
the pain of mind he now felt? A broken bone must be
extremely painful: but he seems to feel as though all
the bones in his body were broken: Lord, deliver us
from sin which caused it! But why does he ascribe
their being broken to God? Did not his fall cause it?
Yes. But he lay many months, as it were, benumbed
by his fall, and insensible of his hurt; but God con-

vinced him of his sins, and quickened him to feel pain.

O ye who make a mock of sin, see, God breaks the bones even of his beloved saints for it: better to groan with broken bones on earth, than under damnation in hell. O think of David's pains and groans under a sense of sin: remember, Peter "went out and wept bitterly" for sin: see hence the exceeding sinfulness of sin, but forget not the Saviour, "whose precious blood cleanseth from *all* sin." 1 John 1 : 7.

JULY 26.—*Behold, the skin of the face of Moses shone, and they were afraid to come nigh him.* Exod. 34 : 30

Here see the glorious effect of being on the mount with God, of having free access to him, and holy converse with him. When we draw nigh to God and he draws nigh to us, our souls catch the splendor and glory of his grace: this revives our countenance and makes our face to shine. Here is something worthy of our attention, for the inspired writer calls upon us, *Behold!* Lord, give us to behold this to our edification and comfort.

When Moses came down from the mount his face shone, but *he knew it not:* O, it is well for us, when we are so wholly taken up with the majesty and glory of our Lord, and see such splendor of grace and love shine in his countenance as not to be looking at ourselves and admiring our own gifts and graces: it is to imitate the worthless fop to look in a glass to admire ourselves.

Though Moses knew not that the skin of his face shone, yet others saw it and were afraid to come near him. Here behold the glory and majesty of the holy law of God; like the face of Moses, it darts its piercing rays of light and terror into the consciences of poor sinners: it works wrath, it fills the soul with the knowledge of sin, the fear of hell, and the dread of damnation: there is a glory in the law, though it ministers nothing but condemnation.

The face of Moses shone so that he was forced to put a veil on it while he was talking to the people. Did so much of the glory of the law shine in the face of Moses, but with borrowed splendor, that they could not behold his face? then how terrifying, how dreadful for sinners to stand before the majesty of divine justice, and to be arraigned by divine truth, as transgressors of the holy law of God? Who can bear the thought without terror? Who can bear the sight without death and destruction from the presence of the Lord? O think of the law in all its dread and terror: see sin in all its exceeding sinfulness; and then consider the ministration of righteousness which exceeds in glory through the love and grace of our dear Mediator: we are called to behold him, but not with a veil upon his face: for " we all with open face behold, as in a glass, the glory of the Lord." 2 Cor. 3 : 18.

Did the Lord cause the face of Moses thus to shine? Eternal praises to him, " he hath shined in our hearts, to give us the light of the knowledge of the glory of God in the face of Jesus Christ." 2 Cor. 4 : 6. In him we see the law fulfilled, its curse sustained, our souls redeemed from all its terror and bondage, and brought into the glorious liberty of the sons of God. " Ye are not under the law, but under grace." Rom. 6 : 14.

JULY 27.—*If we live in the Spirit, let us also walk in the Spirit.*
Galatians 5 : 25

These two things the enemy of souls works powerfully against: To keep sinners from coming to Christ for salvation; and when they come, to prevent their enjoying the comfortable knowledge that Christ is their Saviour: and our own legal hearts and wicked natures join the enemy of our peace and salvation in both. But love lives and reigns above : our Saviour sees how it is with us, and sends the power of his Spirit to help, relieve, and comfort us; the Spirit quickens us when dead in sin, and then guides us in our walk. What need we then of exhortations? Much, very much; for, consider, the walk is ours: to order our steps aright, is by the grace of the Holy Spirit. Our evidence and enjoyment of our interest in Christ are experienced only in a holy walk, or walking in the Spirit. The battle is the Lord's; yet David was to engage and conquer Goliath. " The Lord gave him the victory." 1 Sam. 17 : 47. Exhortations point out our weakness, our need of the Spirit's help, and they excite us to pray for it.

What is it to walk in the Spirit? It is to "mind the things of the Spirit;" those spiritual truths revealed in the Gospel concerning our hope of eternal life by the sin-atoning death and law-fulfilling life of the Son of God; it is to set our affections upon Christ, seek all our happiness in him, and expect daily support from him; to make his precious blood and everlasting righteousness our constant plea, expecting the reviving sense of God the Father's favor and love to us only in him.

Again, it is to go forward, step by step, day after day, looking for and depending on the Spirit's assistance to keep our souls close to Jesus, and to maintain fellowship with him; and to show that our hearts are simple and sincere, we shall be diligent in the means of grace, studious to exercise our graces on Christ, and be uniform in the discharge of every duty—what a blessed walk is this! This is the walk of comfort, peace, and holiness; do you not find it so? Persevere in it; so will you walk above the accusing terrors of the law, the grovelling life of sense, the defiling life of sin, the vain life of worldly pleasures, and the distressing life of Satan's power.

Wouldst thou enjoy spiritual comfort? Th can only be found in a spiritual walk. Dost thou complain for want of it? Examine thy walk; follow the Lamb wheresoever he goeth. Beware lest carnal notions prevail, and by living after the flesh you condemn what is truly evangelical and spiritual. "They who are after the Spirit, do mind the things of the Spirit." Rom. 8:5.

JULY 28.—*If we walk in the light as he is in the light, we have fellowship one with another, and the blood of Jesus Christ his Son cleanseth us from all sin.* 1 John 1:7

The walk of many professors seems to speak this language: "Why cannot we love the world, indulge ourselves in the ways of it, and yet enjoy fellowship with God? Now we have clear notions of the doctrines of grace, of acceptance with God, and justification before him, why need we be so very precise in our conduct?" As though they were desirous to walk as near as possible to the very borders of hell, and yet hope to arrive safe in heaven at last. Such walk not in the light of truth; in the comfort of love; in fellowship with God.

What is fellowship with God? It is a sweet, heartfelt concord, harmony and agreement between God and our souls; a mutual communion of spirits; a free communication from the Lord to us, and from us to the Lord: just as two loving friends have between each other, as though but one soul possessed both. Lord, to what a high, holy, and honorable state are we miserable sinners admitted: eternal thanks to thee, O Jesus, through whom we are admitted; and to thee, O Holy Spirit, who hast formed us for the enjoyment of this inestimable blessing. Lord grant that we may prize this sweet fellowship above all things, yea, above life itself; for what is life without it?

But how is this fellowship enjoyed? By walking in

the light: God dwelleth in the light. We must walk
where God is to have fellowship with him. Christ is *the
light:* God is in Christ: by faith in Christ we walk
with God, and have fellowship with him. Here the
Father is well pleased with us, and we with him: we
communicate to him our wants: he communicates to
us every rich supply out of the fulness of Christ. Christ
shines in the light of truth: in every doctrine which
flows from him and centres in him. Are we loved,
called, justified, sanctified, and preserved unto salvation? It is *in him:* we are to walk in that faith which
worketh by the love of these truths, worketh love to
them, and to God for them; and this faith and love is
contrary to all the darkness of sin and error. Christ the
light shines in all his commands: faith receives them:
in love we obey and walk in them.

But though we walk in the light, yet sin dwelleth in
us. What then? As sure as we have fellowship with
God, "the blood of Jesus his Son cleanseth us from *all*
sin." Did it cleanse us yesterday? So it will to-day, to-
morrow, and to the end of life. Who shall dare to set
bounds to the cleansing virtue of the blood of the Son
of God? No sin too great, no sinner too vile for this
precious blood to cleanse. The chief of all sinners
speaks from experience; let not one despair; for we
sinners "have boldness to enter into God's presence by
the blood of Jesus." Hebrews 10:19.

JULY 29.—*Return, ye backsliding children, and I will heal
your backslidings.* Jeremiah 3:22

Backsliding is a species of apostasy from the faith;
apostasy is the high road to destruction: total apostasy
will certainly end in eternal damnation; for there can
neither be repentance or hope for such a soul. The
Son of God is the only sacrifice for sin; this he once

professed to believe: but now he tramples on his precious blood, wilfully despises and rejects our Saviour; so that now he has only "a certain fearful looking for of judgment and fiery indignation," which shall devour every adversary of Christ. Heb. 10 : 27.

Most striking is the picture of such, drawn by Bunyan in his Pilgrim's Progress as a man in an iron cage who thus confesses: "I was once a fair and flourishing professor, both in mine own eyes and the eyes of others; I was, as I thought, fair for the celestial city, and had even joy at the thoughts that I should get thither; but I left off to watch and be sober; laid the reins upon the neck of my lusts; I sinned against the light of the word and the goodness of my God; I grieved the Spirit, and he is gone; I tempted the devil, and he has come to me; I provoked God to anger, and he has left me; I have so hardened my heart that I cannot repent. O, eternity! eternity! how shall I grapple with the misery I must meet with in eternity!" Lord, enable me to take warning by others, and obey thy gracious words, which prevent thy children's total apostacy from thee.

Observe the conduct of the Lord to such; he arraigns them in the former verses for treacherously departing from him, like a wife from her husband: O what perfidious, faithless conduct! for perverting their way before God; and for forgetting the Lord their God, which is the cause of every evil. If the objects of time and sense drive the memory of the Lord from our minds, though but an hour, how foolishly do we act! Our hearts imperceptibly backslide from the sense of his presence.

But, O the love of our Lord! Though backslidden, yet he owns us as *children*. O Father, thy love ever lives, though folly is in our ways. He calls in love, *Return.* May love cause us to take shame, fall down in sorrow, and cry for mercy. He promises, "I will heal

your backslidings:" I will freely and fully pardon them,
though ever so numerous, heinous, or aggravating, as
though they had never been committed. Backsliding
sinner! believe and rejoice: see the effects of this love
in the next meditation: O Lord my God, lighten mine
eyes, lest I sleep the sleep of death. Psalm 13 : 3.

JULY 30.—*Behold, we come unto thee, for thou art the Lord
our God.* Jer. 3 : 22

Peter was an awful backslider; his crimes deserved
hell; so do yours and mine: both he and we should be
sent there, if love did not reign in heaven, and grace
abound to sinners on earth. One look of love from
Christ broke Peter's heart, made him weep bitterly,
and earnestly return to a crucified Saviour. A bone
broken and set is said to be stronger than it was before:
and surely a heart broken by forgiving love grows
stronger in love. Having much forgiven, we love
much; I have often thought fresh love added speed to
Peter's feet, when he ran to the sepulchre to see his
dear, his crucified Lord. John 20 : 4.

See in the subject of our present meditation the happy
effects of gracious words from a loving Lord. We saw
the backsliding children arraigned, and their conduct
condemned in our last meditation! What was the sentence passed on them? Was it, "Go, ye wretches; ye
have gone from me in your ways, now I will be glorified
in your damnation?" No: break, hard heart; melt, O
frozen soul; bow, stubborn knee, and be as the sinews
of a new-born babe; for love everlasting, immutable
love lives; sovereign unmerited grace proclaims, *Return,
ye backsliding children,* (children still! O matchless
grace!) *and I will heal your backslidings.*

What say gracious hearts to this? Do they reply,
O this is fine doctrine! Come, let us continue to go on

to enjoy the world and sin, and delight ourselves in our happy distance from God? "O no: this is the language of reigning sin and pride. If left to themselves, so would men act; but a spark of free grace within us catches fire from gracious words without, and therefore it is, "*Behold*," see the effects of the Lord's rich grace and precious love; like fire it melts down our hard hearts, makes us lament our base conduct; affects us with the deepest sense of sin; inspires our souls with a hope of mercy and assurance of pardon, and "*we come unto thee.*"

Here we see the actings of a holy faith in the heart; it works by love; by the declarations of a gracious Father and Redeemer it works love in the heart, and it works by love in returning to God; and here is the joyful claim of faith; " FOR," O precious cause! " FOR thou art the Lord OUR God,"—were it not so, thou couldst never have borne with our vile conduct: never had a thought of mercy, or deigned a look of love towards us. O let covenant love and faithfulness ever bind our hearts to thee, that we may never more depart from thee, pervert our way before thee, or ever forget thee, O Jehovah, Father, Son and Spirit, our one God in Jesus.

JULY 31.—*Ungodly men, who turn the grace of God into lasciviousness.* Jude 4

From what the bee extracts honey, venomous insects will gather poison. The word of God, which is food to gracious hearts, is the sport and contempt of profane wits. An ungodly heart will convert the most wholesome truths of God's grace into the most poisonous effects: there ever were such men: there are such at this day, who preach some of the truths concerning the Lord Jesus, and the grace of God abounding to sinners in him, and yet with these maintain the most damnable heresies. They are the "fools who make a mock at

sin." Prov. 14 : 9. Personal holiness they practically
hold in derision : they "declare their sin as Sodom;"
"say unto the wicked it shall be well with him ;" and
they swallow up every unscriptural error in that damn
able heresy, all men shall be saved at the last.

One scarcely knows at which to wonder most, why
such persons should preach at all, or why any who
name the name of Christ can hear them ; but the Scriptures must be fulfilled : "There shall come in the last
days scoffers, walking after their own lusts." 2 Peter
3 : 3. I never knew of but one instance of a person
who had joined himself to these vile antinomians, that
escaped from their soul-destroying doctrines. My soul
rejoiced exceedingly for a visit from this aged disciple
of Jesus, who, through his precious grace, is brought
back into the ways of truth and holiness. When the
preacher asked him why he had left him ? he honestly
answered, "You had well nigh sent me to hell with a
lie in my right hand."

O, brethren ! as you love the holy Jesus, as you value your precious souls, as you prize communion with
God, peace of conscience, and joy in the Holy Ghost,
beware of such ungodly men ; keep at the greatest distance from them ; maintain the utmost abhorrence of
their soul-destroying notions. Why, O why did the
blessed Spirit convince us of sin, and lead us to Christ
for salvation, but that we should love God, delight in
God, enjoy fellowship with God, have no more to do
with the unfruitful works of darkness ; but walk before
him in righteousness and true holiness all the days of
our life. Be assured, if your faith does not influence
you to this, it is not the faith of the holy Gospel, not a
faith in a holy Jesus ; it does not work by the love of
him, but is the faith of the ungodly, whose end is destruction. Philippians 3 : 1 9.

August

AUGUST 1.—*Let God be true, but every man a liar.* Rom. 3 : 4

I have read of one who was dumb; but who, on seeing a violent attempt to murder his father, cried out with great vehemence, "My father." When his heavenly Father's truth and faithfulness are attacked, Paul cannot be mute. Fired with a holy emotion of spirit, he cries out, "Let God be true." Vain, arrogant man, will you dare oppose your carnal reasonings and fallacious arguments to the covenant purposes, faithful word, and precious promises of the Lord? Every such man, be he ever so noble, mighty, wise, and learned, is a liar. Paul's heart was too warm with zeal for the glory of his God to pay any soft compliment to those who act under the influence of the father of lies. The keen satire of Mr. Pope is admirably adapted to such

> ' Snatch from his hand the balance and the rod,
> " Rejudge his justice, be the God of God!
> " In reas'ning pride (my friend) our error lies;
> " All quit their sphere and rush into the skies."

Christian, lay aside thy carnal reason; take up the Lord's word; exercise thy faith upon it. Thou art called to be valiant for the truth of a faithful, covenant-keeping God. Timid silence is criminal when your Father's truth is arraigned and his glory at stake. Know thou hast much within thee, and many around thee, in combination to oppose the mystery of godliness: God manifest in the flesh to bring salvation to miserable sinners, and God's faithfulness engaged to make this effectual by his sovereign grace, in spite of all the unfaithfulness of man. Carnal reason says, how can these things be? Self-confidence exalts herself against them; Arrogance refuses to submit to them; Unbelief pro-

nounces them impossible; Self-love declares against
subjection to them; Pride cries, away with them, totally reject them; and Self-righteousness cries them down
as leading to licentiousness.

These are all professed judges of divinity, but in reality are lying adversaries against your Lord's truth
and faithfulness, and your peace, comfort, and holiness.
Abide by what is written; oppose God's truth to all
their lying suggestions; be simple of heart. Let simple faith prevail. Feed by faith upon God's truth, and
you shall prosper, while others cavil against it and
grow lean. Hold fast "the hope of eternal life, which
God, who cannot lie, promised (to Christ Jesus as our
covenant head, and that we should enjoy it in him) before the world began." Titus 1 : 2.

AUGUST 2. *By faith Moses forsook Egypt, not fearing the wrath
of the king.* Hebrews 11 : 27

Here we see faith opposed by fear, and the victory of
faith over the dread of wrath. Consider Moses' work
and his danger, his faith and his safety.

Moses was engaged in a great work : he was to go to
Pharaoh, and say from the Lord, "Israel is my son, even
my first born, let him go that he may serve me." Exod.
4 : 22, 23. Now might not the king very naturally look
upon Moses as a dangerous, pestilent enthusiast, who,
under the pretence of religion, wished to raise a rebellion
in his kingdom ? Had Moses no fear that the king might
put him to death in his wrath ? "for the wrath of a king
is as the roaring of a lion," Prov. 9 : 12 —most terribly
fierce.

But consider his *faith*; this set him above fear. He
bids defiance to wrath. Forsake Egypt he must; to flee
from the king he was determined; for he had the command of his God for it. Faith is the parent of all holy

obedience. Was his faith nothing more than a strong impulse of his mind, something within him which suggested to him that he must forsake Egypt? This he might have had, and obeyed it too to his own destruction; but he had the Lord's word for the ground of his faith: mind this: "Thus saith the Lord, I will send thee unto Pharaoh, that thou mayest bring my people out of Egypt:" there is the word of his faith.

Consider his safety. Pharaoh could not hurt the hair of his head: why not? Because the Lord added, "certainly I will be with thee." Exod. 3:12. There is the warrant for his safety: thus he believed God, and feared not the wrath of the king.

See here the nature and actings of a true and lively faith. It has the word of the Lord for its object. There may be strong impressions of mind, warm suggestions of fancy, where there is not, Thus saith the Lord. Soul, these will not carry thee out of the Egypt of nature to the promised land; they will forsake thee: then thou wilt not only fear the wrath of a king, but the shaking of a leaf. Faith in the Lord's word delivers the soul from fear of the Lord's enemies; according to the strength of our faith we are set above fears of wrath; we cannot have stronger cause for faith than the Lord's word, nor a better object for our faith than the Son of God. O then, when fear of wrath prevails, look unto Jesus the author and finisher of our faith, with the prayer, "Lord, increase my faith." Luke 17:5

AUGUST 3. *Incline your ear, and come unto me; hear, and your soul shall live.* Isaiah 55:3

Some cannot bear exhortations to duty, whether addressed to saints or sinners: they sound so legal in their ears, they are quite surfeiting to them. But why? Truly they have become "wise above what is written:"

they proclaim their folly in condemning the conduct of Christ, and his Spirit in the prophets and apostles. They have most need of exhortations who see least cause for them: "be not high-minded, but fear." A Chinese philosopher asserted that a man had three ears, one differ ent from those two which are seen; this was counted a great absurdity; but it holds true in a spiritual sense, for naturally we have ears, but hear not: "the hearing ear the Lord hath made." Prov. 20:12. This Christ calls for.

"Incline your ear"—like sentenced rebels and condemned malefactors, be all ear to a sound of mercy and a proclamation of a reprieve from me: though your hearts are bowed down under a sense of your lusts and corruptions, your consciences burdened with guilt, your minds pained with fears, and your spirits dejected with sorrows; yet listen not to the suggestions of Satan, the intimations of carnal reason, or the surmises of your legal spirits; but turn away your ear from all to me. O, it is precious living, thus to hear the voice of Christ! But this call from Christ carries conviction with it that we do not enough incline our ear to him; therefore we are not always happy in him.

Sweet invitation! "Come unto me." "Jesus Christ is the same yesterday, to-day, and for ever." Heb. 13:8. His love is the same; his words are the very same to poor sinners, whether he speaks by his prophets, or by himself in flesh: his loving heart proclaims, "come unto me, all ye that labor and are heavy laden, and I will give you rest." Matt. 11:28. Come, under all your load of guilt, weight of dejection, and burden of sorrow; Christ gives us to feel all this, that we may see our want of him, come to him, and enjoy fellowship with him. Never misconstrue your soul-burdens and spiritual distress as evidences against you; they are love-tokens from Him who says, "Hear, and

your souls shall live ;" not barely live, but enjoy the
vigor of life, the comforts of life, and bring forth abundantly the fruits of spiritual life. All this is by hearing
the voice of Christ, believing the love of Christ, and
living upon the fullness of Christ. See then "that ye
refuse not him who speaketh from heaven." Heb. 12 : 25

AUGUST 4.—*Thy God reigneth.* Isaiah 52 : 7

Christ commissions his ministers to proclaim this
joyful truth to Zion, his church ; that every member of
his may receive it in faith, change the pronoun, and
say, MY God reigneth. Christ's reign is his people's
glory, their triumph on earth, and the song of disem-
bodied saints in glory. Hark, to their acclamations of
joy : "Alleluia, for the Lord God omnipotent reigneth ;
let us be glad and rejoice, and give honor to him, for
the marriage of the LAMB is come." Rev. 19 : 6, 7.

Are we married to the LAMB ? Has he our hearts and
affections ? Then we should constantly "rejoice and
give honor to him," that he who is our God reigneth.
Where ? Where he dwells in heaven for us, and in our
hearts over us ; for as he dwells in our hearts by faith,
he spiritually reigns over all within us. O, what matter of joy and consolation is this !

If our King has set up his throne in our hearts, what
enemy can hurt us ? If Christ reign for us, and in us,
we are sure of reigning eternally in glory with him.
Consider his rich grace in thus reigning : we were once
under the reign of a dreadful tyrant. Sin reigned in
and over us unto death. Rom. 5 : 21. Though we have
sin in our nature, though it warreth in our members,
yet it cannot reign and get the victory over us. It is
under the feet of Christ : it is his vanquished enemy :
he reigns over it : we are under the reign of his grace :
"grace reigns through righteousness unto"—what ! pre-

sent peace, comfort and joy ? Yes, and infinitely more, even unto "eternal life by Jesus Christ our Lord." Is sin our grief and burden ? This is a proof that Christ reigns in our hearts. Do we long for perfect freedom from all sin ? This is a sign that we are partakers of his holiness. Are we afraid sin will destroy us in death ? It cannot : Jesus reigns to give us victory unto eternal life.

Behold, Jesus our King reigns in righteousness. Isa. 32 : 1. "His people shall be all righteous." Isa. 60 : 21. Christ's righteousness is upon us to justify us: his Spirit within us, to make us love righteousness and hate iniquity: if we do not, we only talk of Christ's reign, but have never felt its power. "For he must reign until he hath put all enemies under his feet." 1 Cor. 15 : 25. Therefore rejoice ; all your troubles, temptations, conflicts and distresses, are under Christ's reign. None can hurt you ; and the last enemy, death, shall bring you to reign with him eternally in life. Rom. 5 : 17.

AUGUST 5.—*For thy name's sake, O Lord, pardon mine iniquity, for it is great.* Psalm 25 : 11

Strange plea ! "GREAT is mine iniquity, therefore pardon it !" Such an address at the throne of grace never rose from a self-righteous heart ! No : with the pharisee of old they are ready to say, "Thank God, I am not such a sinner as David was: I never committed the horrid crimes of which he was guilty : his iniquity was great indeed." It was so. But souls enlightened by the Spirit of truth to see the spirituality of the holy law of God, will agree to our Saviour's interpretation of it : that the impure desire is adultery in the heart, and anger a species of murder in the soul. Matt. 5 : 28 "Out of the heart proceed murders and adulteries." Matt. 15 : 19.

Sensible of the desperate wickedness of our heart ;

convinced of the exceeding sinfulness of sin; who wil.
dare plead, pardon mine iniquity, for it is *little*? Is it
against a little God sin is committed? Is a little wrath
revealed against sin? Did a little Christ die for us? Is
a little hell the punishment of sin? Lord forbid that we
should think little of sin, or that iniquity should appear
little in our eyes: the iniquity of every one of us is
great.

"O," says a poor, sin-burdened soul, "Mine iniquity
is great, too great to be forgiven." So the father of lies
might suggest to David; but he believed him not.
Great as his iniquity was, he did not aggravate his
crimes by rejecting God's declarations of mercy, invitations of grace, and promises of pardon: he confesses
his great iniquity; he pleads pardon for it. On what
does he found his plea? *For thy name's sake, O Lord;*
thou hast taken upon thee that precious name, Jesus:
thou wilt be *salvation* to the ends of the earth. Psalm
98:3. Thy blood cleanseth from all sin; wash me in
it and I shall be whiter than snow; ALL manner of sin
and blasphemy shall be forgiven unto men. O, while
these glorious truths stand upon record, I cannot doubt,
I dare not despair; the belief of them causes me to
pray, and plead, and hope: GREAT as mine iniquity is,
GREAT as my distress is, yet thou art *a great God and
Saviour*, to pardon my sin and give peace to my soul.
Was ever any sinner sent to hell with such a plea in
his mouth? No; that is impossible; for the word of
God cannot be broken. "If we confess our sins, God
is faithful and just to forgive us our sins." 1 John
1:9. Therefore heaven rings with acclamations of
joy from such pardoned, glorified sinners. O that we
may join them, in giving glory "unto Him who loved
us, and washed us from our sins in his own blood."
Rev. 1:5

AUGUST 6.—*Go and cry unto the gods which ye have chosen;
let them deliver you in the time of your tribulation.* Judges
10 : 14.

A severe sarcasm from the Lord to apostate professors. It causes a hell upon earth to a renewed soul, to
hear and feel just upbraidings from the Lord of heaven :
this is one of his severest chastisings to his children.
Here is an awful charge and a severe reproof ; the Lord
keep us clear of the one, that we fall not under the other.

Consider *the charge ;* it is idolatry : they had gods of
their own choosing. For the Lord's sake, and for our
souls' sake, let us not think that we are in no danger of
falling into this sin : it is committed by professors every
day ; aged Paul wept over such ; though they professed
Christ, yet they were enemies to his cross ; their flesh
was their God ; their hearts were set upon earthly things.
Phil. 3 : 19. Such are not content with Christ as their
portion, to live in fellowship with him, to walk in love
and obedience before him, and to derive all their comfort and happiness from him : the lusts of the flesh they
gratify ; earthly things have their hearts : thus they depart from the Lord and fall into idolatry against him.
O what a most heinous crime is this ! How much practised ! How little thought of, deplored and deprecated !
Christians, where are your hearts ? Who has your affections—God, the flesh, or the world ? If not God, depend
on it you will soon, very soon hear from him in such
a way as will be awfully distressing.

Consider *the reproof :* a day of tribulation will come ;
when sorrow and distress seize on your minds, then
God is a blessed refuge ; but Oh, then to think, alas ! I
have forsaken the Lord, have preferred other lovers to
him ; chosen other gods beside him ; the world has had
my heart and my hope ; I have lived to the flesh, I have
minded earthly things, and indulged covetous desires

Well, says one, but I read, notwithstanding all this, " the children of Israel cried unto the Lord, saying, we have forsaken our God and served idols." Judges, 10 : 10. Ah ! but mind the Lord's cutting answer, " Go and cry unto the gods which ye have chosen; let them deliver you." A severer reproof is scarcely to be found in the Bible. O lay it to heart : deeply consider its import ; for, even though you may be accepted in Christ, yet he hates your conduct, and will make you smart for it in your conscience. It is said, " the Lord's soul was grieved for the misery" of his children. Judges 10 : 16. But O consider the great misery they must feel to grieve the soul of the Lord : what a compassionate Saviour is ours, " in all our afflictions he is afflicted." Isaiah 63 : 9.

AUGUST 7.—*Whatsoever ye do in word or deed, do all in the name of the Lord Jesus.* Col. 3 : 17

I have sometimes thought, how is it possible that a believer in Christ can ever wilfully and deliberately sin ? It is hardly to be conceived that such can live and walk under the power of sin : all sin is as contrary to the nature of the sanctified soul as heaven to hell ; yet nothing is more plain from the word of God and the experience of his saints, than that sin dwells in them ; but they are solemnly forbid to let it "reign in them, that they should obey it in the lusts thereof." Romans 6 : 12. And if our souls are not striving against sin and pressing after holiness, I know not where to find one text in the word of God to encourage us to believe and hope that we are the children of God. I dread not the frown of licentious antinomians ; do they pronounce this LEGAL ? It only proclaims their unregenerate enmity against God's truth, his grace and his glory.

Ye believers in and lovers of the Lord Jesus, here is a short but most blessed and comprehensive rule for your walk and conduct. Does Satan tempt, the world allure, and the flesh entice? Gratify them if ye can— only see that you do it according to this apostolic rule : yea, go to plays, take your fill of earthly pleasures and sensual delights, and mix with the wicked and profane, only see that you do all this, as here commanded, " *in the name of the Lord Jesus!*" Does your heart recoil? It must, if the name of the Lord Jesus is music to your ears and the joy of your soul: you can no more take delight in these things than in the music of hell.

O the matchless charms of that precious name! Lord, never, never suffer them to fade in our hearts ; thy name charms away the power of sin, the love of the world, and the pleasures of sense : it charms our souls into the presence of God, fellowship with him, and into the joys of heaven: right welcome are we to God, fully reconciled to him, and perfectly accepted with him, in the precious name of the Lord Jesus. O my dear, dear Saviour, it is thy precious name my heart would now indite. O for the pen of a ready writer to display the glories of thy precious name, my King and my Lord ; may the readers of these meditations find the odor of thy name in them, "as ointment poured forth, that they may love thee." Song 1 : 3. To us sinners, "the name of Jesus is above every name." Phil. 2 : 9.

AUGUST 8.—*My meditation of him shall be sweet: I will be glad in the Lord.* Psalm 104 : 34

Sweet meditation causes gladness in the Lord, in spires us with love to him, and inclines us to ascribe the glory of all we enjoy to him. It is said of a christian conqueror, that after God had honored him with many victories, as the effigies of other emperors were set up in a triumphant manner with their victories engraven upon their loins, he desired that his might be

set in a posture of prayer, kneeling, that he might manifest to the world that he attributed all his victories
more to the power of prayer than his sword. This was
the result of sweet meditation.

What great gain do souls reap by spiritual meditation! Strangers to this delighful exercise know not
others' gain nor their own loss. A day spent without
some meditation of the sinner's Redeemer and Saviour,
is a day lost; for Jesus gets no glory from our hearts;
we get no comfort from his love. Paul the aged, exhorts his son Timothy, *meditate on these things*. 1 Tim.
4 : 15. What things? The Scriptures, which testify of
Christ and the peace and salvation which are brought
unto poor sinners by him. O how sweet is this! Saints
in all ages have one and the same delightful object to
meditate upon : the soul under the sweet exercise of
grace knows no end of it; nor how to leave off medi-
tating on HIM who hath loved us poor sinners with an
everlasting love, and saved us with an everlasting salvation.

His person is WONDERFUL, God and man in one Christ;
the love of Christ passeth knowledge; the offices of
Christ, as King, Priest, and Prophet, Mediator, Surety,
Redeemer, Saviour, how glorious in their nature! How
interesting to us sinners! The blood of Christ, how
precious! His righteousness, how perfect! His death,
how affecting! His resurrection, how joyful! The salvation of Christ, how comforting! His intercession,
how prevailing! His grace in the heart, how sin-subduing and soul-purifying! His almighty power in keeping us through faith unto eternal salvation, how animating! and the perfect sight and full enjoyment of Jesus
in glory, how transporting! Contemplations on these
blessed subjects will cause us to cry out with David,
"My meditation of him shall be sweet; I will be glad
in the Lord." Now, do you complain for want of

gladness in the Lord ? It is because your heart is car
ried away after other things; you meditate too much
on them, and too little on your God, who saith, " I will
not forget thee." Isaiah 49 : 15.

AUGUST 9.—*My soul melteth for heaviness: strengthen thou me
according to thy word.* Psalm 119 : 28

While the wicked are gay and merry, many of God's
beloved children go bowed down, from day to day, with
heaviness of soul; and when they compare themselves
with the men of the world in such seasons, they are
tempted to write bitter things against themselves, and
to pass a verdict in favor of others. Souls, in the heaviest season and most dejected frame you ever expe
rienced, say, could you find it in your heart to wish to
change lots with them ? What ! quit your faith in Jesus,
and hope of eternal enjoyment of him ! for what ? the
momentary gratifications and short-lived pleasures of
time ? " Alas !" cries one, " my soul is in such heaviness that I doubt whether I have either a spark of faith
or a ray of hope in Christ. My soul melteth ! it bears no
image nor impression of any grace, or of the power of
any truth; faith fails; hope decays; my heart sinks;
I am burdened with a sense of sin; oppressed with
temptations; and what is heaviest of all, the Lord hides
his face and deserts my soul." David felt all this; Peter
experienced the same; hence he says, "for a season,
if need be, ye are in heaviness, through manifold temptations." 1 Peter 1 : 6.

Mind those words—there is support and relief in
them—*for a season.* Blessed be Jesus, heaviness lasts
not always; he will deliver out of it. " *If need be* ye
are in heaviness—there is cause for it, and good shall
issue from it. What is the remedy when the soul is in
heaviness ? Prayer; pleading God's word of grace,

and promises of love for strength under burdens, and deliverance from soul-heaviness. "Strengthen thou me according to thy word." Says wisdom, "heaviness in the heart of man maketh it stoop." The poor soul sinks under its burden; "but a good word maketh it glad." Prov. 12:25. Where shall we find that good word? In the Gospel of the grace of God; here is a good word, enough to make thy heavy heart leap for joy, and thy burdened soul sing for gladness. O, meditate upon it; pray over it; and may the Lord the Spirit give thee comfort from it. It is the work and office of thy blessed Saviour; in his own time, way, and manner, he will most surely fulfil it: "to appoint unto them who mourn in Zion, to give unto them beauty for ashes, the oil of joy for mourning, and the garments of praise for the spirit of heaviness, that the Lord may be glorified." Isaiah 61:3.

AUGUST 10.—*I have all, and abound: I am full.* Phil. 4:18

Happy Paul! infinitely richer than the most opulent monarch under heaven. Ye poor, wretched, covetous worldlings, whose gold is your god, and who are laboring to add heap to heap—how long? till ye drop into eternity, and for ever lose the idols of your hearts? Behold here a man who has more than ever you possessed: he has *all*; you only obtain a part of what you aim at: you are still in want of more. Rich, happy Paul, possesses *all*. "And," says he, "I abound." Not in want and wish, but in full enjoyment. "I am full." I can contain no more. He had "the unsearchable riches of Christ" for his portion: his wealth consisted in his mind being contented with that as his greatest treasure.

O thou poor murmuring disciple of Christ, who art often fearing and distrusting lest thou shouldst want the bread that perisheth for thyself and family; and thou, my soul, who hast often been exercised with this sore temptation, learn a lesson from rich and happy Paul. Of all the men in the world, would you expect to hear St. Paul say, "I have all things and abound: I am full?" What! he who has been in necessities, in want, in nakedness; who, like his Master, had not where to lay his head, and was treated as the filth and off-scouring of all things? for him to say, "I have all and abound: I am full." O may the Lord contract our wants! They are most of them more imaginary than real.

Lord, enable us to be content with such things as we have! What are they? Come, christian, count up your riches; look over the deeds of your inheritance; see to what vast possessions you are entitled; verily, no less than what Paul once had by faith and now enjoys in full possession, even Jesus, the God of his salvation; Christ is all in all: if he dwells in your heart by faith, he filleth all; you have all; you abound in all; you are full of all. The flesh may covet more, the spirit must be quite satisfied with HIM; for "all things are yours; and ye are Christ's, and Christ is God's." 1 Cor. 3 : 23. Learn hence the use and blessedness of your faith; it brings the unsearchable riches of Christ into your heart. When flesh and sense require to be gratified, here is the work of faith, "Put ye on the Lord Jesus Christ, and make not provision for the flesh, to fulfil the lusts thereof." Rom. 13 : 14.

AUGUST 11.—*Is it true?* Daniel 3 : 14

A question this from a potent monarch backed with a wrathful threatening: enough to have put Shadrach, Meshach, and Abednego to the stand. Their answer must provoke their God, or their King. But did they hesitate a moment? Were they at all in suspense? No; they had faith in their Lord, and they boldly replied,

" O King, we are not careful to answer thee in this matter. Our cause lies before our God: we are not left to ourselves; our present life, our immortal soul is in his hands. If you command us into the fiery furnace, our God will be with us: we shall be safe: he will deliver us: either our bodies that we shall not be burnt; or if they are, the burning furnace shall be only as a fiery chariot to convey our souls to heaven and glory." See the power of faith: according as they believed so it was: the Son of God was with them: the fire could not hurt them. Hence consider:

God may, and sometimes does suffer his dearest children to be brought into great straits, and threatened with the greatest dangers, so that an answer to a single question may perplex them. *Is it true?* Are you one who follow this new way? Do you pretend to be justified by the Son of God only, to be saved by the grace of God entirely, and to have received the Spirit of God freely? On an answer to this, perhaps, depends a parent's regard or a friend's kindness: the one threatens to disinherit, the other to withdraw his favors. Do worldly interest, honor or advantage depend upon the answer of the tongue and the conduct of the life? Do poverty and want seem to threaten, if we declare ourselves for the Lord? Here is the trial of faith. But remember our Lord's declaration; " Whosoever shall be ashamed of me and of my words, in this adulterous and sinful generation; of him also shall the Son of man be ashamed when he cometh in the glory of his Father.' Mark 8 : 38.

Put then this question to your heart: Is it true that God is my Father in Christ my Saviour? Doth the Spirit bear witness to this in the word, and to my heart? Shall I then so fear a worm of the earth as to deny the truth and forsake the Lord, who has promised he will never leave nor forsake me, and that they that seek him

shall not want any good thing? Psalm 34 : 10. My soul
starts, my heart recoils at the thought; rather say, "I
will not fear what man can do unto me." Give up and
forego all for Christ: soon we shall see these dear children: then they will tell us they never were so happy
in their lives as in the fiery furnace; God is most with
his children when they suffer most for him.

AUGUST 12.—*Joseph knew his brethren, but they knew not him.*
Genesis 42:8.

How affecting is the history of Joseph! Who can
read it without emotion? What amazing scenes of providence open to our view! Spiritual minds may see many
things in it typical of our beloved Saviour. Here Joseph's
brethren are introduced to him as governor of Egypt;
he knew them; they knew not him. How does he deal
with them? Does he instantly make himself known to
them? No: though he had the most tender affections of
heart to them and wept tears of joy at the sight of them,
yet he speaks roughly and sends them to prison. Why
this? To bring their sin to their mind, and to affect
them with a deep sense of guilt for their cruelty towards
him. See we not something typical of the conduct of
Christ in all this?

Christ knew us before we knew him; he knew us from
eternity, when we were chosen in him and given to him.
We never seek after him, or come to him, unless we
find a famine in our hearts and are ready to perish for
want of the bread of life. And when we come to him,
does he instantly make himself known to us and assure us
that he is our Saviour? No; for a season he speaks with
the authority of a GOVERNOR, causes his law to treat us
roughly, threatening us with the prison of hell. Why?
Deeply to affect our souls with a sense of our sins and
deserts.

Many trying and afflicting scenes Joseph's brethren passed through before he said, *I am your brother.* Did Joseph do them any real harm by all this? So Christ, though he proves us and tries us, and shows us what is in us before he gives us full assurance of his love and salvation, intends nothing but real good to us: by all this he teaches us humility. Joseph's brethren did not at first come to him as their brother, but as the governor of Egypt; so we come as perishing sinners to Christ, believing him to be a Saviour and praying him to save us: we have faith in him before we have the assurance of his love to us, and know that we are his brethren. All the blessings and comforts of Joseph's brethren flowed from his knowledge of them; so does all our safety and comfort in time and eternity spring from Christ's first knowing and loving us as his brethren. Though true faith may be without special assurance of interest in Christ, yet Christ assures us, "I will manifest myself unto you." John 14: 21.

AUGUST 13.—*Awake to righteousness and sin not.* 1 Cor. 15: 34

What Paul says of natural death, "some are fallen asleep," 1 Cor. 15: 6, may be applied in a spiritual sense to professors: there are many such; but it is a very bad frame to live in and indulge: such bring no honor to God, credit to the Gospel, or profit to their brethren One would think, such sit all the year under that word and heartily obey it, "sleep on and take your rest." Can such be said to be running the heavenly race, fighting the good fight of faith, wrestling with spiritual enemies, and pressing towards the mark for the prize of the high calling of God in Christ Jesus? No: no more than man in a midnight sleep can be said to be active in wordly affairs; but what is worst of all, such sleepers dream that all is safe and well with them.

Paul, like a faithful watchman, cries out to such, *Awake!* "how long wilt thou sleep, O sluggard? when wilt thou arise out of thy sleep?" What do they answer? "Yet a little sleep, a little slumber, a little folding of the hands to sleep." Prov. 6:10. If you jog them and strive to arouse them to the exercise of grace and the discharge of duty, some are ready to answer, "We know the doctrines of grace; do not disturb us with your legal notions about sin and righteousness." The Lord keep our souls from such a dreadful frame. Take heed, O christian, of such; beware lest you catch the infection from them and lie down to sleep by them.

Whence do such slumbering frames proceed? Says wisdom, "Slothfulness casteth into a deep sleep." Prov. 19:15. Slothfulness in the ways of the Lord will bring on deep sleep of soul. Again, sitting under drowsy, lethargic preachers, who aim more to fill the head with notions of light than to warm the heart by the fire of love. So, also, love of this world, and eager pursuits after its riches, honors, and pleasures, are opiates to the soul. O christian, consider the unintermitting zeal and activity of thy Lord for thy salvation! Wrestle hard with him to quicken and keep thy soul alive to righteousness, that thou mayest not sin to dishonor him; but live and walk, love and obey, so as to glorify him. Lord, let us never lose a sense of the exceeding sinfulness of sin, and the dreadful effects of it upon our souls. O, let conscience rather smart with pain than sleep in stupid security.

> "My drowsy powers, why sleep ye so?
> "Awake, my sluggish soul:
> "Nothing has half thy work to do,
> "Yet nothing half so dull."

AUGUST 14.—*Believe in the Lord your God, so shall ye be established. Believe his prophets, so shall ye prosper.* 2 Chron.
20 : 20.

Such was the advice of good Jehoshaphat in a time
of invasion by a powerful army. Precious words; at
all times seasonable. What can a child of God desire
on this side heaven so much as establishment of mind
and prosperity of soul? Both are obtained by faith; as
the mind is established, so the soul prospers.

What is implied in being established? It is to be
fixed and settled in the confidence of one's mind, and
not to halt between two opinions, as those of old did
between God and an idol. 1 Kings 18:21. Their minds
were in suspense, agitated between two objects, and
not steadily fixed upon either. So many sincere souls
are tossed to and fro by every wind of doctrine; they
are like children, not steadily fixed in their judgment,
nor settled in their confidence in the Lord; yet they
delight to hear the truths of God: in hearing, their
souls are refreshed; but when hearing is over, their
minds are shaken, their doubts and fears again return.
O see and rejoice, for

The Lord himself is set forth as the object of our
faith; believe, or trust in the Lord your God; nothing
can establish the soul but faith. "Lord, increase our
faith:" and to prayer we should add earnest diligence
in searching the Scriptures, considering the safeness,
fulness, and suitableness of the promises of the Lord to
us. To believe *in* the Lord, is to trust in and repose
our minds upon his covenant-grace and love in Christ
Jesus: to take him, as he has revealed himself, as our
God and Father: to trust our souls and all our concerns in his hands, just as little children do by their
parents. Their minds have no doubt of their father's
love to them; when they want any thing, they ask for

it ; when in sorrow they tell him of it ; and yet, what parent on earth has such a heart of love to his chil-, dren as our heavenly Father has to us ? Did any one ever so freely, fully, and affectionately manifest it ?

Be ashamed of your unbelief, which keeps your souls from being established in his grace and truth : " it is a good thing that the heart be established with grace." Heb. 13 : 9. Do we desire it, that our souls may prosper ? Then "believe his prophets ;" they testify of God the Father's love ; of God the Son's salvation ; and of peace and joy in God the Holy Ghost. Hear them, and your souls shall be established in grace : believe them, and your soul shall prosper.

AUGUST 15.—*Strong meat belongeth to them that are of full age, even those who, by reason of use, have their senses exercised to discern both good and evil.* Heb. 5 : 14

It is hard for any, who are called to minister or write about the truths of God, to please every one. Babes, who are unskilful in the word of righteousness, can only take milk : they cry out against strong meat, it offends them.

But such should consider that they are not always to continue babes to feed upon milk ; they must learn to eat strong meat, that they may grow thereby.

God's children are not all of equal age : strong meat is as necessary for adult men as milk is for babes. It is necessary to those " of full age," or *perfect*, as in the margin—not so compared with the perfect law of God : there is no one upon earth perfect in this sense, though many, through ignorance of the law and themselves, pretend to it ; but perfect in comparison of babes, respecting the knowledge of the everlasting, immutable love of God in Christ to sinners ; of his freely and fully justifying and eternally glorifying them, through the blood and righteousness of his Son; and of his effectually calling and sanctifying them by his Spirit.

The deep truths of God are held forth in Scripture as strong meat to nourish, comfort, and build up those who are of full age: hence it becomes those who labor in the word to give each their portion; that neither babes on the one hand, nor men on the other, should have reason to find fault. Babes should not expect the strong to come back to their food, but they should press forward to maturity.

How is this to be attained? "By reason of use;" constantly searching the Scriptures, and hearing them opened and explained, just as a learner uses his grammar which contains the rudiments of the language he wants to attain; he cannot get forward without it; he must be perfect in it; he is never to forget its rules. "By the exercise of the senses:" the internal ones of the understanding and judgment: "*Seeing* Jesus." Heb. 2:9. "*Hearing* his voice." John, 10:3. *Smelling* the sweet odor of his love: "his name is as ointment poured forth." Song 1:3. "*Tasting* that the Lord is gracious." 1 Pet. 2:3. "*Handling* the word of life and salvation as held forth in the Gospel." 1 John, 1:1. Thus exercising our senses on Christ, we grow strong to trust him: we discern that all good is in him, and all is evil without him.

August 16.—*They shall take to them every man a lamb.* Exod. 12:3

This was God's appointed means of salvation in a night of sore destruction. Here is a display of the sovereignty of God and the obedience of faith. Lord, enable us to bow to the one, and to learn more and more of the other.

Consider the sovereignty of God in his *severity* upon

his enemies, and his *goodness* to his people : in destroying all the first-born of the former, and in preserving every one of the latter : and this was in a way appointed by his sovereign mercy. There is no mercy from God to any sinner but in the way he appoints. This was a LAMB : "They shall take to them every man a *lamb*." His flesh was to be their food, his blood their salvation. Would not taking the flesh and blood of any other creature have answered the same end ? No : to attempt it would have been a direct act of unbelief of God's word and disobedience to his will ; such a soul would have brought upon himself swift destruction. O beware lest you turn your eyes from the Lamb of God : there is salvation in no other.

See, also, the obedience of faith ; we do not find one Israelite destroyed ; they believed God's word, and obeyed it : they did not dare to reply against God and say, *What doest thou?* Why wilt thou ? Is it just to destroy so many souls in one night ? Why take the lamb and sprinkle his blood as our protection ? Why institute this sign to us only, and not to the Egyptians also ? Why not give them at least a chance of salvation ? O the power of faith ! It kills such arrogant speeches. The grace of faith in the heart subdues the enmity of the carnal mind, bows the rebellious will, stills the turbulency of nature, brings peace to the conscience and love to the heart ; for it takes and feeds upon the flesh, and trusts alone in the blood of "*the Lamb of God* who taketh away the sin of the world :" this is God's appointed way of salvation. O how simple, how happy is the believing soul ! God and he are perfectly agreed. God says, "take the Lamb, my beloved Son, as my free gift for your whole salvation." The Lamb says, "my flesh is meat indeed, and my blood is drink indeed." John 6 : 55. And the obedient sinner says, "Lord, I believe, help thou my unbelief."

Dost thou believe? Hast thou experienced this? O bless the loving Spirit for the gift of precious faith! Faith is the gift of God; feed by faith on the Lamb of God: thus take, thus receive, thus live upon Christ and his fulness every day on earth till you see his face in glory. Yet a little while and he shall come. Heb. 10:37.

> "There is salvation in the Lamb
> "For sinners vile as me;
> "I glory in his precious name,
> "And long his face to see.
>
> "Christ is my food, my robe, my joy,
> "I take him thus by faith;
> "No foes can e'er my soul destroy,
> "Christ is my life, my health."

AUGUST 17.—*If any man suffer as a christian, let him not be ashamed; but let him glorify God on this behalf.* 1 Pet. 4:16

"The disciples were first called *Christians* at Antioch." Acts 11:26. It is a blessed name; we ought ever to glory in it, and never to be ashamed of it; but the bare name will no more avail us in life, death, and judgment, than to be called rich while we are in pinching want.

Christ signifies *anointed:* he was anointed to be our Saviour. Acts 10:38. All who are saved by him and come to him are his anointed ones. So St. John speaks of all Christ's living members, " ye have an unction from the Holy One." 1 John 2:20. To anoint is to consecrate and set apart for holy and spiritual purposes. Christians are consecrated and set apart from the rest of the world, to be a people peculiarly devoted to the glory of Jesus; they are the jewels which compose his mediatorial crown. Are you thus highly honored by the Lord of life and glory? Is your soul anointed by the Spirit of Christ? Then verily the world will also anoint you with their spirit; the more the unction of the Holy

One is manifest in your walk and conversation, so much the more will the wicked one and his children be inclined to reproach and defame you: thus you may suffer as a christian, at least in your good name.

But take heed that you suffer *as* a christian; that it be for confessing Christ and adorning his Gospel. As you love Christ, and have a tender concern for his glory, O let him not be wounded and his cause dishonored by any thing unholy, unjust, or immoral. Remember, the men of the world are vulture-eyed to your faults, glad to espy and eager to proclaim them with an air of triumph, "See, these are your christians." But if you really do suffer as a christian who have given up yourself to be a disciple of Christ, are following him in the regeneration, and therefore are opposed by the ungodly, be not ashamed; be not confounded; do not hang your head with fear, but look up to God with joy; glorify him for thus honoring you; remember on whose behalf you suffer; put all your sufferings for Christ to his account: you have Christ's note of hand; he will surely pay it: but if you are ashamed, it is a sign you cannot credit him. What! is the credit of Jesus, the God of truth, bad in your eyes? Be ashamed for want of faith to trust him: meditate often on that day, when Christ shall come in the glory of his Father to confess them who now confess him. Luke 12 : 8.

AUGUST 18.—*With his stripes we are healed.*   Isa. 53 : 5

A distinguished individual once said to me, "I can never conceive how one man can be made righteous by the righteousness of another." Thus his carnal reason led him to object against Christ's righteousness being imputed to us. I replied, Why then do you profess to believe that your sins can be washed away by the blood of another? He was silent. "Without controversy,

great is the mystery of godliness:" too great a mystery
for human reason to comprehend, but not too great for
divine faith to receive, to the joy of the soul. Sin is a
malignant and mortal disease: the soul must die eternally of it unless healed: this healing of the soul is
the pardoning of sin; this is obtained by the stripes of
Christ.

You feel the evil of sin: you mourn over the guilt of
sin: you groan under the burden of indwelling sin from
day to day. The Spirit of truth, the COMFORTER, here
holds forth a blessed remedy, to which you may look for
pardon of sin, peace of conscience, and healing of soul:
the stripes of Jesus: just as though the Lord proclaimed
to a world of diseased sinners, "This is your only remedy: so sure as you are sinners, and feel sin in your
nature, so truly did the Son of God take upon him the
SAME nature, had all your sins laid upon him, and in that
nature was cursed by the law as a malefactor, wounded,
bruised, and put to death by divine justice: that hereby
your sins, all your sins, may be pardoned, and your
souls as perfectly healed of the disease of sin as though
it had never infected you. Look to any thing but the
stripes of Christ, and you will be miserable: look to
these only and alone, and you shall find health, joy and
salvation."

Sin-burdened soul, what sayest thou to this? "Lord,
increase my faith." This is a precious prayer: that dear
Lord who suffered stripes that thou mightest be healed
of thy sins; that dear Spirit who convinced thee of sin,
and made thee sick of sin, will surely answer the prayer
of faith, and give thee the joy of faith, and thou shalt
say, "Bless the Lord, O my soul, and forget not all his
benefits; who forgiveth all thine iniquities, and healeth
all thy diseases." Psalm 103: 2, 3. O what a marvellous
way is this of healing our souls! It is God's way. Un
convinced sinners care not about it; proud, self-righ

teous souls reject it; licentious spirits abuse it; believing, humble hearts rejoice in it, give Christ the glory of it, and walk worthy of the Lord, to all pleasing. Col. 1 : 10.

AUGUST 19.—*Wherefore take unto you the whole armor of God, that ye may be able to withstand in the evil day, and having done all, to stand.*   Ephesians 6 : 13

Paul was an experienced veteran in the camp of Christ; he had fought many battles under the Captain of his salvation, against his combined enemies, the world, the flesh, and the devil; he warns his fellow-soldiers of their foes and dangers, by exhorting them to take and put on nothing less than "the whole armor of God." The very same armor in which he himself fought is provided for us also. Blessed be God, that as sure as Paul fought his way through, and got safe to glory, so shall we also in this armor of God. O christian, consider, this is not an armor of flesh and blood, not what is natural to man, or is in the power of man to provide for himself; but the Lord of hosts, the God of the armies of the whole earth, hath provided it for all Christ's good soldiers.

What is this armor of God? It is the Son of his love, the Lord Jesus himself; he is the christian's whole and complete armor: in Christ alone he stands his ground, fights and conquers every enemy: without Christ we can do nothing but faint and fly. Take this whole armor: put it on, saith Paul: Christ is yours; he is the gift of God to you; "*put on the Lord Jesus.*" Rom. 13 : 14. Just as one puts on armor for defence, so take, put on, arm your minds with the whole person of Christ, his love, righteousness, and atonement, all his offices, yea, the whole salvation of Christ: this, and nothing but this, what Christ is to us and hath done for us, is proof against every enemy in the evil day of battle. *That ye may be able to stand:* O soldier, Christ is your strength; your standing is by his power: *against all the wiles of the devil.*

Is Satan very cunning and very powerful, full of force and fraud? Is he too much for you to resist and conquer? Remember, Christ is your whole armor. Wisdom lies in the head; Christ is your head; he is to you made *wisdom.* Courage comes from the heart; Christ dwells there by faith. Eph. 3: 17. Thus armed, you are proof against Satan's devices; you never can fall while fighting in his armor, for you shall be strengthened, by the Spirit's "might, in the inner man." Satan must first wound Christ before he can reach you; first conquer Christ before he can conquer you. O then, christian, look at your armor, not at your weak, defenceless self: be strong: be of good courage: shout your victory, "*more than* conquerors, through Christ, who loved us." Romans 8: 37.

AUGUST 20.—*Stand therefore, having your loins girt about with truth, and having on the breast-plate of righteousness.* Ephesians 6: 14

Soldiers of Christ, hear and obey the word of command—STAND. Against every enemy stand to your arms; against all opposition from within and without maintain your ground; face all, fight all, conquer all. Does sin attack, Satan assault, the world threaten? Do corruptions rage, temptations beset, and carnal nature rebel? Are thine enemies many and potent? Is their fury great? Is the battle strong? *Stand* therefore. Why? Because you have put on the whole armor of God. Jesus is with you, upon you, over you, and engaged for you; therefore, "stand fast in the Lord," "and in the power of his might."

Having your loins girt. Long standing makes the loins faint and weak. Here is thy Lord's command; gird up the loins of thy mind; make thy loins strong;

"fortify thy power mightily." Nahum 2:1. How?
Here is a girdle for thee: "girt about *with truth*." What
is truth? Christ answers, "I AM THE TRUTH." John 14:6
Christ, and the truth as it is in him, is like a girdle to the
loins, to brace up and strengthen the mind. Hast thou
not often found it so, O soldier of Christ? When weary
and faint in thy mind under long and sharp conflicts
with the enemy, has not thy soul been revived and thy
mind animated with fresh strength and vigor, by again
girding thy loins with the love, the grace, the truth, and
the salvation of Jesus? This was David's experience;
"Thou hast girded me with gladness." Psalm 30:11
"Thou hast girded me with strength to battle." 2 Sam
22:40. O think not of standing without the girdle of
truth: let Christ and his truth be the strength of thy
loins and the glory of thy soul.

Having on the breast-plate of righteousness; not our
own, that is defective; as well have on a spider's web;
it will not defend the heart; the enemy will wound the
breast through it; no other righteousness than that in
which we stand perfectly justified in the sight of God
can effectually defend our breast against the enemy:
this is the one perfect, everlasting righteousness of him
who is "THE LORD OUR RIGHTEOUSNESS." Jer. 23:6.
Christ, by his obedience unto death, wrought it out.
The Spirit convinces us of our want of it; God the
Father accepts it; the sinner receives it by faith, glories
of it, and rejoices in it; no enemy can stand against it;
it is a guard against Satan, repels his accusations, and
is a security against all condemnation.

———

AUGUST 21.—*And your feet shod with the preparation of the
Gospel of peace.* Ephesians 6:15

Soldiers of Christ, you are not only commanded to
stand against every enemy, but to march on: to follow

the Captain of your salvation in the way to eternal glory. Here you must expect the enemy will strive to retard your march; he will strew the road with difficulties and entanglements, with briers and thorns; make it rugged and almost impassable, as though every step was upon sharp stones and goading spikes.

Your feet must be *shod*, or you will halt when you should march, turn back when you should go forward. "No one can make a shoe to the creature's foot, so that he shall go on easy in a hard way, but Christ; he can do it to the soldier's full content. How does he do it? Truly no other way than underlaying it : or if you will, lining it with the peace of the Gospel. What though the way be set with sharp stones? If this shoe go between the Christian's foot and them, they cannot be much felt."— *Gurnal's Christian Armor.*

Shod with the *preparation* : Dr. Gill observes, this word signifies a base or foundation. Says Paul, "Other foundation can no man lay than that is laid, which is Jesus Christ." 1 Cor. 3 : 11. Christ was laid as the only foundation of a sinner's peace, in the everlasting council and covenant by Jehovah in Trinity : peace is preached by him in the Gospel of peace. When the heart has a solid, scriptural, experimental knowledge of this by faith, it cries out with joy, "Christ is our peace." Eph. 2 : 14. "We have peace with God, through our Lord Jesus Christ." Rom. 5 : 1. This peace in the heart becomes as it were shoes to the feet, to enable the christian soldier to trample upon every difficulty and danger, and to run the way of God's commands with love and delight; for, saith the Lord, "Thy shoes shall be iron and brass," proof against every obstacle, and preservation from every hinderance in the way : "and as thy days, so shall thy strength be." Deut. 33 : 25. Thy days are all in Christ ; thy strength to walk on is from him ; thy Captain, O soldier, sees thy every conflict, eyes thee in every

difficulty and danger; according to his rich love and marvellous grace has given thee exceeding great and precious promises, that by these you might be partaker of
the divine nature. 2 Pet. 1:4. Therefore,

> March on, nor fear to win the day,
> Though death and hell obstruct the way.

"As ye have therefore received Christ Jesus the Lord,
so walk ye in him, rooted and built up in him, and established in the faith, as ye have been taught, abounding
therein with thanksgiving." Col. 2:6, 7.

August 22.—*Above all things, the shield of faith.* Eph. 6:16

When Christ has the heart, it will say, If I can see
nothing of Christ in the text, that text is nothing to
me. Here is a shield of defence. What is it? a mere as-
sent of the mind? a cold consent of the tongue to some
certain propositions? Is this the shield of faith which will
cover my head and defend my heart in the day of battle?
Is it believing a system of doctrines, without having the
heart warmed with love, or the life influenced by the
power of them, that the apostle exhorts me above all to
take? O no: nothing less is this shield of faith than
Christ, precious Christ; never, never have any idea of
faith without including its author and object; otherwise
it is a mere non-entity; a notion which has no real existence but in fancy.

When one hears people insist that *faith* is our righteousness, he is led to think they take up and are in love
with some fancied excellence in themselves instead of
the excellence and glory of *the Lord our righteousness*:
him the grace of faith ever exalts. Have you faith? Is
Christ the glory and excellence of your faith and of your
heart? Then above all, or over all things else, take this
shield of faith. Fiery darts, shot from the burning malice

of hell, are flying thick around us; such as strong temptations, horrid thoughts of God, debasing thoughts of
Christ, distressing and despairing ones of the hope of salvation by him. O how do these fiery darts of the enemy
tend to burn up the peace, hope, consolation and joy of
the soul.

"Ah," says Satan, "you a child of God; you a believer in Christ; you an heir of glory; your faith is
fancy, your hope delusion; you are an accursed sinner
in all you do; you had better give over your profession,
give up your hope, and enjoy yourself in the world, for
all your expectations are only vain!" What can the
poor sinner say? How repel, how quench such fiery
darts? Only by taking "the shield of faith;" holding up
the work of Jesus against them all: "My Saviour's blood
atoned for my sins; his blood cleanseth from *all* sin;
all manner of sin and blasphemy shall be forgiven; in
his righteousness I am justified from *all* things; there
is now no condemnation to me, for I am in Christ Jesus.
Who shall lay any thing to the charge of God's elect?"

AUGUST 23.—*And take the helmet of salvation.* Ephes. 4:17

It is excellently said by Gurnal in his Christian Armor: "Resolve for hardships, or lay down thine arms.
Few come at the beat of Christ's drum to his standard.
Many that enlist by external profession under him, after
a while drop away and leave his colors. It is suffering
work they refuse. Many men are more tender of their
body than of their conscience; they had rather the
Gospel had provided armor to defend their bodies
from death and danger than their souls from sin and
Satan."

All this is because they have not on "the helmet of
salvation." What is this? For an helmet, "the *hope*
of salvation." 1 Thess. 5:8. Do not all naturally hope

to be saved? Yes, some in one way and some in another; but all natural hopes are false hopes; therefore they die and perish. This helmet is a supernatural and divine hope. All men have not faith; therefore they have not Christ, who is the helmet of hope; "the Lord Jesus" is "our hope." 1 Tim. 1:1. We have received him into our hearts by faith: he is the ONLY hope of our souls.

Christian, you are daily, and every day, to take and put on this precious helmet of salvation, that you may lift up your head in every day of battle. Ever lay this down as a fixed maxim in your heart, *whatever* grace the Spirit works in you, as faith, hope, love, it is that you should exalt Christ, the Lord of all grace, out of whose fulness you receive grace for grace. Mind this: you are not to live upon hope as a grace within you; but to take Christ, all that he is to you and has done for you, as the object of your hope and the helmet of your salvation. Many are apt to look more to, and trust more in graces in themselves, than in Christ giving himself for them. The Spirit does nothing in us to glorify us, but to glorify Jesus, to endear him to us, and that we should glory more and more of him and in him.

Take this helmet, for this keeps hope alive in the heart: it is of continual use to us; we are in perpetual danger: it defends the head: it makes the heart happy: inspires with courage: fortifies the mind and purifies the life. No wonder that the enemy strives to rob us of the comfort of hope: no marvel that the Spirit, the Comforter, commands us to take, put on, and keep on, this blessed helmet of salvation, the work of Christ, which is our finished salvation. In that we stand perfect and complete in the will of God: this will guard our heads against corrupt doctrines, and give courage to our hearts in the heat of battle against affliction and distress: "Hope thou in God." Psalm 42:5.

AUGUST 24.—*And take the sword of the Spirit, which is the word of God.* Ephes. 6 : 17

Soldiers of Christ, all hail! Happy are ye: Christ is your whole armor. Christ, who is *the truth*, is the strength of your loins: his righteousness is your breast-plate of defence. He is the sum and substance of the Gospel of peace, whereby our feet are shod to march against the enemy; the author and object of faith; our shield, to quench all the fiery darts of the wicked one; our helmet of hope. Thus, by the grace of the Spirit, put him on as your armor. Then, what dangers may you not face? What enemies have you to fear?

But forget not your *sword:* though but just entered the field, you must know the use of it and necessity for it: it is offensive to your enemy, defensive of yourself. What can you do without "*the sword of the Spirit, which is the word of God?*" By it he conquers the pride of our hearts, the self-righteousness of our spirits, and the rebellion of our nature against Christ and his salvation. He furnishes us with it, and enables us to obtain the victory over our corrupt reason, the injections of Satan, and the objections of carnal men against the mystery of Christ, hope in him, and salvation by him.

Take this sword: hold fast the faithful word; abide by it; stand to it. As a sentinel, with this sword in thine hand, guard thy heart against every intruding, insulting foe, all the lying accusations, soul-dejecting, Christ-dishonoring suggestions of Satan. Not only so, but like Esau, "by thy sword thou shalt live;" live upon what thy sword brings in from day to day out of the precious word of God, out of the fulness of the grace of Jesus, and the precious promises in him. Having such an armor, the Lord forbid that we should be like the children of Ephraim, who turned back in the day of battle! Psalm 78 : 9. Lord, strengthen us, that we may never be ashamed to confess the faith of Christ crucified, but may manfully fight under his banner against sin, the world, and the devil; and so continue Christ's faithful soldiers and servants unto the end of life. Is this the one desire of your soul? O bless the Spirit for it: hold fast the sword which he hath put into your hand: hold up, "Thus saith the Lord—thus it is written," against every foe. Neither men nor devils can stand against the word of the Lord. "It is sharper than any two-edged sword." Heb. 4:12.

AUGUST 25.—*Praying always with all prayer.* Eph. 6:18.

One, by way of banter, said to me, "I will treat you with a play if you will go with me to-night." I thanked him, and told him I would accompany him if I could be sure that it would bring more of the love of Christ into my heart: this, this is worth living for, using any means to promote, and going any where to procure. But, here is a weapon which defends us against all temptations to go to those places, or do those things which are contrary to the peace of our souls and damp the love of Christ in our hearts. That soul who lives in sweet fellowship with God at the throne of grace, is dead to sensual gratifications; the more prayer, the more spiritual life from Christ; the more spiritual life, the more prayer to Christ; the more we enjoy Christ, the less we desire from the world.

Praying: this is the last weapon of our warfare; it will be used by soldiers to the last moment of life. "God be merciful to me a sinner;" "Jesus, save, or I perish," are suitable petitions for a dying soldier of Christ: such prayer of faith we are sure God will answer.

Praying *always:* we are prone to think that we are not always in fit frame to pray. Who but Christ can put our souls in a better? Therefore, pray him to do it. "I am oppressed," said Hezekiah. What then? Did he cease to pray? No: "O Lord, undertake for me."

Isa. 38 : 14. The help of Jesus we want always; therefore should pray for it always.

With all prayer : every kind of prayer : though armed with the whole armor of God, yet we gain no victory without the power of God. The most secret sigh of the soul is heard by God, as well as the loudest cry of the tongue. If your lot is cast into the worst of company, there your heart may pray; God can hear; you then ought to pray that God may keep you. Are you dejected and uncomfortable in your soul? Why is this? That you should call upon the Lord. Do you fear your enemies will prevail? Improve fears into prayers; call on the Saviour; the more prayer, the more victory : the more victory, the more love. Love is heaven below : thus we go on "conquering and to conquer." "The last enemy that shall be destroyed is death:" praying souls may joyfully shout victory over death: in all things "more than conquerors, through Him who loved us." Romans 8 : 37. Is this the state, this the faith of praying christians? Who brought them into this happy state, this joyful faith? The question excites gratitude, and calls forth praise to Jesus, "the author and finisher of our faith." Heb. 12 : 2.

AUGUST 26.—*There is one body and one Spirit.* Eph. 4 : 4

Paul exhorts saints to a holy, loving, peaceful walk : he knew nothing could effect this like the consideration that they all composed one body, of which Jesus is the head. While the power of this truth lives in the heart, love prevails in holiness before God and peace with our brethren. Then, in sweet fellowship we say with Abraham to Lot, "Let there be no strife, I pray thee, between me and thee, for we are brethren." Gen. 13 : 8.

There is one body, saith our Lord : "A body hast thou prepared me." Heb. 10 : 5. As Christ had a natural body, formed by the power of the Holy Ghost, which he was to inhabit, in which he was to atone for sin, fulfil all righteousness, and make intercession for transgressors; so he has also a mystical body, the church, chosen and given to him by God the Father. In and over all these he is head. He was given "to be *head* over all things to the church, which is his body." Ephesians 1 : 22, 23. Believing sinner, art thou a member of this blessed body, united to this ever precious, ever glorious head? Envy not monarchs; covet not earth; study thy dignity; live like thyself; glory in thy head; look down with contempt on all things below Christ and heaven.

There is *one Spirit:* he flows from the head, has united us to the head, makes us like the head, and causes us to rejoice in the head; for Christ is in all his members: by this one Spirit he animates, guides, and comforts them.

Learn hence to love and praise God for the gift of Jesus to be all things to us; and to glory of and rejoice in Christ our head, who has done all for us, and is all to us, "for in him we are COMPLETE." Col. 2 : 10. Give glory also to the Spirit, who convinced us of sin, showed us Christ, knit our hearts to him by faith, and causes us to look to, live upon, and be comforted by Jesus, our covenant head. Endeavor to keep "the unity of the Spirit in the bond of peace" between Christ and his members. Saints' strifes are Satan's sport: they grieve the Spirit and distress our minds. As we expect to live together with our head *above*, "let us follow the things which make for peace, and wherewith one may edify another" *below*. Rom. 14 : 19. The power of this faith, of being one with Christ, is most amazing: it works by the love of Christ, and produces love to him and to all his members, as being one in him: "Lord, increase our faith."

AUGUST 27.—*Now the just shall live by faith.* Heb. 10:38

Then they will highly prize the word of God, for by that "faith cometh." Rom. 10: 17. Prophets and apostles, Old Testament saints and New, speak by one and the same Spirit, one and the same language, of one and the same life. "The just shall live by his faith," says Habbakuk, 2:4. Mind, it is not said, the just, or justified sinner shall live *for* his faith; this would be to substitute faith in the room of its blessed object Jesus, who saith, "Because I live, ye shall live also." John, 14: 19. Nor is it said he shall live *upon* his faith: we are too apt to look more to, and live more upon what we think faith, which is rather the feelings of sense, than upon Christ, the object of faith.

It is said of Esau, "By thy sword shalt thou live." Gen. 27:40. To have lived *upon* his sword would have been hard food indeed; but he lived upon the precious morsels his sword brought in: so the believing sinner, justified in the righteousness of Christ, is to live, as we say, from hand to mouth; upon what faith brings into his mind from the word of Christ, day by day. Eternal praise to the Holy Spirit, who quickened our once dead souls to this holy, spiritual life: and he says, "we shall live by faith." This demands fresh praises every moment, while we thus live in Christ and upon Christ by faith.

Shall live: O what is implied in this! Even that the sinner, "justified by faith," shall never perish; for he is in Christ, who is the way to the kingdom, the *truth* of the kingdom, and the *life* of all the chosen to inherit the kingdom. Hast thou faith, though but as a grain of mustard-seed? Consider not thy faith, though weak, but the author and object of it, Jesus, who is almighty to save: though under the sentence of death for sin in thyself, yet in him thou hast righteousness and justification unto eternal life. "Lord, increase our faith," that we may live more above with thee in heart and affection, in conquest over sin, victory over the world, triumph over the accusations of Satan, the condemnation of the law, and the terrors of death.

Thus the life of faith is a life of present peace, precious love, joyful hope, and holy obedience : for Christ is our life. O let us take heed lest we draw back from this our most holy, humble faith, either to self-righteousness on one hand or ungodliness on the other. Both these oppose the life of faith, the joy of hope, and the comfort of love which are in Christ Jesus.

AUGUST 28.—*And be found in him.* Phil. 3 : 9

What! the heaven-inspired, holy, self-denying Paul, who had the richest experience of grace and manifold gifts of the Spirit, had been caught up to the third heaven, and labored more abundantly than all the apostles, has he got no farther than to have only the hope and desire of such a worthless sinner as I ? What! had he no inherent righteousness, no graces of the Spirit, no holiness, no fruits of good works, no sincere obedience, nothing that he had done to look to, rely upon, and desire to be found in at the bar of God ? No—but he had precious faith in a precious Saviour. Therefore he looks out of himself, out of all that was wrought in and done by him,—he passes it all by; he looks through it all to Jesus ; he renounces it all in point of justification before God, and puts the issue of his eternal life and salvation upon *being found in Christ*, and having on his infinitely perfect and glorious righteousness.

Beza, upon this place, brings in the justice of God pursuing Paul as a malefactor, and Christ as a city of refuge to which he desires to flee. Mr. Burkitt, though not the most consistent expositor, has here one of the many excellent things which he says, " Christ's perfect obedience unto death entitles us to heaven."

From Paul's desire we learn what is the sole object of a convinced sinner's faith : not what he is in himself, not any thing wrought in him or done by him, but wholly and exclusively the person and righteousness of the Son of God. If you have the faith of God's elect, you will rest the hope of your soul only upon Christ, and desire to be found in him in life, in death, and at the judgment.

Let us also beware that we do not slight and decry *the graces and fruits* of the Spirit in us : though we are not to look to these for our justification, yet they are comfortable evidences of our being one with Christ and interested in the Father's everlasting love : they are not bestowed on us to rival Christ in our hope ; but that we should glory in him, and exalt him in our hearts, lips and lives.

Though we desire to be found only in Christ, though our holy walk and good works cannot justify our persons, yet they justify our faith, our profession, yea, and the doctrines of grace, from the unjust charge of licentiousness. O may we be more and more concerned to obey Christ, to let our light of truth " shine before men, that, seeing our good works, they may glorify our Father who is in heaven." Matt. 5 : 16. Paul wishes for the experienced comfort and sensible blessing of being "found in Christ :" this precious enjoyment we also should covet earnestly.

August 29.—*Building up yourselves on your most holy faith.*
Jude 20

Instead of going on comfortably in this work, many are questioning whether they have a most holy faith. Bring this to a point this day. Has the ruinous fabric of nature's self-confidence, self-righteousness, self-complacency, and self-pleasing ever been pulled down ? Has the Spirit convinced you of sin? Do you see yourself a lost, ruined sinner; so lost and so ruined by sin that no one but the Son of God can restore and save you? Do you believe that he came to save sinners? Is it the desire of your heart to be saved from *all* sin by him? If so, you as surely possess a holy faith as you enjoy natural life; and you will get stronger evidence and greater assurance of it, by using every blessed means to prove that you have this most holy faith, while you build up yourself on it.

This will appear to be *a holy faith*, by leading out your soul after a holy Saviour, to be rooted and built up in him, and established in the faith of his perfect love to you and finished salvation for you, abounding therein with thanksgiving. Col. 2 : 7. You will not live a day but praise will rise in your heart to the Father for his unspeakable gift of Christ; to the Son for giving himself for you; and to the Spirit for the gift of this most holy faith to you.

As you believe sin has made you miserable; that it causes God to hide his face; clouds your views of the Sun of righteousness; grieves the Holy Spirit, and damps the joys of faith; you cannot, you dare not seek happiness in the pleasures of sin; you will hate it, strive against it, that you may grow in grace and be *built up* in your most holy faith. As you believe that the earth and all things that are therein are doomed to be burnt up, you cannot love the world so as to set your affections on it and seek your happiness in it. You hear the voice of the Lord, "My son, give me thy heart." When tempted by the honors, riches, and pleasures of a bewitching world, you will say of all, You bid too little to purchase me : I have a holy faith; I believe that my holy God can make me infinitely more honorable, rich, and happy, than all your toys and baubles. The Lord is my portion, saith my soul.

O christian, be this the confidence of thy most holy faith. Bless the Lord that ever it was wrought in you. Bear the fruits of righteousness, knowing that from Christ you shall " receive the end of your faith, even the salvation of your soul." 1 Pet. 1 : 9.

AUGUST 30.—*I die daily.* 1 Cor. 15 : 31

Paul, in a peculiar sense, could say so ; he was daily in danger of suffering martyrdom for Christ : he makes the most solemn oath to it, " I protest by our (not your) rejoicing, which I have in Christ Jesus our Lord, I die daily." He thus virtually appeals to the Holy Ghost, the author of this joy. Happy Paul ! The joy of the Lord was in his heart, the prospect of enjoying his Lord in his eye, the world under his feet, and he daily expecting his Lord's messenger to call him home. This was living indeed in the very suburbs of glory : and pray what should hinder you and I from living as he did ?

Paul was the subject of the same corrupt nature, in which dwelt no good thing, as we are ; we have the same Lord to look to and rejoice in, the same faith and hope to animate us, the same Holy Ghost to strengthen and comfort us, and the same place prepared by Christ for us. Why should not we also " die daily ?" Why should not we live a dying life ? All do in reality : but why should not we in sweet practice and happy experience ? Plainly, we do not believe enough what the Lord has done for us, is to us, and has promised to bestow on us ; therefore we do not look and pray enough to our Lord.

My dear fellow-christians, I will be bold to enter this protest, from the experience of my own soul, that we cannot live comfortably unless we die daily ; as considering ourselves daily subject to the stroke of death.

This hour, this moment may put a period to my existence. Why then all my busy cares, anxious thoughts, corroding fears and ardent desires after the objects of time? Death will soon make me quit my hold of them: but I will anticipate his approach. I will die in heart, hope, and affection to them. Take, ye sons of earth, the riches, honors, and pleasures of a perishing world; grasp them in your hand; clasp them to your heart if you can; but lo, instead of substance you will find shadow; all are but airy bubbles that will elude your hope; I have tried them all; I die to them all; for I have found that above which kills my desires, hopes, and affections to all below. I have found a once crucified, now risen and ascended Saviour. He has possession of my heart; he dwells there by faith; he is to me the hope of glory. The glorious rays of the Sun of righteousness extinguish the faint light of earthly glow-worms: my Lord lives; that is death to all beside. Death is deprived of his terrors: I entertain him as my friend, converse freely and daily with him. Why? Because my Lord introduces him to my heart, not with a sting to wound and kill me, but with the voice of a messenger of peace, to call me from pains and trials to peace and rest, to the full enjoyment of Jesus above, who is my glory and my life below. Col. 3 : 4.

AUGUST 31.—*Honor the Lord with thy substance.* Prov. 3 : 9.

O may this be the daily study of our hearts and the constant practice of our lives! "Let us be glad and rejoice, and give honor to the LORD, for the marriage of the LAMB is come." Rev. 19 : 7. He is our husband: we are espoused to him by faith. Consider the work of honoring the Lord, and the reason for it.

What! can I, a worm of the earth, honor the Lord of heaven? Yes, thou art called to it, and formed for it:

this honor have all his saints : it is our greatest honor on earth to honor our Lord in heaven : "All thy works shall praise thee, O Lord, and thy saints shall bless thee. They shall speak of the glory of thy kingdom, and talk of thy power. To make known to the sons of men his mighty acts, and the glorious majesty of his kingdom." Psalm 114 : 10, 11, 12. So they honored the Lord of old, in displaying the glory of his grace ; this work you are called to, if you have seen the glory of his kingdom, felt the power of it, and entered into it by faith : "Honor the Lord with thy substance."

Do not put such a dry, shrivelled comment upon the word *substance*, as though it meant giving a trifle now and then to the poor. Remember, " the liberal deviseth liberal things, and by liberal things he shall stand," or be established. Isa. 32 : 8. Do not dispense shadow when the Lord requires substance. If thy soul is liberal, thou wilt devise liberal things. This text will not only remind you of liberally dispensing of your substance to the poor and needy ; but also of honoring your Lord by the faith of your heart, the love of your soul, placing your whole affections upon him, and devoting your substance, your whole spirit, soul and body, to him ; you will not be content with notions without life, form without spirit, worship without the heart, religion without the soul.

Consider the reasons for thus "honoring the Lord." God has put the highest honor upon you ; " He has called you into the fellowship of his Son Jesus Christ." 1 Cor. 1 : 9. He has blessed you with *all* spiritual blessings in him. Eph. 1 : 3. There is no blessing God has to bestow, or of which Christ is possessed, but it is treasured up for you in Christ, and shall be received out of the fulness of Christ. Can you walk in the fellowship of Christ and not delight to honor God with your substance ? Again, you received all this freely, therefore you ought to give freely : you are a pensioner upon God, and God is, as it were, a petitioner to you. Can you refuse him who speaks ? Can you withhold any thing from him by whom you enjoy your *all* ? Think also, you have but a little while to honor your Lord : let the faith of this stir you up to exert all your might : only call in and consult faith and love, and act under their influence to God's glory.

September

Sept. 1.—*From that time many of his disciples went back, and walked no more with him.* John, 6 : 66

Thus was fulfilled that saying, how " can two walk together, except they be agreed?" Amos, 3 : 3. This chapter is like a touch-stone ; herein our Lord tries his disciples, to see who are his. Many who are his professed, are not his real disciples. Times of trial will come : they make manifest. The lowest hell is prepared for those who turn their backs upon the Son of God on earth. Lord, grant that our faces may be set like a flint towards thee ; for, blessed be thy name, thou hast said of those who continue with thee in thy temptations : " I appoint unto you a kingdom ; ye shall eat and drink at my table." Luke 22 : 29, 30.

But those who are not agreed with Christ, have not the mind of Christ, and will not walk with him. Some of these disciples followed Christ for the loaves and fishes. John 6 : 26. Those who follow Christ to get food for their bodies and the good things of this life, instead of food for the soul, will soon forsake him.

Christ's blessings are spiritual, their views are carnal. Such are not agreed with him.

Others murmured at him because he said, "I came down from heaven." John 6 : 41. They were ignorant of his mission from the Father. Many people hear again and again of Christ, but have no solid, scriptural judgment of the divinity of his person clothed in human nature, nor of the end and design of his coming into the world; for want of knowledge of him, and faith in him, they soon forsake him.

Others could not receive his saying, "Except ye eat the flesh and drink the blood of the Son of man, ye have no life in you." John 6 : 53. His words were spiritual, their notions carnal: they could not see how Christ could be the spiritual food of souls by faith; so, many in our day cry, "Where mystery begins religion ends:" these left following Christ.

His doctrine of his Father's sovereign grace was galling to the pride of their self-righteous, self-sufficient hearts: "No man can come unto me, except it were given unto him of my Father." John 6 : 65. "From that" speech, (time is not in the original) "many of his disciples went back, and walked no more with him." O how many still oppose the truth of the sovereign love and efficacious grace of God the Father, in drawing sinners to his Son for salvation! Alas, they have not the mind of Christ; they see not the special mercy of being under the efficacious influence of the Spirit of the Father. O disciple, let the falling away of others warn thee: be strong in the Lord: be diffident of self: look constantly to "Him that is able to keep you from falling." Jude 24.

———————

SEPT. 2.—*I labored more abundantly than they all ; yet not I, but the grace of God which was with me.* 1 Cor. 15 : 10

Those journals, diaries, or relations of experience

which do not exalt the riches of the grace of God, but display the self-importance of men, are as tainted food to the palate: they remind of the poet's phrase, "and I the little hero of each tale." Not so Paul, in speaking of himself; no sooner does he advert to what he had done, than he hides himself in the grace of God. Hence this doctrine is plain: the grace of God makes a person labor for God, and yet keeps him humble before God.

To have the grace of God with us, is to have a lively sense of God's free favor in Christ upon our souls; without this we go on heavily in the ways of God, soon tire in his service, and turn back and walk no more with Christ: this was the life and spring of all Paul's labors. Let us see to it, then, that we wrestle with God in prayer, study the precious word of his grace, and be diligent in attending his ordinances, that we may ever have a lively sense of God's pardoning, justifying, sanctifying grace in Christ upon our hearts, ever cautiously avoid all persons, places, and things, which tend to grieve the Spirit and quench his lively influence.

Every private christian is called to labor for God, as well as apostles and ministers. There is such a thing as receiving the grace of God in vain. How? When we profess to esteem and receive the doctrines of the Gospel of grace, and yet they bring not forth in us correspondent fruits. Oh how much is this the case among professors! How greatly to be deplored and deprecated! What! do you profess to know God, and yet in works deny him? Do you believe the love and salvation of Christ for miserable sinners; and yet can you, instead of laboring for his glory, be idle, in not living and walking, studying and striving to please our Saviour and profit his dear children? Have you the grace of God with you? It is to be feared, if you have, that you have sadly lost its life and influence. O then be deeply affected for your state!

Is the grace of God warm upon our hearts? Are we active for God's glory in our lives? Do we labor more than others for God? O let us beware that we do not sacrifice to ourselves, or exalt our own power and faithfulness; for true grace will keep us low and humble: in the light of it we shall see how little we do for God, how much more we ought to do; and in the little we do, how much evil there is in it, and how far short we come in all of his glory: "Be clothed with humility." 1 Peter 5 : 5.

Sept. 3.—*From the rising of the sun, unto the going down of the same, the Lord's name is to be praised.* Psalm 113 : 3

Praise is the incessant employ of glorified saints in heaven: there they fully see and eternally sing of the electing, redeeming, sanctifying, glorifying love of the blessed Trinity. May our souls now catch something of the heavenly flame of love, and imitate them in our praises. This is the work of an humble heart: pride is the parent of murmuring and discontent. A sense of the blessings of the Lord, and a sight of our unworthiness of them, excite praises in the heart.

This is the language of a praising soul, "Why me, Lord? Why am I singled out from the ruins of a fallen race, to partake of thy special grace, peculiar love, and precious salvation? Am I better than others? Have I done more to deserve thy mercies than others? Have I a greater right to challenge thy favor than others? O Lord, why me?" Thus, while the soul sinks in humility, it rises in praises. David describes saints with the "high praises of God in their mouth, and a two-edged sword in their hand." Psalm 149 : 6. What for? To execute vengeance upon the heathen notions of sacrificing any praise to themselves, or ascribing any thing to their own deserts. These are special marks of a regenerate person.

His heart is formed for and his soul delights to praise the Lord at all times; for he sees himself infinitely and entirely indebted to the grace of God for all he is, all he enjoys, and all he hopes for. It is his grief that he cannot praise the Lord as he would; for worthy is the Lord of unceasing praise. His mercies are renewed every morning, continued unto evening, and repeated in the night-season.

But here is a precious word in this Psalm that endears the Lord to us, and excites praise from us: "Who is like unto the Lord our God who dwelleth on high: who HUMBLETH himself"—pause, O my soul, at that astonishing word: how did the most high God humble himself? To the most low and abject state; made himself of no reputation, took on him the form of a servant: yea more, became obedient to the most ignominious death, even the cursed death of the cross. Phil. 2: 8. O my soul, though vile in thine own eyes, though of no repute in the world, consider this: thou canst never want an inexhaustible fund of comfort and a never-failing source of praise. "Bless the Lord, O my soul: and all that is within me, bless his holy name." Psalm 103: 1.

SEPT. 4.—*Come, buy wine and milk, without money and without price.* Isaiah 55: 1.

A free Gospel is the glory of God's grace, the joy of humble souls, the envy of devils, and the contempt of the proud and self-righteous. MILK is the pure, sweet, soul-nourishing doctrines of the Gospel of Christ. WINE is the heart-reviving comfort of pardon of sin and peace with God through the blood of Christ: the Lord knows we cannot grow strong, or be comfortable in our souls, without this precious milk and animating wine. Here is the Lord's open house, public market, free invitation, and fixed price.

Come, draw nigh to me ; keep not at a distance from me, saith the Lord ; make no excuse, nor any delay ; come now, this moment ; here is a free invitation, and a hearty welcome. O the love of our Lord's heart !

Buy. Art thou rich ? Such the Lord sends empty away. Hast thou brought a stock of thine own faithfulness, and good deeds that thou hast done, to buy with ? Then, instead of wine and milk, thou wilt receive a scourge from the Lord. Remember, those who bought and sold he drove out of his temple. "O," saith the poor self-emptied, soul-humbled sinner, "this word *buy* puts me to a stand : I am poor and pennyless ; I have nothing to bring but misery and poverty ; I am perishing for want of comfort." Thou art the very person invited : the Lord "filleth the hungry soul with good." O precious word of marvellous grace !

Buy—*without money and without price*. What ! have I been five, ten, twenty years or upwards in Christ, and have I got no inherent stock of grace, no more worth or value to buy with than I had when I first came to him as a poor, naked, and perishing sinner ? Must I come as at first, poor and pennyless ? Yes : or not at all. The Lord knows what thou art ; he invites thee just as thou art ; his price just suits thy abject poverty. What an affront would it be to a dear friend to bring a price in our hands for a rich entertainment, with a free invitation ? No affectionate mother more freely administers the breast of nourishment to her hungry infant, than the Lord his milk and wine to thirsty souls. Faith works by the love of this : it operates upon the heart, so as to produce sincere love to God and cheerful obedience to his word and will : but base unbelief, with a false humility, raises jealousies and suspicions of the Lord's rich love and free grace. One says, It cannot be for me, I am too vile ; another, I am unworthy of it. Christ says, "whosoever will, let him come." Rev. 22 : 17.

Sept. 5.—*And confessed they were strangers and pilgrims on the earth.* Heb. 11 : 13

O ye worldly-minded professors, can ye read this without being ashamed and reproved? What will bring a man to this confession? Will sickness and a near approach to death? O no: men return from the most dangerous illness to greater love of the world and more ardent pursuit after it. Look at a dying worldling; see him, like a drowning man, clenching the faster what he has grasped for his hope and help. Men not only live fools, but die fools too: their senses beguile them; their reason befools them; they reject the plainest truths before them.

Nothing will kill the love of a bewitching world, in a deceitful heart, but the view of heaven by faith: no man will confess himself a stranger to the world and a pilgrim on the earth, until he sees himself "a fellow-citizen with the saints and of the household of God." Eph. 2 : 19. Admire those ancient heroes of faith: view and imitate their conduct.

What caused this confession? They had not received the promises: the Messiah was not then come from heaven with all the inestimable blessings of his kingdom; yet they believed in him, looked to him, and lived, by faith, upon him as promised. Though they saw the precious promises afar off, yet they were realized to their hearts by faith; the distance of them did not weaken their confidence in their real existence; faith brought them nigh to their minds. They were persuaded of them, and embraced them; they clung to the promises of God as the chief delight and greatest joy of their souls.

Worldly men cry, " O, faith is to do all for you!" No, not so: Christ has done all for us; by faith we enjoy all the comfort of it : hence we become followers of Christ: " strangers and pilgrims on the earth," and travellers to

our Father's kingdom. Have you had no mark of disap-
probation from carnal men? Do they see nothing in
you to which they object? Then you have great reason
to question whether you are a real follower of a despised, crucified Lord: the world will love its own. Are
you striving to keep both God and the world? Of all
men upon earth, you are most to be pitied, for you will
be most miserable: most joyful to say, I am " a stranger
and a sojourner, as all my fathers were." Psalm 39 : 12.

SEPT. 6.—*But now, in Christ Jesus, ye, who sometimes were far
off, are made nigh by the blood of Christ.* Ephes. 2 : 13

If one was asked, " Do you live near the court? Have
you free access to the king?" who would hesitate one
moment for an answer? Consciousness would instantly
dictate one. Pray, is christian experience so dark and
doubtful a matter, that, if one asked, " Are you brought
nigh to God? Do you live near God? Have you free
access to God?" we cannot answer with some degree
of knowledge and certainty? O my dear fellow-christians, though we are brought nigh to God, yet we do not
live near him: hence our doubt and uncertainty: our
hearts and affections rove upon the high roads of earthly honor, riches, or pleasures: here clouds of dust arise,
which so dim our sight and obscure our views that we
can hardly see our way or tell where we are.

Here we are reminded that we " sometimes were *far
off.*" Awful distance! As far as possible from God, because so far from original righteousness. Naturally we
have no desire to draw nigh to him : nay, Satan had possession of us, ruled in and reigned over us: we loved
our master, hated our God, and delighted in our distance
from him. O be covered with shame, be clothed with
humility, yet lift up your head with joy. For

We are *brought nigh* to God. O, says one, I wish I

was sure of this. It is true in the word, that sinners are brought nigh to God: you can only know this for yourself by experience. Consider, then, how we are brought nigh. By the blood of Christ: by faith in him we are reconciled to God, justified before God, and at peace with God.

If you are brought nigh to God, Christ is precious to you; your heart is towards him; your hope is fixed on him. His blood is highly prized by you: you look to his atonement for the pardon of your sins, to cleanse your conscience from guilt, and to bring peace to your soul. You delight to draw nigh to God, making his blood and righteousness your only plea for salvation. And you will live near to God in love, and walk before him in holiness: you will hate the things you once loved, and love the things you once hated; in this way only can you enjoy fellowship and peace with God, comfort from God, and assurance that you are a child of God. Says Christ, "If ye love me, keep my commandments," and the Comforter shall "abide with you for ever." John 14: 15, 16.

SEPT. 7.—*As for me, I will call upon God, and the Lord shall save me.* Psalm 55: 16

I have been often struck with the conduct of blind Bartimeus: when "many charged him to hold his peace, he cried the more a great deal, Thou Son of David, have mercy on me." Mark 10 : 48. Why was this? Truly he had a deep sense of his loss of sight, and by faith he saw Jesus able to restore it. See the consequence of this importunate cry. Did the sun stand still at the word of Joshua? Behold, at the cry of Bartimeus the Lord and Creator of all the host of heaven *stood still.* Jesus knows the cry of his own Spirit; he will hear it, and help the soul that utters it; "His ears are open to our prayers." 1 Pet. 3 : 12.

Look at David's circumstances: was he now on the mount of joy, basking in the sunbeams of comfort? No, he is sighing out a doleful complaint in the vale of distress: "I mourn because of the voice of the enemy and the oppression of the wicked; my heart is sore pained within me, and the terrors of death are fallen upon me; fearfulness and trembling are come upon me, and horror hath overwhelmed me." Psalm 55 : 3–5.

What is his resolution? Does he give up hope in his God? Does he flee his presence and seek for comfort in the world, from its vain pleasures, sensual delights, and from worldly men? No; "*I will call upon God.*" Here is a lesson of instruction for us: the more fears, terrors, pains, and oppression beset us, the more should they impel us to call upon God; seek to no object but God for relief; remember that there is not one of them but is by his appointment or permission; that they are calls from God to us to call upon him; and that when they bring us to God his loving will is answered. He will not suffer his dear people to live at a distance from him without calling upon him; he loves their souls; he delights in their prayers; and his comforts delight them. Psalm 94 : 19. Can you say so?

Then you may confidently take up David's conclusion; "The Lord shall save me." Is not this too bold? Yes, if founded upon any thing in yourself as the cause why God should save you, it is daring presumption; but, from the Lord's absolute declarations, full and free promises given us in Christ, we are divinely warranted thus to conclude. O then take and prize the Lord's word as your blessed charter of salvation; plead before him; expect all salvation from him, even victory over all sin, deliverance from every trouble, the comfort of holiness here, and the joys of glory in eternity, "All are yours, and ye are Christ's, and Christ is God's" 1 Cor. 3 : 23.

SEPT. 8.—*To them who have obtained like precious faith with us through the righteousness of God and our Saviour Jesus Christ.* 2 Pet. 1:1

There may be strong faith where there is no true faith persons may pretend to have the assurance of faith, may believe that their sins are forgiven, without one grain of "precious faith." Who believes more than a deist does? he believes he has wisdom to guide and power to save himself, without either the word or the grace of God. Who has stronger faith than the self-righteous Pharisee had? He believed he had a right to go to God, to plead his works before God, and to assure his heart that he was accepted of God: he wanted no righteousness from God. This is just such a faith as all unregenerate men have. It is not a *precious* faith; it is not obtained through the precious righteousness of Christ; it doth not make his glorious person and everlasting righteousness precious to the heart; it does not cause such to renounce the filthy rags of their own righteousness, and to delight in God, as justifying the ungodly through the righteousness of Christ, and sanctifying the unholy through the Spirit of his grace.

That faith is ever to be suspected, as only a rank weed which grows in the corrupt soil of human nature, the possessors of which do not see the evil of sin which is in them, the curse it has brought upon them, and that nothing can relieve their conscience, support their mind, bring hope to their heart and joy to their spirits, but the one spotless righteousness of Christ, in which sinners stand perfectly justified before God. He who dares open his mouth in objections against justification and sanctification solely by His righteousness, gives fearful evidence that so far from having obtained "like precious faith" with the apostles, his heart is not yet convinced of sin.

"Precious faith" will show itself by its fruits inward

as well as outward: the heart will bow to God's sovereign will, receive his doctrines of grace, in the love of
them, and not carp and cavil against them; it will glory
that salvation, from first to last, is not of works, but of
grace; and it will experience, that "the grace of God
which bringeth salvation," most sweetly and powerfully teaches to "deny all ungodliness and worldly lusts,
and to live soberly, righteously and godly in this present evil world." Most sweetly says one, "Surely there
can be no greater honor to Christ than this: in the sense
of sin, wants, stains and blemishes, to wrap ourselves
in the righteousness of Christ, and with boldness to go,
clothed in his heavenly garments, to the throne of grace."
This is the glory of faith. Lord, grant it may be ours.

SEPT. 9.—*Lord, be merciful unto me : heal my soul ; for I have
sinned against thee.* Psalm 41 : 4

Is this the language of a saint ? Was David a saint
when he uttered it ? Yes, he was a holy man of God :
this confession and prayer show it : his heart was not
hardened through the deceitfulness of sin, nor blinded
by self-righteous pride, so as to say, "I have no sin."
Self-righteous hearts cannot consent that all the Lord's
saints are yet in themselves miserable sinners ; that they
see daily need to confess this, and to sue for mercy and
healing from the Lord. Here is a confession, a plea, and
a prayer.

A confession—"I have sinned against thee." Thus
we must come and confess to the Lord to-day, to-morrow, and every day, till the sun of life sets. Sense of
sin, whether now contracted or long since committed,
abides with us; it wounds and pains a gracious soul.
Here grace discovers itself : that soul waits not for time
to efface the memory of sin, nor strives to stifle convictions for it, but goes humbly to the Lord and confesses

it, with all its aggravations, and with this above all others, Lord, "*against thee* have I sinned." O may my soul never, never lose this conviction, that every sin is against THEE, my Lord and loving Father; THEE, my Lord and precious Redeemer; THEE, my Lord and gracious Comforter: this makes sin exceeding sinful, while it magnifies the super-abounding riches of grace, in receiving sinners, and in pardoning sin.

Consider *the plea:* it is not the pharisee's parade: Lord, I have done this and that, or I have done so and so: Lord, I have been faithful to thy grace, I am not so bad as others: no! but it is the publican's plea: " Lord, be merciful to me," to me a vile sinner, who have done nothing to deserve thy favor, yet plead thy mercy promised to sinners in Christ Jesus: thou canst be just and yet justify the ungodly who believe in Jesus.

Therefore his *prayer* is, " heal my soul." No prayers, no tears, no duties of mine can heal my soul; no, my best works are stained with pollution, my holiest duties are mixed with sin: nothing but the blood of *the Lamb* can bring pardon to my heart, peace to my conscience, and healing to my soul. " The Lord will speak peace unto his people and his saints." Psalm 85 : 8. For, O precious words! he assures us, "*all manner* of sin and blasphemy shall be forgiven unto men." Matt. 12 : 31.

SEPT. 10.—*Light is sown for the righteous, and gladness for the upright in heart.* Psalm 97 : 11

He who never doubts his sincerity to God has great reason to suspect his knowledge of himself. A hypocrite cannot be a christian; yet there is hypocrisy in the fallen nature of every christian. Such are ever suspecting themselves. At times they fear lest they should turn out mere hypocrites at last : this is a proof that their hearts are upright with Christ : their fears and suspicions are a blessed means of keeping them from falling away from him. Righteous souls pass through many dark hours: sometimes they are put to a stand, ready to question if they have any interest in Christ; for they have a nature in which dwells every evil which wars against God, and the peace, holiness, and comfort of their souls: hence they are sometimes in seasons of darkness; they see not things in the light of truth; they enjoy not the comfort of the truth, that they are righteous in the righteousness of Christ, 2 Cor. 5:21, and made upright by his grace.

Upright souls mourn in darkness, and desire ever to walk in the light; yes, says St. Peter, ye "greatly rejoice" in the salvation of Jesus, "though now for a season (if need be) ye are in heaviness through manifold temptations." If need be! O, what need can there be? He tells us, "that the trial of your faith might be found unto praise, and honor, and glory, at the appearing of Jesus Christ." 1 Pet. 1:6, 7. Tried faith is true faith. True faith stands the fire of temptation; trusts Christ in heaviness; stays upon him in darkness; for at all times, in all seasons, under all circumstances, light and gladness are sown for you, and in due season shall spring up in you. Where are they sown? Where every covenant blessing is reaped: in Jesus, the surety of the covenant. Heb. 7:22. All natural light flows from the sun: all spiritual light flows from Christ, the Sun of righteousness, who saith, "I am the light of the world: he that followeth me shall not walk in darkness, but shall have the light of life." John 8:12.

Is light sown in Christ for us? Let us with David claim in faith, "the LORD is MY light, and my salvation." Psalm 27:1. Does gladness of heart spring from Christ? Then say, "My meditations of him shall be sweet, I will be glad in the Lord." Psalm 104:34. Thus faith is tried and proved in the darkest hour: thus it manifests itself to be the faith of God's elect; for it cleaves to Jesus, God's "elect, in whom God's soul delighteth." Isaiah 42: 1.

Sept. 11.—*But that on the good ground, are they, which in an honest and good heart, having heard the word, keep it, and bring forth fruit with patience.* Luke 8:15

Disciple, tread warily on this good ground: speak cautiously about it, lest thy soul be lifted up, and thou shouldst say, I made myself to differ; my nature is better to receive the seed, and my heart more honest and good to retain it than others. Know thyself by nature upon a level with way-side, stony ground, and thorny hearers. See what is predicted of those who "having heard the word, keep it." Let us examine if we are of the happy number: if so, let us fall down in humility and cry, What hath God wrought! Let us give all the glory to the God of all grace!

"That on good ground." It is made good by the labor of the husbandman; tilled, cultivated, and made fit to receive the seed, by the grace of the Spirit, "in an honest and good heart." No man has such a heart naturally: the heart is deceitful above all things, and desperately wicked; see the accursed weeds it brings forth: "Out of the heart proceedeth evil thoughts, murders, adulteries," &c. Mark 7: 21. Such a heart as this can neither receive nor retain the seed of the kingdom, so as to bring forth fruit unto perfection. "A new heart," saith the Lord, "will I give you." Ezek. 36: 26. Precious promise! This is that good and honest heart. Hath the Lord given it thee? If so,

You will "hear the word and keep it." It takes root downward. Thou hast and dost retain an abiding sense of thy own vileness, poverty, and wretchedness; thou wilt be rooted and grounded in the love of Christ, knowing that in him thou art rich, righteous, and happy. As the word made thee thus wise and happy, thou wilt keep it, ponder it in thine heart, meditate upon it day and night: it will be dear and precious to thy soul. This is an evidence of a good and honest heart; it delights in the good news of the word of grace, the faithful prom ises of a covenant God in Christ Jesus.

Such "bring forth fruit with patience." Because they keep the word in their hearts, they go on patient in well-doing, and patient in suffering the will of God. Says David, "Thy word have I hid in my heart." To what end? "That I might not sin against thee." Psalm 119:11. Says Paul, "The word of-the truth of the Gospel bringeth forth fruit in you, since the day ye heard of it, and knew the grace of God in truth." Col. 1:5, 6. That soul in whose heart the word of grace takes the deepest root, brings forth most fruit to God O soul, wouldst thou be more holy and more happy? Keep the word of God: study it: that directs thee to Christ, in whom all thy happiness centres, and from whom all thy holiness springs.

SEPT. 12.—*Unto Him that loved us, and washed us from our sins in his own blood.* Rev. 1:5.

Paul denounces the most dreadful curse upon every one who loves not the Lord Jesus Christ. 1 Cor. 16:22. Why does any sinner love Christ? "We love him because he first loved us." See the awful curses of unbelief: it rejects the love of Christ; it sets at nought his salvation; it seals the sinner under the curse, the wrath due to his sins; and binds him over to eternal damnation. But the unawakened sinner smiles at all this; for he does not believe it. Lord, leave not my soul under this sin of sins, of all sins the most heinous and accursed. O help my unbelief.

See the preciousness of faith: it works by love, even

by the love of Christ manifested to us; it receives and takes home his love to the heart; there it works peace in the conscience, delight in God, access to God, boldness before God, joy in God, fellowship with God, conformity to God, and longing for eternal enjoyment of God.

Our sins, which are the cause of separation and distance from God, are washed away. How? By Christ's own blood. O wonderful to think! O joyful to believe! The holy Son of God has washed us—us unholy, ungodly, hell-deserving sinners, from our sins in his own blood: this precious, this mighty Redeemer hath once appeared, for ever to put away our sins by the sacrifice of himself. Heb. 9:26. What says his Father of him? "In my beloved Son I am well pleased." Matt. 3:17 What saith he of us? "Your sins and iniquities will I remember no more." Heb. 10:17. What say you? Is all this true? Is all this fact, or fable? Upon our belief of this depends our comfort and holiness; and from the faith of this springs glory to God in the highest.

If we firmly believe this, we shall joyfully join the redeemed in earth and heaven, in giving praise and glory to Christ for washing us from our sins in his own blood. But you say, I have sin in me, I mourn over it, and groan under it—the sense of this is needful to keep you humble before Christ: yet faith is above sense; it glorifies Christ for washing away from before God's sight the very sins you feel. You have the sense of fear that you shall perish for your sins: this is a holy fear; this keeps you from sinning. But faith says, "There is no condemnation to them who are in Christ Jesus." Romans 8:1.

SEPT. 13.—*And hath made us kings and priests unto God and his Father.* Rev. 1:6

Christ has done a great work for us: but does he only

call us to believe it, and then leave us just as we were, under the dominion of sin, Satan, and the world? No; he not only washes us from our sins, which he hates, in his blood; but he also dignifies our person, which he loves, by his power.

> "Hail, Jesus, lavish of strange gifts to man!
> "Thine all the glory; man's the boundless bliss."

O miracle of grace! Christ "hath made us kings and priests." *Kings*, to rule over sin, the world, death and hell. Sin brought death into the world: death reigned over all that sinned: but, "they who receive abundance of grace and of the gift of righteousness, shall reign in life, by ONE Jesus Christ." Rom. 5 : 17. O believer, do you forget your regal dignity? Then you do not honor as you ought your *King of kings*. Consider, you are made a king to reign *in life;* a spiritual life over all that is earthly, sensual, and devilish. Do you say, how can I reign over sin who am the subject of sin? "Sin shall not have dominion over you, because you are not under the law, but under grace." Romans 6 : 14. An earthly monarch may have many treacherous and rebellious subjects who envy him and would dethrone him; still, in spite of all, he may keep his throne: so do you over all rebel lusts and traitorous dispositions; for Christ is king over you: you reign by his power, you are a king unto God: you reign to his glory.

"Hath made us *priests*." The priest under the law offered gifts and sacrifices according to the law: under the Gospel we are "a holy priesthood, to offer up spiritual sacrifices, acceptable to God by Jesus Christ," 1 Pet. 2 : 5, even those of "a broken heart and contrite spirit:" our bodies and souls, time and talents, prayers and praises, yea, to sacrifice ourselves, our love of the world, our pride, all our carnal reason and self-righteousness, all and every thing which is contrary to our Lord's will and glory; for as Christ our High Priest has offered up himself to God for us, so we are to offer up ourselves to God by him.

O believer, study more and more your regal dignity and royal priesthood. Will an earthly monarch so degrade and demean himself as to be the companion and gratify the wishes of traitors and rebels? Will any christian priest sacrifice to heathen idols? O, when thy sins rebel and Satan tempts, consider, Christ hath made me a king to reign over them. When worldly vanities allure, remember, Christ hath made me a priest to sacrifice them to his honor and glory.

SEPT. 14.—*Then is the offence of the cross ceased.* Gal. 5 : 11

Another version reads the words as a question, " Is the offence of the cross ceased?" No, nor ever will while there is a christian upon the earth. The cross is put for that ever loving Jesus, who hung upon it as a curse for our souls and an atonement for our sins. O, let us be ever zealous for the glory of the cross, for the sake of the Lamb, who finished our salvation upon it. The cross of Christ is the christian's glory : the offence the world takes at him, is but the natural result of his having taken up the cross of Christ and followed him. This no man can do faithfully, but he must give offence. Settle this well in your mind : sit down and count the cost. Are you willing to be Christ's glory and the world's scorn?

Do you expect all from the cross? Then give up all for the cross. Here nature recoils, flesh and blood rebels, carnal reason pleads that worldly prudence may be consulted : " Look at such and such a professor ; they go on very quietly ; the world takes no offence at them." But why is it? Are they not either quite dead in sin, or fallen into a deep sleep of security? Converse with them : you will perhaps find no sweet savor of Jesus upon their tongue, no warm affections to Christ in their hearts, no burning zeal for his glory in their lives: hence, as the offence of the cross is ceased with them, so the peace, comfort and joy of it is departed from them. For the truth of this I dare appeal to my own and every disciple's heart. When was your soul most active for God, most filled with his love; enjoying most fellowship with him, and peace and comfort in him? Was it not when you lived nearest to the cross, and found most of the offence of the cross of Christ?

Holy Paul seemed to dread the offence of the cross of Christ ceasing. He was jealous lest any should question it. Lord Jesus, hast thou done so much in thy holy life, and suffered so much by thy precious death on the cross for our eternal salvation, and shall we be ashamed of thy cross? Shall we be afraid of confessing the faith of our hearts and the hope of our souls in thee, with our lips and in our lives? O, forbid it! Never shall I forget my late dear friend, Rev. Mr. Jones, when with his usual warmth of affection to Christ, preaching upon the scandal of the cross: "My dear friends, (said he) you who are afraid to lose your good name for Christ's sake, I pity you from my heart. Thank God, my fear of this is gone long ago." "God forbid that I should glory, save in the cross of Jesus Christ." Gal. 6 : 14.

SEPT. 15.—*The righteous is taken away from the evil.* Isa. 57 : 1

Why then do we not rejoice over the dead, who die in the Lord? Why do we, who profess to be in the Lord, fear to die? Death will be the funeral of all our evils, and the resurrection of all our joys. Why then do we dread it? Why so reluctant to be taken from the many evils we suffer here? Why not rather longing to be for ever with the Lord? Plainly, it is for want of faith; the point is not fully settled between our Saviour and our souls whether we are his members or not, and hence we do not walk closely and joyfully with him, and then the fear of death prevails over us. All true believers are living members of Christ, united to him, and one with him. The righteousness of Christ is theirs: they are clothed with it, and stand justified before God. Hence the Holy Spirit is given to us: he enables us to walk in the paths of righteousness, and to bring forth the fruits of righteousness which are by Jesus Christ, to the glory of God. Phil. 1:11.

See the blessedness of the righteous: they are " taken away from the evil." The Lord doeth this for them because he loves them. The words *to come* are not in the original. They are taken from all present evil. They are taken from an evil nature: this is the grief and burden of their righteous souls from day to day; but the death of the body shall quite destroy the body of sin and death; they shall drop this body, and wing their way to endless glory.

They are taken from the evil of sin: though this did not reign over them, yet it raged in them; though they were not under its dominion, yet it warred in their members and made them cry out, Oh wretched! Sin brought death into the world: death shall be the grave of sin: the righteous is not taken away in his sins, but from the evil of them. They are taken from that evil of evils, unbelief: this now dishonors God, causes weak hands and dejected hearts; but in death we shall part with it for ever. From all the evil of this present world: from all pains, trials, and afflictions, of whatever kind, we shall be for ever delivered. This is the negative blessedness of the righteous. Who shall describe their positive happiness? It hath not entered into the heart of man to conceive what the Lord hath prepared for them who love him: this we must die fully to know. O love the Lord, all ye his saints.

Sept. 16.—*Should such a man as I flee?* Neh. 6:11

Nehemiah was engaged in a great work: his God was with him, and gave him success: friends and enemies united against him; by base insinuation, craft and stratagem, they strove to dishearten and deter him from going on with God's work. Opposition is the christian's lot; courage his honor; perseverance his jewel. Look at this man of God: he boldly repels all fear. Instead of fleeing from his work as advised, he flees to his God, and cries, "O God, strengthen my hands." Faith inspires prayer: prayer brings courage to the heart: then he boldly demands, *Should such a man as I flee?* A man so greatly favored, so highly honored, as to be employed by God to work for him? No; I disdain such mean cowardice: I will work on: it is God's cause: let him order the event; I fear it not.

Christian, know your calling: it is to work for God: expect opposition from within and without. This may call up fear and dismay; but consider your dignity; maintain and assert it: "Should such a man as I flee?" A man called by the grace of Jesus to resist the devil, to face carnal men, to vanquish sin, to overcome the world, to obtain victory over death, and to receive a crown of righteousness in endless glory: shall I flee? What, I who am called to be strong in the grace which is in Christ Jesus? O my soul, put on Christ and put off fear: put up prayer and put down dread.

From whom should such a man as I flee? Of whom should I be afraid? Doth not my Lord say, "My grace is sufficient for thee, my strength is made perfect in thy weakness?" O Lord, strengthen my heart to resist Satan, that he may flee from me, and to overcome the fear of man, which is a snare to me. I bless thee for thy precious word: strengthen my heart in the faith of it: "Fear not, neither be faint-hearted." Isa. 7:4. "Hearken unto me; fear not the reproach of men, neither be afraid of their revilings." Isa. 51 : 7. "I, even I am he who comforteth you. Who art thou that thou shouldst be afraid of a man that shall die, and the son of man which shall be made as grass, and forgettest the Lord thy Maker?" "The Lord God will help me: I shall not be confounded: I have set my face like a flint: I shall not be ashamed: the moth shall eat up my adversaries." Isa. 50 : 7.

SEPT. 17.—*And killed the Prince of Life.* Acts, 3 : 15

O dreadful effects of the fall of man! We have not only become enemies to God and rebels against him, but are also so ignorant of ourselves, and so blind to our own state, that we do not see this: we will not own it. "An enemy to God! What, to that good and gracious Lord, in whom I 'live, move, and have my being?' I cannot think that any one upon earth can be so wicked as to be an enemy to God"—such is the language of blind nature: thou that utterest it art the man. Yea, such is the enmity of thine, of every man's nature against God, that were it possible, and in our power, we should *kill God.* Start not at the thought! horrid as it is, here is proof of it. God was manifest in flesh. How was he received? How was he treated by sinful man? Let the annals of his holy life speak the base contempt and hellish treatment he met with from man: let the history of his painful and agonizing death proclaim the enmity of sinners' hearts against him.

They killed, whom? Jesus of Nazareth, a mere man, mighty in word and deed? a great prophet only? Infinitely more, O unparalleled mystery of iniquity! O inscrutable mystery of godliness! they killed the *Prince of Life.* Such the abominable wickedness of human nature, such the total blindness of the human heart, a murderer is preferred to an innocent man; a vile miscreant is spared; the Divine Redeemer, the author of life, is put to death. Here, O soul, behold the true but horrid picture of human nature: such its enmity to God as to take away the life of God.

Dost thou think in thine heart, surely my nature is not so dreadfully wicked, I could not have done so vile a deed? Thou dost not yet know thyself; thy thoughts proceed from blindness and ignorance of the depth of thy totally wicked nature: and as yet thou seest not the amazing heights of the Lord's love. The Prince of Life dies by the wicked hands of men. To what end? That by his death his very murderers should live and not die eternally. O matchless love! Learn, O my soul, to fathom the depth of the enmity of the human heart by the heights of the love of a dying Saviour. Sin has done its worst, slain my Redeemer, that I might live. Satan, thou hast wreaked thy hellish wrath; but thou art conquered in my Saviour's death. Law, thou hast sheathed thy strongest sting, and spent the poison of thy dart in the body of my God; but, glory to my Prince of Life, he lives to love, and loves to save: I am safe. O may the Spirit make this faith kill legal hopes and self-righteous confidence.

SEPT. 18. —*As ye have therefore received Christ Jesus the Lord, so walk ye in him.* Col. 2: 6

It is to the glory of the grace of the holy, blessed, and glorious Trinity, that any poor sinner receives Christ; and Christ is the glory of that heart which receives him: thus there is a mutual complacency and delight between Jehovah, Father, Son, and Spirit, and believing souls. Every one who believes in Christ Jesus has received Christ as his Lord, his atonement, his righteousness, his salvation, as really as Paul or any of his apostles. God is alike the Father of all such; the

Son is alike the Saviour of all such, and the Holy Ghost is alike the Sanctifier and Comforter of all such. O, well may the believing heart cry out in a rapture of joy, Lord, what rich grace is this! What a glorious privilege am I invested with! What hast thou wrought! What am I! Why should Jesus apprehend me, worthless me, that I should apprehend him! Lord, what wouldst thou have me to do?

Hear and obey: *Walk ye in him.* What is meant by this? In one word, seeing Christ is yours, enjoy him more and more—how? How did you receive him? As a perishing sinner by faith: then so walk in him. Walking implies the whole of a believer's life: that his soul should be ever active; that the eye of his faith should be ever looking to, and his heart trusting in Christ Jesus the Lord: so he walks comfortably, holily, steadily, and perseveringly, to the glory of his Saviour.

But shall we meet with no interruptions in thus walk ing *in Christ,* who is *the way?* Not from him; for he is a most smooth, delightful and pleasant way: only keep in him and you are sure of safety; but, from within and from without, you will meet with a crowd of objections and interruptions in your walk; the pride and lusts of the flesh will oppose you; Satan will jostle against and strive to impede your steps; the world will attempt to seduce you. Be simple of heart, know every step that you are as poor a sinner as when you first received Christ: make him the one object of your heart: when you are ready to halt at the sight of your wickedness, poverty and vileness, consider him, look to him, cry to him; so shall you renew your strength: you shall "run and not be weary, walk and not faint." Isaiah, 40 : 31. You are just at your journey's end; you have the shades of death to pass through. What of that? "Though I walk through the valley of the shadow of death I will fear no evil, for thou art with me." Psalm 23 : 4.

SEPT. 19.—*Thy Maker is thine husband, the Lord of hosts is his name; and thy Redeemer the Holy One of Israel: the God of the whole earth shall he be called.* Isa. 54 : 5

In this one verse is a trinity of comforts: all are enjoyed in the unity of faith: the Spirit bears witness of them: let our hearts attend to them. Consider, thou sin-distressed, Satan-accused soul, *thy Maker is thine husband.* Glorious Gospel; faith listen, love awake, hope rejoice. The triune God who made thee hath espoused thee, and is in covenant with thee. How is this relation effected? God the Son comes into the world and takes our nature upon him.

We are peculiarly espoused to Christ, experimentally by faith. We know nothing of the loving, eternal designs of Christ to our souls, till by the grace of his Spirit we are brought to him, receive him, and give him our hearts as our own bridegroom; then we feel the blessings and enjoy the comfort of marriage union: we live in love; walk by faith; rejoice in hope. O Christ, make us and keep us chaste virgins to thee!

Christ is our REDEEMER: he took our nature, that in our nature he might redeem us to God his Father: he has effectually done it by his precious blood: being redeemed by him and married to him, the Father owns the relation, glories over us in him, and the Spirit sanctifies and comforts us in him. Therefore, as an affectionate bride glories in the person and rejoices in the titles of her husband, so, O soul, do thou in thy heavenly bridegroom.

He is thy *Maker:* he who was almighty to create, is almighty to preserve. He is *the Lord of hosts:* what can all the powers of earth and hell do against him? He is *the God of the whole earth:* the Lord God omnipotent is thy Redeemer; ever glory in him as equal to the Father. Fools deny this: the wise unto salvation believe, adore, and glory in Christ as such; "who only hath immortality" to bestow upon poor sinners, "to whom be honor and power everlasting, Amen." 1 Tim. 6:16. Ever remember we are married to Christ, that we should bear fruit unto God. Rom. 7:4.

SEPT. 20.—*Having food and raiment, let us be therewith content.* 1 Tim. 6:8

Man wants but little; that little not long; but unbelief multiplies our wants and magnifies our discontent. God rains down manna; the people are delighted with it, but are not content to trust God for the morrow's supply; they gather more than would serve for one day; what was the consequence? "It bred worms and stank." Exod. 16:20. Here distrust and unbelief prevailed, and abundance occasioned discontent. O ye rich and great, is it not so with you?

And thou, O my soul, thy pittance is more than Paul here requires. Art thou content? No riches without Christ and the riches of his grace can bring content to the mind. But when Christ vouchsafes to fulfil that precious word, Rev. 2:17, "I will give to eat of the hidden manna," then we shall have true contentment, though we have no more coats than backs, and but just food enough to satisfy our hunger; for faith supplies all: it brings the Supplier of all into our hearts: we feed upon him by faith. The supply of our wants does not fix content in the mind: most of them are not real, but imaginary: as wants increase so does discontent:

> "That cruel something unpossess'd
> "Corrodes and leavens all the rest."

True content arises from the mind being brought to our state. Have we little or much? The Lord gave it: he sees best to give no more. When his will is the law, the mind is content.

See Paul's reasons for content. Look back to your birth : " we brought nothing into the world ;" if we have nothing, we have all we were born with. Look forward to your death : " it is certain we can carry nothing out of it." Think of your naked birth and naked death ; all we possess we shall soon leave behind. Would you be rich ? Paul says, this is to " fall into temptation and a snare, and into many foolish and hurt. ıl lusts which drown men in destruction and perdition ; for the love of money is the root of all evil." O for Agur's prayer : " give me not riches." Prov. 30 : 8.

What is the greatest gain ? " Godliness with contentment :" having Christ for your food, and his righteousness your raiment, this brings true content of mind. One who had nothing but bread and water, cried out in an ecstasy, " What, all this and Christ too !" Learn more to live by faith on the Son of God : all God's promises are yours in him : this one is enough to silence murmurings and quell the risings of discontent : " I will never leave thee, nor forsake thee." Heb. 13 : 5.

Sept. 21.—*I stir up your pure minds, by way of remembrance.*
2 Peter 3 : 1

All the children of God have in some degree a pure mind ; many of them complain of bad memories : all need to have their minds stirred up, and their memories quickened. There is no doubt but Peter had such a mind when he denied his Lord ; but he seems to display a very treacherous memory, in sadly forgetting himself, his Lord, and his words. Forgetfulness of dangers causes one to fall into them : forgetting our own weakness to stand, causes us to fall.

Consider what is a pure mind : that of which we are all destitute by nature : our " mind and conscience is defiled," "and unbelieving." Tit. 1 : 15. Our mind is made pure, when our hearts are sprinkled from an evil or guilty conscience by the blood of Christ, through faith. Heb. 10 : 22. So that a pure mind is a believing mind, which receives the truth as it is in Jesus, in the power and purity of it; and holds the mystery of faith in a pure conscience.

Such pure minds need to be aroused: do you not find it so day by day? Alas! how prone are we to neglect, forget, and let slip from our minds the glorious truths and precious promises of our Lord! Then we grow weak in faith, dejected in hope, cold in love, and negligent in duty: this is not right; it is an offence to our Lord, and uncomfortable to our souls; it is neither a fit frame to live or to die in. When a fire burns languidly, we stir it, to promote flame and heat. Lord, grant that our souls may not languish, but flame in love to thee.

"I stir up." Could Peter stir up their minds? Doubtless, instrumentally. Beware of that accursed notion begetting sloth, that because you have not the power to do any spiritual act effectually, you may therefore neglect the means. Paul calls on Timothy, "Stir up the gift of God which is in thee." 2 Tim. 1 : 6. He could use the means, and so ought we, as those alive to God, to use them, and look to God's power to bless them: this is the genuine acting of a lively faith.

Notice the manner of doing this: "by way of remembrance." Refreshing the memory is stirring up the mind. Says Peter, "I think it meet as long as I am in this tabernacle" to do this: we have all need of it; we ought also to stir up our own and one another's mind, by word and epistles, of the everlasting love and precious promises of God in Christ to sinners; of his finished salvation for them; the eternal glory which awaits them, and which they shall soon enjoy in his kingdom. The Lord help us thus to stir up each other's minds while in these tabernacles.

SEPT. 22.—*By one offering Christ hath perfected for ever them that are sanctified.* Heb. 10:14

We have two remarkable instances of Paul's holy zeal for the glory of his Lord: one against a gross sin in the church of Corinth, which brought a scandal upon the holy Gospel of Christ; another against a legal, self-righteous spirit which obtained in the church of Galatia: this depreciated and dishonored the finished work of Christ, and perverted the faith of his members. It is hard to say whether Paul's zeal was strongest against the former or the latter; hence learn that profaneness and spiritual pride are equally contrary to the faith of the Gospel: as a holy faith brings Christ and his salvation into the heart, it casts out the love of sin as well as self-righteous hopes.

Here is a glorious truth for precious faith to fix upon O that, through the Spirit, it may bring joy and peace to our souls. Consider who are said to be "sanctified" here? Those who are separated and set apart by God the Father, according to his electing love, Jude 1; and sanctified by the Holy Spirit, to possess a holy faith in Jesus and a holy life from him.

In what sense has Christ "perfected them for ever?" My dear reader, it is for want of faith in this that we feel so much distress in our consciences, so little love to Christ in our hearts, and enjoy no more peace with God in our souls. Sin causes all this: but Christ has "perfected for ever them who are sanctified:" that is, he has so perfectly freed them from all the charges of law and justice, that there is now no condemnation against them.

How has Christ done this? "By one offering." O the love of Christ in this offering for sinners who deserved it not! O the willingness of Christ in it! "He gave himself for our sins." Gal. 1:4. O the pains and agonies he endured for our salvation! O the glorious efficacy of his offering upon the cross! He made there (by his *one* oblation of himself *once* offered) a full, perfect and sufficient sacrifice, oblation and satisfaction for our sins: thus he hath once for all and for ever satisfied the justice of God, appeased his wrath, and perfectly reconciled his holiness to us.

But, how is the comfort of this enjoyed? By faith. Is this true? Yes, says Paul, we have the most infallible evidence for its veracity, "Whereof the Holy Ghost is a witness to us." Heb. 10:15. Then, as we value peace of conscience, the hope of heaven, and the love of God, we are bound to honor the Spirit of truth, by *faith unfeigned*. 1 Tim. 1:5.

SEPT. 23.—*I am not ashamed of the Gospel of Christ.*
Romans 1:16

Says Bunyan in his Pilgrim's Progress, "Of all the men that I met with in my pilgrimage, SHAME, I think, bears the wrong name: this bold-faced Shame would never have done; I could scarce shake him out of my company; he would be continually haunting me and whispering me in the ear; indeed this Shame is a bold villain."

Have not you found the same? Lord, pardon thy servant, that this shame still cleaves unto me. Lord, I am ashamed of myself, that I ever should be ashamed of thee and thy Gospel. Lion of the tribe of Judah, drive away this shame from my heart.

Consider its origin. It is begotten by pride. We are proud of our good name, fair character, our reason and understanding, among the men of the world. If we openly profess the Gospel of Christ, and live and walk under its influence, we cannot act like the rest of the world. Hence we shall soon be reproached, and perhaps deemed fools, madmen, and enthusiasts. Pride cannot bear this: it is ashamed of it. Then it works by fear. Fear says, take heed to yourself: do not go too far: keep your Gospel to yourself: you will surely suffer for it: you will lose your friends, character, and business: you will set all the world against you, and then, how will you live.

Hence you see that pride and fear are the offspring of atheism and unbelief: they banish the Providence of God and the promises of his grace from our mind. Hence it is plain that faith, a living faith in the Gospel of Christ, will drive pride, fear and shame out of the heart. O consider the dishonor it is to Christ to be ashamed of his glorious Gospel. Does it bring to our souls the glad tidings of the pardon of our sins, peace with God, justification before him, and eternal enjoyment of him through the salvation of Christ? Did he make himself of no reputation for us? Did he endure the cross and despise the shame of hanging upon it as an accursed malefactor to save us? And shall we be ashamed of him? Where then is our faith in him and love to him?

It is one thing to be beset with shame and another to give way to it. A lively faith begets warm love. Then shame dares not show his base head. Without thee, O Jesus, we can do nothing. Through thy strength we can do all things. Lord, strengthen our souls in the faith and love of thee. O suffer us never, never to be ashamed of thee and of thy cross. But let us ever glory in thee, and of thee. And, dear Lord help us, that we may never be a shame *to* thee and thy Gospel, by an unchristian life and unholy walk.

———————

SEPT. 24.—*Wash me, and I shall be whiter than snow.*
Psalm 51 : 7

Here is majesty in misery: a king in penitence: a monarch of the earth at the footstool of mercy. David, as a miserable sinner, polluted with the complicated

crimes of adultery and murder, is here ascribing honor
to the blood of the Lamb by the pleading of faith. Had
you now asked David what he thought of the pleasures of sin? he would have read the most affecting lec-
ture on its exceeding sinfulness, and the terror and horror it brought upon his spirit. Though invested with
the government of a kingdom, yet he could not command away its terrors from his mind, its burden from
his conscience, or its pollution from his soul. He now
found the words of his son fully verified, "Whoso
breaketh an hedge, a serpent shall bite him." Eccles.
10 : 8. He had broken through the hedge of God's law,
and that old serpent who tempted him, now stings and
torments him.

But when Nathan had convinced David of his transgressions, so that he cried out, "I have sinned," did not
the prophet add, "The Lord also hath put away thy
sin?" 2 Sam. 12 : 13. Yes. Nevertheless, this peniten-
tial psalm was written after this. Hence we learn that,
though sin is put away by the Lord Jesus in the court
of heaven, yet the poor sinner may not enjoy the comfort of its removal from his own conscience. There
may be true faith in the blood of the Lamb, that it
cleanses from all sin, and yet the soul be left to cry out
under the pollution of sin; for a truly regenerate soul
is as much concerned to be cleansed from the pollution
of sin as to be comforted with pardon for sin.

True faith manifests itself in the heart, by its turning
away from every other ground of deliverance, and turning to that blessed fountain opened for sin and uncleanness. Not my tears of repentance, but thy precious
blood, O Lamb of God, can wash me. Precious word!
"The blood of Jesus Christ cleanseth from ALL sin." 1
John 1 : 7. Faith ascribes the utmost efficacy to it,
"Wash me, and I shall be whiter than snow." I shall be
as free and as fair from the least stain of sin in God's

sight, as if I had never sinned: "without spot or wrinkle, or any such thing." Eph. 5 : 27.

Hence as you value the sense of God's love and peace of conscience, beware of sin. If you sin, flee instantly to the blood of the Lamb to be cleansed, and to no other remedy. Believe, watch and pray. No power can forgive sin, or cleanse from it, but the Lord, against whom it is committed. "If we confess our sins, he is faithful and just to forgive us our sins, and to cleanse us from all unrighteousness." 1 John 1 : 9.

SEPT. 25.—*The joy of the Lord is your strength.* Neh. 8 : 10

This is a precious, evangelical chapter: glorious gospel truths are here held forth to us: Lord, help us to see them and feed upon them. Here is, 1st. A solemn observation of the feast of tabernacles: this was appointed by the wisdom of God the Father. Lev. 23 : 34. Did God solemnly command the people to dwell in booths for eight days, but for some glorious end? No: Christ is the substance of the whole law: here is a shadow of him: here is typified God's beloved Son, who was to tabernacle in our flesh, and all the Father's glory to dwell in him. 2d. "The people gathered together as one man." So, "Unto Shiloh (the Messiah) shall the gathering of the people be." Gen. 49 : 10. 3d. Ezra the priest reads and expounds to them the law in the open street, (much like field-preaching,) the people were convinced of sin and wept: the law ministers death and condemnation to them. Here is the office of the Holy Ghost in convincing of sin and comforting them by faith.

Again, Ezra preaches the Gospel to them, and says, "Weep not, neither be ye sorry." What! Not when their hearts were wounded by sin, the terrors of a broken law fell upon them, and when they saw justice armed with vengeance to destroy them? No: for "*The joy*

of the Lord is your strength." How so? A glorious ray
of Christ's rich love and marvellous grace to poor sinners beams forth here: see what is the joy of the Lord.
Our precious Lord Jesus, the author and finisher of our
faith, "*for the joy that was set before him* (of saving us
miserable sinners) endured the cross, despising the
shame." Heb. 12:2. Look unto Jesus; meditate on this
joy of your Lord. Though he was to suffer the most
excruciating pains and agonies on the cross, and to be
exposed to public shame and infamy as a malefactor;
yet such was his joy in saving his dear people from hell,
to be glorified with him eternally in heaven, that he patiently endured and cheerfully despised all this.

O, did such love, such grace, such joy dwell in the
heart of our incarnate God! Sinner, this joy of the Lord
is your strength and mine: the faith of this creates the
highest joy in our souls; and this joy inspires our hearts
with strength and courage against all our enemies; for
we are more than conquerors, through Christ, who loved
us, and had such JOY in saving us. O, to think "I am a
poor weak and vile sinner from day to day, surrounded
by the most subtle and powerful foes," is enough to
make our hearts faint, our knees feeble, and our hands
hang down: but O the joy, the strength with which it
inspires the soul to know, "The LORD thy God in the
midst of thee is mighty." Zeph. 3:17.

SEPT. 26.—*Men shall be blessed in him: all nations shall call
him blessed.* Psalm 72:17

"Cursed is every one that continueth not in all things
which are written in the book of the law to do them."
Gal. 3:10. This curse God has never revoked: every
man is naturally under it; but the greatest curse is, men
neither believe it, feel it, nor care for it. Hence they
slight and disregard HIM who was made "a curse for

us," that we might be blessed in him. Says our Lord, "Search the Scriptures, they testify of me." John 5 : 39. Here is a sweet testimony for our mind, and precious food for our faith: Jesus, Master, bless me while I meditate on it.

See all blessedness in Christ. Well might Luther say, "I will have nothing to do with an absolute God:" that is, God without a mediator. O sinner, O saint, there is nothing but curse and wrath for us out of Christ : there is a hell of sin in our nature : pride and lust dwell in our flesh. Spirit of God, give us to know this more and more, to the humbling of our hearts and to the prizing of our dear Immanuel: for in Christ there is nothing but blessedness: we are blessed IN him. "Blessed be the God and Father of our Lord Jesus Christ, who hath blessed us with all spiritual blessings in Christ, according as he hath chosen us in him before the foundation of the world." Eph. 1 : 3, 4.

Here are precious foundation-truths of our blessedness : faith receives them, and works by the love of them. Not only blessed *in* but blessed *by* Christ : as our covenant head, he has every blessing for time and eternity to bestow upon his members. We have not only the knowledge of this, but the enjoyment of it. Christ is the author of our faith: he gave us faith, that we might feed on him in our hearts, have fellowship with him in our spirits, and have all things in common with him, which our Father's love can bestow, to make us blessed and happy.

"Men," miserable, sinful men shall not only be blessed in Christ, but shall bless themselves in him. This is a sweet art: Holy Spirit, teach it us from day to day : though we find ourselves vile, miserable and cursed, yet let us bless ourselves in the Lord ; boast of him, glory in him, and rejoice for what Christ of God is made to us. Men shall call Christ blessed : the most blessed object their eyes ever saw, or their hearts ever knew. But language fails: Lord, make up in spirit what is wanting in words. There is no end of speaking, dear Lord, of thy blessedness.

Sept. 27.—*One Mediator between God and men, the man Christ Jesus.* 1 Tim. 2 : 5

O, my fellow-sinners, I heartily congratulate your soul and my own for this blessed truth! Lord, help us to live upon it in our consciences from day to day: it is not a speculative, but an experimental truth: it enters into the very essence of our faith, is the very life of our hope, lies at the foundation of our peace, and is the source of every blessing and comfort. If we are not continually looking to this ONE Mediator, JESUS, we lose the peace of faith, the comfort of hope, the fellowship of love, become perplexed in our minds; and then we do not draw nigh to God with confidence, stand before him with boldness, nor cheerfully walk with him in love and holiness.

Consider, *a mediator* stands as a middle person, interposing between two parties at variance, to make peace and reconciliation: this Christ has perfectly done: he has for ever made peace by the blood of his cross. Colossians. 1 : 20. Sin was the cause of variance between God and us: but Christ hath "put away sin by the sacrifice of himself." Heb. 9 : 26. Thus the work of reconciliation is finished in respect to God. But Jesus hath a work to do with us; for we are naturally alienated from God and enemies to him in our minds: this is manifest by our wicked ways: but, says the apostle, " you hath he now reconciled." Col. 1 : 21.

Is it so with you? Has Christ, by the persuasive eloquence of his tongue, the affecting oratory of his love, and the sweet power of his Spirit, conquered the rebel-

lion of your will, subdued the stubborn pride of your
heart, and gained your affections for God? Yes, say
you: but I am such a miserable sinner, I fear God will
not receive me; I have so much sin in me, I think he
cannot be reconciled to me and at peace with me. Nay,
but if Jesus had not been a Mediator for miserable sinners full of sin, Paul and all the apostles, and every
saint now in glory would have been in endless torment: all the comfort of Christ's mediation is enjoyed
by faith.

Christ lives to continue perfect reconciliation between God and us. O that is a most precious text:
"For if when we were enemies, we were reconciled to
God by the death of his Son, much more, being reconciled, we shall be saved by his life." Rom. 5 : 10. Look
back to the atonement of Christ on the cross; look up
to the intercession of Christ at the right hand of a reconciled God; look forward and see heaven open to
receive you, and the arms of a loving Father to embrace you.

SEPT. 28.—*Fear ye not. Stand still and see the salvation of
the Lord.* Exodus 14: 13

Now were the people of God in a great strait, even
at their wits' end: perish they must, to all human appearance. A wide ocean is before them. Inaccessible
mountains surround them. An enraged monarch pursues
them: death in various shapes presents itself to them:
yet, for all this, says Moses, "Fear not." Unbelief and
carnal reason might suggest, What! not be afraid when
inevitable destruction must be our doom? Why will
Moses talk to us after this enthusiastic rate! But, in
the view of apparent destruction, Moses tells them of
certain salvation, and commands them to stand still and
behold it: we do not hear one word from Moses to

soothe their fears or comfort their minds, from any considerations of what they were in themselves, or what they had done to entitle them to the Lord's favor. No; but they were at this very moment indulging the murmurs of unbelief: "Why hast thou brought us forth? Better to serve the Egyptians, than to perish here."

Hence observe, in times of difficulty, in seasons of distress, when sin rages, conscience accuses, the law condemns, unbelief prevails, and we poor sinners are at our wits' end; seeing justice pursuing, all hope and help failing, and despair at the door, then the salvation of Jesus is our only resource: in such seasons how does this quell our fears, compose and comfort our minds!

But, what is it to *stand still* and see the salvation of the Lord? Is it to cease from prayer and all other means of grace, and, as some say, be still; stir not in the way of duty? No; for, contrary to this, the Lord ordered the people to "go forward." What is it then, but in the midst of fears, in the sight of dangers, and in the dread of destruction, to cease from all self-confidence, to attend to the voice of the Lord, to rely upon his gracious promises, and quietly to hope for his great deliverance; for, O precious word! says Moses, "The Lord shall fight for you:" and what then? "Ye shall hold your peace."

How soon, how effectually did the Lord do this! He destroyed their enemies, saved them, silenced all their unbelieving fears and unreasonable murmurings: they saw their enemies no more for ever. Stand still, O soul, admire, adore, love, and confide in a gracious, wonder-working, sinner-saving Lord: look on thine enemies as the foes of thy Lord: he has promised their destruction and thy salvation. Rejoice to think of that day, when thou shalt see thy Lord in glory, and thine enemies no more for ever.

Sept. 29.—*I will greatly rejoice in the Lord, my soul shall be joyful in my God, for he hath clothed me with the garments of salvation, he hath covered me with the robe of righteousness.* Isaiah 61 : 10

It would be surprising to see a malefactor going to execution singing and rejoicing all the way. But if, when he came to the fatal place, he should produce the king's free pardon, with royal promises of being admitted to his presence, and appearing at court in the richest robes of the king's providing, our wonder would cease; we should own that he really had abundant cause for joy. Come, my fellow-condemned malefactors, though sin has stripped you of your innocent dress of righteous clothing; though you are under the sentence of death; yet behold, here is a pardon for you, the best robe to be put upon you, and a sure promise of admission into the king's presence in it. Read it and rejoice. *Grace reigns through righteousness unto eternal life.* Rom. 5 : 21. The God of righteousness clothes us naked sinners with the garments of salvation, and adorns us with the robe of righteousness, which our heavenly bridegroom wrought for us : this is the blessing of being united to Christ by faith; this is the joy of faith; this causes joy of soul, and great rejoicing in *the Lord our righteousness.*

When all sense of comfort and joy in nature is dead; yet, in Jesus our covenant head we have a never failing source of comfort, and an inexhaustible spring of joy : faith leaves nature behind, with all its sins and miseries; it looks neither to works nor worthiness in self, but considers what Christ is to the soul, and what the soul is in him, righteous, perfectly and everlastingly righteous. O then joy, great joy springs up.

See the claim of faith, " *my* God." Though faith doth not meritoriously cause the Lord to become our God, nor adopt us into his family; yet it claims that peculiar

and precious interest in him, which the word of his
grace reveals. The Father draws us by his Spirit to his
Son for his righteousness; the Spirit bears witness that
we are righteous in his Son: then faith makes the claim,
boasts of it, and glories in it: then Jesus has our hearts
and our hopes; our affections are placed on him; our
hopes centre in him. Then we find our God in Christ;
we call him MY God; Abba, Father: we are at peace
with him, and joyful in him; we proclaim our joy in our
God. What! clothed with the garments of salvation
which we wrought not; covered with the robe of righteousness which we spun not, and not be joyful? O believers, be ashamed of your unbelief: it damps your joy;
it withholds the glory of your heart.

SEPT. 30.—*But the body is of Christ,* (*or is Christ.*) Col. 2 : 17

There is not a greater instance of the depravity of the
human mind, and the corruption of the judgment, than
its seeking happiness in the shadow instead of the substance. What is all created good but the shadow of
him that created it? Yet we are prone to grasp at the
shadow, and seek to be satisfied with it, while we neglect God the substance. But all, like a shadow, eludes
our embrace; still we are restless and pursuing: it is
just the same in spiritual things: we are prone to take
up and rest satisfied with the shadow of things, without the body, which is Christ: yea, so foolish are we,
that unless we are kept, even after we have known the
substance and fulness of Christ, and see that we are
complete in him, we turn again to trust in the shadow
of our own works and duties. This is awful! "But the
body is Christ."

Jehovah, Father, Son, and Spirit, have put the glory
of every attribute and perfection of the godhead in the
body of Christ: "In him dwelleth"—not the fulness

merely—" ALL the fulness of the godhead bodily." Col.
2 : 9. God the Father says, " Behold mine elect, in whom
my soul delighteth." Isa. 42 : 1. God's soul can delight
in nothing but where his glory is. Again, " This is my
beloved Son, in whom I am well pleased, hear ye him."
Matt. 17 : 5. God cannot be well pleased with any one
who is not, like himself, perfect in holiness, righteousness, and truth : of these, not one of all the human
race is possessed : therefore, God is so far from being
well pleased with us, as we are in ourselves, that he
hates and abhors us.

But here is our special mercy, God loves us, he hath
chosen us, and blessed us with all spiritual blessings in
the body of Christ : by Christ's body we are redeemed
from all our sins, he " bare our sins in his own body on
the tree." 1 Pet. 2 : 24. In Christ's righteous body we
are justified and sanctified : " we are sanctified through
the offering of the body of Christ, once for all." Heb.
10 : 10. Yea, " by one offering he hath perfected for
ever them that are sanctified." Heb. 10 : 14.

Of this "the Holy Ghost is witness to us." Heb.
10 : 15. This is his blessed office, to glorify Christ to
our view and in our hearts. The Father calls on us to
behold Christ and to *hear him.* The Holy Spirit enables
to this, and fills us with all joy and peace in believing.
Here then things are brought to one single point : all
our righteousness, holiness, peace, comfort, and joy, are
in Christ. Are we reconciled to God ? Has God put all
his glory in Him ? Then let us seek all our happiness
there

October

OCT. 1.—*Of whom I am chief.* 1 Tim. 1:15.

What a mighty change does grace make! Paul was once in his own eyes, the chief of saints. But now that he is really an eminent saint in Christ, he confesses himself the *chief* of sinners. Why so? Did he love sin, and glory in sin? No, far from it; he was now saved from all his sins: but he now sees the exceeding preciousness of Christ his Saviour; the exceeding sinfulness of sin, which dwelt in him; and the infinite holiness, spirituality, and perfection of the law of God: therefore he makes this public declaration; not I have been, but I now *am* the *chief* of sinners.

He as it were stands forth and challenges the whole race of sinners, and says, I will give place to no one: of all of you I will be the first, and stand foremost in the rank. "But is not this glorying in sin, which was his shame?" Self-righteous hearts may think so; they cannot understand Paul's feelings. When any sinner adopts Paul's language, and says, " of sinners I am chief," they ignorantly reply, There can be but one chief. Who then is that one? Why every one who drinks into the same spirit with Paul, has the same views of himself which he had.

They see sin, not only in its fruits, but as a root; not only its actings, but as a nature in which dwells no good thing. Though sin has not dominion over them, yet sin dwells in them. When they look at their sinful actions, they take into view their present nature also, and therefore abuse themselves: they have done with self-admiration and self-justification. I AM the chief of sinners: I see myself: I think no one has so wicked a heart and so bad a nature as I have.

Such from their hearts give glory to the holy, blessed Trinity. O how is God the Father glorified for his everlasting love to such sinners! How is God the Son's grace exalted in dying to save them. How is the Holy Spirit's kindness magnified, in convincing them of sin, bringing them to Christ to be saved from sin, and sanctifying them, by the faith of Christ, over the power of sin!

Such, all such, and none but such, do cordially embrace and live upon this "faithful saying and worthy of all acceptation" (with the deepest humility and highest joy,) "Christ Jesus came into the world to save SINNERS:" therefore, as they are not under the power of sin, so they are delivered from the pride of their own righteousness. A sinner's righteousness! They are ashamed that they should ever be so arrogant and ignorant as to talk of it, trust in it, or expect to be justified by it, either in whole or in part.

OCT. 2.—*This is his commandment, that we should believe on the name of his Son Jesus Christ, and love one another.* 1 John 3:23

When a weary traveller has lost his way, what joy must the sight of a directory afford him! How must his joy be increased if it informs him he is near a dear friend's house who will kindly receive him! Weary pilgrim, look at this directory and rejoice: you are nigh a dear friend who will kindly receive and heartily welcome you. Obey this command, and enjoy the blessing.

Consider who commands. God the Father; that God against whom you have sinned, and by sin have become miserable: he would have you both holy and happy; you can be neither without believing: both are enjoyed in faith.

Consider the command: *believe.* By the ten commandments you are condemned; you are brought in guilty by them; the law ministers nothing but wrath and condemnation. God shows us mercy. O the love and grace of the law-giver! He here gives us one command, which ministers life and salvation to our guilty souls: only believe. You mourn under a sense of sin, and are dejected and distressed: you look one way and another: you strive to do this and that: you pray, read, hear, converse—still your soul is not happy and joyful. Why not? Because you do not obey your Father's command, *believe*.

Consider the object of faith: "*The name of his Son Jesus Christ.*" God the Father doth not command, believe on me, come to me, but only as he is in Christ: therefore he says, "hear my beloved Son." Mark, 9:7. Believe on him; go to him; receive him; look to him; venture your souls on him; constantly and continually exercise your minds on him for all salvation: so shall you enjoy my peace, my favor, and my love. All centres in his name, JESUS; your sin-bearing, sin-atoning, law-fulfilling Saviour. *Christ:* anointed, sent and appointed by God the Father, to do and suffer his will; to finish your salvation, and to save and make you ever happy in the sense of the Father's reconciled love IN HIM.

Who are commanded thus to believe? Sinners, lost and perishing sinners, who have no righteousness to justify, no strength to save themselves. This is your character and mine, and will be so all through life: therefore this command is ever to be obeyed by us. Are you in a doubting, fearing, condemned, dark, distressed frame? Your Father's loving command just suits you: obey him: believe in his Son, for light, joy, and peace, and they shall spring up in your conscience: then love shall prevail in your soul to God and to his children. This is the prayer of faith, "Lord, increase our faith." Luke 17:5.

Oct. 3.—*Saul answered, I am sore distressed; for the Philistines make war against me, and God is departed from me.* 1 Samuel, 28 : 15

A more awful speech is scarcely to be found in the Bible : a more dreadful state a soul cannot be in on this side of hell : to have powerful enemies in battle array ; to have the guilt of abominable sins staring us in the face ; and to be sensible that the Lord is departed from us, how horrid the thought ! Here see the awful effects of trifling with God and disobeying his commands !

We read that the Spirit of the Lord came upon Saul : that God gave him another heart; that he was turned into another man ; and that he prophesied. 1 Sam. 10 : 6. And yet, such was his dreadful conduct as to bring upon himself sore distress. How does he act under it ? Does he humble himself as heretofore before the Lord ? No : but adds this evil to all his abominations ; he seeks to the witch of Endor, and desires her to raise up Samuel to him : the form of Samuel appears, and tells him of his sudden destruction by the Philistines.

Learn hence, that as the Lord's mercies are sure, so also are his judgments : though he may delay for a season, yet a day of vengeance will surely overtake every impenitent, sin-hardened soul : though it was not long before, that Saul disobeyed the Lord's command in not totally destroying his enemies, the Amalekites ; yet the Lord had neither forgotten it nor forgiven him.

See how a sin-hardened soul acts ; not like David, who goes to the Lord with an humble heart, a broken spirit, and a sorrowful cry, " O Lord, pardon mine iniquity, for it is great." Psalm 25 : 11. But, like Saul, who applied to one possessed with the devil for relief.

We do not hear one word from Saul of the cause of his distress, SIN : his eyes were so blinded by it that he saw not the evil of it : his heart was so hardened by its

deceitfulness that he felt no sorrow in his soul on account of it; for the Lord was departed from him. O that
we may dread and deprecate the Lord's departing from
us. But let not any sin-distressed, broken-hearted sinner write bitter things against himself in view of this:
for, if sin causes sorrow of heart and mourning of soul,
and excites a cry, " God, be merciful to me—save, Lord,
I perish:" the Lord is not departed from that soul: it is
not hardened through the deceitfulness of sin. O love
the Lord: praise him for his grace, which keeps you;
and that his promises still invite and encourage you:
" for if any man sin, we have an advocate with the
Father, Jesus Christ the righteous," and "his blood
cleanseth from all sin." 1 John 2 : 1, and 1 : 7.

OCT. 4.—*Peter was grieved, because he said unto him the third
time, Lovest thou me?* John 21 : 17

Peter had grieved his Lord by three denials of him:
now his Lord grieves Peter with three questions of his
love to him. We may often read our sins in our punishment; Peter's Lord suffered him to fall, to lower his
pride and self-confidence; and having been brought by
his sins into the valley of humiliation, our Lord lets the
burden of them rest upon him for a season. A little
while ago he boasted of his superlative love to Christ,
above all the rest of his disciples: "Though all men
shall be offended because of thee, yet will I never be
offended—I am ready to go with thee both to prison
and to death—though I should die with thee, yet will I
not deny thee." Brave words! Who can doubt of the
sincerity of Peter's heart in all this?

Hence learn that the warm frames of young converts
are often attended with great self-confidence; there is
much of nature's fire in them. My heart has often rejoiced and been warmed with love to hear the ardor and

energy with which some in their first love have spoken of "a precious Saviour: but I have thought, their sifting time will come; the Lord keep your poor hearts humble before him."

See the unchangeable love and sovereign grace of Christ to his dear disciples. He told Peter of his fall, and warned him against it; yea, set before him every particular aggravation of it. How blind are those who see not here the divinity of our Lord! Notwithstanding this, Peter abates nothing of his self-confidence. Must his fall cure him? Not that, but Christ's grace raised and restored him. Falls into sin naturally harden through the deceitfulness of sin: take heed of looking to saints' falls to make you think little of your own. Peter's fall was a damnable sin; he deserved hell for it: Christ snatched him as a brand out of the fire. His grace brings good out of the evil of sin. Let us glory in grace, but beware of sin.

Souls raised by the grace of Christ are grieved for their base sins and falls; though the subject between Christ and Peter was LOVE, yet it grieves: no threats of damnation wound new born souls like love: "*Lovest thou me?*" saith the Lord. Look back, soul, to thy past conduct; say, was there warm and generous love to thy Lord in it? O, the thought of past unkindness to Christ grieves the soul before him. As Christ repeats the question, grief is enlarged. Never think you are truly raised from your falls and restored to the love of Christ, if you have not grief of heart for them: Christ's grace melts into love; love sinks into humility, while it kindles the fire of joy and excites a godly jealousy.

OCT. 5.—*Moses endured, as seeing Him who is invisible.*
Hebrews 11:27

What a paradox! "Seeing Him who is invisible." Is

not this the very height of enthusiasm? Enthusiam! I love that term, and in the very sense in which worldly men use it too; for they mean one who has the zeal and fire of godliness in his soul. Is it any marvel that scriptural, experimental truths are foolishness to the spiritually blind, and that they can neither endure the persons nor the language of the children of faith?

Consider, *What* did Moses endure? What you, and I, and every enlightened soul are called to endure, "the reproach of Christ," and "suffering affliction with the people of God." Now this is opposed by "enjoying the pleasures of sin for a season." So that if you will enjoy the pleasures of sin with the men of this world, you may escape "the reproach of Christ" and avoid suffering affliction from them. Now, which is your choice? If Christ is in your eye, you cannot hesitate one moment: Moses' choice will be yours: "Give me Christ—welcome reproach—afflictions I embrace for him. O let me have Christ within me, and his mark upon me. Faith makes all easy: love makes all pleasant: hope makes all joyful." Well, but how could Moses endure the reproach of Christ, before Christ was born in the flesh? Why, the promised Messiah was the object of his faith, his hope, his love and his joy: so he was of all these heroes of faith recorded in this chapter. "Jesus Christ, the same yesterday, to-day, and for ever," is the one only object of every sinner's faith since the fall of Adam to this day: take away Christ, and faith has no existence.

How did Moses endure? Just as you and I must, *seeing:* this implies a continued act of the mind constantly fixed upon an object. We cannot be steadfast in faith, joyful in hope, abounding in love, and enduring reproach for Christ, unless we are continually "looking unto Jesus, the author and finisher of our faith, who, for the joy that was set before him, endured the cross, despising the shame, and is set down at the right hand of the throne of God." Heb. 12:2. Though he is invisible to the eye of sense, yet we see him by the eye of faith: see him as our forerunner, entered into heaven for us—having removed out of the way all things that hindered us—ever living to pray for us—ever ready to keep us—and waiting to receive us to himself, that where he is there we may be also. O, this constant *looking* makes hopeful, holy, joyful living, and comfortable dying.

Oct. 6.—*Whose names are in the book of life.* Phil. 4:3

How did Paul know that? Had he seen the book of life, when caught up to the third heavens? No; but he very plainly and evidently saw the work of God's Spirit upon these persons' souls, by their fruits of faith and labors of love to the glory of the Lord Jesus: hence he speaks so confidently of them. This furnishes us with some glorious truths.

The names of all God's chosen people are registered in the book of life, called the LAMB's book of life. Rev. 21:27. This implies the eternal love of God to them; choice of them, personal knowledge of each of them, value for them, care over them, and their certain enjoyment of God in heaven and glory: for, says the Lord of hosts, "they shall be mine in that day when I make up my jewels." Mal. 3:17. But may not the name of a believer in Christ be blotted out of this book of life and he suffered to perish? No, saith the LAMB, "I will not blot his name out of the book of life." Rev. 3:5. It is his book: they are too dearly loved and too dearly bought, to be blotted out. Not all the powers of sin, earth and hell, can make him a liar: he has said, "I give unto my sheep eternal life; they shall never perish, neither shall any pluck them out of my hand." John 10:28. Say, believer, what hadst thou done to deserve that thy name should be enrolled in the annals of eternal love? What canst thou do to merit its continuance in the book of life? Methinks thy generous, loving soul recoils at these thoughts. Love did the mighty deed: grace reigns: salvation from first to last is all of free-gift to the glory of God.

Those whose names are written in the book of life may attain to a comfortable knowledge of it. How? Not by seeing this book; not by any voice, visions, or fresh revelations from heaven: but says Paul of these, "They labored with me in the Gospel." This implies faith in the Lord Jesus, love to him, delight in him and in the Gospel of his grace. When the Gospel is indeed good news to us miserable sinners; when we see the glory of the Father, Son and Spirit, shine in it; when it captivates our affections, enlivens our hearts, invigorates our minds, animates our hopes, brings peace to our consciences, and subdues the whole man, to give up all for it, and to live under its influence, we may be well assured that our names are written in heaven: for the power of God hath effected this upon our heart, as a consequence of it, and a sure evidence to prove it. "We are chosen from the beginning to salvation, through sanctification of the Spirit and belief of the truth." 2 Thess. 2: 13. Without a holy faith in Jesus, a holy life from him, and a holy walk before him, we can enjoy no comfort from electing love. But these are evident tokens of the salvation of God. Phil. 1: 28.

OCT. 7.—*I am the Lord, I change not, therefore ye sons of Jacob are not consumed.* Malachi 3: 6

Religion without feeling is like a body without a soul: feeling without truth is only nature warmed by fancy. Those are the only precious feelings which are caused

by the word of God: it is well when we can say "I rejoice at thy word, as one that findeth great spoil." Psalm
119:162. Why such exceeding joy? Because the word
of God testifies of the immutable nature and unchangeable love of a covenant God to poor sinners. "I am the
Lord,"–Jehovah, Father, Son and Spirit,–"I change not."

Here is the believer's security from destruction: in
this consists his safety unto salvation; for alas! we are
poor changeable creatures. Now, our souls are strong
in confidence, warm with love, joyful through hope, enlarged in prayer, with Christ in our view and glory in
our eye; anon, a cloud arises in the horizon of our
hearts, unbelief prevails, corruptions rage, all nature is
in a ferment, and the soul in distress: then, what has
it to look to for hope and support? An unchangeable
God, who is of one mind; with whom is no variable-
ness, neither shadow of turning. Job 23:13. James
1:17. A precious Jesus, who is "the same yesterday,
and to-day, and for ever." Heb. 13:8. "The Lord thy
God in the midst of thee, is mighty: he will save, he
will rejoice over thee with joy: he will rest in his love:
he will joy over thee with singing." Zeph. 3:17. The
different frames and feelings which distress us do not
affect God nor cause any change in his love to us. A
changeable God must be an unhappy being like ourselves; but God never changes in his love, purposes,
and grace to us.

He did not love us, choose us, and set his heart upon
us on account of what he saw in us, but as he viewed
us in the Son of his love. We are unrighteous sinners
in ourselves; but he sees in Christ an everlasting atonement for our sins, an everlasting righteousness to justify us: therefore he is ever pleased with us in Christ;
ever of one mind concerning us; ever rests in his love
to us and joys over us: no change in us can ever affect
his mind, his love, or his joy.

Hence learn not to live upon any thing you are in yourself. Bless God for lively frames and comfortable feelings; but know, these are not Christ; they do not make you acceptable to God. Look to what you are in Christ: that is your glory. God so views and loves you. Look here, live here, and rejoice. So you will be like God, of one mind with Jesus, live upon him, and walk to the glory of your God and Father in him.

OCT. 8.—*My son, be strong in the grace that is in Christ Jesus.*
2 Timothy 2:1

Paul had known what it was to be strong in vain confidence and self-righteous hopes; to be strong in rage and persecution against Christ and his people : but his poor soul had severely smarted for all this. Now that Christ had taken possession of his heart, He was all in all to him; he thought he could never enough recommend Him and His grace to his dear friends. O let us imitate him.

" The grace that is in Christ Jesus:" Because of our low, scanty thoughts of his rich grace, we are low in courage against our enemies, and weak in the joy of our souls. There is much more in this than many suppose, as though Christ came into the world to procure some grace for us, then leaves us to be faithful to it, and thus to secure our own salvation. What kind of grace is this? Not saving grace: if this were all, it would end in our certain destruction; but the grace, or favor that is in Christ towards us, is nothing less than the everlasting love of God to us : an everlasting atonement for our sins : an everlasting righteousness to justify our persons : an everlasting salvation for our souls; and the everlasting consolations of the Holy Ghost, all promised to us in the everlasting Gospel, and enjoyed by faith.

Be strong in this grace: fortify your mind: fence yourself round with it: entrench yourself in it: let your confidence be strong in it against all opposing enemies; be bold in faith; strong in hope; firm in the grace of Christ: rest not in any degree of grace received; but be strong in the fulness of the grace that is in Christ. Are your lusts and corruptions strong? Oppose the almighty grace of Christ to them. Are your doubts and fears strong? Be strong in the precious promises which are in Christ Jesus yea and amen, to the glory of God. 2 Cor. 1 : 20. Are your conflicts, temptations, and distresses strong? Flee for refuge to Jesus, the hope set before you: there is *strong consolation* for you! God knowing our distress and dejection through the prevalence of unbelief, has graciously confirmed his council and promise by his *oath*. Can you, dare you think it possible for God to lie? Then, whatever in nature, sense and feeling oppose, "stagger not at the promise of God through unbelief;" but "be strong in faith, giving glory to God." Rom. 4 : 20.

Oct. 9.—*Fight the good fight of faith, lay hold on eternal life.*
1 Timothy 6 : 12

The soldiers of an earthly monarch are regularly enlisted to fight under his banner: they wear his livery and are furnished by him with arms: in the day of battle they prove their courage and faithfulness. So the Captain of our salvation chooses and enlists his own soldiers: he puts on them a livery whereby they are known to his enemies: he puts an armor on them and weapons into their hands. From the moment they enlist under him, they enter the field of battle: there is never any peace with the enemy; the fight is the good fight of faith; the prize is eternal life; the daily word of command is, *fight*—stand to your arms—give no quarter to the enemy—beware of the least truce with them; for the danger is great, the effects will prove awful.

It is a *good fight:* it is in a good cause; under a good Captain, who gives good encouragement, and has assured us of certain victory over the worst of enemies. Fight this good fight for the glory of Him, who, in dying for us, has for ever conquered all who are against us. But they are not all dead yet: fight on.

It is a good fight of *faith.* Dost thou say I have no faith? Then pull off thy soldier's livery. What hast thou to do in the ranks? But who told thee that thou art destitute of faith? Why, thou hast laid down thy shield, and art in the enemy's camp; he has seduced thee by his deceitful insinuations, and will prevail over thee. No faith! What meanest thou? Instead of fighting against the enemy, thou art parleying with him. Dost thou believe that Jesus is the Son of God, the Saviour of sinners? Yes, sayest thou, but I have not the comfort of knowing that he is *my* Saviour! What then? Wilt thou deny thy faith for want of comfort? Desert thy Lord's banner till thou hast assurance of his love? Fight on against thy worst foe, unbelief, and cry to thy best friend, "Lord, increase my faith." The battle is the Lord's: thy strength is from him: "be of good courage, and he shall strengthen your heart, all ye that hope in the Lord." Psalm 31:24.

Lay hold on eternal life; it is the free gift of God. Lay hold of it by faith; possess and enjoy it now in the belief of thy heart; hold it fast in hope: quit not thy confidence in it; so shall thy heart be warm with love, thy spirit filled with joy, and thine arms made strong to fight, until thou art crowned in eternal glory. Remember, "the joy of thy Lord is thy strength." When death, the last enemy comes, hold fast thy faith, and thou shalt sing victory in death.

Oct. 10.—*Having a form of godliness, but denying the power thereof, from such turn away.* 2 Tim. 3 : 5.

Paul says, " The Gospel is the *power* of God." Rom. 1 : 16—and " Christ is the power of God." 1 Cor. 1 : 24—- and " our faith standeth in the power of God." 1 Cor. 2 : 5. Hence it is plain that godliness is powerful upon the soul : it consists not in form and shadow, not in notion and speculation, but in the real enjoyment of Christ in the heart ; and in an experimental knowledge of the grace of the Gospel through faith : it is the grand concern of every living member of Christ, to enjoy more of the light, life, liberty, and power of Christ and his Gospel.

While those who have only the form of godliness are content if their heads are clear in the notions of divine truth ; if they can but see a harmony and consistency in the plan of salvation, give a good account of the doctrines of grace, talk fluently about them, and contend earnestly for them, they are content, and seek nothing more. They place all religion in head knowledge, while they are careless about real heart experience : such persons are visible and manifest by their life and walk ; they talk high, but live low; they soar aloft in notion, but live in earthly pleasures and sensual delights. O they have the form of godliness in their heads, but their hearts are devoid of the power of the Spirit, the warm influences of the love of God, and the grace of Christ : they deny all this ; if not in word, yet in life and action.

What does the apostle advise concerning such persons? To aim to convince them, and strive to convert their hearts to the power of the truth? No : they are so fortified with head knowledge that you cannot reach their hearts ; it would be but lost labor to attempt it ; therefore, from such *turn away :* leave them ; you can do them no good : they may do you much harm.

You may imbibe their spirit and temper: it is conta-
gious. We may say of such as Solomon says of the
furious man, "Make no friendship with him, with him
thou shalt not go, lest thou learn his ways, and get a
snare to thy soul." Prov. 22 : 24, 25. Such professors
greatly damp the zeal of faith, the joy of hope, and the
comfort of love, which are enjoyed in communion and
fellowship with God and his Son Jesus Christ. As they
have no heart to it, nor relish for it, their conversation
will not savor of it; so that you will get no help forward, but rather be driven backward. You will be in
danger of supposing that you can enjoy God and the
world; have fellowship with both in your heart, if you
but have knowledge in your head; and of learning many
specious, but carnal reasons, for throwing off all self-
denial, and indulging a light, trifling, worldly spirit.

OCT. 11—*Behold, here am I, let him do to me as seemeth good*
unto him. 2 Samuel 15 : 26

Here is majesty in distress, a kingdom in confusion,
and the king's royal heart struck with panic. Every
circumstance concurs to heighten poor David's sorrow:
his own son had stolen away the hearts of his subjects,
raised a most unnatural rebellion against his royal father, and caused him to flee from his city. Very excellently says one, "Let a child of God be but two or three
years without an affliction, and he is almost good for
nothing; he cannot pray, or meditate, or discourse as he
was wont to do: but when a new affliction comes he
finds his tongue; he comes to his knees with fervency,
and lives at another rate."

Perhaps David was never more weaned from self-
confidence, nor did his faith ever run higher, nor was
his soul bowed lower, nor did he ever breathe with more

humble submission to divine sovereignty than at this time. O how does his grace shine in this speech! As though he had said to Zadok the priest: "Return with the ark: I hope I shall have the Lord's real presence with me, though I have not the symbol of it: I see myself in his hands: I firmly believe God's everlasting love to me: he is my Saviour and my salvation: I know my immortal soul is safe: how he will direct the event of this dark providence I know not. If it appears that the Lord has no delight in me as the king of his people, if he suffers my crown and kingdom to be taken from me, his will be done; he has a sovereign right to put down one and set up another. By him kings reign: by his will they are deposed. Behold, here I am, let him do unto me as it seemeth good unto him. Love makes all things work together for good."

O christian, dost thou not admire David's faith in God, his resignation to the divine will, his submission to sovereign purposes, and his unreserved acquiescence in the counsel of the Lord? Let that man blush who would dare impeach the character or speak of the faith of David, as though it was not to be compared with the faith of a christian. O for more of the grace of faith, to follow the bright example of this Old Testament saint. Though his own beloved son, though his own dear subjects were against him; though driven from his palace, yet the presence of his God and the power of his Spirit were with him. Well might David say, "It is good for me that I have been afflicted." Psalm 119 : 71. Ever remember, O soul, whatever thy afflictions may be, whoever may be against thee to heighten them and aggravate thy sorrows, yet the Lord hath said, "I will never leave thee, nor forsake thee." Heb. 13 : 5.

18*

Oct. 12—*Jesus said, Why are ye troubled? And why do thoughts arise in your hearts?* Luke 24 : 38

Help, O help us, thou blessed Redeemer, who didst speak these words to thy affrighted disciples, to gather some sweet consolation from them to our hearts; Thou didst pray for all who should believe on thee. John, 17 : 20; O speak in life and power these words to our troubled hearts, and forbid the rising thoughts of dis tress. Thine is the power; thine shall be the glory.

We here see that, though their dear Lord is present, his beloved disciples are troubled: yea, and though he had but that moment pronounced *Peace unto you*, yet fears again arose in their hearts: they were as we are, flesh as well as spirit: men of like passions with us. The dread, fear and trouble to which nature is subject reach the hearts even of disciples. But they do not alter our state, nor separate us from the love of Christ: this is a cordial under heart troubles, and the rising of all evil, blasphemous, or horrid thoughts.

Christ is touched with the feeling of our infirmities: he sympathizes with us in what is distressing: he asks, Why are ye troubled? Why do ye give way to unreasonable fears and terrors, which distract and distress your mind? He takes pains to remove them: "Behold my hands and my feet, that it is I myself;" no other than your dear and loving Saviour. O the condescending grace of Christ! He manifests himself to us. A sight of Christ by faith dispels trouble and fear from our hearts.

Whatever troubles, fears, or distress arise in our hearts, we are encouraged with all freedom of soul and boldness of hope, to *go to him*. Now, to the shame of our hearts and the sorrow of our souls, have not you and I acted contrary to this? Instead of simply going to Christ with our distresses, have we not questioned his love to us and care for us? Thus Satan gets an advantage over us ; and the Saviour gets no glory from us. O, fools that we are, and slow of heart to believe that Jesus died for our sins, rose again for our justification, and that he is "able to save them to the uttermost that come unto God by him, seeing he ever liveth to make intercession for them." Heb. 7: 25. Let faith then live, and fear be banished : away with all thoughts that trouble our hearts. Look from within : look up. Jesus is before the throne *for us :* "in the multitude of my thoughts within me, thy comforts delight my soul;" "though I walk in the midst of trouble, thou wilt revive me." Psalm 94: 19, and 138: 7.

Oct. 13.—*The Lord Jesus Christ be with thy spirit.*
2 Tim. 4: 22

A most precious benediction ! How blind are all who deny the divinity of Christ ! How miserable are all who live without the presence of Christ ! How ignorant are all who know not that such a blessing may be enjoyed ! How stupid are all those who seek it not ! Art not thou, O christian, wanting, in not more earnestly seeking and constantly praying for more of the presence of thy Lord ? Consider what is implied in this wish. It is heaven in the heart, glory in the soul, to have Christ with our spirits : it disposes and qualifies the soul for heavenly glory.

Christ's presence sweetens our bad tempers, and subdues our unruly passions. Boisterous waves are changed into a profound calm ; rough winds are at peace : foaming billows are still : there is the calm sunshine of heartfelt joy within : all is serene and happy without. Christ's presence banishes haughty pride and furious anger It fills the soul with love : love to God and man. We cannot enjoy the presence of Jesus without loving him as our Lord. It is love that causes him to be present with our spirits, and our spirits catch the flame of love from him: and if we love God, this love will diffuse itself to our brethren also.

Christ's presence counsels and directs us in all our difficulties. We are often in the dark, both as to providence and grace: in things temporal and spiritual: as to our bodies and souls: but the presence of the Lord causes light; solves every difficulty, and makes our way plain before our eyes. It enables us to bear up under all our distresses, and comforts our hearts while afflictions bow down our spirits.

Christ's presence fortifies us with strength to fight manfully against the world, the flesh and the devil. We can do all things, through Christ strengthening us: it is out of his fulness we receive grace for our every need. His presence animates us in the discharge of every duty, and enlivens the exercise of every grace. His presence makes sin hateful, our souls humble, the world contemptible, temptations tolerable, self-denial easy, the cross glorious, Satan to flee from us, vanquishes hell, conquers death, makes the passage to glory delightful, and heaven most earnestly longed for, that without interruption we may be ever present with the Lord. O, use every means to enjoy the Lord's presence. Avoid all things which may cause him to withdraw it: "Grieve not the Holy Spirit of God." Eph. 4 : 30.

Oct. 14.—*Earnestly contend for the faith which was once delivered unto the saints.* Jude 3.

When Paul was preaching the most important truths of the everlasting Gospel at Corinth, he was brought before the judgment-seat and accused for his doctrine. Poor Gallio would not concern himself about the matter: he looked on it all as a strife of words, and a contention about names. "I will be no judge," said he. He "cared for none of these things:" his heart was totally unacquainted with the faith of God's saints. Art thou a partaker of like precious faith with the apostles? And canst thou be a Gallio too? Know, if thou wilt not contend for the faith, that hell and earth are in arms to contend against it.

What is the faith here spoken of? It includes the doctrines of faith revealed in the word of God; the whole scheme of evangelical truth, inspired by the Spirit of truth: these are received by faith; are the rule, the warrant, the support, and the glory and joy of faith: such as the doctrine of the Trinity in unity: the everlasting covenant of grace: the result of God's everlasting love to his people: the incarnation of the Son of God to save us: our regeneration by the Spirit; and full and complete salvation by grace. It includes also the great object of faith: Christ received into the heart by faith, by whom we have peace with God, pardon of sin, justification, boldness to draw nigh to him, and sweet fellowship with him. Now these truths are delivered to, and received by saints.

Says Jude, "Beloved, it was needful that I should exhort you"—to what? To *contend earnestly*, heartily, with warmth of zeal, with a holy glow of affection, in good earnest. Disciple, improve this word of exhortation. Consider that the doctrines of the Gospel and your receiving them are of the greatest moment to your wellbeing as a christian. Some ignorantly call the doctrines of the Gospel mere opinions; just as if it was indifferent whether they are believed or not. Stand reproved, ye Laodicean spirits, who have not a word to say in defence of your most holy faith, but under a pretence of peace, are cool and indifferent about the truth. Truth is too great a price at which to purchase peace. But remember, faith works *by love:* contend only with the fire of love in your heart: eye Christ in all: aim at his glory by all: pray to have his mind accompany all: with love

and pity to all, pray him to bless all who oppose you,
if peradventure he may give them repentance to the ac
knowledging the truth. Titus 1 : 1.

_____

Oct. 15.—*Why weepest thou? Whom seekest thou?*
John 20 : 15

Profession of Christ, without affection to him, leaves
the heart in dead formality. What is religion without
the affections ? What the highest pretensions, the greatest depth of knowledge, without love to our dear Saviour ? Here poor Mary discovers her affection to her
Lord, by weeping for him, and seeking after his crucified body. The fire of love in the heart carries out the
soul beyond itself. Tell me, sir, said she to Jesus, (supposing him to be the gardener,) where thou hast laid
him, and *I will take him away.* Poor weak being, her
affections went beyond her strength ; but, to her inexpressible joy and comfort, Jesus manifested himself to
her. This was written for our instruction. Come, ye
weeping, disconsolate souls, learn a lesson of encouragement from your sister's conduct and your Lord's
dealings with her.

Observe, Christ's beloved disciples have their seasons
of weeping and seeking him. They weep because they
love Christ : they seek him because they cannot be
happy without him. So the church, "I sought him
whom my soul loveth : I sought him but I found him
not." Song 3 : 1. Seeking Christ is an evidence of love
to him ; seeking him sorrowing and weeping, shows the
ardency of affection. Poor distressed sinner, who seest
thy want of Christ, knowest that thy all is in him, and
canst not be happy without him, be assured that this
sorrow of thine heart is an evidence of his love : there
is a mutual affection between Christ's heart and thine.
Jesus was near to Mary, though she knew him not ; so

is he near to every weeping, longing soul, though they have not the comfort of it.

Christ discovers his affection by his questions: "Why weepest thou? Whom seekest thou?" Our fears are seen; our sorrows are felt by our sympathizing Lord; our most silent sighs enter his ears and pierce his heart: but he will know the cause of our sorrows *from our own lips.* Pour out then your hearts before him; tell him your complaints. Do this in the assurance of faith that he will manifest himself to you. He did so to Mary: he called her by her name, MARY, which signifies exalted: she was exalted to know Christ's voice, to taste his love, to be his sister and spouse, and to live in sweet union to him and communion with him. O soul, see whence your seeking, sorrowing spirit springs! See the blessed end in which it terminates. O, bless Jesus for a heart to seek him; bless him, though you seek him "sorrowing." Thy Lord has assured thee, "Every one that asketh receiveth, and he that seeketh findeth." Luke 11:10.

OCT. 16.—*They crucified him.* Matthew 27:35

A short sentence, replete with the greatest import-ance to a world of sinners: each word in it contains matter of sorrow, wonder and joy. Here is a fund for meditation. O christian, time can never explore its depths: it will be the glory of eternity to sing of, won-der and adore a once crucified Jesus. Let us consider the agents—the work—and the subject.

They crucified him. Who? Angels? No; they gaze and wonder at the cruel, awful deed, but share not in it. Devils? No; they instigate to it, they shout and applaud the deed, but effect it not. No; the work is done by beings a little lower than the angels, by men —men of devilish natures, cursed passions, and wicked hands: with these they seize the innocent victim, doomed to direful agonies and an accursed death.

"They *crucified*." O the bloody deed! Heaven that hour let fall a tear. There hangs—who? A man like us? Yes, but immaculate, innocent: yea more, the Son of God: God and man in one Christ. The Lord of life and glory hung a spectacle to men and angels: nailed his innocent hands and tender feet to the transverse wood, to bleed, and groan, and die.

Consider the subject, HIM: Jesus Christ, the anointed Saviour. As God, he loved sinners from all eternity: as man, he was born to make sinners righteous by his obedience unto death. The work is done: on the cross he finished it. What are the effects?

> "Seest thou, O sinner, where hangs all our hope?
> "Touched by the cross, we live."

Ever view then, O soul, the sovereign cure of death, the eternal source of life; God and man in one Christ, on the accursed tree, to make thee blessed and happy. Such is the love of thy Saviour: such is his salvation. Where is your faith? O look, and look, and look again, till your whole soul loves him. Is sin your grief and burden? O, the load of pain and grief which Jesus bore! "The iniquities of us all:" he has taken them away by his *one* sacrifice. Remember this: plead this before the Lord; the faith of this brings hope to the most desperate and vile: the best of saints have no other. With this faith and this hope thou mayest draw nigh to God; plead boldly before him; face death, and resist and repel Satan with thy Saviour's dying words, "*It is finished.*"

OCT. 17.—*I am found of them that sought me not.* Isa. 65: 1.

Every display of the Saviour's grace is a jewel in his mediatorial crown. O what hearts have we, that we are not more humble before him, more thankful to him, and more joyful in him! Jesus, help us sinners to look back, to look within, to look up, and to look forward, that it may excite humility, thankfulness, and joy of heart.

Look *back*, O my soul: view thy state by nature; asleep in the arms of the wicked one, dead to God, under the power of sin, in love with the world, blind to the charms of Christ, without a single desire after him, or the least care for thy immortal soul.

Look *within:* dost thou find affection to Jesus and desires for him? Is the language of thy heart, "None but Christ; I look to none but him; I expect salvation from him, and him only?" O, whence this mighty change? Say, did you first seek Christ, or Christ you? Did your desires first go out after Christ, or his desires toward you? O, in the fervor of love you must cry out, I should have sunk to hell, without a single desire of salvation by Jesus, if he had not sought me and made himself manifest to me: his grace was first in the work.

Then, look *up*, give Jesus all the glory. O, to think, when there was nothing in us to invite the loving Spirit down, but every thing to cause him to depart from us: yet, O matchless love and sovereign grace! he showed us Christ, drew us to Him, and caused us to receive Him. Rejoice, love, adore and praise. Who can resist divine attraction? Who is proof against divine love? Who that loves can love enough?

Look *forward!* Heaven is before you: Jesus stands ready to receive you: God the Father to embrace you: God the Son to glory in you: and God the Spirit to triumph over you. Glory shall complete what grace has begun. O, to study the grace and love of Jesus, this is our heaven below; to praise him for it will be our eternal employ above.

But one thing remains, give God the glory of all this amazing grace: study from day to day, and from hour to hour, to do it by the faith of your heart, the words of your lips, and the obedience of your life. No consideration whatever can beat down your native pride, sink you into genuine humility, animate with holy love to all cheerful obedience, like this, "God commendeth his love towards us, in that while we were yet sinners, Christ died for us." Rom. 5 : 8.

Oct. 18.—*I know thou wilt bring me to death, and to the house appointed for all living.* Job 30 : 23

What sweet familiarity does grace make between God and believing sinners! How freely can they speak to him upon that solemn event, death. In the exercise of faith, we think of it without terror, and speak of it with delight. Why so? Because we have no sin, and are not sinners? No : but because we know Christ, the friend of sinners, who has taken away our sins, conquered death for us, subdued the fear of death in us, brought life and immortality to us, and is ever before the throne pleading for us.

We know also that *He* will bring us to death. O, this is soul-comforting knowledge! What, wilt thou, my loving God, my precious Saviour, who bore my sins in thine own body on the tree, bring me to death? Are the issues of life and death in thy hand? Cannot death approach me till thou give him commission, and bring me to death? I thank thee, my dear Lord, for this knowledge : then, death, thou art no more the hideous monster, the frightful king of terrors to my soul. No : my best Friend brings me to thee, that I may salute thee as an angel of love, and embrace thee as a messenger of peace.

Fond parents carry their children to see fine sights, to delight them : they avoid spectacles which would terrify them ; so doth our heavenly Father by us ; he *brings* us to death that we may see and be delighted with the glorious victories of his beloved Son. Here we behold him a triumphant conqueror over sin and death, and over the devil, who had the power of death. Our Father, God, *brings* us to the field of battle ; he carries us through it ; he shows us the spoils of his Son's glorious conquests ; there, says he, see, reap and wear the blessed trophies of his victorious cross ; all are for you, my children ; your enemies are all slain ; a crown of glory is won for you eternally to wear ; a kingdom of glory is obtained for you, where you shall for ever reign. No sooner are we brought to the field of battle, and carried through it, than shouts of victory await us. Hark, hark to the immortal spirits above : we shall soon be brought to join them in eternal shouts of *Salvation to God and the Lamb*. Now this is the life of faith : believing in Christ, the fear of death is conquered, the hope of life is enjoyed, eternal life is possessed, and we cry out, " O death, where is thy sting ? O grave, where is thy victory ?" " We have an house not made with hands, eternal in the heavens." 2 Cor. 5 : 1.

Oct. 19.—*Peter said unto him, Lord, why cannot I follow thee now? I will lay down my life for thy sake.* John 13 : 37

Peter seems now in a high frame indeed : all is the warmth of love and sunshine of joy. Ecstasies carry us out of ourselves ; we forget what we are, where we are, to what we are exposed, and what may soon befal us. Like Peter on the mount, we are apt to speak without due consideration ; we know not what we say ; the fire of passion exceeds the bounds of solid judgment. " Why cannot I follow thee *now?* Let the way be strewed with ever so many difficulties, let ever so many dangers oppose, nothing is able to dismay or dishearten me : I have just now such fervent love to thee, that I could face death in the most frightful form, and lay down my life with the greatest pleasure for thy sake."

What thinkest thou ? Is Peter's language becoming him or not ? Is it not a noble and generous declaration ? Art thou ready to say, I wish I could boldly say so too ? Ah, soul! whatever thou mayest think of these high-flown expressions, our Lord soon brought poor Peter low. Do not be discouraged at hearing professors speak great swelling words. I was once where a person said, " This world is nothing to me ; it is quite under my feet ; I have so much love that I care no more about the world than if I was not in it." Lord, thought I, what a wretch am I! Not fit to be thy disciple. But, alas! in a little time the world attracted that same person (I fear) from Jesus, under its power.

Beware of self-confidence ; live low, lie low, think low, speak low of thyself, let thy frames be what they may. Now hear our Lord's reply to Peter : " Wilt thou lay down thy life for my sake ?" I do not question thy sincerity, but I do thy strength ; I pity thy vain confi-dence ; I am concerned for thy self-sufficiency : poor vain man, thou hast turned thine eye from my love to thine own, thou trustest in the glow of thine affections, thy confidence is in thy fine frames and warm feelings, instead of my love to thee and my power to uphold thee : " Verily, verily, I say unto thee, (instead of laying down thy life for me,) the cock shall not crow till thou hast denied me thrice." What shall we say to this ? "Verily, every man at his best state is altogether vanity. Selah." Consider this. Psalm 39 : 5. And ever remember the unchangeable love of Christ to such poor, vain, change-able creatures. Well may he say, "I am the Lord, I change not, therefore ye are not consumed." Mal. 3 : 6.

Oct. 20.—*Worthy is the Lamb.* Rev. 5 : 12

This the song, this the glory of angels and redeemed sinners in heaven. To know, to believe in, love and fol-

low the Lamb, constitutes our heaven upon earth. Sin
is our hell: but the Lamb of God taketh away our sin;
then heaven is in our souls. O that ever we should be
ashamed of this Lamb, who is heaven's wonder and
heaven's glory! Is not the thought of being ashamed
of the Lamb of God like a dagger to one's heart?
Lamb of God, have mercy upon us!

Why is our dear Saviour called a LAMB? Because of
his immaculate purity; he was holy, harmless, undefil-
ed, separate from sinners, without a spot of sin or stain
of impurity. He was also meek and inoffensive like a
lamb. A lamb has no weapon of hostility: it never
hurts any one: it cannot defend itself against assaults:
it becomes an easy prey: all this Christ was in his life.
Like a lamb he was also taken and slain: he was the
very paschal lamb, to take away our sin by his blood.
As a slain lamb is precious for food and useful for clothing: so the flesh of Christ is meat indeed; his blood is
drink indeed; his righteousness is the clothing of our
souls: we live by feeding on him; we are justified in
him; our sins are washed away in his precious blood;
our souls are perfect before God, in his glorious righteousness.

Can you say from your inmost soul, *Worthy is the
Lamb?* Then you have the grace of heaven in your
heart. Proclaim it *aloud*, as they do in glory, with your
lips; and show it forth in your life: study to walk worthy of the LAMB; look at your sins; humble yourself
before the LAMB; honor him by believing that he has
atoned for them, and taken them away from before God,
by his blood. Look at yourself as a sinner; glorify the
LAMB for redeeming you to God by his blood, presenting
you before God in his righteousness, and making you
one with God by his grace; look constantly on yourself
as a sinner saved by the LAMB: have nothing to do with
any other name under heaven for salvation from sin,

death and hell. Of all the faith of your heart, the love of your soul, and glory of your life—*worthy is the Lamb.* And, O let it be the daily joy and rejoicing of your spirit, that you, a vile sinner, shall soon join the redeemed around his throne, incessantly and eternally to shout his praise who hath " washed us from our sins in his own blood."

OCT. 21.—*Most gladly, therefore, will I rather glory in my infirmities, that the power of Christ may rest upon me.* 2 Cor. 12 : 9

Though Paul is not now in the third heavens, yet he is not content to speak any language below the superlative degree, *most gladly.* O, says he, " I have had the richest experience of my own weakness and impotence : I should be most glad every day to be thus emptied and laid low at the feet of Christ, that the all-sufficiency of his grace and the power of his strength might be made perfect in me.

What does he mean by *infirmities* ? All that weakness, feebleness and inability which he found in his nature to withstand sin and Satan, to bear up under crosses, trials and distresses, to run the way of God's commandments, to fight the good fight of faith. I will rather *glory* in these. What means he ? I will glory, rejoice and be glad, that self is laid low, my proud nature debased, my self-exalting views brought down, and that I am entirely emptied of all self-sufficiency. I will *rather* glory in this than in any thing else. Why so ? " That the power of Christ may rest upon me." When full of the pride of nature and self-sufficiency, the soul sees not the need of Christ's grace. The full soul loaths the honey-comb. When strong in nature's power, the strength of Christ is not sought : but when Satan buffets, infirmities prevail, nature fails and sinks, hope and help from self forsake us; then the Saviour is sought; the soul goes humbly to the Lord.

The sinner's extremity is the Lord's opportunity. When Peter begins to sink, self-confidence forsakes him, and he cries, Lord, save or I perish: then Christ exerts his power and saves him. When Satan thinks to buffet Paul out of his faith and hope in the Lord, he only buffets him out of his self-exalting and self-confidence: he drives him to the throne of grace: he besought the Lord again and again: the Lord delivers not, but only tells him, "My grace is sufficient for thee:" Paul felt the power of Christ resting upon him. Learn hence, O soul, not to be distressed at thy infirmities, a sense of thy weakness and emptiness: glory in them, that Christ may be glorified by thee, in causing his power to rest upon thee: for mind that precious word of his, let thy weak and infirm spirit hang upon it from day to day: "He giveth power to the faint; and to them who have no might he increaseth strength." Isaiah 40 : 29.

Oct. 22.—*The great trumpet shall be blown, and they shall come which were ready to perish.* Isaiah 27 : 13

One trumpet has been blown at the giving of the law on Mount Sinai; the voice of it sounded long and waxed louder and louder: it made even Moses to fear and quake exceedingly, and all the people tremble. Soon, very soon—who knows but it may be the next moment, in the twinkling of an eye—the last trumpet shall sound and the dead shall be raised. 1 Cor. 15 : 52. Tremendous voice! Most solemn sound! The prophet asks, "Shall a trumpet be blown in the city, and the people not be afraid?" Amos 3 : 6. If the alarm of war and the approach of an enemy be sounded in the dead of night, what fear and terror seize us? Must we hear the sound of the last trumpet calling us to judgment?

Blessed, eternally blessed be our God, for the blowing of this great trumpet of Gospel grace; it is the sound of great love: it proclaims a great salvation—to whom? Even to great sinners; such as see their sins so great that they are *ready to perish*. The sound of this great trumpet expels the legal fears of the first, and the awful terrors which arise in our minds by the sound of the last trumpet; for it proclaims that "the great God" is "our Saviour Jesus Christ." Titus 2 : 13. Our judge is our advocate, our Saviour, and friend.

Do we see ourselves ready to perish without hope and help in and from ourselves? Are the curses of a broken law upon us, and is the glittering sword of justice brandished over us? The great trumpet sounds, Come, come to Christ, ye sinners, who are ready to perish, and must perish if ye do not come. Saith Jesus, "All that the Father giveth me shall come to me." John. 6 : 37. Therefore this great trumpet of Gospel salvation shall not be blown in vain. Those who never saw themselves ready to perish can perceive neither music nor charms in its sound: it is foolishness to them: but to those who feel themselves to be perishing sinners, it is a joyful sound; it proclaims victory over sin, the law, Satan, death and hell, through Jesus, who loved us and gave himself for us. Nor less doth it proclaim holiness than happiness: for it calls us to war with our sins, to peace with God, and to walk in sweet fellowship with God the Father, and his Son Jesus Christ. 1 John, 1 : 3. This great Gospel trumpet, like those of old, is all of one piece. Numbers 10 : 2. It does not give an uncertain sound; but it proclaims a free, full and finished salvation by Christ, to the glory of God, yea and amen.

Oct. 23.—*Joseph sought where to weep.* Gen. 43 : 30

To weep! What! when he saw his beloved brother Benjamin, and heard that his affectionate, aged father was alive and well? Yes, the sight of the one and the news of the other created such an ecstasy of joy in his heart as was too great to bear. He sought where to vent it by tears. O, had one followed good Joseph to his chamber, and heard what passed there between his God and his soul! Methinks I see the dear man fall prostrate, crying out in a flood of grateful, joyful tears, "O what a God do I serve! What amazing scenes of his providence have opened to my view! How has the Lord appeared graciously in my behalf! How strangely has he exalted me in life! And now, to crown all and complete my happiness, I see my beloved brother, and hear of the welfare of my honored father." Doubtless he wept, he prayed, he praised, he rejoiced, he loved, he adored his God, his kind preserver, his bountiful benefactor, his dear Saviour.

Methinks we cannot meditate on Joseph's conduct without calling to mind some sweet weeping seasons of spiritual joy with which our souls have been refreshed: when in some highly favored moments the blessed Spirit has brought some joyful tidings, some tokens of love from our once crucified, but ever-living Redeemer. O then what joy has sprung up in our souls! too big for utterance. When he has assured us of his love to us; that we shall soon see him as he is, be with him where he is, and eternally enjoy him and his Father and our Father in glory—O, the rapture of this faith! Then we are ready to fly the world and all its concerns, and even our brethren in Christ too: we seek to be alone to pour out our souls, to give vent to our joy in a flood of loving, grateful tears. Then, like the disciples on the mount, we cry out, It is good to be here: this is sweet: methinks my soul is drowned in tears of love!

Now are we not ready to wish, O that it were always thus with me! But neither Joseph, you, nor I, could live in such ecstasy and rapture: the body could not support them: my weak body could not. Neither are they always good for the soul: if so, we should be always favored with them. Of this we are fully assured: for "no good thing will the Lord withhold from them that walk uprightly." Psalm 84:11. But these God withholds. You never read of one saint in the Bible always in an ecstasy of joy. He who freely gave us his Son, "how shall he not with him also freely give us all things?" Rom. 8:32.

Oct. 24.—*Lord, increase our faith.* Luke 17:5

Men of the world tauntingly say, "O, you don't mind good works, faith is to do every thing for you." Truly, faith is all, for it includes the object of faith, the Lord. Faith has no existence without its object.

Consider, Is it not *a good work* to forgive an offending brother? This is what our Lord teaches in the preceding verses. The apostles were made truly sensible that they could not do this without faith; nay, not without the increase of faith; therefore they prayed for it. Real believers are "created in Christ Jesus unto good works, which God hath before ordained that we should walk in them." Eph. 2:10. They are "a peculiar people, zealous of good works." Tit. 2:14. Thus they love to glorify their heavenly Father.

They know, too, that all good works *proceed from* faith, and from the increase of faith: for Christ dwells in our hearts by faith. Eph. 3:17. This is the source and spring of all comfort, and every good work. Without this, what is life to a Christian? Verily, but an uncomfortable breathing, not worthy the name of life. Christ dwelling in the heart constitutes heaven upon earth. Just as uncomfortable as this world would be if the sun were blotted out of heaven, would the christian be without the in-dwelling of Christ. How hast thou found thy soul, O christian, this day? Hast thou found "Christ in thee the hope of glory?" If not, it is for want of faith. If thou hast, dost thou not desire to enjoy more of it? It is to be had by the increase of faith: pray for it.

Faith sickens the soul to the love of sin and the love of this world. The increase of faith kills the love of both; "for this is the victory, even our faith." 1 John 5:4. Faith brings the prospect of heavenly glory into view. The increase of faith brings fuller assurance to our hearts of our enjoyment of it, quickens our diligence in the way to it, and excites ardent desires for the full fruition of it, that we may be "absent from the body and present with the Lord."

See who is "the Author and Finisher of our faith." Do you complain that your faith is weak, and your corruptions strong? Remember, that Redeemer who died for your sins can strengthen your faith. Look unto Jesus: cry unto him to increase your faith; so shall your heart be happy, your life holy, and your soul "strong in the grace that is in Christ Jesus." 2 Tim. 2:1.

OCT. 25.—*Behold my hands and my feet, that it is I myself.*
Luke 24:39

Amintas had done valiant acts, and lost part of his arm in the field of battle for his country's good. His brother Æschylus was about to be condemned to die. Amintas came into court, spoke not a word, but only lifted up the stump of his arm without a hand; as though he had said, See what I have lost in my country's cause His silent oratory prevailed, and saved his brother's life How much more affecting a sight does our Lord here present to his disciples! He called upon them, he calls upon us: *Behold!* they by the eye of sense; we by the eye of faith. Consider the reasons for this.

To compose and comfort their minds: they were terrified and affrighted; they took him for a spirit. Christ is touched with the feeling of our infirmities: he sympathises with us in all our troubles. One cause of them is misapprehension of the nature of Christ: we too oft forget that he was *man*, like unto us in all things, except sin: "Behold my hands and my feet" with the print of the nails: "it is I *myself:*" the very same man, with the same flesh and blood, who lately hung upon the cross. Handle me; feel me.

It was to confirm their faith in his dying for their sins and rising again for their justification: he died as a weak man; he rose as the almighty God: as God-man he atoned for sin, conquered death and hell for us. The faith of this is the source of all hope and the spring of all peace to our souls.

He says, *Behold*, that he may quicken our love. O soul, can you behold by faith, and think of the love and sufferings of Jesus for your salvation, and not love him? His pierced body, hands and feet, are the marks of his great love and the agony of his sufferings for you. O love, rejoice and adore. Does he not deserve the whole love of our heart and the affections of our soul? *Behold*—that all your hope may be in him. Beware of the fatal error of some, who pretend to believe in Christ for the pardon of sin, but for final justification hope in their own works. No, my Lord, the sin-atoning, soul-justifying work is thine, and thine alone. I will hope in no other. My soul, I charge thee, fix, constantly fix all thy attention, for all thy hope, upon thy once-pierced Lord. My conscience, I charge thee, when base intruders would rival his glory, banish them: cry with abhorrence, Get ye hence; "what have I to do any more with idols?" Hosea 14 : 8.

Oct. 26.—*Peter said, Man, I know not what thou sayest.*
Luke 22: 60

No, Peter! Why, he speaks plain enough: he is confident of thy person, knows thy voice, and the very brogue of thy tongue: he boldly affirms, "Of a truth thou wast with Jesus." It is downright falsehood to reply, "I know not what thou sayest." Peter is ashamed of his Lord. Is he not ashamed of himself? Not yet. No; he "began to curse and to swear, saying, I know not the man." Might we not expect to hear next that he was damned eternally? He deserved it. Was he here now he would confess it from the very depths of his heart; but he is above, confessing his desert of damnation, and ascribing "salvation to God and the Lamb." For, "the Lord turned and looked upon Peter." O, who can say what there was in that turn and that look? Lord, give us to feel its grace and power, that we may improve it.

Consider: Sin is sin, in God's saints as well as others: yea, their sins exceed all others: yes, and God sees sin in them as well as in others; and he will visit them, too, for their sin. To his people of old he says, "You only have I known (with the love of a tender father) of all the families of the earth, *therefore* I will punish you for your iniquities." Amos 3: 2. Who can say what a hell of agonies Peter felt when he "wept bitterly?" He experienced that truth which he afterward preached to others, "Judgment must begin at the house of God." 1 Peter, 4: 17. A sense of condemnation for sin is awakened in the heart and conscience; the clear sight of it; feeling, mourning, groaning under a sense of it; looking up to God with a broken heart, a contrite spirit, a sorrowful soul, sighing out, "Against thee, O Lord, have I sinned, and done evil in thy sight. Nothing but thy blood, O Jesus, can cleanse me! O my

God, let thy grace pardon me, and thy Spirit comfort me.

What affects any sinner thus? The Saviour's turning and looking upon the soul. Sin naturally hardens the heart and sears the conscience. Peter, after his awful fall, would have run away from Christ; given himself up to the service of sin and Satan, till. he fell into hell, if the Lord had left him to himself. So would you and I. But Jesus *turns* from his anger against our sins; turns to us in love. He *looks:* instead of frowning us into eternal despair, he looks with love; he speaks love into our hearts; he melts our hearts into sorrow and remorse for our sins, and with hope of mercy and pardon; "for where sin abounded, grace much more abounds." Romans 5 : 20.

Oct. 27.—*I know that my Redeemer liveth.* Job 19 : 25

Matters are sometimes brought to a close point between God and the soul: it is stripped of all its comforts: the soul is in heaviness. 1 Peter 1 : 6. It is broken in the place of dragons and covered with the shadow of death, as the Psalmist most affectionately paints the scenes of horror and affliction. Psalm 44 : 19. So that as he says, " I had fainted, unless I had believed." Psalm 27 : 13. Nothing within, nothing without, for the soul to stay itself upon, but the word of the Lord and the Lord revealed in the word. Then is that sweet word fulfilled, "they shall hang upon HIM all the glory of his father's house." Isaiah 22 : 24.

This was Job's tried, tempted, afflicted, yet blessed state : though all his comforts are dead, still his " Redeemer liveth:" in the midst of all his losses he had not lost this blessed knowledge: I *know:* it is a matter of the greatest certainty to my soul, that there is a Redeemer for lost sinners ; I know he is my Redeemer: I have seen my want of him, and my certain destruction without his redemption. *He liveth;* while he lives my hopes cannot die, my soul cannot despair; stript of all things beside, nothing can separate me from the love of Christ. I know that Christ liveth at the right hand of God, because he lives in my heart by faith. Such is the language of this Old Testament saint. Says Luther, "I had utterly despaired had I not known that Christ was head of the church." "Head over all things to his body the church." Eph. 1:22.

But how is the soul enabled to say, with Job, Christ is *my* Redeemer, or, with Paul, he "loved me and gave himself for me?" By the word of grace we know there is a Redeemer; by the testimony of the Spirit of truth, through faith, the sinner is enabled to say he is *mine*, my beloved, my friend. There are two infallible evidences of this: Christ has both our hearts and our hopes: our heart is set upon him; our hopes centre in him. He is precious to our *hearts:* we have fellowship with him by faith; we know that he liveth, because we enjoy the comfort of his life and love in our souls; we know him both as dying for us and also as living in us; he dwells in our hearts by faith; he sends his tokens of love; he draws our affections to himself, from the world of sin and vanity. And our *hopes* are in him: his Spirit gives us to see such perfection in his glorious work and finished salvation as sickens to every other hope; yea, kills self-righteousness and self-confidence: we become "dead to the law by the body of Christ." Rom. 7:4. We may as soon place our confidence in the righteousness of the thief on the cross, as in any righteousness of our own: "We know that he abideth in us, by the Spirit which he hath given us." 1 John 3:24.

Oct. 28.—*By the obedience of One shall many be made righteous.* Romans 5:19.

Joyful truth to *miserable sinners.* O that this passage were ever upon our minds, "My thoughts are not your thoughts, neither are your ways my ways, saith the Lord." Isa. 55:8. Our thoughts are to make ourselves righteous by our own obedience; and our ways are, to be justified before God by our own righteousness: but the Lord calls us to forsake these unrighteous thoughts as well as wicked ways, and to submit by faith to his thoughts and his ways, to be made righteous by the obedience of One.

Consider, this negative is implied, no other obedience can make any sinner righteous. O sinner, for what art thou seeking? What art thou striving to be and to do? What is the end of thy praying, reading, hearing, and of thy striving against sin and to excel in obedience? Is it to make thyself righteous? Then it all proceeds from unbelief of the truth that "by the obedience of *One* shall many be made righteous," and by no other obedience whatever. "Then," say some, "there is an end to all good works." No: from the faith of this all good works begin. There is indeed an end to all the evil works of unbelief, which are done to supplant the *one* spotless obedience of Christ in making sinners righteous, and to establish the filthy rags of man's righteousness. Taught by the Spirit of truth, through faith, my soul abhors this. "Whatsoever is not of faith, is sin." Rom. 14:23. "Works which do not spring of faith in Jesus Christ, have the nature of sin." (*Church Article* 13.) Hence, O my soul, no obedience of thine, before faith in Christ, can make thee righteous. Nor doth obedience after faith make thee righteous; for then thou art made righteous by the *one* obedience of Christ. Settle this matter well in thy conscience: the glory of thy God and the comfort of thy soul demand it. It is positively asserted, "By *the* obedience of *one*," or the *one* obedience of Christ, "shall many be made righteous." The faith of God's elect takes the comfort of this, and will love Christ, live upon his righteousness, and give him the glory of it.

But who are made righteous by Christ's one obedience ? *Many:* The many sons whom Christ shall bring to glory. Heb. 2 : 10. Even *all* who see themselves miserable sinners, and believe in Christ for righteousness unto justification of life. What a glorious way is this of making sinners righteous ! It secures all the glory to Christ ; it keeps the sinner humble before him, dependent on him, and prevents all self-righteous boasting ; while it gives the poor sinner "boldness and access with confidence" to God, and inspires warm love to Christ, and the cheerful obedience of faith.

Oct. 29.—*She said, Truth, Lord; yet the dogs eat of the crumbs which fall from their master's table.* Matt. 15 : 27.

Here is blessed reasoning: it produced admiration in the Lord: "O woman, great is thy faith !" It also obtained a rich grant from him: "Be it unto thee even as thou wilt." Great faith ! How does it appear ? We do not find that she came to Christ in full assurance of faith, saying, I know thou art *my* Saviour, I am assured thou hast loved *me* and wilt save *me*. No. Still there was great faith without this. Look at her faith : imitate it : she honored the Lord by it ; he honors her for it.

She was in trouble : she flies instantly to Christ ; she tells him of her sorrows : "Have mercy upon me, O Lord, for my daughter is grievously vexed with a devil." To cry to Jesus for mercy, in trials and under a sense of sin, is the prayer of faith, and honors the Lord of glory.

Here were great discouragements : Christ answers

her not a word: the disciples desire him to cure her, that they might get rid of her: but Jesus answers, (not her, but his disciples,) "I am not sent but to the lost sheep of the house of Israel." Was not this repulse enough to strike her dumb and send her away in despair? Instead of this, her faith grew stronger and her importunity greater. She falls at his feet, with, *Lord, help me.* O that was putting it home to the loving heart of our dear Lord: she brought her case to a point: Jesus, you can help me; none but you can: if you do not, I am miserable. Have you no compassion for a poor miserable sinner? Lord, help me. Thus casting herself upon the Lord's love and power, she at last gets an answer from him: but, O such a one as was like a dagger to her heart, "It is not meet to take the children's bread and cast it to the dogs."

Does she now turn away in despair? No. She had a child's heart, and a child's faith too: she again puts her case home to the Saviour. Mark it: I am a dog, a vile, unworthy creature; let me be fed as such upon the falling crumb: I know I do not deserve even that from thee. See what perseverance, faith and prayer will do: it overcomes all difficulties, surmounts all obstacles, obtains the sought-for mercy. Some in our day would have thought this woman undervalued herself: but Jesus humbles those sinners to the very lowest whom he raises to the very highest. O take up this resolution, "I will wait upon the Lord, who hideth his face: I will look for him." Isa. 8. 17.

Oct. 30.—*Wherefore, lift up the hands which hang down, and the feeble knees.* Heb. 12: 12

Are you saying, my troubles are many, my burden is great, and hope deferred makes the heart sick? True, a faint heart makes weak hands and feeble knees; then afflictions become intolerable, duty tiresome, prayer irksome, the ordinances unprofitable, the lamp of spiritual life seems expiring, the poor sinner grows dejected and dispirited, is ready to give up hope, and to give way to despondency. *The Comforter* inspires a work for such, "Lift up the hands which hang down." Do you say, the advice is good, but the practice hard? Paul supposes it; for he introduces it with *Wherefore*. O, I dearly love these Scripture adverbs! Much courage and comfort are gained by attending to them. *Wherefore*, or for which reason, lift up your weak hands, or the weak hands of others. Consider why, or wherefore, we should do this.

We have Jesus to look unto for patience. He is the author and finisher of our faith; be bore our sins; he hath for ever taken away the curse due to them; he has made our peace with God; God is in him reconciled to us. He who endured the cross for our sins, and despised the shame of being treated as a malefactor, is now before the throne of God praying for us. O, this look is reviving!

Consider Jesus, the captain of our salvation, lest ye be weary and faint. He was "made perfect through sufferings, that he might bring many sons unto glory." He is bringing you, "through much tribulation," into his kingdom. Consider the love and sorrows of Jesus for you. Look on yourself as a suffering member of a once suffering head: so shall your weak mind be strengthened and your weary mind refreshed.

Forget not, but consider the exhortation, *My Son*. Precious appellation! God is your Father; he loves you with the same everlasting and unchangeable love as he did his only begotten Son: he treats you in love; he chastises you as his child. Why? Because he is in wrath against you? No; but to make you more like himself in holiness. O then "lift up your hands" to your God and Redeemer in confident faith, in humble prayer. Though all within is clouded dejection, yet all above is sunshine, joy, peace, and consolation. Consider your hope. It is as "an anchor of the soul." On what is it fixed? It "entereth into that within the vail, whither the fore-runner is for us entered, even Jesus." Hebrews 6 : 19, 20.

Oct. 31.—*He saw his glory, and spake of him.* John 12 : 41

Ministers who do not preach Christ, and sinners who do not speak of Christ, are objects of pity, not of our wrath; their eyes are blind to his matchless glory; their hearts do not understand his unparalleled love. But when once Christ's glory is displayed and his love believed in the heart, the tongue will speak of him. So Isaiah found it. So did the poor woman of Samaria, "she ran into the city," she took hold of one and another, she eagerly cried, "'Come, see a man who told me all things that ever I did; is not this the Christ?' Surely it is, 'what think ye?'" John 4 : 29. She had sweet experience. Here was no self-exalting; no cry, "See me, admire me; what fine experience I have had." One is sometimes grieved to read or hear people tell of their experiences, when they tend only to make the poor sinner appear somewhat glorious in his own eyes, and to be admired by his fellow-sinners: this is not right. If the sinner's vileness is not fully explored, and the Saviour's glory *only* exalted, such souls know not as they ought to know; such experiences are not profitable, they are not worth attending to.

When sinners see Christ's glory, they will *speak of him* to God the Father; they will come in his name; they will plead his blood only for the pardon of sin, his righteousness alone for the justification of their souls, his intercession for their obtaining every blessing in earth and heaven. Thus we come boldly to a throne of grace; thus we expect freely to obtain mercy to relieve us and grace to comfort us: thus we are sure, perfectly sure, that we are welcome to God; for he hath told us so. "It pleased the Father" that in Christ all fullness (of grace and glory) should dwell, Col. 1 : 19; that "out of his fulness we should receive." John 1 : 16. Having seen Christ's glory, we come to him for this grace.

The sight of Christ's glory blinds us to our own fancied glory. The more we see of Jesus, the less we like ourselves: we grow out of love with ourselves. What glory is there in a cage of unclean birds? Worse, inexpressibly worse are our hearts. Yet, astonishing love! Jesus displays the glory of his grace to us. Nothing but unbelief prevents our beholding it : "Said I not unto thee, if thou wouldest believe, thou shouldest see my glory?" John 11 : 40.

November

Nov. 1.—*Behold, this day I am going the way of all the earth.*
Joshua 23 : 14

Though fully assured of his near dissolution, yet with what calm composure does Joshua utter these words! Though you are a sinner and must fall under the sen tence of death for sin, yet you need not be under bon dage all your life-time through *fear of death.* Why should you? Has not the sinner's Friend gained a complete and everlasting victory over death, the sin ner's enemy?

Consider what Christ hath done for us sinners; for

sinners we are, and shall be, though redeemed by the
blood and sanctified by the Spirit of Christ, when the messenger of death calls us to glory. Honor thy Lord's work
by the faith of thy heart: so fear and terror shall flee from
thy soul. By his death he has appeased divine justice.
As Jonah, his type, being cast into the sea, quelled the
storm; so Christ, being cast into the furnace of Divine
wrath, quenched the flames. God is just, while he justifies the ungodly who believe in Jesus. Rom. 3: 26.
He has silenced the accusations of the law. He has "redeemed us from the curse of the law, being made a
curse for us." Gal. 3: 13. Upon this follows the removal
of guilt: "He put away our sins by the sacrifice of
himself." Heb. 9: 26. "We have redemption through
his blood, even the forgiveness of sins. Eph. 1: 7.
He hath wrought out and brought in an everlasting
righteousness for us. We are "made the righteousness of God in him." 2 Cor. 5: 21. He hath conquered
Satan: by his death destroying "him who had the power of death, that is, the devil." Heb. 2: 14. He hath opened heaven to us. We lost a paradise by sin. We gain heaven by the cross of Christ. It is our "purchased possession." Eph. 1: 14. He hath obtained victory over sin and
death, so that we may joyfully cry out, "Thanks be to
God, which giveth us the victory through our Lord Jesus
Christ." 1 Cor. 15: 57. Now, if Christ has appeased justice, silenced the law, taken away the guilt of sin, is made
righteousness to us, has conquered Satan, opened hea
ven, overcome death, and obtained victory for us, what
have we to fear? Why should we not triumph in the
view of death?

We cannot thus triumph without the work of the
Spirit in us. But if he has made the work of Christ
glorious in our eyes; if he has given us to see our need
of it; to believe in and rely upon Christ's life and death
as our title to heaven and glory; by the faith of this he

has sanctified our souls, as vessels of honor, to the glory of Christ. It is our privilege to rejoice in him; to look upon his victories as our own; to triumph over every enemy, and over death as the last enemy; for though he is an enemy to the flesh, he is the best friend to the soul.

Nov. 2.—*We walk by faith, not by sight.* 2 Cor. 5:7

Thus we quit sense for faith: so we overcome "the lust of the eyes." To gratify this is contrary to the walk of faith. Then is it any marvel that we lose the peace, comfort, and joy of faith? But this is not what is here meant by sight, as opposed to faith. Here is an infallible truth: Though a christian, by the eye of sense, can neither see. God, nor Christ, nor the things of the heavenly world, yet he walks in the firm belief of what the word of God tells him of them; and hence they have the supreme affection of his soul from day to day. Faith supplies the sight of them. They are as real to the mind as though seen by the bodily eye. Thus, a lively hope of enjoying them is kept up in the heart: "We are always confident," we are as sure of the existence of spiritual, heavenly, and invisible objects, as we are of our own being. O ye sons of carnal sight and sense! ye deride us—we pity you. Ye look only at shadows, we at eternal substance: "The things which are not seen are eternal." 2 Cor. 4:18.

See the preciousness of faith. Though we do not now see, nor ever have seen Christ, yet we love him; believing in him, we rejoice with joy unspeakable and full of glory. 1 Pet. 1:8. We see in ourselves nothing but sin and misery; but by faith we know we are righteous in Christ, accepted in him, justified, presented without spot of sin. We see our bodies under the sentence of death, daily dying, hasting to the grave: natural sight can look no farther: the body turns to dust; but by faith we look through death and the grave, and " we know that if our earthly house of this tabernacle were dissolved, we have a building of God, an house not made with hands, eternal, in the heavens." 2 Cor. 5 : 1.

Though we cannot explain the manner of the Spirit's work upon our souls, any more than we can tell whence the wind cometh, or whither it goeth; yet by sweet experience we can say, "He that hath wrought us for this self-same thing, is God." 2 Cor. 5 : 5. For we find ourselves formed to live by the faith of the Son of God, " who loved us, and gave himself for us." Gal. 2 : 20. Hence we are dead to the sinful pleasures of sense and the joys of carnal mirth; for, we see Jesus at the right hand of God, where are "fulness of joy, and pleasures for evermore." Psalm 16 : 11.

Nov. 3.—*Give us this day our daily bread.* Matt. 6 : 11

Happiness, that inestimable jewel, springs only from contentment. Christian contentment is founded in humility. The humble christian lives upon the fulness of God: thence he seeks all his supplies. Our Lord not only teaches his disciples the word of prayer, which any one may use, but he also gives the spirit of prayer peculiar to themselves only. This consists in knowing our wants; in seeking a supply of them from the Lord, and in *daily* looking to him for all the blessings of providence and grace needful for us as men and christians.

Do we know our wants? A proper sense of them will make and keep us low and humble in our own eyes, for we shall go out of ourselves and live out of ourselves. Do we want daily bread to support our bodies? Have we no spring of life in ourselves but what must be fed and nourished from the food we receive from day to day ? Just so it is with our souls. Christ saith, "I am the bread of life." John 6 : 48. We have no inherent stock of spiritual food in ourselves; the man who thinks otherwise is as foolish as he would be who should say he has within himself a supply of natural food, he needs not pray for it.

Do we seek a supply from our Lord ? He says, "Blessed are they which do hunger." Matt. 5 : 6. Their blessedness consists in coming empty to him to be filled: *Give us*. Lord, I am just the same hopeless, helpless, miserable sinner in myself, as I was when I first heard of thee and came unto thee. *Give* me this day my daily bread : thy flesh to eat and thy blood to drink. Thy flesh is meat indeed : thy blood is drink indeed. John 6 : 55. Lord, thou hast said, "He that eateth me, even he shall live by me." John 6 : 57. O that in feeding on thee by faith, I may know that I have eternal life, and that thou wilt raise me up at the last day.

This feeding is vastly preferable to disputing. True, we are exhorted to contend earnestly for the faith ; but then it should be with a desire that our own souls and the souls of others may be edified, fed, and nourished by the faith of Jesus ; else it is but vain jangling. Who would not contend for his natural food ? How jealous, how watchful should we be against every enemy who would prevent our feeding upon Christ, the bread of life ! The more we feed upon this bread, the less appetite we have for the pleasures of this world and the vanities of sense. Our spiritual food transforms us into the image of our Lord, and causes us to aspire after him and long to be with him. Precious promise ! "Jesus shall feed his flock like a shepherd." Isa. 40 : 11.

Nov. 4.—*The blood of Jesus Christ his Son cleanseth us from all sin.* 1 *John* 1 : 7

Most precious truth for guilty sinners ! Lord, help us

to consider what is implied in these words. See the exceeding sinfulness of sin. It has brought upon us, loss of God's image; obnoxiousness to his wrath; rejection from his presence. We are by sin totally unclean. The pollution of sin has brought the curse of God upon us, armed his justice, shut his kingdom against us, and opened the gates of hell to us. The bitter cries and torments of the damned in hell will eternally proclaim the malignity of sin. The everlasting songs of the saints in glory will proclaim the praises of the Lamb, who washed them from their sins in his own blood.

This proves the curse and defilement of sin. The blood of Jesus Christ, and that alone, cleanseth from all its deepest stains. O the infinite love of the Son of God, to shed his blood for guilty sinners! O the infinite virtue of his precious blood to cleanse us from all sin! Remember, God's justice would have been eternally glorified, and thy soul eternally suffering his wrath due to thy sins, if the blood of his Son had not cleansed thee from all sin. Reflect on this, and say, canst thou think light of sin, or count the blood of Jesus of little value? O, see sin's crimson dye in the purple gore of the Son of God, which was shed to atone for it and cleanse from it.

"Cleanseth us." Not only hath cleansed and shall cleanse, but it continually does so; whereby we stand before God as without spot in his sight, and freed from all condemnation.

"The blood of Jesus Christ." This means the last act of the tragedy in the life of our anointed Saviour; his blood being the ransom of our souls, the price of our redemption, and the expiation of our sins.

"His Son:" the Son of God: very God of very God. Here let faith fix and conscience be satisfied: not only the blood of the Son of the Virgin, but it is the blood of the Son of God. Neither the greatness nor the number of sins can expose any sinner to wrath who believes in the Son of God : no guilt so great but it can cleanse ; no stain so deep but it can remove. Unbelief shuts this blood out of the conscience. By faith we receive its cleansing virtue and peaceful effects on our souls.

Nov. 5.—*Jesus said, What manner of communications are these that ye have one to another, as ye walk and are sad ?* Luke 24 : 17

Time is the best remedy for most diseases, whether of body or mind. A present hour may cause sadness, the next may bring joy. This is a living comfort in saddest seasons : Christ knows both our sorrows and the cause of them : he is always near to us, though we see him not : his sympathising spirit manifests itself in the question here recorded.

Here were two disciples communing together and reasoning with one another : this is right. It is pleasing to our Lord to see his dear members converse with and strive to edify each other in the faith of him : and endeavoring to bear each other's burdens. Jesus joined company with them. Disciple, how often have you found it so ? Christ delights in the fellowship of his saints.

Christ inquires of their conversation and the cause of their sadness. Disciples of Christ have their sad seasons : it is good that they should converse freely with one another about them. But whence do they spring ? Chiefly from unbelief. These poor souls were sad Why ? They did not believe their Lord was risen. But, ah ! there was another reason for sadness ; they had basely forsaken and deserted him : this also arose from the same cause, unbelief. Well, notwithstanding all this, O the free grace of Christ ! he follows them, though they forsook him ; he owns them, though they denied him ; he cares for them, though they showed no care for him ; he comes to comfort them, though they had grieved him.

Says the Prince of peace, "Why are ye sad?" Then they opened their minds to him; they told him of the ray of hope and the gleam of confidence which they possessed: "*We trusted* it had been he who should have redeemed Israel." But delays begat doubt. Luke 24:21.

What was the consequence? Christ chides them for their unbelief. Expounds the Scriptures to them. Causes their hearts to burn within them. O christians, though you are perplexed in your minds, walk and are sad, yet forsake not the assembling of yourselves together; expect and pray for your Lord's presence: this, like the rising sun, will scatter the clouds of doubt, fear and sadness, which hang over your minds. Remember, with the confidence of faith and the joy of hope, your Lord's precious promise, "Where two or three are gathered together in my name, there am I in the midst of them." Matthew 18:20.

Nov. 6.—*For when I am weak, then am I strong.* 2 Cor. 12:10

We have heard of Paul's "revelations" and exaltings —here we have his humbling. He is brought down to his right place, low in himself; and to his right feelings, weak in himself. Hence we see the true nature and blessed end of christian experience: it keeps the soul from being puffed up with pride, lest it fall into the condemnation of the devil: it sinks it low in humility, under a sense of weakness, and it leads it out of itself to look for all its strength in Christ. Here the strength of faith is opposed to the weakness of sense. "When I am weak, then am I strong:" this, though a difficult lesson, yet is a precious one.

Do we see ourselves weak? Christ is held forth to us as our strength, and he calls upon us to be strong in him: "Trust in the Lord for ever, for in the Lord Jehovah is everlasting strength." Isa. 26:4. But surely folly is bound up in the heart of the weak; for, instead of obeying and trusting in him, how many are saying, I am the weakest of the weak; I have no might, no power? You are the very person here addressed. You can get no strength but from the Lord. By trusting in the Lord, you will say, though weak, I am strong; I have everlasting strength.

To encourage to this, the Lord commands, "Let the weak say I am strong." Joel 3:10. Let them believe it in their hearts and confess it with their lips. What! if they find no strength in themselves? Yes, it is a command to the weak; yea, to the weakest of the weak. Then this exactly suits you and me. "Hast thou not known, hast thou not heard, that the everlasting God, the Lord, giveth power to the faint, and to them that have no might he increaseth strength." Isa. 40:29. Here we are rebuked and reproved—"faint, and have no might:" this is our state. Have you never heard nor known how the Lord dealeth with such? O look up to him. Though not sufficient of yourself to do any thing as of yourself, know your sufficiency is of the Lord: though we can do nothing of ourselves, yet we can do all things through Christ, who strengtheneth us. Phil. 4:13. How do we get strength from Christ? By believing his promises, going to him in the faith of them, pleading them before him, and praying him to fulfil them in us: thus we put our cause upon the strength of Christ's truth: he is faithful; he cannot deny us; he will say, "According to your faith, be it unto you" Matthew 9:29.

Nov. 7.—*Then were the disciples glad when they saw the Lord.*
John 20:20

"Truly the light is sweet, and a pleasant thing it is for the eyes to behold the sun." Eccles. 11:7. But, O how much more sweet and pleasant to see the light and behold the glory of *the Sun of righteousness!* This inspires the heart with gladness. These disciples had lost their dear Lord, and mourned in darkness for his absence: tongue cannot tell their inexpressible joy at seeing him again: their sight was by the eye of sense, ours is by the eye of faith: yet our sight is not less real than theirs, and it brings the same gladness to our hearts; therefore it is highly prized by us, for we can neither live comfortably, walk holily, nor die happily without seeing the Lord Christ.

A sight of Christ by faith brings peace to the conscience. There is ever a war within, between the flesh and the Spirit, grace and nature, the old man and the new. The motions of sin in our members are ever warring against the law of holiness in our minds. Wicked nature is like the troubled sea, which cannot rest; it is continually casting up mire and dirt: but the winds and seas of corrupt nature obey Christ; he says, " Peace, be still," and there is a great calm in the soul; for Christ is our peace, he hath made our peace with God by his blood, he makes and keeps peace in our souls by his presence; our stubborn lusts will fight and reign if Christ be absent from our hearts. Therefore we cannot but be glad when we see the Lord.

The sight of Christ quells our doubts and dispels our fears. Our poor hearts, seeing sin and all manner of evil dwelling in us, are ready to fear and doubt whether we are the children of God. But O, when we see Christ by faith, our consciences are satisfied; our minds are divinely assured that Christ hath "redeemed us to God by his blood;" for we cry out, This is our Beloved and our Friend in whom we have redemption, even the forgiveness of our sins. We believe and are sure that he is the Christ of God, the Saviour of sinners.

The sight of Christ gives victory over death, opens the kingdom of heaven to our view, and gives us to see a smiling God and Father ready to receive and embrace us. O most joyful sight! If so, O christian, beware, beware of gratifying your sight with any vain, sinful, and carnal pleasures. These will draw away your sight and take off the attention of your mind from looking unto Jesus, and prevent your gladness of heart and joy of soul in and from him; "Turn away mine eyes from beholding vanity." Psalm 119 : 37.

Nov. 8.—*I know that in me* (*that is in my flesh*) *dwelleth no good thing.* Rom. 7 : 18.

This is the knowledge which puffeth not up; but like love, it edifies the soul in deep humility, while it excites overflowing gratitude in the heart to Christ for his righteousness to justify such vile sinners: it is the knowledge of regenerate souls. *I know;* not only doctrinally, in notion and theory, but it is a confirmed truth, by heart-felt experience; I know it from day to day; I have proved it again and again, "that in my flesh dwelleth no good thing." Paul's judgment of himself was confirmed by experience.

But, was not Paul a most eminent apostle and holy saint? Yes: still he confesses publicly before God, angels and men, that he was the subject of a nature which is "earthly, sensual and devilish." If no good thing dwelt in his flesh, is it not implied that every evil dwelt there? Doubtless he would be so understood. Were "evil thoughts, murders, adulteries, blasphemies" in the flesh of this holy saint? Yes, his knowledge of the total corruption of his fallen nature agrees with his Lord's doctrine. Matt. 15 : 19. He had been a murderer and blasphemer by practice; then he was in a state of ignorance and unbelief; but now he was regenerated, his state changed, and his practice altered, therefore, surely his flesh could not be so bad. Yes, it was just the same: the flesh, the old man, the corrupt fallen nature is and ever will be the same in the regenerate: "It ever lusts against the Spirit." Gal. 5: 17.

Why is this woful experience of Paul's left upon record? For our profit. That we might judge and try ourselves by it. If we are taught by the same Spirit, we shall have the same humbling views of our flesh. Our flesh is not worse than Paul's, nor was his better than ours. If we are left in nature's pride, we shall join the ignorant cry of those who say, "all who are convinced of sin greatly undervalue themselves."

We also here learn not to be cast down with despondency, nor to give way to despairing thoughts, though we find every evil and nothing but evil in our flesh; for this cures us of all confidence in the flesh, to which we are prone, but it opposes the faith of the Gospel.

Look then and go entirely out of yourself: look wholly to and trust entirely in the Lord Jesus and his righteousness, that though you have no confidence in the flesh, you may ever rejoice in him; this is the character and conduct of a true believer. Phil. 3: 3. Adore the Holy Spirit, who, when you had no goodness to deserve it, no fitness to qualify for it, but all in you to oppose it, gave you a new birth into Christ, in whom you have every spiritual good. Therefore, "walk in the Spirit, and ye shall not fulfil the lust of the flesh." Galatians 5: 16.

Nov. 9.—*We are perplexed, but not in despair.* 2 Cor. 4: 8

God's dear children have not all the same clear judgment of truth; they are not all of one mind and the same sentiment in all points: yet they all have one Lord, one faith, and one hope; and there is a uniformity in their experience, in regard to the exceeding sinfulness of sin, the depravity of their nature, their perplexities from the world, the flesh, and the devil; their love of the

Scriptures, and the exceeding preciousness of Christ: this proves that they are taught by one and the same Spirit. We have perplexities of a spiritual nature, besides those in common with others, to which natural men are utter strangers: these are no weak evidences of our spiritual birth. To be perplexed with a body of sin and death, with a sense of unbelief, with deadness, formality, wanderings in spiritual duties; with Satan's temptations, accusations, corrupt reasonings, and carnal pleadings: being sensible to all these makes it manifest that the soul is born of God, and alive to God; for when dead in sin we felt nothing of them. How absurdly and foolishly then do many act? Because thus perplexed, they are ready to give up hope, cast away confidence, and deny that they are God's children; but their sense of these things, and groaning under them, are evident tokens of salvation: "Perplexed, but not in despair:" O take heed of yielding in the least to despair: of desponding: of letting go your confidence in Christ: of giving up, for one moment, hope in Christ.

Consider the evil of this. You hereby slight the everlasting love of God the Father to sinners. You dishonor the work and salvation of the Son of God. You grieve the Holy Spirit, the *Comforter* of sinners. You disregard the Gospel of grace, glad tidings to sinners: and set at nought all God's precious promises in Christ. You give the enemy all possible advantage over you. He stands and cries, "There, there, so would I have it." You give sin all its strength against you. You perplex, distress, and darken your own soul, whereby you are hindered from running the way of God's commands with love and delight. A thousand evils are connected with indulging despondence; away then with all false humility. Hold fast this faithful saying, for it is worthy of all acceptation at all times, under all circumstances, "Jesus Christ came into the world to save sinners."

1 Tim 1 : 15. Till the adversary can blot that truth **out**
of God's word, or make you worse than a sinner; you,
as a quickened sinner, have the same reason as Paul,
or any other apostle, to say, "*I am always confident.*"
2 Cor. 5 : 6.

———

Nov. 10.—*Christ was in all points tempted like as we are,
yet without sin.* Heb. 4 : 15

O, says a soul in heaviness through manifold temptations, surely no one was ever tempted and tried like me!
Paul answers to the contrary: "There hath no temptation taken you but such as is common to man." 1 Cor.
10 : 13. Is this any relief and support to you? If not,
consider the text.

Temptation was common to Christ, as man: he was
tempted "in all points like as we are." View him beset
by Satan: see the hellish arts he practised upon him:
he tempted him to the lust of the eye, to self-murder,
to idolatry, to distrust God, to tempt God, yea, in *all*
points, like as we are. You cannot feel a trial or temptation but what Christ felt before you. Though he had
no sin in his nature, yet he doubtless felt all the assaults
with which the power and malice of hell could attack
him. Still he remained without sin: therefore temptations are not sins. Though, as God, Christ knew all things
intuitively, yet he could only, as man, have an experimental sense of the nature and power of temptations.

This is very comfortable to his tried, tempted members, for he is "*touched* with a feeling of our infirmities." "Being tempted himself, he is able to succor
them who are tempted." Heb. 2 : 18. O think of this
under all your temptations and trials. What! did Christ
feel all that I feel before me and for me? Had he the
most quick and pungent sense of temptation? And was
all this that he might be able to succor me? Think, O

my soul, thy crowned Head in glory feels for all his
tempted members on earth. Consider Jesus, once a MAN
as thou art, and now, as seeing thy poor panting heart
and laboring breast bowed down with one temptation
and another. Methinks we hear him say, "Thus it was
with me when in the flesh: my heart yearns, my bowels
move with tender compassion to that my brother in
flesh: I am touched with a tender sympathy for him."
Is it so? Then go and lay all in thine heart open to thy
Lord: be neither afraid nor ashamed:

> "He knows what sore temptations mean,
> "For he has felt the same:"

confess the vile lusts and corruptions of thy nature
Remember, ever remember Christ's blood is the fountain opened for sin and uncleanness. Zech. 13 : 1.

Nov. 11.—*Behold, I have erred exceedingly.* 1 Sam. 26:21

In this chapter we have an account of an heroic act
of David's faith in the Lord, his invincible courage, and
his tenderness towards Saul, his enraged enemy, by
which he melted his heart and overcame his cruel wrath.
Let us view his conduct, and pray for grace to get good
from it.

View his faith. Here was Saul, with three thousand
chosen men, in pursuit of David, thirsting for his blood;
they were at a very small distance from him. Behold,
David proposes to go to Saul's camp in the dead of
the night, and asks, " Who will go down with me?" Does
not this seem to the eye of natural reason to be a most
rash and dangerous attempt? Though it were at midnight, though they might be fallen into a dead sleep,
yet, out of such a number of men, one or more might
awake and seize on David. Surely, it was going into
the very jaws of death; but David's faith surmounted
his fears; his trust in his God prevailed. O precious

gift of precious faith! Lord, increase it in our souls.
Abishai consents to go with him ; they pass the king's
life-guards ; enter Saul's camp : for behold, they were
all like dead men. David and Abishai converse together :
not a man hears or stirs. Why was this? How can we
account for it ? Why ? "Because a deep sleep from the
Lord was fallen upon them." O, my soul, learn courage
from hence. When Giant Despair attempted to pursue
the pilgrims he was seized with his fits. All thy enemies are under thy Lord's power ; he can cast all into
a deep sleep, or into the long sleep of death ; and he
will, sooner than thou shalt perish by them. Up faith—
down sense—away with all carnal reasonings :

> " March on, nor fear to win the day,
> " Though death and hell obstruct the way."

Now see how David's faith wrought by his works.
When they got safe into the camp Saul lay sleeping,
and his spear stuck into the ground at his head. Now
for a strong temptation. Abishai said to David, " God
hath delivered thine enemy into thy hand this day ; let
me smite him, I pray thee, with this spear to the earth
at once, I will not smite him a second time." See this
specious reasoning. He begins with God, who had delivered Saul into David's hands. Here was a fair opportunity to revenge himself of his cruel enemy and
put an end to his troubles. And he promises to do it
effectually, at a stroke. Now, who but a man after God's
own heart could have withstood this? But David had a
better way to kill his rage and save his life. Here see
an heroic act of faith working by love and producing an
unshaken obedience to God : he durst not stretch forth
his hand against the Lord's anointed. See how conspicuous the grace of God shines in the Old Testament saint
O blush, ye who regard David's faith as nothing compared to the faith of a christian !

See the effects of David's conduct: he carried away Saul's spear and cruse from under his head, and upbraids the captain of his host for not watching over his royal master. Saul hears of the affair and cries out, " Is this thy voice, my son David ?" Struck with David's fine reasoning; melted down at his noble, generous conduct; and doubtless recollecting that his life had been once before in David's hands, when he cut off the skirts of his robe in a cave, 1 Sam. 24 : 4, Saul replies, " Behold I have played the fool, and erred exceedingly." Thus faith works by love and patience : this will overcome, when wrath and resentment only add fuel to an enemy's rage.

Nov. 12.—*My soul fainteth for thy salvation: but I hope in thy word.* Psalm 119 : 81

David's words furnish us with these observations, 1st. That it is a sure evidence that a sinner is savingly convinced of sin by the Spirit of God, when the salvation of Jesus is the desire of his heart. 2d. That the soul, though destitute of the joy of faith, in the assurance of interest in Christ's salvation, yet may have the grace of *hope* in lively exercise. 3d. That when the soul faints, the word of the Lord is the sure support of hope. Study these points : settle them in your hearts : the Lord give you comfort from them.

When a person faints, the blood returns to the heart; it ceases to flow through the veins : hence the spirits sink, nature fails, the eyes see not, the limbs cease to move, life and strength depart. Have you not experienced it thus with your soul ? Have you not been ready to give up hope and let all confidence go—just at the last gasp ? See the actings of a gracious soul. Learn experience by David's conduct : he thinks of his best Friend, his dear Saviour ; he looks up to him ; he tells him what he faints for, *thy salvation :* for fresh knowledge of his interest in it ; for the joys and comforts of it. What, when his sins stared him in the face? when his conscience was burdened with guilt? when his soul fainted within him, and without assurance in his heart of interest in Christ's salvation? is this a time to go to Christ? Yes, the very time, the proper time, the time of *need*, in which we are exhorted to "come boldly." Heb. 4 : 16.

O, my fainting fellow-sinner! What a precious Saviour is Jesus! What a glorious salvation hath he finished for us! What a special mercy it is, that the Spirit excites desires in our souls for the enjoyment of it! Well, though David's soul faints, yet says he, "I hope in thy word." What, without faith? No : he had living faith in his heart, though he fainted for the joy and comfort of faith : he believed the word of grace and salvation, and he hoped for the fulfilment of the promises of his Lord, to the reviving of his soul : he honours his Lord's word, trusts in his faithfulness, and casts the anchor of his hope upon his truth. Go and do likewise ; "for we are saved by hope." Rom. 8 : 24. "Which hope we have as an anchor to the soul, both sure and steadfast, and which entereth into that within the vail, whither Jesus is for us entered." Heb. 6 : 19, 20.

Nov. 13.—*My soul shall make her boast in the Lord : the humble shall hear thereof and be glad.* Psalm 34 : 2

There was a poor vain-glorious boaster, who had arrived to the summit of his happiness, and attained the zenith of his glory : the sun of prosperity shone with great splendor upon him ; he bade adieu to all care, and sat down to solace himself : "Soul," said he, "thou hast much goods laid up for many years, take thine ease, eat, drink, and be merry." But, awful moment! dreadful doom! God said unto him, "Thou fool, this night thy soul shall be required of thee." Luke 12 : 19, 20

O how many such are there, who think the soul can be made happy in outward ease, eating, and drinking, and earthly enjoyments! Alas! one moment dashes the honey of their comforts into the gall of disappointment. Not so that soul who boasts in the Lord. This was not a transient fit of David's, caused by a glow of the passions; for, says he, "I will bless the Lord at *all times:* his praise shall be *continually* in my mouth." This is living indeed like a son of God and an heir of glory. Paul, like David, sets us the same example. Christ and free grace, says Luther, was ever in his mouth; he never thought he could mention the precious name of Christ too often; he repeats it in every verse of the ten of the first chapter of 1 Corinthians.

If Christ is the boast and glory of our souls, his name will ever be uppermost in our hearts and upon our tongue. It was the martyr Lambert's motto, "None but Christ, none but Christ." It is said of some one, that he seldom or never mentioned the name of Jesus without a tear. A martyr who was judged to be dead, being burned as black as a coal in the fire, moved his scorched lips, and was heard to say, "Sweet Jesus," and fell asleep. These were all poor, needy sinners, like ourselves; they saw their want of Christ; they believed what he had done for them, and was to them; they gloried in him, and made him the boast of their souls. The humble are glad to hear of this; it delights their souls to hear the name of their Saviour and his sacrifice gloried in, his righteousness exalted, and his salvation made the triumph of sinners; their hearts catch the sound, and with a glow of the fire of love they join the heavenly cry, "Worthy is the Lamb that was slain to receive honor, and glory, and blessing." Rev. 5 : 12. O how vastly different is this from self-exalting and self-boasting: "God resisteth the proud and giveth grace to the humble." James 4 : 6.

Nov. 14.—*But God, who is rich in mercy, for his great love wherewith he loved us, even when we were dead in sins, hath quickened us together with Christ ; (by grace ye are saved.)* Ephesians 2 : 4, 5.

My dear brethren in Christ, and thou, O my soul, one chief reason why at any time we have so little comfort and are so low in joy is, that we do not enough believe and live upon the *love* of God. Let us never think of or look for any mercy from God without considering that it flows from love. Is God rich in mercy to any ? It is because he loves them. Great love, everlasting, unchangeable love is the source and spring of rich mercy. It was rich mercy for God to give us his beloved Son to be our Saviour. This was because of his great love to us before time : he loved us from eternity in his Son : he loves us through time and under all states and circumstances : yea, when we were forlorn, helpless, hopeless, even "*dead in sins,*" he loved us with *great love,* too great to be conceived or expressed : he manifested it by bestowing *rich mercy* upon us ; mercy so rich, so free, so liberal, that it came to us unsought, unasked, undeserved.

His great love for us was the parent of his rich mercy to us. Mercy without love may be exercised by an enemy ; but the mercy of God flows from the heart of a Father : he saw our souls dead in sin, dead under his law, dead to himself. Did he leave us ? No. He loved us with great love, therefore in rich mercy he "quickened us." "Quickened us !" says one. "Is that all ?" A quickened soul, some think, is in a very inferior degree of grace ; it is neither justified nor sanctified—but such persons are great strangers to the rich mercy and great love of God ; they do not consider that souls are quickened *together with Christ.* In Him is the sweetness of quickening mercy enjoyed. Quickened souls see their sinfulness, know their poverty, feel their misery and wretchedness, and groan under a body of sin and death : but here is their glory, joy, and comfort; they are one with Christ; his life is theirs, his death is theirs his righteousness is theirs, his holiness is theirs, his fulness is theirs. Though sin is not dead in us, yet being one with Christ, we are "dead indeed unto sin and alive to God." *By grace ye are saved :* not by your own deeds or righteousness. Therefore rejoice ; "quickened together with Christ," your salvation is not precarious and uncertain; you shall reign with him. O, may love, mercy, and grace be the constant theme of our souls!

Nov. 15.—*Mine iniquities are gone over mine head : as an heavy burden, they are too heavy for me.* Psalm 38 : 4

Though there may be pleasures in sin for a season, yet, at the last, "it biteth like a serpent, and stingeth like an adder." O come hither and see how the venom of sin has overspread poor David's whole frame : read this Psalm : mark the anguish of his conscience and the distress of his soul : and say, is not sin "exceeding sinful?" What pain out of hell can be compared to the pain of a guilty conscience? But better, infinitely better, to smart for sin here, than to cry out of the smart of sin in hell. Conviction of sin by the Spirit is in order to cleansing from sin by the blood of Christ. Better to weep from the disquietude of one's soul on earth, than to sleep secure in sin till we weep for sin in the bottomless pit : one or other will be the portion of all flesh.

Two comparisons are before us expressive of David's distress. "Mine iniquities are gone over mine head." He was like a man in the greatest danger of drowning : overwhelmed in distress, like one whose head was under water : his iniquities caused his soul to sink within him. They were "as a heavy burden." He had greater weight upon him than he could bear. He cries out, as though ready to be crushed by its ponderous load, " they are too heavy for me."

Look at his cry, and hear upon whom he calls: " Make haste to help me, O Lord, my salvation." Psalm 38 : 22. Though pressed down with iniquities on his conscience, yet he had salvation in view, and the Lord of his salvation as his hope. O Lord, *my* salvation. Now, can you be in a worse state than David was? Can you be in more distressing circumstances? He was sinking in deep waters. In such a state, you may discover whether your convictions are evangelical and you possess the faith of God's elect or not. Legal convictions only fill the soul with terror, drive it from God, and leave it in despair. Convictions from the Spirit, the Comforter, lead the soul to Christ; and the faith, hope and cry of the soul will be after the help and salvation of Jesus *only :* for he is " the Lamb of God who taketh away the sin of the world." Behold him, O my soul, under every sense of guilt; believe him, under every dejection of soul; for he hath assured us, " All manner of sin and blasphemy shall be forgiven unto men." Matt. 12 : 31.

Nov. 16.—*But as many as received him, to them gave he power to become the sons of God.* John 1: 12

Man lost paradise by receiving a gift from Satan. There is no way to regain it but by receiving Christ, the gift of God. Am I one of the many who have received Christ? This question is of eternal moment. If I have not received him, no matter what I profess, by what name I am called, what I think of myself, or others think of me; for I am certainly in a state of wrath, exposed to eternal damnation. What answer does conscience return to this important question? God may this day require my soul. I may be in eternity before the light of another morning. Have I received Christ or not?

What is it to receive Christ? Many precious souls are sadly perplexed and greatly distressed on this point. But why should they be? St. John plainly tells us, that to receive Christ, is to believe on his name, that he is the anointed Saviour of lost sinners. Do you receive this truth into your heart? Does your mind go out after Christ? Do you hunger and thirst to know him as your Saviour? Then you do believe in Christ's name Bless the Holy Spirit, who has opened your eyes to see his glory and your heart to receive this precious Jesus: hear and rejoice: he gives you, and all such, " power to become the sons of God." Not merely puts it in the power of your free-will to choose whether you will become a son of God or not; but he actually bestows this heavenly honor upon us. He gives us the *right* (or *privilege*, as in the margin of our Bibles) of enjoying the comfort and blessing of being the adopted sons of God. O the riches of new covenant grace and love! What a miracle of mercy is this! Of the children of wrath and heirs of hell, Christ makes us sons of God and heirs of heaven!

Why then do you ever live uncomfortably, or walk unholily? It is because you do not assert your *right*, maintain your *privilege*, and live up to your *power*, in your mind and conscience. Hence love to and delight in your Father God, and your Saviour Jesus, are wanting. O remember, ever remember, as you received Christ by faith, all your power, peace and comfort flow from him through faith: study, strive and pray to the Spirit to keep faith lively in act and exercise, that you may live and walk on earth so as to glorify your Father who is in heaven: for if you are a son of God, by faith in Christ, you have the heart of a son; the fear, the love, the hope, and the delight of a son of God; and you will rejoice to think that you shall soon be at home with your heavenly Father.

Nov. 17.—*We also joy in God through our Lord Jesus Christ, by whom we have now received the atonement.* Rom. 5:11

Having obtained the king's free pardon for a poor man sentenced for transportation, I carried it to the jail to him: seeing the poor fettered creature fall down upon his knees to return thanks, caused a burst of tears from mine eyes of heart-felt joy. I thought, this is just what thou, O my precious Saviour, hast done for me: thou hast obtained a free and full pardon of all my sins, set my soul at liberty, and filled it with peace and joy, by the one atonement of thy precious blood. The poor convict had not read his pardon: he had not seen the king's name to it. I only made the report to him that I had it: he believed me; hence he was happy, joyful and thankful. Thus he received his pardon.

Now here is a simple and plain idea of faith—of receiving the atonement of Christ and of joy in God. You are a poor sinner: the Spirit of God comes and convinces you of sin: you are arraigned, tried, brought in guilty, and condemned in the court of conscience: you are concluded under sin and shut up in unbelief: here you wait in sorrow and distress for the sentence of the law to be executed upon you: you find you can do nothing that can obtain pardon and liberty for your poor soul: but, the Gospel brings the glad tidings of the atonement of Christ to your ears, and that by it a full and free pardon is obtained for sinners.

Now, what reception does it meet with in your heart? Say you, I believe it from the very bottom of my heart, but I fear it is not for me? It is free for all who will receive it by faith. You believe it, therefore you have received it: you ought to joy in God for it. Examine into the grounds of your fears and doubts. Is the atonement of Christ sufficient to satisfy divine justice and obtain pardon and peace? This you cannot doubt. Is it not free for all sorts of sinners? Of this you can have no fear: "For this is a faithful saying, and worthy of all acceptation, that Christ Jesus came into the world to save *sinners*." 1 Tim. 1:15. Do you fear that you are too great a sinner? This cannot be. Paul says, of sinners *I am chief:* yet he received the atonement, and was saved by it. Learn hence, that all joy in God springs from the *one* atonement of Christ for sin, and that *only,* exclusive of every thing else. Every one who believes in Christ has *now* received this atonement; and therefore ought constantly to joy in God the Father's everlasting love.

Nov. 18.—*Stand fast therefore in the liberty wherewith Christ has made us free, and be not entangled with the yoke of bondage.* Gal. 5:1

Here is something enjoyed, the danger of being deprived of it, and the necessity of standing fast in it. Let us consider these three points, looking unto Jesus.

What is enjoyed? *Liberty:* one of the most precious blessings in life; but this, of all liberties, the most precious; for Christ hath made us free in our consciences, from the guilt and power of sin; from the condemnation of the law; and given us access to God as righteous persons. He hath washed away the guilt of our sins by his blood, and subdued the power of them by his Spirit; "He hath redeemed us from the curse of the law, being made a curse for us." Gal. 3:13. So that there is now no condemnation to us, being in Christ Jesus. Rom. 8:1. He presents us before his Father in his perfect righteousness. We are "accepted in the beloved," as righteous, "to the praise of the glory of his grace." Eph. 1:6

Thus Christ hath freed us from the law, sin, death and hell: he has brought us into this blessed liberty by his Spirit. We enjoy this precious freedom in our consciences by faith. O brethren, let us glory in our inestimable privilege: let us ever rejoice in Christ Jesus, and give him the glory of our hearts, lips and lives.

See your *danger* of being entangled again with the yoke of bondage. We who now enjoy the precious liberty of Christ, were once slaves to the law; a most dreadful yoke it was. We felt wrath working in our consciences, and dread and terror hung over our guilty heads from day to day. O how did we then pant and cry for Christ to set our souls at liberty. We were tied and bound with the chain of our sins, fettered by the law, shut up in unbelief. My soul deeply felt this distress. O beware of bondage again. There is danger on the right hand and on the left. The pleasures of sin, and the pride of our hearts seeking, either in whole or in part, justification by the law of works, are both equally contrary to our freedom in Christ.

Let us therefore stand fast in the liberty of Christ Oppose your happiness in Christ to all the pleasures of sin, which are but for a season. Stand fast in your freedom in Christ, against all the corrupt notions of self-righteous men, who are under the law, seeking to be justified, in whole or in part, by their own works. Stand fast against all the accusations of Satan: we overcome him by the blood of the Lamb. Stand fast against all the legal workings of your flesh: for we are the Lord's freemen: we are no more under bondage.

Nov. 19.—*And he requested for himself that he might die.*
1 Kings. 19: 4

"Elias was a man subject to like passions as we are." James 5: 17. This request proves it. It arose from fear and discontent. Both were occasioned by the threats of a weak, but wicked woman. Jezebel threatened his life. O how soon and by what weak means are the elevated joys of God's children interrupted. What, Elijah! that great prophet of the Lord, who had wrought so many miracles in the name of the Lord, who had been so miraculously fed by ravens, according to the command of the Lord—he, who had courage to say, "As the Lord of hosts liveth, before whom I stand, I will surely show myself to incensed Ahab to-day"—what, he! who had zeal to face four hundred and fifty of Baal's priests, and to command them all to be slain—what, does he request to die because of the threatenings of Jezebel? What shall we say to this? Verily, human nature is the same in all, whether prophets, patriarchs, or apostles: all men are not the same at all times: the flesh is part of themselves: it lusts against the Spirit: this is manifest in all, none excepted. What is man when left of God? What are the best of men when left to themselves?

And yet the same apostle James says, "Take, my brethren, the prophets who have spoken in the name of the Lord, for an example of suffering affliction, and of patience." James 5 : 10. But where shall we find a perfect character? Paul might well say, "We have this treasure (all the gifts and graces of God's Spirit) in earthen vessels." Why? That the excellency of the power might be of God, and not of us. 2 Cor. 4 : 7. If men were not sometimes left to themselves they would forget this. Elijah, like Paul, was in danger of being exalted above measure for his eminent gifts, graces and miraculous works: he is left to be buffeted, that he might know his own sinfulness and impotence.

Learn now a lesson from this: prophets, apostles, ministers of Christ, are men of like passions, frail sinners like yourselves. Paul forbears glorying; "lest any

man should think of me above what he sees me to be."
2 Cor. 12 : 6. If we so judge of ministers, we shall be
in great danger of harm thereby. We shall over-rate
them, look to them, instead of looking through them to
God : we shall rest on their teaching instead of God's ;
and then, if we see those infirmities in them which are
common to men, we shall under-rate them and be pre-
judiced against them, so as not to be profited by them.
Cease ye from man : look unto the Lord.

Nov. 20.—*Behold, he prayeth.* Acts 9 : 11

In many trades it is customary to show samples or
patterns : by these men judge of the goodness or quality
of the whole. Paul sets himself forth as an example of
the free, distinguishing, unmerited grace of God, that
we should judge of its nature by its efficacy upon him :
" for this cause I obtained mercy : that in me, first Jesus
Christ might show forth all long-suffering, for a *pattern*
to them who should hereafter believe on him to life
everlasting." 1 Tim. 1 : 16.

Thou hast seen this pattern of free grace. What dost
thou think of it ? The whole is like the pattern. Grace
finds no more pre-requisites or fitness in any than it did
in Paul ; and it produces the same effects in others as it
did in him. Grace and mercy from Jesus makes Saul
pray to Jesus : there is the emphasis : this is the main
point : " *Behold, he prayeth.*" To whom ? Doubtless he
had prayed much and often, while an unconverted
pharisee ; but it was to an unknown God. He knew
there was a God : he knew it was his duty to pray to
him ; but he knew him not. But now Jesus speaks to
him : God manifests himself to him in Christ : therefore,
behold, take special notice of this, " Behold, he prayeth,"
to Jesus ; to God in Christ. He no longer dares to come
to God in his own name, to expect access to God and

acceptance with him on account of his own sincerity or works of righteousness, but in the name, blood and righteousness of the Son of God *only*.

So he prayed, so he proved his conversion to Jesus: hence the true spirit of prayer manifested itself in him; his prayers were agreeable to, and sprung from his knowledge of himself as a poor sinner, and faith in the Son of God as the only Saviour. This is the prayer in which God delights, and which he especially notices as an evidence of true conversion. Hence know that prayerless souls are Christless. Prayer, without the knowledge of Christ, faith in him, hope of eternal life by him, and acceptance through him, is only lip service and formal duty. But the spirit of prayer arises in the heart from a discovery of God in Christ; the knowledge of him, by believing his word of grace and truth, and expecting his mercy and salvation, according to his great and precious promises given in Christ. Dost thou pray thus? Then it may be truly said of thee, behold thou art converted; thy prayers evidence it: the God who heareth prayer hath manifested himself to thee as he does not unto the world.

Nov. 21.—*But one thing is needful.* Luke 10:42

Happy, most happy for that soul who can simply bring all things to centre in one point. More than one object perplexes the mind. We stand and pause, doubting where we shall begin, and neglect both. What is the *one thing needful?* It is plain that by it our Saviour means that the soul maintains intimate communion with himself. This Mary did: she "sat at his feet and heard his word." Every thing else is but a drudgery compared with this; for this one thing comprises all the holiness, happiness and heavenly-mindedness of the soul.

O, if we have the presence of Jesus, guilty fears

vanish, doubts are scattered, legal terrors are silenced, anxious cares subside, strong temptations lose their force, Satan is resisted, afflictions are sweetened, turbulent passions calmed, raging corruptions subdued, pride is brought down, humility is excited, peace with God is enjoyed, holiness promoted, the fear of death is conquered, the terrors of hell chased away, the prospect of glory in the full fruition of Jesus is sought and longed for, earth loses its charms, heaven is in the heart, to be absent from the body and present with the Lord becomes the one desire of the soul.

Say, O christian, what *one thing* else can produce so many, and such blessed effects, as close communion with our Saviour? Is not this the *one thing*, above all others, needful? Needful at all times and in all seasons; needful in the hour of prosperity and in the day of adversity. O, if this *one thing* is maintained in the soul, your sweet communion with Christ cannot fail to subject the will, attract the affections, and beget holy conformity to him. You will not wish or dare to follow any thing which is contrary to your Lord, while you live near him and dwell in holy fellowship with him. Thus religion is brought to a single point; holiness and happiness resolved into *one* thing. There is but *one* Lord to make you holy and happy, but *one* faith by which you know him and cleave to him; but there are a thousand things to prevent this. O may this " one thing needful " rise superior to all! Think, O my soul, of Mary's choice. Remember thy Saviour's approbation of it. O, do thou also choose this good part, which shall never be taken away.

Nov. 22.—*The salvation of the righteous is of the Lord, he is their strength in the time of trouble.* Psalm 37 : 39

We may say of righteousness as Job says of wisdom, " Where shall *righteousness* be found? And where is

the place of understanding ? Man knoweth not the price
thereof, neither is it to be found in the land of the liv
ing." Job 28 : 12, 13. The patriarch says, It is not in
me. The prophet says, It is not in me. The apostle
says, It is not in me. The Lord saith, " All flesh hath
corrupted his way." Gen. 6 : 12. " There is none that
doeth good, *no*, *not one*." Psalm 14 : 3.

Why then do the Scriptures speak so much of the
righteous, if there are no such persons upon earth ? Indeed there are. This is a point of great importance :
the Lord settle it well in your heart and mine. We are
poor sinners in ourselves ; we have no righteousness of
our own ; yet, saith the Lord Jesus, the righteous one,
" Their righteousness is of me." Isa. 54 : 17. We are
made the righteousness of God in Christ. 2 Cor. 5 : 21.
When we are taught this by the Spirit of truth, instead
of looking into ourselves for righteousness, we cry out
in the joy of faith, I have found it : " In the Lord have
I righteousness." Isa. 45 : 24. Then we have a living
union with *the Lord our righteousness*, by faith ; being
perfectly righteous in him, we have righteous hopes,
fears, desires, a righteous walk, and righteous expectations ; for we know our salvation is of the Lord. The
Spirit of truth does not leave us to the unrighteous notions of salvation on account of our own works, duties,
and performances, either in whole or in part ; but he
shows us such matchless glory in our Lord's *one* everlasting righteousness, that we renounce all our own
righteousness, and all dependance on it for salvation.
The Lord increase our faith in this righteousness : Lord,
quicken our love to thee for making us righteous.

But though thus righteous, yet sin is in us ; therefore
we have our troubles : " many are the afflictions of the
righteous." Are we in trouble from the number of our
enemies, the greatness of our sins and corruptions, the
weakness of our graces, the strength of our tempta-

tions, a sense of desertion, or the want of comfort, peace and joy from the Lord? These are righteous troubles. The righteous Lord is our strength to support us under them: he has power to remove them: he neither wants love nor power to save us from them, for the Lord delivereth the "righteous out of all his troubles." Psalm 34 : 17.

Nov. 23.—*Take heed and beware of covetousness.* Luke 12 : 15

It is said, that if a person seeks for the *philosopher's stone* (which is fabled as turning all metals into gold) with a covetous desire to be rich, he may be sure not to find it. We are sure that precious jewel, contentment, is not to be found in a covetous heart. Let philosophers and moralists reason ever so persuasively against the evil of covetousness, yet the love of money will rise superior to all. What mighty charms are there in gold! But the voice of our Beloved here speaks: his words are spirit and life. Hear them, O disciple : " Take heed and beware."

Consider this admonition of thy Lord's. It is redoubled : " *Take heed ; beware.*" Just as the loving parent, seeing his dear child running into the jaws of danger, cries out with vehemence, Take care! Take care! Fix this in thy mind ; there is great, very great danger here : our Lord sees it : his love speaks with the utmost earnestness, that we may avoid covetousness.

What is covetousness? One gave a good definition of it, who being advised to leave off business, as he had enough, replied, " What is enough? It is *a little more than a man has.*"

Consider the evil of covetousness. That insatiable desire prevents present contentment, destroys thankfulness, yea, and keeps the enjoyment of Christ out of the heart. Can a covetous mind be happy in God? No ; no more than Dives could have been happy in the miserable circumstances of Lazarus, full of hunger and sores. Will any one ask, What harm is there in the love of riches? Paul expressly answers. "A covetous man is an idolater." Eph. 5:5. Is there no harm in this? Our Lord says, "Seek ye first (principally, chiefly, and above all other things) the kingdom of God, and all these things shall be added unto you." Matt. 6:33. Is there no harm in reversing Christ's command; and slighting his kingdom of love, righteousness, peace and joy in the Holy Ghost; by preferring riches?

Soul, consider, What is your profession? Are the unsearchable riches of Christ enough to satisfy your mind, or are they not? Can the enjoyment of fellowship with Christ make your heart happy or not? Have you faith to believe this, or have you not? Does Christ here caution you to no purpose, where there is no danger? O, lay this to heart; cry to the Lord. Covetousness is natural to us: lively faith in Christ will kill it; for it will enable the soul to say with Paul, "I am full and abound." Phil. 4:18.

Nov. 24.—*And Israel said unto Joseph, Now let me die, since I have seen thy face, because thou art yet alive.* Gen. 46:30

Strange request! What, just come to the sight and embrace of thy long-lost son, and yet wish to leave him at the very first interview? One would have thought the language of Jacob should have been, Happy man! I not only see my beloved son, but also see him governor over all the land: I hope I shall live long to enjoy his riches and grandeur. But no: the good man had lived long enough to make an estimate of the uncertainties of life; to know the evil of days, the vicissitudes of time, and how soon the day of brilliant joy might be changed into an eclipse of gloom and sadness. The sight of his son was the summit of his wishes: that granted, he sought no more; he wished to be at home with his Lord

Happy christian, thus to hold as subordinate all creature enjoyments, even when at their highest flood, and to have the mind go out in longings for the heavenly world: this bespeaks the spirituality of the affections. Many have for a time manfully withstood the frowns of the world; but its smiles have caressed, enchanted, and at last overcome them. To choose death, to be with Jesus, when all things around are inviting and engaging, shows that Christ has the supreme affections of our hearts.

Here see the nature of christian faith. It confesses that Christ is come in the flesh: that though he was dead, yet he is alive for evermore, and hath the keys of hell and of death: and that he has opened the kingdom of heaven to all believers. Therefore, as Israel rejoiced to see his beloved son, and could depart in peace, so the believer rejoices at the sight of Christ by faith. Christ is the glory of the believer's soul. He can die peacefully, viewing the death of Christ for his justification, and the intercession of Christ prevailing for his eternal glorification.

This faith is more than a notion in the head: it brings victory into the heart. "For this is the victory that overcometh the world, even our faith: who is he that overcometh the world, but he that believeth that Jesus is the Son of God?" 1 John 5: 4, 5. It is impossible to overcome the world, in any other way than by seeing greater glory and happiness in the Son of God than this world can bestow: but by faith we see this; therefore we exchange shadows for substance, baubles for jewels. O, rest not in a dead faith, which brings not the glory of Christ into the heart, and brings no glory to Christ in the life.

Nov. 25.—*Lest Israel vaunt themselves against me, saying, Mine own hand hath saved me.* Judges 7 : 2

Thus the Lord reasoned with Gideon : he knows what is in man : he sees the pride of the human heart, and how prone we all are to boast in an arm of flesh. The Lord is jealous of his own glory. Gideon's army of two and thirty thousand is brought down to three hundred : by this handful of men, and no more, did Gideon gain the victory over the Midianites. The Lord's wisdom in this was, " Lest Israel should vaunt themselves against me and say, mine own hand hath saved me."

Here are two little words of great import : *against me.* Remember, christian, whenever thou dost boast of thy power, thy goodness, thy works, duties, and perform- ances in order to be saved, thou art then, as it were, *two and thirty thousand strong :* thou vauntest thyself *against the Lord :* thou art glorying in some measure or degree in thine own arm of might and power to save thyself Thou art trusting to thy works, to save thee in whole or in part. Be assured thy Lord will bring thee down, and weaken thy numbers, that he may have the sole glory of thy salvation.

The Lord proclaimed, that all who were afraid should depart. Two and twenty thousand returned. So he will proclaim the terrors of his just, holy, and righteous law in thine ears, and cause thy heart to tremble. Then shalt thou get rid of much of thy self-righteous confi- dence : it shall depart from thee. Again he brought the people down to the water and tried them by lapping. Here also he reduced their numbers to prevent their vaunting. So he will try thee by the waters of affliction. Here he will cut off the strength of thy vain confidence and prevent thy vaunting thyself against him. Thus, when thou findest the commandment come with power, and sin revive, then wilt thou die to self-confidence, and glory alone in the Lord. When the pruning-knife of affliction has cut off thy luxurious branches of pride and vain glory, then wilt thou say in deep humility, Wretch that I am, that I should trust in myself and depart in heart from the Lord. I thank thee, my dear Saviour, for all the pains thou takest with my proud nature, to bring me to glory only in thee, and to say, "In God is my salvation and my glory." Psalm 62 : 7.

Nov. 26.—*He that lacketh these things is blind, and cannot see afar off, and hath forgotten that he was purged from his old sins.* 2 Peter 1:9.

It is hard to say whether Peter here draws the character of a mere formal professor, or of one who has really tasted that the Lord is gracious, and has awfully backslidden : be it which it may, it holds forth a solemn lesson of instruction to our souls. We may hence lay it down as a sacred truth, that whatever profession a man makes of faith in Christ, justification by him, and hope of salvation through him : yet if he is destitute of the graces of the Spirit and the fruits of righteousness in his life, he is blind to the glorious end of the Gospel of peace, and is a stranger to the purifying grace and pardoning love of Christ to his soul. Think of this. Pardoning love, purifying grace, and sanctifying influences are inseparable. Where there is the root of grace, there will be the fruits of righteousness : this is as natural as for any cause to produce its effects.

But may not these words be applied to some who we have good reason to hope are the children of God, but are sadly backslidden from him ? Do we not see awful instances around us ? He who *lacketh* these things, viz ' virtue, knowledge, temperance, godliness," &c. (not totally, for there may be a partial lack of them) has sadly departed from the steadfastness of faith, and that degree of spiritual life he once had; has left his first love, and has lost the sweet savor of Christ from his heart: hence there is a lack, in not abounding in these things. There may be true faith, and yet somewhat lacking in it. 1 Thess. 3:10. But such a soul is in sorrow, concern, and distress about it: so the life of grace manifests that it is not quite extinct.

Again, he is *blind*. Not entirely so, for he may see, but not far off: he only sees himself and his own misery and unprofitableness: this causes him to weep and bewail himself. But he cannot see, he does not enjoy the love of Christ and the sweet peace of God: his sight is dimmed and his comforts marred. He "has forgotten that he was purged from his old sins:" he has lost the sense of pardon in the blood of Christ: though he remembers there is such a thing, yet he has lost the comfort of it; it is to him as though it had never been. Satan has obtained the advantage. So false prophets seek "to cause my people to forget my name, saith the Lord." Jer. 23:27. That is, the pardon and comfort of his name. Is not this an awful state? O how much to be deplored! how greatly to be deprecated!

Nov. 27.—*So an entrance shall be ministered unto you abundantly, into the everlasting kingdom of our Lord Jesus Christ.* 2 Peter 1:11

Our last meditation was gloom and sadness: here the sun of comfort arises and sheds splendor, glory and joy upon us. O that we may now enter by faith into the joy of our Lord. Come, christian, it seems you and I must tarry a little longer on earth, absent from our Lord. How shall we employ ourselves? In studying the word of his grace; in being diligent in the use of means; in exercising ourselves unto godliness. What then? O blessed assurance! So an entrance shall be ministered unto us *abundantly*. When? Both in life and in death.

In life. We shall find a free and open door into the kingdom of Christ's grace, love, and peace even *now*: we shall have joy in the Holy Ghost, and " the peace of God, which passeth all understanding," in our hearts. Thus shall we sweetly and swiftly pass the voyage of life. All is enjoyed in being diligent in the ways of Christ. Soul, thus press on, let who will say it is *legal*. What! legal to live and labor in the kingdom of love? Say, deluded objector, did you ever expect to enter your Lord's kingdom any other way than by Christ, who is the *door*? Do you expect to enjoy the comfort of his love and the assurance of his favor in a walk and way contrary to his word and will? Are we not to walk in Christ, abounding in the work of faith, the patience of hope, and the labor of love? Diligence of soul to enjoy his presence, and to be conformed to his image, is our delight below. To have every holy temper and heavenly disposition from Christ, puts the soul into a right frame to enjoy him: this is to have a constant and an abundant entrance ministered to us into the kingdom of Christ. So living and abiding in his kingdom of grace and love, our souls become dead to the kingdom of this world.

We rejoice also to think of an entrance into Christ's kingdom being abundantly administered to us at *death*. Fellowship with Christ, and diligence in his ways, makes us think of death with pleasure, and familiarizes it to our minds. By faith we see heaven open to admit us, God our Father with open arms to embrace us, Christ to welcome us, and the Spirit to enable us to sing victory in death.

Nov. 28.—*Death is yours.* 1 Cor. 3 : 22.

" O Death, how bitter is the thought of thee to a man who is at rest in his possessions; to the man who has nothing to vex him; and who has prosperity in all things!" "O death, how sweet is the remembrance of thee to a man who is alive to God, dead to the world: who longs to be absent from the body and present with the Lord: to see the glory of Jesus, and to reign eternally with him!" Christian, here is a precious legacy left thee by the Lord: a covenant-gift from the God of thy salvation: "Death is yours." He is your conquered enemy; your faithful friend.

He is your *conquered* enemy; you need not fear him; he has neither strength nor sting. Christ, the victorious Captain of your salvation, has disarmed him of both; he can neither destroy nor wound your soul: yea, "he hath *abolished* death." 2 Tim. 1:10. There is no substance in him; he is changed into a shadow. It is not the enemy death which seizes a believer, but the shadow, or emblem of it, *sleep.* Weary soul, tired out with the burden of sin, corruptions, afflictions, accusations, temptations—is sleep an enemy to you? Do you dread sleep? Are you afraid of rest? What! fear to fall asleep in Jesus, to awake in his presence, to be satisfied with perfect likeness to him, and eternally to enjoy him! "O fools, and slow of heart to believe" the victory of Christ over death! And thou, too, O my soul, take the rebuke to thyself, and be ashamed of thy folly.

"But I am not afraid of death, but of dying!" Why? Are you afraid of sleeping? But "O! the insupportable pains of the body in that hour!" Who told you they are insupportable? How many have sweetly sung *victory in death?* O, says one, Is this dying? it is sweet, it is pleasant: "Though I pass through the valley of the shadow of death, thou shalt be with me." That is the claim of faith, upon the warrant of the Lord: "When thou passest through the waters I WILL be with thee." Isa. 43:2. The presence of the Saviour will beguile thy pains and fill thy soul with comfort. For,

Death is *thy faithful friend*. Hast thou not found sleep so to thy weary body ? Thus shall death be to thy weary soul: it will at once deliver thee from all thy burdens and sorrows, and introduce thee into joys unspeakable and full of glory. Death is that and no more to the soul, than God calls it in his word, and faith makes it to the heart. If you really and truly believe that death is swallowed up in the victory of Christ : if you firmly believe that his precious blood has atoned for sin and his righteous life has fulfilled the law, you may undauntedly sing, " O death, where is thy sting ? O grave, where is thy victory ?"

Nov. 29.—*We believe, and are sure.* John 6 : 69

Here is both faith and assurance. " O that I had them," is the language of many a doubting heart, while both this very faith and assurance are in possession. This assurance is essential to faith ; without it faith has no existence. Consider the nature of this faith and assurance : " *We believe, and are sure.*" Of what ? That their names were written in heaven ; that they were the elect of God ? No : but says Peter to our Lord, " We believe and are sure, that thou art Christ the Son of the living God, and that thou hast the words of eternal life." Their minds were as sure of this truth as of their existence ; so must ours be at all times, and in all circumstances.

" But is this faith and assurance ? Then, blessed be God, I am a partaker of both : I do believe, I am sure that Christ is the Son of God, and that he, and he alone has the words of eternal life ; but I want to be sure of my own interest in the Son of God." Bless the Spirit for revealing Christ in the word, and revealing him in thine heart according to the word. Go on with thy present blessed faith and assurance. It will make Christ precious to thy soul: it will cause thy soul to cleave to him: thou wilt say, "None but Christ." In due time the Spirit will fully manifest thy interest in his love and salvation.

Consider the *blessedness* of this faith and assurance: it was for want of this that "many disciples went back and walked no more with Christ." John 6 : 66. It is believing and being sure that Christ is the Son of God, and that he has the words of eternal life, that causes any poor sinner to follow him, to cleave to him, to call upon him, to hope in him, and to expect all salvation from him. Little as some may think of this faith, low as some may rate this assurance, yet our Lord honors it: he pronounces Peter blessed for it. Peter does not say, I believe and am sure that I am a child of God, and that my sins are forgiven ; but, "*Thou art Christ, the Son of the living God.*" What says our Lord to this? "*Blessed art thou:* for flesh and blood hath not revealed this unto thee, but my Father which is in heaven." Matthew 16 : 17.

Rejoice, O believing soul! thou hast a revelation from God thy heavenly Father, even whilst thou art doubting. All thy salvation depends on this truth; all thy comfort results from belief and assurance of it. The more steadily and confidently you believe and hold this truth in your conscience, the more solid peace, holy comfort, and heavenly joy.

Nov. 30.—*Therefore I will look unto the Lord; I will wait for the God of my salvation; my God will hear me.* Micah 7 : 7

Here is a soul crying out of the very worst of foes: "A man's enemies are the men of his own house." Under such experience, behold and imitate the conduct before us. Here are two acts of the mind, and the cry of faith.

"I will look." The Lord is the object looked to Blessed be the Spirit, he opens our eyes to see him, and our hearts to believe his love to us and care for us: then we know the voice of Christ and obey it. He says, "Look unto *me*, and be ye saved." Isa. 45 : 22. Whenever distressed with enemies from within or without, sin, Satan, or the world, here is our warrant, to look unto the Lord. He assures us of salvation from them. We shall find and feel these enemies to the end of life. Therefore, looking unto the Lord is to be the constant work of life. O the special mercy to have such a Lord to look to! Shame to us that we look no more to him: happy for us when we look to him only. We are sure of comfort from him, and safety by him, from all the power, malice and fraud of every enemy.

But I see enemies beset me : I am not saved from them : I grow impatient ; unbelief prevails : doubts and fears arise. Here is the remedy : "I will wait for the God of my salvation." Time will prove God's truth, Satan's lying suggestions, and the groundless suspicions of my own heart. "He who believeth shall not make haste." Isa. 28 : 16. It is "the God of my salvation" I wait upon, and wait for : "My times are in his hands." Psalm 31 : 15. Every promise has its season for accomplishment, every providence its hour, every vision its appointed time. O, this waiting faith honors the Lord's word greatly : it has the Lord's word for its support. The Lord honors it. Behold his absolute, precious promise to it : "They that wait upon the Lord shall renew their strength." Isa. 40 : 31.

But this was not silent looking and dumb waiting. Here is the cry of faith : "My God will hear me." O the preciousness of faith ! It claims the Lord, and makes a special appropriation of him : *My* God, vile and sinful as I am; wretched and miserable as sin has made me; however beset and distressed by foes within and enemies without, yet, O my soul, thou hast a covenant God in Christ to look to, wait for, and call upon: he will hear me, I am sure of it; for he put it into my heart to cry to him.

December

Dec. 1.—*The kingdom of God is not meat and drink, but righteousness, and peace, and joy in the Holy Ghost.* Rom. 14:17

How much did our dear Saviour bear, what pains did he take with his first disciples to teach them the nature of his kingdom! Their notions were carnal and worldly: his kingdom spiritual and heavenly. We are just like them. Blessed be his name, the Lord is the same in patience and love to teach us also. There ever was, now is, and ever will be a cry, Lo, here is Christ with us: lo, there is the kingdom of God: it consists in this external mode, that outward rite, ceremony or institution. But what says our Lord? *Behold,* take special notice, "The kingdom of God is within you." Luke 17:21. It consists in nothing carnal nor external. Its blessings are inward, spiritual, and substantial: "righteousness, peace and joy."

Righteousness. Glory to Christ, he restores righteousness to us; he gives us a better righteousness than that we lost: we lost but a creature's righteousness; we gain the righteousness of God's only Son; the righteousness of God and man in one Mediator. Satan ruined us by sin, Christ saves us by his righteousness. The kingdom of God is established in righteousness upon the ruins of sin and Satan: the subjects of this kingdom are all righteous. Isa. 60:21. As we possess this kingdom in our hearts by faith, so Christ's righteousness is called the righteousness of faith; for we receive it by faith: we do not work it out, it is "the gift of righteousness." Rom. 5:17. O how gloriously are our souls arrayed in the righteousness of the King of saints. Let us glory of this righteousness *only;* for the more we believe it in our hearts, the more we live in the spirit and temper of righteousness in our lives.

Peace. We were once at peace with the world, the flesh and the devil, and at war with God; now that we are in his righteous kingdom and righteous in his Son; we are at peace with God and at war with them: the effect of this righteousness is peace and "quietness, and assurance for ever." Isa. 32:17.

Joy in the Holy Ghost. Being righteous in Jesus and at peace with God, the Holy Ghost gives us the joy of this; he teaches us to joy in all Christ is to us and has done for us; yea, "he fills us with all joy and peace *in believing.*" Rom. 15:13. "Wherefore, we receiving a kingdom which cannot be moved, let us have grace whereby we may serve God acceptably, with reverence and godly fear." Heb. 12:28.

DEC. 2.—*Then said one unto him, Lord, are there few that be saved?* Luke, 13:23

Peter's fervent prayer, "Lord, save or I perish," was much better than this curious question: it was an unprofitable one. Suppose our Lord had given a direct answer to it, and told the inquirer how many will be saved, what good would he have gained by it?

Learn hence, that unprofitable questions are to be avoided; they proceed from a vain curiosity. Indulge no thoughts above, beyond, or contrary to what is written: they may amuse and perplex, but cannot edify thy soul. Observe also the wisdom of thy Lord: he does not give a direct answer to this vain question, but improves it for general usefulness, as though he had said, "Friend, thy question is impertinent; thou art prying into a matter that concerns thee not; thou hast a notion of salvation in thy head, and hast put a curious question with thy tongue, but thy heart is unconcerned about thy own salvation; rather than answer this question I will improve it to general use, '*Strive to enter in at the strait gate.*'"

Disciple, here is an admirable lesson for thee and me Let us learn to improve every curious question for godly edification; nice and subtle distinctions for practical and experimental conversation. You can scarcely begin to speak of the grace of God and the salvation of Christ to poor blind sinners, but they will seek to divert atten tion from the subject by some question as to the doc trines of the Gospel. I am persuaded it is best to fol low our Lord's conduct: give no answer to the ques tion; set forth the exceeding sinfulness of sin, the deplorable state of sinners, the absolute necessity of a Saviour, the matchless glory of his person, the riches of his love, the fulness of his salvation, and the need we have of faith in him, to be clothed in his righteousness, justified before God, and eternally saved by him: this, this is the way to instruct poor sinners' minds, and to warm and enliven our own souls. Dry disquisitions promote jar and discord. Let Jesus, "the strait gate," be in our view. "Let us consider the end of our conversation, Jesus Christ, the same yesterday, to-day, and for ever." Heb. 13 : 7, 8. Let us look to him every day and every hour, to save us from the deceitful pride of our hearts, the abominable wickedness of our nature, and from all the lusts which war against our souls.

DEC. 3.— *And Israel said, It is enough.* Gen. 45: 28

His soul seems fully satisfied with the Lord's dealings and dispensations: he could ask no more: there
was a perfect calm in his mind: he sings a sweet re-
quiem, like David, when he said, " Return unto thy rest,
O my soul, for the Lord hath dealt bountifully with
thee. For thou hast delivered my soul from death, mine
eyes from tears, and my feet from falling. I will walk
before the Lord in the land of the living." Psalm
116 : 7–9. Most precious resolution, awakened by such
great bounties!

Come, christian, canst thou now say with the hoary-
headed patriarch, " *It is enough* ?" What could God
have done for me, which he hath not done? Could the
tidings sounded in the ears of Jacob, " Joseph is yet
alive," cause a transport of joy too impetuous to be resisted! How should the blessed tidings, *Jesus is yet alive*,
transport thy soul! Was Joseph governor over all the
land of Egypt? The government is upon the shoulders
of your Redeemer. Isaiah 9 : 6. All power in heaven
and earth is committed to him. Matt. 28 : 18. He saith,
" I am he that liveth, and was dead; and behold, I am
alive for evermore, Amen: and have the keys of hell
and of death." Rev. 1 : 18. Is not here cause for thee
to cry out, " It is enough: I can desire no more.
Surely this is sufficient to cause thy dejected spirit to
revive.

Did Jacob believe when he saw the presents of his
son? Did he say, " I will go and see him before I die?"
O christian, is thy Saviour ascended into his kingdom?
Has he " received gifts " for thee, and poured down
love-tokens upon thee? Has he given thee repentance
to turn to him, and faith to embrace him? What is thy
language? It is enough: Jesus ever lives, eternally
loves, incessantly prays. Then I shall surely see him—
but not before I die : but I shall soon shake off this mor-

tality, and sing victory in death. Then, O then I shall behold him eye to eye, and face to face. Then I shall say with the highest rapture of soul, "It is enough." Then death shall be swallowed up of life, and I shall cast down my crown before the Lamb. O then I shall eternally see him, "whom having not seen, I love: in whom, though now I see him not, yet believing, I rejoice with joy unspeakable and full of glory." 1 Peter 1:8. O, that in the same spirit with Paul I may ever say, "Doubtless I count all things but loss for the excellency of the knowledge of Christ Jesus my Lord." Philippians, 3:8.

DEC. 4.—*He that receiveth me, receiveth him that sent me.*
Matthew 10:40

It is very natural to think, "If the Son of God were now upon earth, O how gladly would we receive him into our houses." If you really would, you now cordially receive the report of him into your heart: you now welcome it by faith as the most precious truth that ever saluted your ears.

What is it to receive Christ? There is endless perplexity in the conscience of many poor sinners, whether they have received Christ, when they received him, what it is to receive him, how they received him, and whether they received him aright. Satan thus gets great advantage over many. You would have no difficulty to tell whether you received a dear friend, how your heart stood affected towards him, and what reception you gave him. How is it between Christ and your soul? Do you see him, believe on him, and trust in him as a Saviour just suited to your ruined, desperate, hopeless state? Bless the Holy Spirit for this; for you have received Christ.

Now consider the blessedness of this. You have also

received Him who sent Christ, that is, God the Father :
he gave Christ for us : he sent Christ to us. Therefore,
God is now your loving Father in Christ : he is reconciled to you : all his attributes are engaged for you : he
declares, "I will be merciful to your unrighteousness :
your sins and your iniquities I will remember no more."
Heb. 8 : 12. You are safe from the curse of sin, the
condemnation of the law, and the power of Satan, for
your Father's right hand is your defence. If he stretch
it forth to chastise and afflict you, it is all in love. O
the joy of faith! For,

You are his child in Christ. Though in yourself you
are sinful and miserable, have wicked thoughts, vile
lusts, and the workings of unbelief, these all spring from
your flesh, in which dwells no good thing ; these are
common to all the children of God : therefore think it
not strange that you are made to groan under a body
of sin and death from day to-day ; let not these mar
your comfort, nor prevent your joy of being accepted
in Christ. You ever have access to God, and may come
with all holy boldness before him. Ephesians 3 : 12.

DEC. 5.—*The Lord gave, and the Lord hath taken away ; blessed*
be the name of the Lord. Job 1 : 21

Meek Moses, righteous Lot, patient Job, were as wicked by nature as any sinners. True, they were eminent
saints ; but who made them so ? The same Saviour who
sanctifies you and me. "Cease ye from man :" look
upon the most holy saint as a sinner in himself, but only
distinguished by the grace of God. When grace eminently shines in any sinner, remember it all proceeds
from the fulness of the Saviour ; look to him for grace
for yourself. While Job suffers the loss of all, yet he
glories in the possession of all : though he could not now
say, my children, my possessions, my health, yet he could

say, "My Redeemer liveth." Job 19:25. The belief of this sweetened every cross; made up every loss; kept his head from sinking in the deep waters of affliction, his heart from fainting under the greatest tribulations, and fortified his mind with the greatest patience under the severest calamities; he saw his Lord in all, therefore by his grace he submits to all.

Job is here set before us as most eminent for his *patience*. To what end? Doubtless that we may imitate him. But remember, patience is a gift from the God of all grace. View the saint, but look to the King of saints to be like-minded. "The Lord gave." Sweet consideration! Look upon all you enjoy as the free gift of a covenant God; hold the Giver fast, but hold the gifts with a trembling hand. Perhaps ere to-morrow's sun you may be constrained to say of some of your sweetest enjoyments, "The Lord hath taken away." Love saw that they would do you harm, and that it is best for you to be without them; therefore in love God takes them away. Love is the same in God when giving, as when taking away; therefore, what good reason have we to say for both, "Blessed be the name of the Lord!"

Here you see the work of faith. It sees the Lord's name written upon every enjoyment; it owns the Lord's right to give or take away; it bows to the Lord's sovereign will, and says, Lord, thou doest all things well; though what thou doest I cannot now know, yet I shall know hereafter; I am sure there is a Father's love and wisdom in all: O that all may be sanctified to me, and I profited by all. Thus, as faith in Christ brings us to the knowledge of God, to enjoy peace with him, so it teaches submission to his will, and to bless his name at all times. Rejoice in the Lord.

Dec. 6.—*He that hath received his testimony, hath set to his seal that God is true.* John 3 : 33

Wherein consists the essential difference between the righteous and the wicked ? In this : the heart of the former receives the testimony of Christ, and thereby honors the God of truth ; the latter rejects it, and thereby makes God a liar." 1 John 5 : 10. No marvel then that it is declared, " He that believeth not the Son, shall not see life, but the wrath of God abideth on him;" John 3 : 36 ; and that " God is angry with the wicked every day." Psalm 7 : 11. They live in this daring, provoking sin of unbelief of the testimony of the Son of God. This is the greatest sin under heaven. O the long-suffering of God toward such stout-hearted rebels.

Consider, what is this testimony ? It is the witness which Christ bears to the children of men, that he is the Son of God ; that he came forth from God ; that he came to fulfil the law of God ; to honor the justice of God ; to bring glory to all the attributes of God, by saving sinners according to the *truth* of God.

What is it to receive this testimony ? Simply to credit it ; just as one does by a person who in a solemn manner gives a plain and faithful evidence in court of what he knows of the cause on trial. Now here we see what a simple thing faith is : it is no other than receiving Christ's testimony ; believing him to be what he declares he is, the Saviour of lost sinners ; righteousness to us who have none of our own ; an atonement for sins which must have sunk us to hell ; redemption from the curse of the law, which we could never avert ; and the hope of eternal life, which we have forfeited. Thus we receive the testimony of Jesus as a reprieve for condemned malefactors, an act of grace for rebels, tidings of mercy for miserable sinners. But alas! how do we puzzle our heads and perplex our hearts! For, instead of blessing Jesus for this precious testimony, considering its suitableness, and deriving our comfort from it, we set ourselves to questioning our faith: whether we have received it and do believe aright. This is our folly.

See the blessedness of receiving this testimony : " He hath set to his seal that God is true." Or, as some read it, God hath sealed him (by his Spirit) because he is true. As we set our seal to God's truth, he will seal our hearts with his consolations. We cannot honor God more, nor please him better, than to hear and believe his beloved Son.

Dec. 7.—*The God of the whole earth shall he be called.* Isa. 54: 5

An affectionate wife cannot bear to hear her husband reproached. The Church, consisting of all true believers, is " the bride, the Lamb's wife." Rev. 21 : 9. Her Redeemer is said to be her *husband.* These four names are given to him: " thy Maker: the Lord of hosts: the Holy One of Israel: the God of the whole earth." In view of these Divine appellations, who can be so bold, so reckless or wicked as to deny that Jesus Christ is truly and essentially God? Jealous of our dear *Husband's* honor and glory, we cannot bear to hear him so traduced and blasphemed. While we pity, we would flee from such, and take shelter under the wings of our *Redeemer,* and the protection of our *Husband.* The Godhead dignity of his person is the glory of our souls. The humility of his appearing in flesh adds charms to his matchless beauty. Though he is our Husband in our nature, our Redeemer incarnate ; though we have free access to him, sweet converse with him, and are indulged with holy fellowship by him as *man,* still we honor and adore him as "*the God of the whole earth.*" A poor sinner can never get near God, enjoy him, have any peace with him in his conscience, or comfort from him in his soul, but when he has simple, believing views by faith of an incarnate God—God in Christ his Redeemer.

Is he *Thy Maker?* Then give him the glory of thy existence. Is he the *Lord of hosts?* Then glory in him, and rejoice, for thou art more than conqueror over all the powers of darkness and the hosts of hell, through him who hath loved thee. Is he the *Holy One* of Israel? Then study to be like him, pray for conformity to him, and walk in holy fellowship with him, so as to derive all holiness from him. Is he " *the God of the whole earth?*" Then be assured, being married to him, and redeemed by him, thou shalt want nothing which his infinite wisdom sees best to give : for his everlasting love will supply all. Live daily upon the fulness of thy *Husband*, and the grace of thy *Redeemer*. Behold your precious, gracious charter : " No weapon that is formed against thee shall prosper, and every tongue that shall rise against thee in judgment, thou shalt condemn. This is the heritage of the servants of the Lord, and their righteousness is of me, saith the Lord." Isa. 54 : 17.

DEC. 8.—*Good and upright is the Lord, therefore will he teach sinners in the way.* Psalm 25:8

Here are two most opposite characters : a good and upright Lord—wicked and perverse sinners. Good and upright as the Lord is, he might justly give sinners up to perdition ; but no, O condescending grace ! he will not leave them to perish in their ignorance and obstinacy : he will teach them. It is said of one, that after his conversion he could scarcely mention the name of JESUS without a tear. O, had it not been for his redemption, no sinner would have had divine teaching ! But all whom Christ has redeemed by his blood, the Spirit teaches by his power : this is his office in the covenant of grace. This implies, that sinners are so ignorant of divine truth that no teaching besides that of the Lord the Spirit can instruct and make them wise unto salvation. Come, sinner, come down from the heights of thy fancied wisdom and boasted knowledge, and learn this humbling truth. If thou seest thy own ignorance and thy want of Divine teaching, rejoice at this declaration. Cry to the Spirit, Lord, teach me.

He will teach. Whom? Only such as are good and upright like himself? No; but *sinners:* whose carnal minds are enmity against his holy law, who are "sold under sin," and in whose "flesh dwells no good thing." Is this thy character? The Lord will teach such—*in the way.* What way? Not in the way of sin, that is contrary to his holiness; not in the way of self-righteousness, that is contrary to his truth: but in the knowledge of Christ, who is *the Way*, the way of access to God, acceptance with him, justification before him, and everlasting life as the free gift of God, according to the covenant-grace and everlasting love of God.

By repentance unto life in this way of peace, in this walk of faith, in this path of love, truth and holiness, the Spirit will teach redeemed sinners on earth, till he brings them to glory: his teaching shall be as effectual to their glorification as the death of Christ for their salvation. Poor sinner, who, like me, art oft distressed and dejected with thy wicked nature, take comfort from these two truths: till Satan can blot them out of God's book, or make us worse than sinners, they stand on record for our comfort: "Christ Jesus came to save *sinners.*" God will teach *sinners.* Look then to the finished salvation of Jesus: look to the Spirit to teach thee the glory of it, to bear witness to thy soul of interest in it, and to fill thee with joy and peace by it.

Dec. 9.—*Come and see.* John 1:39

Thus replies the Lamb of God to the inquiry where he dwelt. How came these two disciples of John to make this inquiry? John had pointed them from himself to Jesus with, *Behold the Lamb of God!* Just as though he had said, "Look at that dear MAN: take special notice of him: he has a world of sinners to save: he loved them from all eternity: he is come, an innocent, meek LAMB, to be slain as a sacrifice for them; and his precious blood taketh away all their sins. You and I are poor miserable sinners. We have no object to look to but that LAMB. Nothing can take away our sins, nothing can bring pardon to our hearts, peace to our conscience, and salvation to our souls, but his blood: nothing can make us holy and happy here on earth but looking to and living upon this *Lamb of God.*" They believed this: no wonder then that they followed Jesus and asked him, "Where dwellest thou?" He said, *Come and see.* O what a sweet, free, and loving invitation is here!

Just so are disciples now gathered to Jesus. His ministers preach of Him. They point lost sinners to him: they tell of the love of his tender heart, the virtue of his precious blood, and the lamb-like meekness of his nature to receive all who come to him: hence dejected, distressed hearts and troubled minds hear, are encouraged, and follow him. He turns and sees, and asks them, "What seek ye?" They ask him, "Where dwellest thou?" Then saith Jesus, *Come and see* Come and live with me, upon all the fulness of grace which I have for your needy souls. *Come and see* all the fulness of my salvation for your ruined souls; the full atonement my blood has made for your sins; the glorious righteousness I have wrought out to justify your persons; the peace I have made on the cross for you. *Come and see* that this is effectually and for ever done, and is fully to be enjoyed by faith.

Hence learn that there cannot an inquiry arise in a poor sinner's mind concerning Christ, but he has a meek and tender answer to give. He has compassion on the ignorant and them who are out of the way. Do we inquire where Christ dwells? He answers, *Come and see*. I, the high and lofty One who inhabit eternity, dwell also in your nature: I became flesh for you, that you may freely come to me, joyfully see, and richly partake of my fulness to supply all your wants and all your need. Here is a free invitation. You have nothing to bring. Come, see and enjoy all freely, "without money and without price." Jesus will soon say to you and me, Come and see all the glory of my kingdom above. Glory be to thee, O Lord.

Dec. 10.—*Behold my servant, whom I uphold ; mine elect, in whom my soul delighteth.* Isa. 42 : 1

Angels reproved disciples of old with, "Why stand ye gazing up to heaven?" Acts 1 : 11. How much do we deserve this reproof, Why stand ye gazing upon the vanities of the earth? Soul, at what art thou looking? What is the present object of thy attention? Be it what it may, God calleth to thee, and demands audience and attention. It is for your comfort and his glory. The Majesty of heaven speaks to sinful worms of the earth.

Behold ; take off your eyes and thoughts from every object: be all eye, ear and attention to me. Ye poor, miserable, condemned souls, behold *my Servant*. Wonder, adore, rejoice and love. My beloved, my co-equal Son, who is Lord of all, becomes man, takes on him the form of a servant to do my will perfectly, and to finish your salvation completely.

Whom I uphold : carnal reason, bow: pride, avaunt: high thoughts, submit to faith's mystery. Christ, as perfect man, was too weak to sustain the load of a world of sin, and to support the suffering of divine wrath, in atoning for sin and satisfying divine justice : therefore all the fulness of the Godhead dwelt in him to uphold his manhood. O sinners, in your precious Saviour behold the man : adore the God.

Mine elect. Christ was chosen to the office of God's servant and our Saviour; chosen in the eternal counsel, before time, to assume human nature in the fulness of time. *In whom my soul delighteth.* Says St. John, " We know that we are of God." 1 John 5 : 19. How? By this sure mark, this infallible evidence, we are of one mind with God. Doth God's soul delight in the person and work of his beloved Son : so doth ours. Is God's soul delighted that Christ hath satisfied his justice, magnified and made honorable his law, and finished salvation for miserable sinners? So is ours. Then as surely as our souls delight in Christ, the Lord's soul delights in us. We are called Hephzibah, that is, the Lord's pleasure is in thee. Thou art married to him. His soul delighteth over thee. Isa. 62 : 4. He hath given his Spirit to thee : for, says Christ, he shall receive of mine, my love, my atonement, my redemption, my righteousness, my salvation, my resurrection, ascension and intercession, and shall show it unto you. Thus ye shall glorify me in your eyes and in your hearts. John 16 : 14.

Dec. 11.—*By faith the walls of Jericho fell down.* Heb. 11: 30

To see Joshua and his army, with seven priests blowing ram's horns, marching round Jericho once every day, and on the seventh day seven times, what could the men of Jericho think? Doubtless that it was the foolish parade of a set of weak-headed men. Had they told them, behold, on the seventh day's blowing of the ram's horns, the strong walls of your city shall fall down at our shouting, without any human power, they would have laughed them to scorn as a set of dreaming enthusiasts. The obedience of faith is the scorn and ridicule of carnal men. What of that? Our Lord was pleased with it. They had his word for their warrant; they believed his word; they did as he commanded; the event was as he promised: the Lord soon made it manifest who were the fools and madmen.

But why is it said, "*By faith* the walls of Jericho fell down?" Was not this effected by the power of God? Yes, but it was according to the faith of the Israelites, and agreeable to the word of God, which was the ground of their faith. Divine faith and divine truth are inseparable. So it is said, "by faith" we are "justified," and "have peace with God." Rom. 5 : 1. Yet "it is God who justifieth." Rom. 8 : 33. Faith no more procures justification than the Israelites threw down the walls of Jericho! The righteousness of Christ solely obtains this for us. But as they did, so we do by faith shout, Christ and salvation. All opposition from sin and Satan fall before us; we see the kingdom of heaven open to us.

Here was the *obedience* of faith. Though to carnal sense and reason the means commanded were even ridiculous, yet they obeyed. Study the Lord's word; obey his will; attend his ordinances; look to the Lord for the promised blessing.

Here was the *patience* of faith. They encompassed the city seven days, and repeated their work. O christian, be not weary; hold on and hold out till the seventh day, the Sabbath of thy eternal rest, comes. Says Bishop Hall, "A good heart groans under his infirmities: fain would he be rid of them; he strives and prays; but when he hath done all, until the end of the seventh day, it cannot be." At God's time the walls fell: not one moment sooner. His word cannot fail. So, believer, at God's appointed time (you are immortal till then) shall your body, the prison-walls of your soul, fall. O, then faith may shout, " There remaineth a rest for the people of God " Heb. 4 : 9.

DEC. 12.—*He received from God the Father honor and glory, when there came such a voice to him from the excellent glory, This is my beloved Son, in whom I am well pleased.* 2 Peter 1 : 17.

These words furnish us matter for sweet meditation. Spirit of truth, help us to see the honor and glory of the Father and Son in them, and to gain comfort from them.

Here is a silencing answer to that objection, you rob God the Father of his honor and glory by ascribing so much to Christ. Have you never felt this temptation ? It comes from the enemy of God and sinners. Our faith puts all the honor and glory of our salvation upon God's beloved Son : there God himself places it : in his beloved Son God is well pleased, and with us also in him. Here see the nature of faith : it causes the soul both to imitate and obey God, and to be well pleased with Him in whom God is well pleased—the beloved Son of God.

Though to the eye of nature Jesus appeared as a mere man, in abject poverty and lowest abasement ; yet the Father gives him the highest honor and glory, because he magnified his holy law and made it honorable ; satisfied his divine justice, and brought everlasting honor and glory to every attribute and perfection of his nature So that now, " God is just, and the justifier of sinners who believe in Jesus." Then under a sight and sense of your ruined nature, innumerable sins, and dreadful apostacies from God, put honor and glory upon the Son of God : with his work and salvation God is well pleased : it has satisfied heaven for thy sins ; let thy conscience be satisfied with Jesus, and glory in him alone.

For thy encouragement herein, consider Peter, who wrote these words: he was honored to be on the mount; saw his Lord's transfiguration; heard these words from the excellent glory; and yet, with oaths and curses, he denied that he knew the man whom God the Father had so lately honored and glorified: there was an inexpressible fulness of grace in Jesus even for him. Out of Christ's fulness Peter received grace upon grace, whereby he was recovered from his fall, restored to repentance, and preserved to salvation. O may the dear Saviour look our hearts into godly sorrow and holy love, that we may say, " This is my beloved Saviour, in whom I am well pleased."

DEC. 13.—*I was alive without the law once : but when the commandment came, sin revived, and I died.* ROM. 7 : 9

Would you read the best experience of a true believer in Christ ever written ? I believe it is here in this chapter. Try your own : judge of others by this. If we are taught by the same Spirit, our experience will answer to that of Paul in the following particulars :

A sense of *sin* will be revived in the conscience, which no human palliatives or lulling opiates can any longer hush to silence. You will so see, and be sensible of its dread and terror, that you will confess yourself to be totally destroyed by it, and that your case is desperate.

This is effected by *the law*, " for by the law is the knowledge of sin." Rom. 3 : 20. "When the command ment came "—that is, when the purity and spirituality of the holy and perfect law of God comes into your heart and conscience, then you see that it requires truth and perfection of obedience in the inward parts as well as in the outward life. You see you have it not : you find it is impossible for you, a sinner, to ful fil God's holy law.

Then you *die:* you become as a dead man. Seeing the exceeding sinfulness of sin in you, and the dreadful curse of the law hanging over you, all hope of life forsakes you. Sin and the law live within you; they pierce your soul to the quick. The law adds strength to sin. You can no longer flatter yourself that your state is good, that you can do any thing to bring yourself upon good terms with God; you have now done with all works of righteousness to that end; you can have no more hope from your obedience to the law, than from your transgressions against it: you see sin in all that you are, and in all that you do.

But the hand of the Comforter is in all this. His loving design is to bring you to live by the faith of the Son of God. Instead of looking to your own righteousness, and living by it, you are to live wholly and solely upon his life and by his righteousness. But while " alive without the law," and striving to fulfil the law, you overlook Christ, slight his righteousness, and think it better to trust your own than his. Now the Spirit keeps alive sin and the law in you for this very purpose, to make you wretched in self and happy in Christ. All experiences that do not effect this are vain. Christ is the end of the law for righteousness to every one that believeth. Rom. 10 : 4.

DEC. 14.—*Be content with such things as ye have : for he hath said, I will never leave thee, nor forsake thee.* Heb. 13 : 5

Preach contentment to a covetous, carnal man, and you will have no better success than if you bid the surging billows be calm, or the boisterous winds be still. He possesses nothing which can give true content to his mind. Has he riches ? They are a curse to him; for he himself is under the curse of the law. O believer, were not this, in a certain sense, your case also, you would stand in no need of this exhortation, " Be content." You are the subject of a carnal nature : this is under the curse of the law ; for it is ever dissatisfied, craving for more, murmuring against the dispensations of the Lord. Know and consider this : be humble : be watchful.

Consider what good things of this life you have. Be they little or much, do you deserve them ? Have you a right to challenge more from God, the giver of them ? Here rest, and let conscience answer nature's cravings.

Consider what spiritual things you have. You have the everlasting, unchangeable love of a covenant God and Father. You have the life, death, and intercession of God the Son for your righteousness, atonement, and salvation. As a consequence of this, and that you may know and be sure of it, the Spirit has bestowed his graces upon you. Hence you have faith in Christ, hope towards God, love to him, delight in him, a heart to cry to him, a will to please him, a desire to walk holily before him. And to encourage and enable to this, you have all his precious promises in Christ : these are the staff of your faith, the support of your hope, and the joy of your soul. What want you more ? Paul sums up all in one word : " *All things* are yours." 1 Cor. 3 : 22.

Is not this enough to make you content ? Ah, say you, I find myself such a vile sinner, I am afraid I shall forfeit all these things. So you would before the next setting sun if you stood in yourself ; but here is a covenant promise from a faithful God for you : " I will never leave thee nor forsake thee." This is a most precious word for you : fasten upon it : draw comfort, derive content from it. Some say this regards things of this life only. Well, surely if God loves his people's bodies, he will never forsake their souls : and to silence all the cavils of unbelief, the words run, *No, I will not leave thee ; no, no, I will not forsake thee.* Here are five negatives. " Be not faithless, but believing." John 20 : 27.

DEC. 15.—*These all died in faith.* Heb. 11 : 13

An officer in the navy, who held me in derision on account of religion, fell dangerously ill. To my great surprise he sent for me. I found him in distress of soul: spoke freely to him of our lost estate, of Christ's love and salvation, and prayed with him. He wept sore, and clapping his hands to his breast, cried out, " O my God, have I a soul ?" as though he had never known it before He soon added, " Where have I lived that I never heard these things before ? O, I shall never forget what I have heard this night !" I visited him to his last moments, and trust he died in the faith, and hope to see him in glory. " Heaven is a house full of the miracles of Christ's grace," says one. There is the once idolatrous Manasseh ; the murdering David ; the persecuting Saul ; the Christ-denying Peter. O my God, shall wretched I be there ? Yes, if I die in the faith of Christ, my vileness, sinfulness, and unworthiness his blood shall wash away. Christ, by his grace, qualifies me for heaven.

See the nature of this faith : it looks to precious promises : though seen afar off, yet it brings assurance of their existence into the mind, and the soul embraces them. O christian, when you complain of your faith, you forget the great and precious promises which are its ground and support. It not only views Christ in the promises, but it receives Christ, in whom " all the promises are yea and amen, to the glory of God." 2 Cor. 1 : 20. When Christ dwells in the heart by faith, we con fess ourselves strangers and pilgrims in the earth : we see that we have a heavenly inheritance, and are only passing through this world to it. This world is not our

home: we are not of the world: our hearts are above
the world: our souls cry to be at home with our Father,
God; with Christ; and with our brethren in glory. Like
Abraham, we see the day of Christ. He saw the first
coming of Christ long before his advent: we by faith
see his second coming to take us to himself in glory;
hence we rejoice. O the comfort of living, O the joy
of dying in this faith: it realizes heaven and glory to
the soul: *hope* is its constant attendant; and by faith
and hope in the promises, *love* springs up in the heart.
Thus the sinner is fitted for the enjoyment of God. Die
when he may, he dies in faith—dies in the Lord, and
shall live eternally with the Lord. "By grace ye are
saved, through faith." Ephes. 2 : 8.

DEC. 16.—*The times of refreshing shall come from the presence
of the Lord.* Acts 3 : 19

To whom shall these times come? To every sinner
who repents and turns to Christ for salvation. From
whence shall they come? From "the presence of the
Lord." Here then see whether you have repented and
turned to the Lord. If so, your soul will delight in God's
presence. You will earnestly long for and highly prize
these refreshing seasons. You will say with David,
"Thou art my God, my times are in thy hands: I will
bless the Lord at all times: his praise shall continually be in my mouth." Psalm 31 : 15; 34 : 1. Hence you
will turn from your sins, your self-righteous hopes, carnal pleasures and worldly vanities, to seek all your happiness in the enjoyment of the presence of the Lord;
and you will wait in the patience of faith for the coming of refreshing seasons, assured that they shall come.

Is it now a night of gloom and sadness? Are we
tried and afflicted, bowed down and dejected? Is the
sun of comfort set? Does the moon withhold its shin-

ing, and the stars their light? Yet times of refreshing *shall* come. Believe this: hang on this word; bless the Lord for it. That blessed COMFORTER who brought us to Christ, will refresh our souls with a sense of the love of Christ, the peace of God, and the joys of the heavenly world: he will refresh us with his witness to our hearts that we are the children of God and heirs of glory. He does preserve in our minds a sense of the precious truth, that Christ is both an able and a willing Saviour: that he calls our weary, laboring souls to him, and promises us eternal rest. This is refreshing to our hearts.

Is sin our burden? Do we want rest? Are our souls troubled for want of peace? Are our spirits distressed for want of refreshment? Christ says, "Come unto me." But more precious times of refreshment shall soon come: yet a little while, and we shall behold, and be in the eternal enjoyment of the presence of the Lord. O, a lively view of this by faith is refreshing indeed! Then we long to be absent from the body and present with the Lord: we are sick of the world: sick of ourselves: we triumph over sin and Satan, smile at death and welcome its approach. "And now, Lord, what wait I for? My hope is in thee." Psalm 39: 7. "Looking for that blessed hope, and the glorious appearing of the great God, and our Saviour Jesus Christ, who gave himself for us." Tit. 2: 13, 14.

DEC. 17.—*I, even I, am he that blotteth out thy transgressions for mine own sake, and will not remember thy sins.* Isa. 43: 25

With tears of joy and love, my once dearly beloved and much honored friend, now with Jesus, the late reverend Mr. Jones, minister of St. Saviour's, told me that the awful charges which precede, and the free and unmerited grace which is proclaimed in this text, made the first impressions of the Saviour's love upon his heart. O that the Lord of all grace may grant some comfort from it to-day. Here grace shines with meridian splendor: here grace gloriously reigns over all the aboundings of sin: here grace sweetly triumphs over all the baseness and unworthiness of the sinner

In the two former verses God arraigns the sinner, reads a black catalogue of indictment against him, and concludes with, Thou hast made me to serve with thy sins, thou hast wearied me with thine iniquities." The sinner is struck dumb: he dares not deny it; the Judge proceeds to pass sentence. What is it? Vengeance and damnation? What else could be expected? Be astonished, O heavens! shout for joy, O sinners upon earth! *I, even I, am he*—what? who will be avenged of thee? Yes: but it is love which takes vengeance upon thy sins, and will melt down thy hard, thy base heart—*that blotteth out thy transgressions.* What, my soul, the very God whom thou hast "made to serve with thy sins and wearied with thine iniquities," will HE blot them all out? Yes, as a black cloud is dispelled by the sun, or driven away by the wind; or as an immense debt is discharged by the stroke of the pen of a merciful creditor, never, never more to appear against or be demanded of the debtor.

For, O wonder of love! he saith farther, *And will not remember thy sins.* I cannot forget my sins; how then can my Lord? He laid them upon his Son, thy surety. They were all atoned for by him. Why all this? For the sake of thy works, or any thing thou hast done? Spurn the thought. Hear thy Lord, *For mine own sake,* I have blotted out thy sins through thy Redeemer's blood. The Father blots them out for the sake of his righteousness and truth. The gracious Spirit blots them out of the conscience, for the glory of the Father and the Son, and because he is *the Comforter.* O what boundless bliss is here! Believe, rejoice, and love.

Dec. 18.—*If we sin wilfully after that we have received the knowledge of the truth, there remaineth no more sacrifice for sins, but a certain fearful looking for of judgment and fiery indignation, which shall devour the adversaries.* Hebrews 10 : 26, 27

Awful words! enough to make one's heart tremble, excite a holy fear, and provoke a godly jealousy. Wilful sins bring on woful complaints. Yes, some one replies, I find it so by woful experience. I have received the knowledge of the truth of salvation by Christ Jesus, and Oh what have I done! Sinned wilfully; and now I must perish eternally ; there is no hope or help : my sin is unpardonable ; there remains no more sacrifice for sins, but a certain fearful looking for of judgment ; I am shut up in despair ; I wait with terror my dreadful doom

Stop a little: write not such bitter things against thyself. True, you are condemned for your past wicked conduct : it is fit you should take shame to yourself, humble yourself, and repent as in dust and ashes ; but this text never was intended to drive to despair, even the wilful sinner, who sees and truly repents of his vile conduct. Consider, that if every wilful sin committed after a person has received the knowledge of the truth is unpardonable, the whole world must be lost ; not one sinner would be saved ; and the word of God could not be true, "The blood of Jesus Christ cleanseth from *all* sin." 1 John 1 : 7. Then all backsliding sinners must perish without hope. God himself must prove false to his word, "I will heal their backslidings." Hosea 14 : 4. And Christ must be a false prophet when he declares, "*All manner of sin and blasphemy* shall be forgiven unto men." Matt. 12 : 31.

Consider well two words in this text: "There remaineth no more *sacrifice* for sins." Now this wilful sin is rejecting the one sacrifice of Jesus, treading under foot the Son of God, accounting his blood an unholy thing, and expecting to be saved some other way. Here is total apostacy and final unbelief; whereas your guilty conscience seeks no sacrifice beside the one offering of the Son of God. Again, it is the *adversary* who is to be devoured. Is your heart set against Christ? Do you turn from him? Do you desire to have nothing to do with him? O no! the one desire of your soul is to be pardoned through him, accepted in him, and saved by him. Then you are not, in the sense of the text, the adversary of Christ, and this text belongs not to you. But this does, "It is a faithful saying, and worthy of all acceptation, that Christ Jesus came into the world to save sinners." 1 Tim. 1: 15.

DEC 19.—*Ye have not received the spirit of bondage again to fear; but ye have received the Spirit of adoption, whereby we cry, Abba, Father.* Rom. 8: 15

The Spirit of God never was, never is, nor ever can be "the spirit of bondage" to any soul: some have asserted it, but it is a mistake; it is contrary to his name, *the Comforter:* he is a free Spirit, a spirit of liberty to the soul: he takes of the things of Christ and shows them to us; testifies of Christ; brings us into the liberty of Christ; enables us to glory in the adoption of children, and to call God Father, in the faith of Christ. When he convinces of sin, it is not to bring the soul into bondage, but to break the bondage of sin, of the law, of death, and of Satan in the conscience, and to cast away the cords thereof, that the soul may be united to Christ by faith. In all this he is *the Comforter*.

What then is this "spirit of bondage?" It is the spirit of the law: just as the Egyptians made the children of Israel to serve with rigor, and made their lives bitter with hard bondage. Exod. 1: 14. Do what they would, they could never please, never get a good word from their task-masters. So let the poor sinner labor, tug and toil from day to day to fulfil the law, and to be made righteous by obedience to it, yet, like hard-hearted Pharaoh, it says, "'Ye are idle, ye are idle;' pay me what thou owest me, my full due : I am not satisfied : you have not fulfilled my righteous demands: you are still cursed." Thus a legal spirit is always in bondage : his soul is always subject to fear. Though he works like a slave, yet he gets nothing but slavish dread of God, and fear of perdition at last; for the law works only wrath in the conscience. Rom. 4 : 15. This is fearful bondage indeed.

Glory to the Spirit of adoption for bringing us from it, and enabling us to cry, Abba, Father. How does he effect this? We receive the Spirit of adoption by the faith of Jesus : we see a righteous law perfectly fulfilled by the one obedience of Christ : by this we, sinners, are made righteous. Rom. 5: 19. Here our hearts take refuge : through this righteousness the Spirit brings peace to our conscience; discharges from the condemnation of the law; frees us from guilty fears and terrors of God; and instead thereof, breathes this precious cry in our hearts, "Abba," my loving, my adopted Father in Christ. Now love reigns in the soul. The Spirit of adoption does not again become a spirit of bondage : but if you do not walk in faith and love, he may leave you to the awful bondage of your own spirit, and under the terrors of a broken law. "Grieve not the Holy Spirit of God." Eph. 4 : 30.

Dec. 20.—*Can a woman forget her sucking child, that she should not have compassion on the son of her womb? Yea they may forget, yet will I not forget thee.* Isa. 49 : 15

"Lord, remember David in all his afflictions." Psalm 132 : 1. How comprehensive is this short petition!

What a holy boldness, what a filial confidence breathes in it! Yes, says a poor doubting, dejected soul, it came from an eminent saint; but I am a miserable sinner; I am afraid the Lord hath forgotten and forsaken me. Is your mind pained at the thought of this? This is a godly sorrow, to which the wicked are strangers. This is one of the afflictions of the righteous.

"Lord, remember me," is the prayer of faith to a covenant God. Here is a precious cordial, a heart-reviving answer from the Lord. "Look at that woman with her smiling babe at her breast: see how fond she is of it, how delighted with it: it is part of herself: its innocent look and helpless cry call forth her tenderest affection and regard. Can she forget it? Can she refuse to show compassion to it? Will she neglect to administer to its wants, and to preserve from danger the dear and tender son of her womb? Is it possible?" Here is an image in nature which strikes one with the most tender affection, to set forth the love and care of the Lord to his people.

But strong and striking as it is, it fails. There have been those who have not had compassion upon the offspring of their womb. Therefore, knowing the fears and surmises of our nature, the Father of love and the friend of sinners, as it were, corrects himself, "Yea, they may forget"—the comparison fails—this image, yea, all nature is too weak to borrow a representation from. *Yet will I not forget thee.* O, may faith fasten and live upon this precious word. May love be excited and joy increased by it. As though our dear Lord had said, "I have loved thee with an everlasting love," saved thee with an everlasting salvation, called thee by my grace, made thee know thy poverty and vileness, thy hopeless and helpless state: shall I ever be unmindful of thy distress, deaf to thy cry, and unwilling to relieve thy wants?

Is the tender infant part of its mother? Remember, "we are members of Christ's body, of his flesh and of his bones." Ephes. 5 : 30. Was the infant born in pain and sorrow? O, what agonies did it cost our Lord to redeem us! Has he brought us to himself for salvation; and will he leave us to perish by sin, to be overcome by the world, or to be a prey to Satan? Ever remember the riches of his love: "Behold, I have graven thee upon the palms of my hands." Isa. 49 : 16.

Dec. 21.—*My Beloved is mine.* Song 2:16

Here is a knowledge worth more than heaven and earth; for heaven and earth shall pass away, but this knowledge endureth for ever. O happy souls, who are favored with it, give glory to your beloved to-day. Ye who are seeking it, rejoice; for he hath said, "Every one that seeketh findeth." Matt. 7 : 8. Happy Job was favored with it when he was "in heaviness through manifold temptations," "broken in the place of dragons and covered with the shadow of death:" then he must have utterly fainted had he not believed. Time was, when Job could say, *my* health, *my* wealth, *my* honors, *my* children, *my* comforts; but these were all dead and gone: he had nothing within nor without on which to stay his soul, but the word of the Lord and the Lord revealed in the word. This was his support and his glory: though I have lost all things, "I know that *my Redeemer* liveth;" while he lives I cannot die: he has redeemed me; I cannot despair: I will rejoice in him, though stript of all besides.

O, how does the whole world lie fast asleep in the arms of the wicked one, without the least thought or desire after the knowledge of this precious Redeemer! Yet how many poor sinners are saying: "O that I knew this Redeemer was mine; that I could say, I know that my Redeemer liveth. Nothing in all the world could give me such comfort as this." Bless the Holy Spirit, for he hath given you peculiar knowledge of Christ. It is special grace that you are brought to see your misery as a sinner, and your want of a Redeemer, and to make Christ the choice of your soul. You know that you believe the Redeemer liveth. All this is in consequence of his love to you: he chose you: he loves you: he died for you: he lives to pray for you: therefore he has blessed you, by sending his Spirit to you. Why then should unbelief so prevail in you as to keep you from honoring him, by claiming him as your beloved and rejoicing in him as your friend?

O the unspeakable mercy to have such a Redeemer! "We have redemption through his blood, even the forgiveness of sins:" perfect peace with God and a sure title to glory. Blessed be God for Jesus Christ. Study the work, the finished, everlastingly glorious work of Christ's redemption: believe his precious word of invitation, "Come unto me:" his precious promise, "I will give you rest." What could Christ have done more than he hath to manifest his love to sinners? Why then should you or I, or any poor sinner, be kept from claiming him by faith, saying, "This is my beloved and my friend?" Song 5:16.

Dec. 22.—*Underneath are the everlasting arms.* Deut. 33:27

It is fabled of Antæus, that every time Hercules threw him to the ground, he rose up the stronger; for he obtained new strength by touching his mother, the earth. So the christian: when assaulted and thrown down by the enemy, he falls into the Lord's everlasting arms, and gains fresh strength: he cannot be thrown down lower than God suffers; for "underneath are the everlasting arms." His word is full of grace, his arms almighty, his love everlasting. Here is the wisdom, here the glory of the Lord's people—to look from themselves, to go out of themselves for safety and salvation. For they rest upon God's word: they believe the Lord to be all that to them which he has said. This is living by faith; honoring the Lord's truth; glorifying the Saviour's name.

Why are we told, "Underneath are the everlasting arms?" Because we know and see ourselves deserving of hell, and liable to fall into the pit of destruction. Therefore the Lord would have our hearts strong in him, and in the power of his might, that we may not fear the face of any enemy, nor be dismayed under the sense of our own vileness and insufficiency to stand.

Drooping believer! Why dost thou hang down thy head? Why those distressing doubts and fears? Look back to the everlasting covenant: there everlasting love presided. Then wast thou viewed, and thy case provided for. Look up; there sits a God of love on a throne of grace; there stands thy blessed advocate, Jesus, ever pleading thy cause. Look underneath, there are the everlasting arms to sustain and support thee. What power then shall prevail against thee? Neither sin, death, nor hell can snatch thee out of the everlasting arms of thy almighty God, thy reconciled Father: out of the arms of thy gracious Redeemer: out of the powerful arms of the Holy Ghost, thy sanctifier. In the everlasting arms is everlasting safety. Here is a covenant declaration. Exercise upon it the covenant grace of faith. "The eternal God is thy refuge:" flee to him in distress. His everlasting arms are underneath: rejoice in thy safety. He will thrust out every enemy before thee, and speak destruction to them. Happy art thou, O believer! Who is like unto thee, saved by thy Lord?

DEC. 23.—*Keep thy heart with all diligence.* Prov. 4 : 23

Camden reports, that " Redwald, king of the East-Saxons, the first christian prince of this nation, allowed 'n the same church an altar for Christ and another for the heathen idols." How many professed christians imitate him. Their hearts are not whole with Christ : they are sons of folly. This is a charge of Wisdom to all her children : consider, there is but one object can make your heart happy ; there are a thousand that promise happiness, but only yield misery : keep thy heart " in the love of God." Jude 21.

Give all *diligence* to this blessed end : unless you do, vanity may prevail in the mind, error in the understanding, perverseness in the will, the affections may be inordinately set upon other objects than thy Lord, and so thy conscience contract fresh guilt. Then thou mayest be left to bemoan a hard heart and an absent God : darkness may surround thee : fears and terrors haunt thee ; the remembrance of long-departed sins may distress thee ; the prospect of death and eternity appear awful to thee ; the day of judgment dreadful, while Satan triumphs over thee, " There, there, so would I have it." Then may thy heart upbraid thee that all this is come upon thee because thou wast not diligent to watch its motions, to keep out the enemy, and maintain sweet communion and holy fellowship with thy best friend, thy Saviour.

Lord, stir up my soul to " give all diligence." Though we shall not be saved for our diligence, yet, we shall thus escape many snares and evils, and enjoy safety and comfort : " The soul of the diligent shall be made fat." Prov. 13 : 4. Such shall feed upon heavenly truth, grace and love ; their soul shall prosper and be in health ; while careless triflers with God and their own souls shall go to rest with dejection, rise with distress and live in awful suspense.

Dec. 24.—*Lo, this is the man who made not God his strength.*
Psalm 52 : 7

The following fact I had from my late beloved friend
and faithful minister of Christ, Mr. Jones : A poor infidel
had conceived a strange notion that men need not die
unless they would. Upon his death-bed he affected to
be resolute and to bid God defiance. In his last moments he sprang up, gnashed his teeth, and with looks
of horror cried out, " God, I will not die !" With these
words he expired. Oh the fearful death of the ungodly,
who make not God their strength ! O the joyful end of
the righteous, whose strength is in the Lord ! They
have hope in their death ; for they make God their
strength in their life.

What can a vile sinner do to make God his friend ?
to make God his strength ? God is all that to every poor
sinner which his word reveals him and faith receives
him to be. Consider this. You say, I am a weak, needy
creature. What saith the Lord ? " Let him take hold
of my strength." Isa. 27 : 5. " Thou hast been a strength
to the poor : a strength to the needy in his distress."
Isa. 25 : 4. Again, in that sweet 52d chapter of Isaiah,
the title of which is, *Christ persuadeth the church to believe his free redemption,* the Lord calls upon poor and
needy sinners, " Awake, awake, put on strength." Ver. 1.
Thus, for the encouragement of our hearts, and to the
joy of our souls, we see that the Lord is the strength of
that soul who believes in him, chooses him, and receives
him as such. Faith is the hand that takes hold of God's
strength. Faith claims God as the strength of the poor
and needy. And, because our poor hearts are apt to
grow heavy, neglect and forget the strength of our heart
and our portion, lo, he crieth to us with a mighty voice,
" *Awake, awake.*" Lift up your eyes : look unto me, who,
" when ye were without strength, in due time died for
the ungodly." Rom. 5 : 6.

Put on thy strength. Thou hast no inherent strength. Know thy strength is perfect weakness. Put on the Lord Jesus Christ: he is "the Lord Jehovah, in whom is everlasting strength." Isa. 26 : 4. Learn daily that blessed art, to say with St. Paul, "When I am weak, then am I strong." 2 Cor. 12 : 10. The Lord commands you, "Let the weak say, I am strong." Joel 3 : 10. "Be strong in the Lord, and in the power of his might." Ephesians 6 : 10.

Dec. 25.—*Behold, a virgin shall conceive, and bear a son and shall call his name Immanuel—God with us.* Isaiah 7.14; Matthew 1 : 23

On this prophecy hang all the hopes of fallen sinners. Had this failed, we had all been lost: horror eternal had awaited us; hell eternal must have been our doom. "God with us" must be born a babe in time, or sinful man for ever dies. But, O my fellow-sinners, all hail! I give you joy. This day is this Scripture fulfilled. This virgin hath conceived; this Son, this Immanuel, is born God in our nature—God with us, God for us we behold in Him.

He says, "I was set up from everlasting," (as the covenant head of my people,)— my delights were with the sons of men." Prov. 8 : 23, 31. Now he hath shown how he delighted over us, how he rested for ever in his love to us. For he visits us in our flesh. "He took not on him the nature of angels," but became a babe in human flesh, a man; born to save, he lived to justify; he died to redeem—whom? fallen angels? No, they are left, reserved in chains of darkness. But, unto us, sinners, us miserable apostates from God, in the very same desperate state as devils; behold, "unto us a Child is born; unto us a Son is given:" that we, who are filthy by birth and polluted by nature, might have a holy birth and a sanctified nature in him. "The government is upon his shoulders." He is our King. He reigns over us, for us, and in us. Our souls and all our concerns are safe in his hands. "His name is Wonderful." In his conception, birth, person, God and man in one Christ: in his life, death, resurrection, ascension, and intercession, wonderful: in his love to and salvation of us, wonderful. "Counsellor." He powerfully pleads our cause above; he sweetly counsels our hearts below to come to him, and find rest in him. "The mighty God." None less could save us. Jesus is the God of our salvation. "The everlasting Father." He begets us to himself, by the word of his grace. The most tender parent on earth never loved his children as Jesus loves us. "The Prince of Peace." Isaiah 9:6. He is ever at peace with us, made peace for us, bestows his peace on us.

> "For ever hallowed be this happy morn!
> "God dwells on earth, the Son of God is born."

The birth of Jesus—behold it, says the prophet; dwell on it in your own minds; feed on it in your hearts. This makes you happy all the year round. For this brings "glory to God in the highest, on earth peace, good will towards men." Luke 2:14.

DEC. 26.—*Emmanuel, God with us.* Matt. 1:23

This is the mystery which holy angels pry into—-devils envy—proud infidels reject with derision—humble sinners glory in—and for which all the redeemed around the throne above are incessantly shouting and everlastingly triumphing.

The sin-convinced, spiritually-enlightened christian is ready to exclaim, O how did we talk of God in nature's darkness, when we were without Christ, "having no hope, and without God in the world." But now, O wonder of converting grace, we see, we believe, we know, *God with us.* This is the chief glory of our faith, the chief joy of our hearts. In the eternal counsel he had our persons in view, our case at heart, and undertook to be our surety, our Jesus. Lo, we were then given to him by the Father. In the fullness of time he appears in our flesh. Lo, he is born: see the babe: adore the God: rejoice in "Emmanuel, God with us."

He came to accomplish that in our nature, without which we must have perished eternally; but for which we are everlastingly saved: namely, to "finish transgression, make an end of sin, bring in an everlasting righteousness, and suffer, the just for the unjust, that he might bring us to God." 1 Peter 3 : 18. This is sweet in the history: but, O how much more so in the experience of the christian.

God with us, living in our hearts, hopes, and affections by the Spirit, through faith. We know, we taste, we feel the reality, power, and comfort of this truth, *God in Christ* reconciled, "not imputing our trespasses to us." 2 Cor. 5 : 19. *God with us,* to oppose all who are against us? Rom. 8 : 31. Now, may we not stand forth and challenge all the powers of sin, earth, and hell, "Who shall lay any thing to the charge of God's elect?" For God the justifier, and we the justified, are one in Christ: "I in them, and thou in me," says our Lord. John 17 : 23. Hence we meet in love, mutually embrace, and have fellowship one with another. This is the glory of Christ's nativity, brought into our hearts. "Christ in us the hope of glory." Col. 1 : 27.

Dec. 27.—*To reveal his Son in me.* Galatians 1 : 16.

Hence begins spiritual life: a life from God, in God, with God, and to God. By the Gospel the Son of God is revealed to us: by the Spirit he is revealed in us.

External revelation by the word, and internal by the Spirit, are both necessary to salvation. Though Paul was "separated from his mother's womb, and called by the grace" of God, yet he had not this inward revelation of Jesus Christ to his heart, till he heard the external word of Christ, saying, "Saul, Saul, why persecutest thou me?" Acts 9 : 4. Hence learn to prize both the outward testimony of the word, and the inward testimony of the Spirit.

But the chief glory of our souls is the revealing Christ *in us*. O for the reviving influence of this while we consider it. To reveal Christ in us, is to make such a clear discovery of the matchless charms and inestimable glory of his person to our souls, unknown to us before, that our hearts are enamored with him ; we choose him, love him, delight in him, and cleave to him in all his offices and characters ; for by the eye of our soul we "behold his glory, the glory as of the only begotten of the Father, *full of grace and truth*," to us miserable sinners : hence he is the ONE beloved of our souls.

Without this revelation of Jesus Christ in us, alas ! what is all external profession ? No more than mere dry formality and drudgery. O my soul, O my dear friends, be not content to live without a constant revelation of Christ to your souls : this makes the conscience peaceful, the heart happy, and the soul joyful: this inspires love, subdues lust, captivates the affections, makes the whole man happy in God, and creates heaven in the soul If Christ is in the heart, all will be right and well in the life. If you believe in Christ, as revealed in the word, this blessed promise is for you ; pray for its daily fulfilment, "I will manifest myself unto him." John 14 : 21

DEC. 28.—*Ye are all one in Christ Jesus.* Gal. 3 : 28

Will a covetous man be content with the *idea* that

he is rich? Were your body in pain, would it give you ease to *think of* a remedy without experiencing its salutary effects? What avails all the refined notions of external union, unless the soul is vitally united to Christ by the power of the Spirit, through faith? O my soul, I charge thee not to rest satisfied with the notion of the doctrine of union, without the comfort of the grace of being united to Christ and being one with him in heart and affection. O, my Saviour, to thee I look and pray, to find and feel more and more the sweet experience of this: grant it to my soul out of thy fulness.

Consider the persons here spoken of, *ye :* ye Jews, who had the form of godliness without the power : ye Gentile sinners, who once had neither the form nor the power of Christianity : ye apostate sinners, who yesterday were haters of God, at enmity against his law, rebels against his government, in league with sin, death and hell ; fighting under the prince of darkness : see what ye are *now.* Behold what grace has done for you : see into whom it has implanted you.

"In Christ Jesus." Not only in the knowledge of him, faith in him, hope in him, and love to him : though all this is precious ; but much more, ye are spiritually united to Christ even as your soul is to your body, your body to your head, or your hand to your body. Now Christ is your life, your husband, your wisdom, righteousness, sanctification and redemption. 1 Cor. 1 : 30. "Ye are complete in him." Col. 2 : 10. Simply believe this : look to Christ for the comfort of this : glorify the Spirit for the grace of this.

"Ye are all *one* in Christ," whether Jew or Gentile, of one religious denomination or another : "we being many, are one body." 1 Cor. 10 : 17. Christ is the head: we are all members in him, and of one another. As Luther says, "We have the same Christ ; I, thou, and all the faithful, which Peter, Paul, and all the saints had." We are all in the same Jesus: have all one Father, one Comforter, and are of one Spirit. Then let this faith quell all unholy strife, and excite all heavenly love to each other. O let us make it manifest that we are in Christ, by following him who is our peace, and by holding "the unity of the Spirit in the bond of peace," "let us consider one another, to provoke unto love and good works." Heb. 10 : 24.

DEC. 29.—*When Christ, who is our life, shall appear, then shall ye also appear with him in glory.* Col. 3 : 4.

I have read a book consisting of stories, said to be told to the Sultan of Arabia, to prevent a bloody purpose of his against his Sultaness. The relator of the tales was her own sister. She always contrived to leave off in the midst of her story, which he was so delighted with as to promise not to destroy her sister till it was ended ; and thus by protracting the execution she saved her sister's life. Methinks there is no end to the history of Christ. Every fresh relation of him delights the believing soul, and kindles the desire to hear more of him again and again ; for he averted the bloody execution of law and justice against us ; every fresh tale of him strengthens our faith, sets our minds more and more against every evil, and excites us to every good : for *Christ is our life.*

O soul, can you ever believe too much of him, or hope too much in him ? It is our fault, our shame, our misery, that we dwell no more on him and converse no more with him. Is Christ thy *life*, O my soul ? What sort of a life do I live ? Jesus, wash me in thy blood. Lord, pardon me by thy grace. Favor my soul with fresh experience that thou art my life ; so be the death of all my sins and the life of all my graces. O appear

appear in the power of thy Spirit again and again in me,
before thou shalt appear in thy power and glory to me.

Christ shall appear. What are we looking at? Why
stand we gazing on perishing objects? What are we
waiting for? The Saviour? He shall appear. Perhaps
the very next moment, as the Lord of life and death, he
may say to his angel death, Go, bring that saved sinner
to me, his Life. O joyful word! Learn to welcome it;
faith will; for, "we shall appear *with him in glory.*"
How shall we appear? In what we wore by faith, were
not ashamed of, but gloried in here: "Arrayed in fine
linen, clean and white:" the rich robe of Christ's obedience unto death, which is "the righteousness of
saints." Rev. 19 : 8. Mind, this is granted to us. If it
be our own righteousness, we have a right to appear in
it; there needs no grant of it: but it is Christ's righteousness, therefore a gift, by grant, to us. O remember
we *shall* appear (all the powers of hell cannot prevent
it) with Christ in glory. *Only believe,* and you will love
Christ, rejoice to obey him, and long for his appearing.
O Jesus, my life, appear to my soul in all the power of
faith, the joy of hope, the comfort of love, and the fellowship of peace.

DEC. 30.—*Old things are passed away.* 2 COR. 5 : 17

Such is the blessedness of every new creature in
Christ : every believer in him is a new creature. Mind,
Paul does not say, old things are passing away, but are
passed away. We are not to understand him in an absolute, but in a qualified sense; for if none were new
creatures till all old things are passed away, we should
not find one on this side heaven. Now the year is near
its close. Do not you find your old corruptions cleaving
to you? Yea, the old man of sin still alive in you, just
as you did at the beginning of the year, or at the be-

ginning of days when you first believed in Christ and was made a new creature in him ? Do not you also see the same reason to comply with these exhortations as at first ? " Put off the old man, which is corrupt." Eph. 4 : 22. " Cleanse yourself from all filthiness of the flesh and spirit." 2 Cor. 7 : 1.

But if all this be so, how can it be said, " Old things *are* passed away ?" Consider, Paul is not speaking of the old creation of fallen nature, but of the new creation in Christ Jesus. As men, and descendants from fallen Adam, all the sin and misery of our old nature abides with us. We are still in the flesh : in that dwells nothing but sin and evil : it is under the sentence, and must receive the wages of sin, death. But as believers in Christ, " we are passed from death to life." John 5 : 24. Being in him by faith, we are new creatures in a new creation.

Observe, in the foregoing verse Paul is speaking of knowing Christ and men after the flesh ; but now says he, We have done with carnal views and fleshly knowledge : we are spiritual : we view and know things by faith, as new creatures in Christ. Hence, as we are passed from our old state, old things *are* passed away from us : our old notions of God, of Christ, of salvation, of our own righteousness, salvation by works in whole or in part—are all passed away. Yea, our delight in our old companions, in the vanities of this world, which is under the curse, and our manner of living and walking in it, are passed away. Our old way of keeping Christmas holidays, and concluding the old year in card-playing and vanity, is passed away : and if, for conscience sake, we do not keep days by any religious observance of them, we do not spend them in our old way, by " making provision for the flesh, to fulfil the lusts thereof." O, says one, I would not keep Christmas for the world : it is superstitious. Pray then do not keep it for the devil and the flesh : " If we live in the Spirit, let us walk in the Spirit." Gal. 5 : 25.

DEC. 31.—*He that endureth to the end shall be saved.* Matt. 10 : 2

We have now reached the end of another year. Look back with humility: look up with hope: look forward with joy : for consider what great things God hath done for us : "Now is our salvation nearer than when we (first) believed." Rom. 13 : 11.

Salvation, O the joyful sound!

But, before the Sun of Righteousness arose upon us and displayed the glory of his finished salvation to our hearts, alas! what dark, proud, ignorant notions of salvation did we entertain ! Instead of seeing righteousness as a gift by Jesus Christ, and justification of life coming by free gift, and eternal life the gift of God through Jesus Christ, Rom. 5 : 17, 18 ; 6 : 23—we vainly thought that salvation was to be procured by some deeds or righteousness of our own. In our natural state of blindness, before we saw Jesus, we thought enduring to the end might give us a claim to be saved; now we see that we are " saved in the Lord with an everlasting salvation." Isa. 45 : 17.

We began the year *seeing Jesus.* O, in this blessed sight let us endure to the end. In him we see a complete salvation. We hear and believe his cry from the cross, " *It is finished.*" We hear him proclaim from his throne in glory," *It is done.*" " I am Alpha and Omega, the beginning and the end." Rev. 21 : 6. In him we are " chosen to salvation, through sanctification of the Spirit, and belief of the truth." 2 Thess. 2 : 13. He " of God, is made unto us wisdom, righteousness, sanctification and redemption." 1. Cor. 1 : 30. In the faith of this we persevere. By faith we " endure (every fight of affliction) seeing him who is invisible." Heb. 11 : 27. We " run with patience the race set before us, looking unto Jesus, the author and finisher of our faith." Heb. 12 : 2. Consider these precious words, ye who tremble lest your faith shall not endure to the end : the same Jesus who is the author is also the finisher of your faith. It is the glory of gospel faith to live upon Jesus, who is our life and salvation; and to enjoy life and salvation in Christ every step we take in the way to endless life and glory: where in spite of all the deceitfulness of sin, and the art and malice of Satan, we shall "receive the end of our faith, the salvation of our souls." 1 Pet. 1 : 9.

Now, christian reader, I commend thee to God, and to the word of his grace, wishing thee sweet comfort in perusing these daily meditations. If our Lord give thee as much in reading as I have found in writing them, thou wilt have great cause for love and praise. Accept them, as the labor of one who is "no prophet, neither a prophet's son," but who would glory in being a saved sinner, by the cross of Jesus.

Glory be to God in the highest. Grace be with all who love our Lord Jesus in sincerity. Amen.